SCRIPTURAL TRACES: CRITICAL PERSPECTIVES ON
THE RECEPTION AND INFLUENCE OF THE BIBLE

29

Published under

CW00954278

LIBRARY OF HEBREV
OLD TESTAMENT S'

709

Formerly Journal for the Study of the Old Testament Supplement Series

THE LAND WITHOUT PROMISE

The Roots and Afterlife of One Biblical Allusion

Katerina Koci

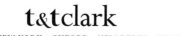

LONDON · NEW YORK · OXFORD · NEW DELHI · SYDNEY

T&T CLARK

Bloomsbury Publishing Plc

50 Bedford Square, London, WC1B 3DP, UK

1385 Broadway, New York, NY 10018, USA

29 Earlsfort Terrace, Dublin 2, Ireland

BLOOMSBURY, T&T CLARK and the T&T Clark logo
are trademarks of Bloomsbury Publishing Plc

First published in Great Britain 2021
This paperback edition published 2023

For legal purposes the Acknowledgments on pp. ix–x constitute
an extension of this copyright page.

Cover design: Charlotte James
Cover image: untitled, 2011. Oil & pencil on paper © Daniel Domig.

A catalogue record for this book is available from the British Library.

Library of Congress Cataloging-in-Publication Data:
Names: Koci, Katerina, author. Title: The land without promise :
the roots and afterlife of one biblical allusion / by Katerina Koci.
Other titles: Library of Hebrew Bible/Old Testament studies ; 709.
Description: London ; New York : T&T Clark, 2021. | Series: Library of Hebrew Bible/Old
Testament studies, 2345-678X ; 709 | Includes bibliographical references and index. |
Summary: "Katerina Koci charts the development of the Promised Land motif, starting from its
biblical roots and examining its reception over the centuries until the present day"--
Provided by publisher.
Identifiers: LCCN 2021002343 (print) | LCCN 2021002344 (ebook)
| ISBN 9780567696298 (hardback) | ISBN 9780567696304 (pdf) Subjects: LCSH: Brueggemann,
Walter. Land. | Steinbeck, John, 1902-1968--Themes, motives. | Bible--Reader-response criticism.
| Bible and literature. | Religion and geography.
Classification: LCC PN56.B5 K63 2021 (print) | LCC PN56.B5 (ebook) | DDC 809/.93522--dc23
LC record available at https://lccn.loc.gov/2021002343
LC ebook record available at https://lccn.loc.gov/2021002344

ISBN: HB: 978-0-5676-9629-8
         PB: 978-0-5677-0132-9
         ePDF: 978-0-5676-9630-4

Series: Library of Hebrew Bible/Old Testament Studies, ISSN 2513-8758, volume 709
Scriptural Traces, volume 29

To find out more about our authors and books visit www.bloomsbury.com and sign up
for our newsletters.

To Noemi and Elias

CONTENTS

ACKNOWLEDGMENTS

My passion for the Bible and for literature goes back a long way. As a teenager, I spent every minute of my free time reading novels, and although it was just the 'One Book' that would provide the key for my academic career, the many others that are influenced by the Bible in some way or another kept reappearing in my research.

It is no coincidence, then, that my work on this book has been deeply influenced by Brian Doyle, Robert Evans and Vik Doyen, all scholars with an expertise in literature (and much else). I would like to thank them for their professional guidance and friendly advice and for putting their trust in my project.

I cannot fail to acknowledge the support of Bradford Manderfield and Carrie and Jared Schumacher, my friends and colleagues from KU Leuven, who by posing questions from various angles, especially out of their genuine American interest in the theme, opened up horizons that might otherwise have remained hidden to me.

For their hospitality during my Junior Jan Patočka Visiting Scholarship, I am indebted to the academic and administrative staff at the Institute for Human Sciences in Vienna. Special thanks go to Ludger Hagedorn for his invaluable support and to Marci Shore for showing me that academia and motherhood are not necessarily mutually exclusive enterprises. I would also like to thank the Protestant Theological Faculty at Charles University in Prague for hosting me during the final phase of composing and editing my book.

My humble thanks go to my proof-readers and English editors, Stuart Nicolson and especially Tim Morgan, who helped to elevate my manuscript to the 'level of literature', which given my passion for reading is such an important factor.

Last, but certainly not least, I would like to thank my family: my husband Martin, who as an academic himself knows how it feels when it's time to finish up, edit, reread or submit a book or paper regardless of the day of the week or the time of day; my children Noemi and Elias, who are the true light and meaning in my life and a constant connection to the world beyond academia; and my parents, who have given me unfailing support in everything I have ever done in my life.

Some ideas in Chapter 2, in the section 'Reception of the Promised Land in the New Testament', appeared earlier in my article 'Reception of the "Promised Land" in the Pauline Letters', *Communio Viatorum* 56, no. 1 (2014): 35–55.

Parts of Chapter 4 – namely the sections entitled 'Curing One's Conscience but What Comes Next? Brueggemann and Liberation Theology' and 'Killing the Land and Marching Further West: *The Grapes of Wrath*' – are adapted from my article 'On the Legacy of the Land: Ideology Criticism of Walter Brueggemann and John Steinbeck', *Theology Today* 78, no. 1 (2021): 13–28.

Publication of this monograph was generously supported by the research project 'Christianity after Christendom: Paradoxes of Theological Turns in Contemporary Culture' PRIMUS/HUM/23 and by research project 'Christianity after Christendom: Exploring the Human Condition in the Digital Age' of the Theology and Contemporary Culture research group, Protestant Theological Faculty, Charles University.

The final touches to the monograph were completed within my research project 'Woman without a Name: Gender Identity in Sacrificial Stories' (M2947-G) funded by Austrian Science Fund (FWF).

INTRODUCTION

The Bible and literature

The promised land is a concept that rings bells with almost everyone in our Western culture and prompts passionate discussions on various ideas that may concern the motif only obliquely. This book will offer ways of interpreting the motif of the promised land and suggest how and why this elusive and utopian concept contains an inherent contradiction. The central pillar of the research is a dialogue between 'the novelist' and 'the biblical scholar' on the theme of the promised land, a trajectory towards which the whole book is directed, including the chapters on methodology and the biblical and literary background to the motif. The book will explore the basic principles for constructing a world in which art and science can meet together and combine to offer a unique hermeneutical tool for interpreting biblical motifs.

The experience of religious believers has been portrayed in countless works of fine art, literature, architecture, sculpture and music. Some authors and artists have sought to convey broad theological concepts, others particular biblical motifs. While exploration of the former category has generally been the domain of systematic theology, the latter is in the purview of biblical studies, particularly the field of reception history of the Bible. Although the biblical motif has this long tradition in works of art, and great theologians down the ages have been fascinated by such works, attempts by biblical scholarship to define and categorize instances of the Bible in literature are more recent.[1]

Of course, the Bible *and* literature have maintained a courtship of sorts for a good deal longer. As early as 1901, Hermann Gunkel's *The Legends of Genesis* arranged the stories within the book of Genesis into literary

---

1. 'Reception history…is usually – although not always – a scholarly enterprise consisting of selecting and collating shards of that infinite wealth of reception material in accordance with particular interests of the historian concerned, and giving them a narrative frame'. Jonathan Roberts, 'Introduction', in *The Oxford Handbook of Reception History of the Bible*, ed. Michael Lieb and Emma Mason (New York: Oxford University Press, 2011), 1.

genres in an attempt to discern their origin. Although Gunkel analysed the literary form of the narratives – rather than any particular artistic or literary feature – in order to determine their *Sitz im Leben*, his progressive literary method certainly paved the way for the synchronic literary approaches which dominated biblical scholarship in the second half of the twentieth century. There is little doubt that one of the most important contributions to the marriage of biblical and literary studies and to a literary analysis of biblical texts has been made by Robert Alter, a professor of Hebrew and comparative literature at the University of California. In his best-selling *The Art of Biblical Literature* (1992), *The Art of Biblical Narrative* (1981) and *The Literary Guide to the Bible* (1987), among other titles, Alter deals with the phenomenon of the Bible *as* literature, seeking out literary features within the Bible and interpreting the Bible according to its literary value. Alter takes a different path in *Canon and Creativity* (2000), here looking for the Bible *in* literature: exploring the paradigmatic literary works of art in Western history and teasing out the biblical influences to be found there. Another significant literary scholar to have focused on the Bible is Northrop Frye, whose original specialism was English literature. In his masterpiece *The Great Code: The Bible and Literature* (1982), Frye set out the paradigmatic biblical stories that have influenced Western culture. The ground-breaking works by each of these literary scholars presented the Bible not only as a piece of literature which can be analysed – and even criticized – using all the usual literary methods, but also as a work of art with literary value in itself.

Alter and Frye were pioneers in and sources of influence for synchronic literary approaches in biblical studies. Alter nonetheless criticizes the current tendency in biblical studies to exchange the dominant philology and archaeology (the domains of the historical critical method) for linguistics and semantics (the domains of synchronic literary methods), in other words the tendency to exchange one deficient method for another. As early as the 1990s, Alter observed:

> A French-inspired vogue in literary theory sought for a while to displace the living author with a notion of the text as a playground of impersonal literary codes, but that view seems increasingly one-sided, and the assumption of ordinary readers about an informing authorial presence is confirmed in the practice of most critics, even at this postmodern moment. The author addresses us with a representation of or reflection on life spun out of densely tangled stuff of his own lived life, and thus the act of reading is a kind of colloquy – the author speaking, the reader thinking back – between him and us.[2]

2. Robert Alter, *The World of Biblical Literature* (London: SPCK, 1992), 2.

No wonder, then, that the younger generation of scholars in the field have defined themselves against both the historical-critical method and the synchronic literary method and found each of them equally and inherently oppressive. Yvonne Sherwood – a literary scholar by training – and her colleague in biblical studies, Stephen Moore, react critically to the praising of deconstruction, the creed of the poststructuralists, and suggest that any theory that must be observed to the letter inevitably becomes self-referential, even idolatrous, and will meet the same end as the historical-critical method. Moore confesses: 'Derridean discourse is…an extension of the discourse of modernism'.[3] Sherwood and Moore believe that biblical studies must be liberated from its colonial bondage of hegemonic 'theories' on the one hand and white male Euro-American academia on the other. While Sherwood and Moore specialize in freeing biblical studies from 'theories', Norman Habel, Rasiah Sugirtharajah and Fernando Segovia, three of the many academics to emerge from the former European colonies, seek to liberate biblical studies from the bonds of the 'standard' omnipotent white male Euro-American perspective and shift the discourse towards the margins, to aboriginals and the socially disadvantaged. Although they use deconstruction as their natural method, they nonetheless seek to overcome what they see as its 'methodolatry', and argue that synchronic literary approaches such as formalism and new criticism, despite their passionate attempts, failed to free biblical studies from the oppressive context and methods of colonialism. As part of our exploration we will see whether liberation theologies and postcolonial methods fared any better than deconstruction in liberating biblical studies from colonial ideology, or whether in fact at least the former of the two fell into a trap of its own making. Could it be that a radical contextu-alization of analysis and an exclusive focus on liberating the margins creates its own 'inverted' ideology? Does such an approach in fact deepen and widen the abyss between the oppressor and the oppressed, intensify their respective traumas, guilt and victimization, and lead, ultimately, to an exchange of roles between the two?

Reception history, the method pursued here, can be divided into two basic streams that more or less follow the development of literary studies in German and Anglo-Saxon academia. While the Anglo-Saxon path tends to follow the strict synchronic literary approach described above, the Germanic path incorporates the diachronic line,[4] although it does not

3. Stephen Moore and Yvonne Sherwood, *The Bible in Theory: Critical and Postcritical Essays* (Atlanta, GA: SBL, 2010), 12.
4. The suggestion that Anglo-Saxon tradition is strictly a synchronic reader-response approach and that the German tradition is predominantly diachronic is a

focus on the composition of the biblical text and its development within the canon, but rather on the life of the biblical text after it had taken its final form. Synchronic reception history takes a single novel and analyses the interpretation of the biblical motif without considering the development of that motif through the colourful history of its reception. The diachronic approach on the other hand composes a 'synopsis' of the history of reception and sketches the development of the biblical motif over time but does not discuss particular receptions in detail. Each of these approaches refers to itself as reception history and each offers interesting insights. Neither, however, fulfils the potential offered by this overall approach, which leads me to believe that the best way to interpret a biblical motif in a literary work is to combine the synchronic and diachronic approaches. These pages will therefore offer a synopsis of the history of the reception of the chosen biblical motif and will do so using the example of the interpretive method employed by a single author.

The pre-eminent and arguably the most eloquent scholar in this field is the German philosopher Hans-Georg Gadamer, author of the ground-breaking *Truth and Method* (1960) and champion of the hermeneutical approach. Jean Greisch has described Gadamer's hermeneutics as 'phenomenological' as they focus on 'the *experience* of understanding'.[5] Gadamer's approach is unique in combining the diachronic and synchronic methods; it is reader-oriented but takes text and author equally seriously. Gadamer emphasizes both the historicality of every understanding (the diachronic, universal, and thus objective line) and the uniqueness of a personal experience and application of the text (the synchronic-diachronic, particular, and thus subjective line). This methodological cocktail, mixed in the optimum proportions, offers the ideal approach for the purposes of this book. Chief among Gadamer's followers, and the scholar largely responsible for introducing reception history into biblical studies, is Ulrich Luz, author of the pioneering commentaries *Matthew in History: Interpretation, Influence and Effects* (1994) and *Das Evangelium nach Matthäus* (EKK,[6] in four series: 1985, 1990, 1997, 2002).

This study combines the best from the synchronic and diachronic approaches to reception history. First, it takes an important motif in the

schematic generalization that does not always correspond to reality: there are English and German scholars in both camps. The labels are nonetheless used in methodological discussions to make this rather contested field a little neater.

5. Jean Greisch, 'Ou Passe Le Rubicon? Un Problème de Geographie Spirituelle', in *Une Analytique de Passage: Rencontres et Confrontations Avec Emmanuel Falque* (Paris: Editions Franciscaines, 2016), 322.

6. Evangelisch-Katholischer Kommentär.

Hebrew Bible – the promise and loss of land – and analyses it in the Hebrew Bible, the New Testament, and through history up to the present day. Secondly, it is carried out from the very beginning through the lens of its ultimate goal, an exploration of the motif of the promised land as interpreted in the novels of John Steinbeck.

I have three main reasons for choosing Steinbeck. First, he is a representative of American culture, which is clearly one of the most prominent heirs of promised land ideology. American religion, politics and culture testify to the assumed exceptional nature and 'chosen-ness' of the American nation, an assumption that has been a feature of American life since the first Puritans stepped onto the New World in the seventeenth century. Secondly, Steinbeck refers to biblical themes openly and without apology. In seeking an exemplar for interpreters of biblical motifs, it is more straightforward, therefore, to use Steinbeck than to use authors whose biblical allusions are weaker and whose theological concepts are more (indeed overly) complex, such as William Faulkner or Hermann Melville. Jackson Benson, an authoritative Steinbeck biographer, illustrates this point:

> Before leaving Paris, Steinbeck gave Buck a package saying, 'Here – I'm giving you the source material for all stories. You'll have no problems after this.' Buck said, 'What is it, John?' 'The Bible'… The imagery and implications of *Pilgrim's Progress* were very real to him, and the image of a stern grandfather (a memory he could not have possibly had) reading solemnly and with all finality from the Bible came back periodically to haunt him.[7]

Finally, of all the American authors who deal with the motif of the promised land, I chose Steinbeck because his literary style, the setting of his novels and the fact that he deals with everyday human issues make him more accessible to and popular among a broad audience, including outside America.

The promise and loss of land is a prominent biblical motif and Steinbeck employs it liberally in his novels. Interest in the biblical themes in Steinbeck's novels began as early as the 1950s. The first literary scholars to embark on such an exploration were Martin Shockley in *Christian Symbolism in The Grapes of Wrath* (1956), Peter Lisca in *The Wide World of John Steinbeck* (1956) and *John Steinbeck: Nature and Myth* (1978), Joseph Fontenrose in *John Steinbeck: An Introduction and Interpretation* (1963) and Warren French in *John Steinbeck* (1975). Each

---

7. Jackson J. Benson, *The True Adventures of John Steinbeck, Writer* (New York: Viking, 1984), 710, 20.

of these works presents a systematic synopsis of a different biblical motif (in both the Hebrew Bible and the New Testament) in Steinbeck's novels. Most, however, stop short of interpreting Steinbeck's own re-interpretations of the original biblical motifs. A step towards this goal was taken by the Native American scholar Louis Owens. In *Steinbeck's Revision of America* (1985) and *The Grapes of Wrath: Troubles in the Promised Land* (1989), Owens explores the issue of the promise and loss of land in America – the rise and fall of the American dream in Steinbeck's novels – in relation to the original biblical motif.

Before outlining the structure of the book, I will offer some reasons for promoting reception history ahead of other approaches to interpreting Scripture. Using art as a hermeneutical tool, in literature in general and Steinbeck in particular, challenges traditional biblical scholarship in both the methods used and the themes chosen for interpretation. Alter suggests that literary authors approach sacred texts from the perspective of constructive criticism: 'The engagement of modern writers with the Bible is especially instructive because it cuts sharply two ways. They frequently translate biblical motifs and themes into radically redefining new contexts, and...their stance toward the Bible can sometimes be positively combative'.[8] Alter's position is helpful and reflects my own experience with the novels of John Steinbeck.

The best way to evaluate an approach that some scholars deem to be still in its youth – and therefore 'innovative' – is by appealing to a scholar who is well-established in the field and whose work is broadly accepted rather than controversial. I have therefore provided Steinbeck with an interpretive partner from his close historical, religious and socio-cultural context, namely the Hebrew Bible scholar Walter Brueggemann, who is not only a devoted reader of Steinbeck's novels – as he confesses on the pages of his commentaries – but also a passionate interpreter of the motif of the promised land in the Hebrew Bible. In *The Land* (1977 [2nd edn 2003]), Brueggemann claims that the land is a symbol of the relationship between God (YHWH) and God's people. He also acknowledges the significance of the motif in American culture.[9]

We should acknowledge some of the weaknesses in reception history. In his introduction to *The Oxford Handbook of Reception History of the Bible*, Jonathan Roberts suggests that reception history scholarship opens up two thorny methodological issues. First, since the well of possible

8. Robert Alter, *Canon and Creativity: Modern Writing and the Authority of Scripture* (New Haven, CT: Yale University, 2000), 8.

9. Walter Brueggemann, *The Land: Place as Gift, Promise, and Challenge in Biblical Faith*, 2nd ed (Minneapolis, MN: Fortress, 2003).

receptions of biblical motifs in culture is undoubtedly bottomless, it is necessary to make choices and to select the receptions that are to be included in any synopsis. Reception history therefore urges us to discern whose responses to the biblical motif are relevant to the analysis and whose can be disregarded. Secondly, as such a selection can clearly not be random, it must be justified,[10] and, if it is to avoid suspicion among advocates of the more conservative biblical critical methods (such as the historical-critical method), it must be credible. These conditions are more easily satisfied by this current study than are some other forms of reception history as the aim here is to explore and interpret a single author: all the historical receptions chosen for the synopsis,[11] beginning with the biblical motif, create a trajectory of interpretation that ends with John Steinbeck; the trajectory itself also serves as a justification for the selection.

Aims and methods

The book is divided into four thematic chapters. Chapter 1 deals with the methodologies used in exploring literary works (novels) as interpretations of biblical texts. There are three main areas of methodological inquiry: the first relates to the role played by art in the hermeneutical process; the second regards the choice of methodological approach to be applied; and the third, if we are to question the use of the 'go-to' but (I would suggest) deficient methodology of reception history, regards how and when we should introduce the approach that resolves such a deficiency, namely reader-response criticism. Our exploration of these three points will include the work of the philosophers Hans-Georg Gadamer, Robert Alter, and Theodore Adorno and the literary scholars Hans Robert Jauss, Stanley Fish, and the biblical hermeneutics of Anthony Thiselton, Robert Evans, and David Clines.

Chapter 2 leaves the territory of pure methodology and moves towards the main theme, the promised land. The chapter is devoted to the reception of the promised land in Scripture, both the Hebrew Bible and the New Testament. It begins with a thematic analysis of the motif of the promised land and identifies two Bible verses that appear to provide the most likely foundation for its reception in the rest of the Bible. Next comes an historical-critical analysis of the two verses in question. The chapter concludes with an outline of the reception of the motif of the promised land in the Hebrew Bible and the New Testament.

---

10. Roberts, 'Introduction', 1.
11. Ibid., 3.

Chapter 3 follows the motif of the promised land in extra-biblical material from Antiquity to the present day, using a careful and colourful selection of authors whom we will use to track the trajectory of reception, beginning with the biblical text and ending with John Steinbeck. This history will include the Hebrew Bible scholar Walter Brueggemann as an interpretive partner for John Steinbeck. Literary authors will include those representatives of the motif's literary trajectory who influenced Steinbeck's interpretation of the motif in his novels. Finally, several Puritan ministers from seventeenth-century America will provide a foreshadowing of the religious-cultural and political mindset of twentieth-century America into which both Steinbeck and Brueggemann were born and which influenced their understanding of the promised land motif.

Chapter 4 discusses the interpretation of the promised land in Steinbeck's novels and in Brueggemann, who quotes Steinbeck in his commentaries and thus makes the connection between the two authors still more organic. Brueggemann sets the initial framework for a discussion on the tension between the promise and loss of land, but Steinbeck is by no means the weaker partner. The two writers clearly use different means of interpretation but, as we will see, sometimes reach quite similar conclusions. Our aim here is to present the ways in which Steinbeck's artistic freedom and distinctive hermeneutics could be instructive for Brueggemann and perhaps for other biblical scholars.

My motivations for writing this book were my passion for all matters methodological and my desire to advocate on behalf of a method I truly believe in. It is possible to read individual chapters as self-contained units that provide their own rationale, but I would rather readers came with me on a journey through the whole book, seeking not only the inner logic of each chapter but also their interdependence, and to see the unique contribution that reception history can bring to the interpretation of Scripture. I will also seek to deflect the suspicion from within some other biblical disciplines that the methods used in reception history are unclear and questionable. I will trace the motif of the promised land across the centuries and argue for the logical context-related development which results in its specific interpretation in the novels of John Steinbeck. To make Steinbeck still more credible as an exemplar and to make the method even clearer, I will compare Steinbeck's interpretation with that of his compatriot, the Hebrew Bible scholar Walter Brueggemann. This will show us that within his discourse of the promised land, Steinbeck hits upon themes and findings that would be discussed by biblical scholarship only some decades later.

Chapter 1

THE ROLE OF ARTISTIC INTERPRETATION IN BIBLICAL HERMENEUTICS

That biblical texts have always been sources of influence for art of every kind, including literature, is beyond doubt.[1] Robert Alter suggests that, 'The Bible, once thought of as a source of secular literature yet somehow apart from it, now bids fair to become part of the literary canon'.[2] Current biblical scholarship generally recognizes the benefits of literary interpretations of biblical texts, but what has always been a matter of fervent discussion among biblical scholars is the most appropriate approach to analysing such interpretations. The *status quaestionis* of this study consists in the work of the German scholar Hans-Georg Gadamer. Gadamer is a natural choice as interlocutor because his hermeneutics suggest that both art and science provide a path towards understanding and knowledge.[3] Unlike his great teachers among the modern hermeneutists, Kant and Dilthey for example, for whom art belongs to transcendental categories and does not therefore participate in knowledge, Gadamer holds that neither science nor art is superior to the other and that both therefore demand our attention. Gadamer's life-long project was to rehabilitate art as a hermeneutical tool: 'art is knowledge and experiencing an artwork means sharing in that knowledge'.[4] Moore agrees with Gadamer that

1. Alison Jack, *The Bible and Literature* (London: SCM, 2012), 1.
2. Robert Alter and Frank Kermode, *The Literary Guide to the Bible* (Boston, MA: Harvard University Press, 1987), 3.
3. Hans-Georg Gadamer, *Truth and Method* (London: Continuum, 2004), xxii–xxiii.
4. Ibid., 84. Also: 'They are concerned to seek the experience of truth that transcends the domain of scientific method wherever that experience is to be found, and to inquire into its legitimacy. Hence the human sciences are connected to modes

during modernity, art as a hermeneutical tool was forcibly removed from the process of understanding:

> Aesthetic modernism – the crisis of representation that erupted in nineteenth-century art and literature – can thus be seen as a crisis of philosophical and scientific modernity's analytico-referential paradigm. The iconoclastic aesthetic of nascent modernism amounted to a rejection of the early modern épistème and the canons of representation that it legitimized.[5]

The conviction that art and science are of equal importance is the cornerstone of this study. It is something to which I will adhere throughout the book as I focus on the artistic interpretation of biblical texts in the form of literary works of art, namely novels.

The respective outcomes of these two paths towards understanding are qualitatively different. Unlike artistic explorations, scientific accounts represent a plurality of views based on a critical discussion. I will follow this more scientific route in my research on historical-critical scholarship in Chapter 2. Of course, 'qualitative difference' refers not to a 'difference in quality' but to a different kind of response from that offered by standard biblical criticism. Supporting the relevance of art in hermeneutics, Theodore Adorno stresses that art is not a 'non-binding cultural supplement to science'; rather it has its own specific role, that of criticism.[6] The philosophical hermeneutics of Gadamer and of those who came before and after him are thus by far the richest sources of argumentation for the approach I will use in this study.

The role of art in the hermeneutical process

Applying Gadamer's hermeneutics to the exploration of a biblical text received in a work of art, we find both a scientific component (epistemological experience), the territory of traditional biblical scholarship (academic research with its claim to objectivity), and an artistic component (aesthetic experience), which can be attributed to the work of art represented by the novel. The novel is thus representative of the culture or formation – the *Bildung* – which participates in knowledge of the biblical text. One must always bear in mind, however, that even this

---

of experience that lie outside science: with the experiences of philosophy, of art, and of history itself. These are all modes of experience in which a truth is communicated that cannot be verified by the methodological means proper to science.' Ibid, xxi.

5. Moore and Sherwood, *The Bible in Theory*, 13.

6. Theodore Adorno, *Aesthetic Theory*, Athlone Contemporary European Thinkers (London: Continuum, 2002), 95.

representation is to a large extent objectifiable through 'common sense'.[7] Merold Westphal points out the benefit of both epistemological and aesthetic experience by drawing on the double hermeneutics of Nicholas Wolterstorff. Westphal speaks about two 'worlds' created by the author of either the (biblical) text or the work of art:

> On one hand, it refers to the world in which the author lives and out of which the work emerges, what the theologians call the *Sitz im Leben*... On the other hand, there is the world created by the author (but not ex nihilo) and presented to us by the work. It is what Ricoeur calls the world in front of the text in contrast to the author's inner life behind the text.[8]

Gadamer sees the hermeneutics of a work of art as a 'play' between the author-interpreter and the work itself, a process which takes place in the 'fictitious world' but which imitates reality. Alter argues similarly:

> As with literature elsewhere, meaning is here deepened and in a sense is discovered, through the exploration of form. Because the working of literary form is a kind of work that involves a dimension of free play, biblical literature, like its counterparts elsewhere, repeatedly offers us insights and pleasures that exceed the strict limits of ideological intentions.[9]

7. Gadamer, *Truth and Method*, 16–37. See also the 'interpretive community' in Fish's terminology (see Stanley Fish, *Is There a Text in this Class? The Authority of Interpretive Communities* [Cambridge, MA: Harvard University Press, 1980], 11) and the 'horizon of expectations' in Jauss's terminology (see Hans Robert Jauss, ed., *Toward an Aesthetic of Reception* [Minneapolis, MN: University of Minnesota Press, 1982], 21–2).

8. Merold Westphal, *Whose Community? Which Interpretation? Philosophical Hermeneutics for the Church* (Grand Rapids, MI: Baker Academic, 2009), 93. See also: 'A full interpretation of the Bible [or any of its parts] would have to answer two questions: What did the human author say to the originally intended audience? What is God saying to us now through the very same text?' Merold Westphal, 'The Philosophical/Theological Response', in *Biblical Hermeneutics: Five Views*, ed. Stanley Porter and Beth Stovell (Downers Grove, IL: IVP Academic, 2012), 162. See also: 'An essential characteristic of a literary work, and of a work of art in general, is that it transcends its own psychological conditions of production and thereby opens itself to an unlimited series of readings, themselves situated in different socio-cultural conditions. In short, the text must be able, from the sociological as well as the psychological point of view, to "decontextualize" itself in such a way that it can be "recontextualized" in a new situation – as accomplished, precisely, by the act of reading.' Paul Ricoeur, *From Text to Action: Essays in Hermeneutics* II (London: Athlone, 1991), 83.

9. Alter, *The World of Biblical Literature*, 45.

Gadamer refers to the ancient Greek concept of 'mimesis' (imitation),[10] which is central to more or less all of the post-modern reader-oriented approaches and was re-discovered by the German literary scholar Erich Auerbach.[11] The concept of mimesis, a process whereby imitation partici- pates in knowledge through recognition of the original work, is broad and complex. Gadamer suggests that the most common type of mimesis is the metaphor. Brian Doyle speaks of metaphors having the capacity not only to create new meaning but also to depict the reality hidden in the metaphor.[12] Metaphors help us describe the relationship between the biblical text and its interpreter through his or her artistic interpretation. But what is the theoretical basis of the mimetic relationship between the original and its artistic interpretation? There are many different perspec- tives from which to approach this question. Doyle combines two seemingly distinct approaches, the rhetorical (Bourget) and the cognitive (Stienstra), but stresses that each has its truth. Neither the rhetorical approach nor cognitive understanding, promoted especially by Lakoff and Johnson, covers the whole spectrum of possible functions and interpretations of a metaphor.[13] Lakoff and Johnson rightly pointed out that metaphors are used every day by almost everyone and that they are therefore a natural part of our lives.[14]

According to Ricoeur, the literary work of art, or more precisely 'fiction', is one of the best means of re-defining reality because poetic language is the most appropriate means of imitating it, and it is the re-creation of reality which helps us reach its most profound essence.[15] For Gadamer, the re-creation of a work of art is as important as its

10. Gadamer, *Truth and Method*, 112–13.

11. Erich Auerbach, *Mimesis: The Representation of Reality in Western Literature* (Princeton, NJ: Princeton University Press, 2003). I have not incorporated Auerbach's analysis as he builds on the romantic hermeneutics of Dilthey and therefore follows a different path.

12. See Brian Doyle, *The Apocalypse of Isaiah Metaphorically Speaking: A Study of the Use, Function and Significance of Metaphors in Isaiah 24–27*, Bibliotheca Ephemeridum Theologicarum Lovaniensium 151 (Leuven: Peeters, 2000), 133.

13. Ibid., 49–144.

14. George Lakoff and Mark Johnson, *Metaphors We Live By* (Chicago, IL: University of Chicago Press, 1980). Lakoff and Johnson's work on metaphors proved to be seminal.

15. Ricoeur, *From Text to Action*, 86. Also: 'Through fiction and poetry, new possibilities of being-in-the-world are opened up within everyday reality… Everyday reality is thereby metamorphosed by what could be called the imaginative variations that literature carries out on the real.' Ibid.

creation as it helps to reveal a deeper truth about the work by offering a new perspective, revealing that which could not have been seen before: 'In recognition, what we know emerges, as if illuminated, from all the contingent and variable circumstances that condition it; it is grasped in its essence'.[16] Adorno is persuaded that the mimetic relationship between the original and its artistic interpretation must always be critical: 'The desideratum of intuitability wants to conserve the mimetic element of art while remaining blind to the fact that this element survives only through its antithesis, the works' rational control over everything heterogeneous to them'.[17]

The concept of play as developed by Gadamer is taken over and developed in the methodological approaches of reception history and reader-response criticism. Each of these approaches can be called 'dialogical' because, like the concept of play, they involve both the text and the author/reader in the process of interpretation.[18] What we said about the exclusion of the aesthetic experience from the search for truth can also be applied to the concept of the mimesis that functions within it:

> Thus imitation, as representation, has a special cognitive function. For this reason, the concept of imitation sufficed for the theory of art as long as the cognitive significance of art went unquestioned… By contrast, for nominalistic modern science and its idea of reality, from which Kant drew agnostic consequences for aesthetics, the concept of mimesis has lost its aesthetic force.[19]

The recognition of the validity of aesthetic experience in the process of understanding and knowledge represented a paradigm shift that became a portent of post-modernity. Jürgen Habermas sees the turning point towards post-modernity and the change of paradigm in the work of Friedrich Nietzsche and his disciple Martin Heidegger: '[Nietzsche] renounces a renewed revision of the concept of reason and bids farewell

---

16. Gadamer, *Truth and Method*, 113.

17. Adorno, *Aesthetic Theory*, 96. Also: 'Mimesis in art is the pre-spiritual; it is contrary to spirit and yet also that on which spirit ignites. In artworks, spirit has become their principle of construction, although it fulfils its telos only when it emerges from what is to be constructed, from the mimetic impulses, by shaping itself to them rather than allowing itself to be imposed on them by sovereign rule.' Ibid., 118.

18. Roberts, 'Introduction', 3.

19. Gadamer, *Truth and Method*, 114–15.

to the dialectic of enlightenment'.[20] Influenced by this concept, Gadamer explains the role of hermeneutics as a 'corrective by means of which the thinking reason escapes the prison of language, and it is itself verbally constituted'.[21] Moore adds that, 'Historical criticism of the Bible, an offshoot of the scientific revolution and the Enlightenment (modernity in the expanded sense), is currently in the grip of an epistemic crisis'.[22]

There is one crucial dimension to art which we did not find in Gadamer and which later will call some of our findings into question. Adorno rightly points out that art is often critical, interruptive, and even provoking; it is the interruptive component that elevates 'mere' aesthetics to the level of art. Nietzsche even speaks about the prophetic role of art.[23] The question then arises regarding whether a work of art is a re-creation or interpretation of the original that can be seen in line with its other representatives or is unique and original. The role of art, according to Adorno, is to question that which has been taken for granted, to plant a seed of productive doubt, and to offer new and previously unconsidered perspectives.[24] Alter ascribes the artist as having a critical and creative role and observes that, 'literary tradition might often offer enlivening occasions for continuity as well as serving as a battleground for warring creative egos'.[25] Art is thus appealing because it uses original means to communicate the truth about the original. These means are not at the disposal of the original, which comes from the empirical world. Art speaks through these particular and original means and communicates with the empirical world – it is dependent upon it and deduced from it – but its nature lies in sharp criticism.[26]

20. Jürgen Habermas, 'The Entry to Postmodernity: Nietzsche as a Turning Point', in *Postmodernism: A Reader*, ed. Thomas Docherty (New York: Columbia University Press, 1993), 53. Also: 'Heidegger is faced first of all with the task of putting philosophy in the place that art occupies in Nietzsche (as a counter-movement to nihilism), in order then to transform philosophical thinking in such a way that it can become the area for the ossification and renewal of the Dionysian forces – he wants to describe the emergence and overcoming of nihilism as the beginning and end of metaphysics'. Ibid., 55.

21. Gadamer, *Truth and Method*, 403.

22. Moore and Sherwood, *The Bible in Theory*, 13–14.

23. Fridrich Nietzsche, *Kritische Studienausabe*, vol. 8, 189, frgm 11/2.

24. Adorno, *Aesthetic Theory*, 8–10.

25. Alter, *Canon and Creativity*, 8.

26. Ibid., 10–14.

Although Gadamer does not address the question of whether art is affirmative or critical, his exposition allows both of these options. Where Alter acknowledges both variants, many of Gadamer's followers argue either for affirmation or for criticism. Those in the first camp see the mimetic relationship between the original and its artistic interpretation as being affirmative and the interpretation as merely developing new significances. This idea is held and developed further by the literary scholar Hans Robert Jauss, Gadamer's own student and follower. It is also adopted by biblical scholarship through Anthony Thiselton, one of the principal advocates of reception history. The second camp sees the mimetic relationship between the original and its artistic interpretation as including a critical distance. This stream developed as a reaction against Jauss and his followers and was promoted by Stanley Fish, a representative of synchronic literary criticism. Robert Evans aims to protect Gadamer's legacy from both poles – from Jaussian continuity and from the discontinuity described by critical theory and exclusively synchronic approaches. Like Alter, Evans takes the middle path and is convinced that there is enough space for 'freedom' or originality of interpretation within tradition because every understanding is historical and takes place at the crossroads of the objectivity of tradition and the subjectivity of the interpreter: 'The interpreter is not subject to tradition, though it conditions his/her "anticipation" of the meaning to be discovered, but participates in it. Understanding is the "interplay" between "the movement of tradition" and "the movement of the interpreter".'[27] Following Alter and Evans, this book will acknowledge that the nature of a work of art as a representation of reality is both affirmative and critical and is also responsive to the current context.

Jauss, a reception history scholar, bases his literary theory on Gadamer's philosophical hermeneutics, builds upon it, develops it, and makes it more practical and more applicable to literary theory and biblical hermeneutics. He criticizes the praxis of historical positivism in literature and the removal of the aesthetic dimension from the literary work of art,[28] and draws art and aesthetic experience into the process of interpretation. Art gets to work in us and creates an aesthetic experience which participates in understanding and knowledge. Two hermeneutical acts contribute to the process of interpretation: understanding, which is immediate, and

27. Robert Evans, *Reception History, Tradition and Biblical Interpretation: Gadamer and Jauss in Current Practice* (London: Bloomsbury, 2014), 4.
28. Jauss, *Toward an Aesthetic of Reception*, 49.

interpretation, which is reflective.[29] Jauss adopted Gadamer's theory of
'three steps of interpretation', which he calls the 'method of three successive readings': understanding, interpretation, and application.[30] The
artistic element, of particular interest to us here, pertains to the first step.
The aesthetic reading creates a 'pre-understanding' of the text. Although
it is seen as an act of perception, it nonetheless has an impact on the
interpretation of the text.[31] The moment of experience pre-conditions
and initiates every hermeneutical process. In other words, experience
precedes interpretation: there is no hermeneutics without phenomenality.
This is not to say that these aspects of the hermeneutical process happen
separately: on the contrary, they always go hand in hand. The second
reading is synchronic literary or textual analysis, which requires the
reader to know literary theory[32] and read the literary signs and grammar
of the text, and to be attentive to what has been emphasized or left out
and able to fill in the gaps accordingly. The third reading is historical-
philological and involves a synopsis of the history of interpretation of
the text.[33]

Building on the philosophical hermeneutics of Gadamer and the
literary theory of Jauss, reception history in biblical studies describes
the history of the interpretation of biblical texts and states that every
interpretation participates in knowledge of such texts. Scholars such as
Luz and Thiselton employ reception history to show different interpretations of the same biblical text in different eras.[34] Jauss's model of three
successive readings simply represents three readings of the biblical text.
It requires a minor adaptation, however, and this was developed by
Thiselton. The first step remains unchanged. It is an aesthetic reading,
which is perceptive and creates a 'pre-understanding' of the text. Here we
meet the appreciation of art and aesthetic experience in the hermeneutical
process. The second step, a critical reading, becomes historical-critical
exegesis. The third step involves an historical reading which asks, 'What
did the text mean?', and an applicatory reading which asks, 'What does
the text want to say to me now?' This step includes a synopsis of the

29. Ibid., 141.
30. Ibid., 139–40. See also Gadamer, *Truth and Method*, 306–7.
31. Ibid., 143.
32. Ibid., 145.
33. Ibid., 145–7.
34. Ulrich Luz, *Matthew in History: Interpretation, Influence, and Effects*
(Minneapolis, MN: Fortress, 1994). See also Anthony Thiselton, 'Reception Theory,
H. R. Jauss and the Formative Power of Scripture', *Scottish Journal of Theology*
65, no. 3 (2012): 289–308; Anthony Thiselton, *1 & 2 Thessalonians: Through the
Centuries*, Blackwell Bible Commentaries (Chichester: John Willey & Sons, 2011).

history of interpretation of the biblical text as well as an interruption in the form of the 'hermeneutics of suspicion', which stresses the originality of the artistic interpretation.[35] Thiselton articulates an adjustment to Jauss's methodology in order to allow a measure of interpretative freedom; the idea of a hermeneutics of suspicion comes from Paul Ricoeur.[36]

However, drawing on Gadamer's and Ricoeur's appreciation of the role of art in hermeneutics, reception history is also employed to investigate a work of art as a receptor of a biblical text.[37] Our analysis will also require some adjustment to Jauss's model as we are not producing a new interpretation but rather evaluating one that is already before us: an artistic interpretation in the form of a novel. The first of Jauss's three steps again remains unchanged. The historical-critical analysis of the second step is enhanced by the reception of the text within the Hebrew Bible and the New Testament. Robert Evans suggests that in reception history, historical-critical analysis reconstructs the first horizon of expectation.[38] He does not see the analysis as resulting in a single final and unchangeable meaning but rather as involving the 'scholarly task' of a 'projection of the horizon of the past'.[39] However, the biblical world and its context are at such a remove from our current situation that despite all the groundbreaking findings of biblical archaeology, our imperfect knowledge of the context of ancient Near Eastern people prevents us from accurately reconstructing the horizon of expectation.

Because novelists tend to allude not to a particular verse from the Bible but to some more general motif, we will conduct a thematic analysis of the motif in order to identify the concrete sources. This analysis will include later receptions of the motif in the Bible, and some of these may

---

35. Thiselton, 'Reception Theory', 299–300.

36. Ibid., 300.

37. Michael Lieb and Emma Mason, eds., *The Oxford Handbook of the Reception History of the Bible* (Oxford: Oxford University Press, 2011). See also Niko Huttunen, 'The Bible, Finland, and the Civil War of 1918: Reception History and Effective History of the Bible as Contextualized Biblical Studies', *Studia Theologica – Nordic Journal of Theology* 65 (2011): 146–71; Kirsten Nielsen, 'The Holy Spirit as Dove and as Tongues of Fire: Reworking Biblical Metaphors in a Modern Danish Hymn', in *Gåder Og Billeder: Studier Til Ære for Tryggve N. D. Mettinger*, ed. Göran Eideval and Blazenka Scheuer (Winona Lake, IN: Eisenbrauns, 2011), 239–56.

38. Evans, *Reception History, Tradition and Biblical Interpretation*, 34–40.

39. 'They do not produce the "primary datum" in the sense of a single and unchallengeable "meaning" of the text to which other meanings are later added…but they contribute to the "scholarly task" of a "projection of the horizon of the past", which for Gadamer is "one phase in the process of understanding"; and for Jauss, this is a strategy to render the "horizon of a specific historical moment comprehensible".' Ibid., 39.

appear more fitting to the allusion made by the novelist. Because this study asks a bolder question than other studies within reception history, namely whether an artistic interpretation of a biblical text contributes to a more complex understanding of that text, the step that requires most adjustment is Jauss's third. The historical reading – the question of 'what the text meant' – will cover both the history of biblical scholarship on this text and the history of its reception in art. The applicatory reading as the completion of the history will be covered by (i) a representative of biblical scholarship, and (ii) a representative of the history of reception in art. This last step in our analysis is indeed the most important of the three as it is not only a completion of the historical reading but the main purpose of the whole analysis. In this study I will argue that the artistic reception of the biblical text complements the scientific reception and perhaps in some way sheds light on some as yet unanswered – or even unasked – questions. In order to answer the question, 'Is the artistic reading of the biblical text illuminating?', it is important to choose an interpretive partner from the field of biblical scholarship who comes from a similar context to that of the artist and who asks similar questions, otherwise any comparison would be worthless and we would learn little or nothing from the whole exercise.

Thiselton's suggestion of adopting the concept of the hermeneutics of suspicion fully conforms to our special requirement of an original artistic interpretation – in our case the novel – with a prophetic, interruptive role, rather than simply a modification of what has gone before.

The text and the reader: partners in a dialogue

The role of art in hermeneutics consists in producing an aesthetic experience in the interpreter, and this is an essential component in every process of understanding. Art therefore requires a partner who acknowledges their own subjectivity and is allowed to play an appropriate role in hermeneutics. Such an 'involved interpreter' can be represented by a novelist who produces an artistic interpretation of the biblical text. Because novels are both subjective and objective in their interpretation of biblical texts, the appropriate approach to any analysis of such an interpretation should also be both objective and subjective. This dual condition for the analysis – an involved interpreter and both subjectivity and objectivity – requires the application of two analytical approaches: in our case reception history and reader-response criticism.

The text and the reader/interpreter interact with and influence each other. They are players who interact in the creation/re-creation of the work of art, co-workers in the hermeneutical process, and partners in a dialogue. Each creates a reaction, or in literary theory a 'response', in the other. The biblical text is neither a dead text (an object) subjected to a totalitarian quest for a single original meaning intended by the author, nor is it the omnipotent creation of a 'dead author'[40] which can dictate its meaning to the interpreter (the subject). The text is one partner in a dialogue and co-creates meaning.[41]

Gadamer's dialogical hermeneutics is one of the predecessors of postmodern literary and biblical approaches. Although Gadamer was noncommittal on the degree of subjectivity involved in an interpretation, he clearly opened a space for the development of reader-oriented approaches. Gadamer himself insisted, as did many formalists, that the 'players' do not bring their own subjectivity to the interpretation: the 'players' or 'readers' have to *die* in a work of art.[42] Talking about the non-existence of the personality of the player (Gadamer), the death of the reader (Georges Poulet), and the imprisonment of the reader in the text (Walker Gibson, Michael Riffaterre, Gerald Prince) are all approaches which seek to avoid the risk of subjectivism.[43] A similar idea was suggested by Andrew Hass, a well-known Hegelian, who reverses the master–slave dialectic of his teacher and argues that it is in fact the artist who is bound to the created work:

> It is only when the slave recognises her labour as her own, or when she recognises that the fruits of her labour, the objects into which she has poured herself on behalf of the lord, are in fact more an extension of herself than they are an extension of the lord, that she can make a break towards a freedom from enthrallment. Converted back into terms of self-consciousness, the self, in recognising its own self as part of the dynamic of othering, need no longer fear the other as oppressive, since it requires that otherness to fulfil its own true independence.[44]

40. Roland Barthes, *The Rustle of Language* (Berkeley, CA: University of California Press, 1989), 49–55.

41. Louise Rosenblatt, *The Reader, the Text, the Poem: The Transactional Theory of the Literary Work* (Carbondale, IL: Southern Illinois University Press, 1978), 5, 16.

42. Gadamer, *Truth and Method*, 111. See also Jane Tompkins, 'An Introduction to Reader-Response Criticism', in *Reader-Response Criticism: From Formalism to Post-Structuralism*, ed. Jane Tompkins (Baltimore, MD: Johns Hopkins University Press, 1980), xv.

43. Ibid.

44. Andrew Hass, 'Artist Bound: The Enslavement of Art to the Hegelian Other', *Literature and Theology* 25, no. 4 (2011): 382.

This process brilliantly describes the means by which we overcome not only the master–slave dialectic but also the inequality that is inherently bound to this concept. Although formalism intends to leave the author out of the analysis – and from the perspective of modern hermeneutics it does just that – the author still somehow enters the analysis from a different angle. Poulet perceives the role of the author as 'incarnated' in and through the text: 'Thus a book is not only a book, it is the means by which an author actually preserves his ideas, his feelings, his modes of dreaming and living'.[45] Formalists have developed various concepts to help them grasp the nature of the reader's role as they understand it. Walker Gibson, for example, developed the concept of a 'mock reader'[46] who is little more than a puppet, led through the text by a puppeteer, the 'speaker' in Gibson's terminology, who executes the author's will. Mock readers fulfil only the roles ascribed to them by the author: they are, 'prisoners of the author's consciousness'.[47] Formalists are prepared to admit that the text attains value only when it is read, but they are reluctant to ascribe to the reader a more significant role. Poulet describes reading as a process whereby the 'real reader', a reader with some expectations, literary abilities, and aesthetic values, is swallowed up by the 'mock reader'.[48]

As we saw earlier, formalism is criticized by Sherwood and Moore, who contend that the 'theory' which rules such literary analysis oppresses the real reader. The literary scholar Stanley Fish formulated his approach in the same spirit. Fish was formed by new criticism, and his whole literary work is marked by attempts to critically distinguish his own approach.[49] One of the merits of his approach is that he seeks to describe the state of literary criticism as he perceives it and to make this the starting point for his analysis. He does not see his role as a corrective one. On the role of the reader in new criticism, Fish sees the concepts of 'informed reader' and 'mock reader' as constructs. The informed reader has all the competences necessary for uncovering the hidden message of the text and thus functions as a counterpart to the

---

45. Georges Poulet, 'Criticism and the Experience of Interiority', in Tompkins, ed., *Reader-Response Criticism*, 46.

46. Walker Gibson, 'Authors, Speakers, Readers, and Mock Readers', in Tompkins, ed., *Reader-Response Criticism*, 1–11.

47. Tompkins, 'An Introduction to Reader-Response Criticism', x–xv.

48. Poulet, 'Criticism and the Experience of Interiority', 41–5.

49. Fish, *Is There a Text in this Class?*, 9–11.

mock reader. A real reader, according to Fish, is a mixture of these two neighbouring constructs.[50] Fish also argues that the relationship between the text and the reader should not be seen as dialectical:[51] the meaning is created neither in the 'mind of the reader', as subjectivists suggest, nor in the 'structures of the text', as the formalists would have it. This being so, we might criticize Fish for favouring the role of the reader over the role of the text in the process of shaping its meaning. However, faithful to the creed of the abolition of the dialectical subject–object relationship between the text and the reader, he developed the concept of the 'interpretive community' in order to avoid the threat of subjectivism, and in so doing shifted the discussion to a different sphere: 'Indeed, it is an interpretive community, rather than either the text or the reader, that produces meanings and is responsible for the emergence of formal features'.[52] An interpretive community is made up of those who share the same strategies for interpreting a particular text.[53] Fish also confirms the postmodern abolition of the subjective and objective categories since his legitimizing concept of the interpretive community lies simultaneously in both:

> An interpretive community is not objective because as a bundle of interest, of particular purposes and goals, its perspective is interested rather than neutral; but the very same reasoning, the meanings and texts produced by an interpretive community are not subjective because they do not proceed from an isolated individual but from a public and conventional point of view.[54]

Fish is seeking 'legitimization' rather than 'objectification', which is a desirable movement for this study. As we saw earlier, Gadamer presented a similar concept of 'common sense' when discussing the formative role of culture.[55] Jauss is certainly less bold than Fish in his acknowledgment of the reader. Jauss draws his inspiration from Michael Riffaterre[56]

---

50. Stanley Fish, 'Literature in the Reader: Affective Stylistics', in Tompkins, ed., *Reader-Response Criticism*, 86–90.
    51. Fish, *Is There a Text in this Class?*, 13–14.
    52. Ibid., 14.
    53. Ibid., 13–14.
    54. Ibid., 14.
    55. Gadamer, *Truth and Method*, 16–37.
    56. Michael Riffaterre, 'The Stylistic Approach to Literary History', *New Literary History* 2, no. 1 (1970): 39–55.

and Wolfgang Iser,[57] and his approach is a critical response to them.[58] In Jauss's methodology of three successive readings, the second step is devoted to synchronic literary analysis and corresponds to filling in gaps in meaning through the formal activity of literary or textual criticism.[59] Here Jauss formulates his concept of an 'historical reader'[60] who knows the text or narrative well but is not so advanced in historical and linguistic competence and therefore 'wonders' and formulates questions for a 'commentator' who has all the necessary scholarly competence to answer them. There is thus a question–answer relationship in the process of interpretation, and this deepens the aesthetic impression of the reader.[61] Such a relationship recalls that between the 'speaker' and the 'mock reader' in Gibson's terminology.[62] However, Jauss's historical reader is not completely mock as he or she is competent enough to formulate questions and is certainly determined not to be 'swallowed up'. Regarding the process of the legitimization of the interpretation, Jauss introduces the concept of a 'horizon of expectations',[63] which somewhat resembles Fish's interpretive community. Jauss developed his concept from the phenomenology of perception applied by Husserl and Gadamer to the experience of consciousness. There are always two horizons at work, an individual experience and a methodological understanding, and these horizons are continuously engaging with each other.[64] Paul de Man summarizes Jauss's concept by suggesting that the horizon of expectation 'mediates between the private inception and public reception'.[65] Inception takes place in the here and now and is oriented synchronically: '[it is] an entirely contingent and syntagmatic relationship between two elements that happen to coincide in time but are otherwise entirely alien to each other'.[66] Reception on the other hand is a relationship between the work and its historical setting and is oriented diachronically.[67] Thus, we see that

57. Wolfgang Iser, 'The Reading Process: A Phenomenological Approach', in Tompkins, ed., *Reader-Response Criticism*, 58.

58. Jauss, *Toward an Aesthetic of Reception*, 143–5.

59. Ibid., 145.

60. Ibid., 144.

61. Ibid.

62. Gibson, 'Authors, Speakers, Readers, and Mock Readers'.

63. Paul de Man, 'Introduction', in Jauss, ed., *Toward an Aesthetic of Reception*, xii.

64. Ibid.

65. Ibid., xiii.

66. Ibid., xiv.

67. Ibid.

a horizon of expectations is both objective and subjective: it involves the subjectivity of the interpreter but still mediates a means of legitimizing the interpretation. Evans clarifies:

> The fusion of horizons [*Horizontverschmelzung*] is not a formation of a single horizon, but it involves an experience of tension between the text and the present... In fact, neither the horizon of the present reader nor of the historically situated text exists in isolation.[68]

Regarding acknowledgment of the reader/interpreter in the herme-neutical process, reception history and reader-response both tend to rely on literary scholarship. For our analysis, the most appropriate balance between the roles of the interpreter and the interpreted text is described as an ongoing mutual influence between the interpreted text and the interpreter as presented by Fish and Jauss. The interpreter is granted considerable space. As Clines, a significant supporter of reader-response criticism, observes: 'reader-response criticism regards meaning as coming into being at the meeting point of text and reader'.[69] However, the interpretation is not subjective overall, because the producing 'I' of the interpreter is, as Evans clarifies, to a large extent formed by his or her interpretive community within the horizon of expectation. In our research, the novelist is a member of an interpretive community which helps him or her understand and interpret the biblical text. The novel that functions as an artistic interpretation of a biblical text is a product of an involved interpreter, but any such interpretation should nonetheless be legitimate.

Clines discerns various approaches towards identifying the role of the reader in the hermeneutical process, but the most appropriate approach for our analysis builds largely on the literary theory of Fish. Clines calls his own approach a 'comparative interpretation'.[70] According to Clines, two elements determine the interpretation. The first is the indeterminacy of meaning. Unlike researchers in reception history scholarship (Jauss, Thiselton), Clines is persuaded that there is very little determinacy of meaning over time: 'Whatever a text may mean in one context, it is almost

---

68. Evans, *Reception History, Tradition and Biblical Interpretation*, 5.

69. David Clines, *On the Way to the Postmodern: Old Testament Essays, 1967–1998* (Sheffield: Sheffield Academic, 1998), 39.

70. See also David Clines, *Interested Parties: The Ideology of Writers and Readers of the Hebrew Bible* (Sheffield: Sheffield Academic, 1995), 178. Ideology critique will be discussed in detail in the final part of this chapter. We focus here only on matters connected with the relationship between the text and reader/interpreter and with the process of legitimization.

bound to mean something different in a different context'.[71] The second element is the interpretive community. For Clines, as for Fish, 'There is no objective standard by which we can know whether one view or the other is right; we can only tell whether it has been accepted'.[72] What is acceptable and therefore legitimate is determined by the interpretive community:[73] no legitimate interpretation arises out of the blue.[74] According to Clines, an interpretive community can be 'an academic community, which establishes norms by which it will allow certain interpretations and disallow others. Or it may be a church community, which will decide on what kinds of interpretations are suitable for its own purposes'.[75]

Thiselton, a researcher in reception history scholarship, is much more conservative when it comes to acknowledging the role of the reader/interpreter in the process of interpretation.[76] Although his training was through the Sheffield school of reader-response criticism, he has been greatly influenced by the German school of reception history, that is, by Jauss. Unlike Clines, Thiselton sees much more determinacy in meaning in the text and adheres to the approaches of Iser and, mainly, Jauss. However, the main difference between Clines and Thiselton lies in their respective perceptions of the time horizon and the role of tradition. Thiselton sees some continuity in meaning over time:

> Tradition mediates *judgements* concerning textual content. Even if Fish could claim that these are no more than reactive constructions by earlier reading communities, at least these would constitute 'something outside' Fish's self-sufficient reader or reading community.[77]

What is the relationship between the interpreter (the novelist) and the interpreted text (the biblical narrative) that gives rise to the artistic interpretation of the biblical text in the form of the novel? My conviction is that the novelist is surely not a mock reader who would 'die' in the text and fail to contribute any new insight, nor an informed reader who would

71. Ibid.
72. Ibid., 179.
73. Clines, *On the Way to the Postmodern*, 39.
74. Clines, *Interested Parties*, 178–9.
75. Clines, *On the Way to the Postmodern*, 39.
76. Anthony Thiselton, 'Communicative Action and Promise in Interdisciplinary, Biblical and Theological Hermeneutics', in *The Promise of Hermeneutics*, ed. Roger Lundin, Anthony Thiselton, and Clarence Walhout (Grand Rapids, MI: Eerdmans, 1999), 133–239.
77. Ibid., 157.

decipher the grammar of the text and generate an objective response to any 'gaps'.[78] The novelist is in fact a combination of the two: someone with the appropriate literary competence who is drawn into the text but still able to ask critical questions. However, perhaps not every meddlesome question can be answered from the structure, the grammar, or any other signals in the text. Regardless of my own perspective on this issue, the most suitable approach seems to be a combination of Jauss's reception history, adjusted for biblical scholarship by Thiselton and Evans, and the post-structuralism of Fish, and its application in biblical studies within reader-response scholarship.

The struggle between synchrony and diachrony

The methodological query which Alter sets out to resolve is that of the relationship between different paradigmatic books within the 'Western canon'. Alter's conviction is that a literary work of art can be in both continuity and critical discontinuity with its predecessors in a particular literary tradition.[79] As we shall see, it is indeed the case that different authors in different eras deal differently with their biblical sources of influence.

The task of reception history scholarship in biblical studies is often narrowed down to a synopsis of the history of the reception or interpretation of the given text, which gives us a perspective on why a text is currently read the way it is.[80] Thiselton goes further and builds on Jauss's complex and well-developed approach. Our interdisciplinary analysis here, however, offers a critical evaluation of our chosen novelist's work as an interpreter of the biblical text and of the work of his interpretive partner from the field of biblical studies, and I will evaluate their analysis through the legitimizing means of reception history and reader-response criticism, that is, through interpretive communities and the horizon of expectations. The first step of this analysis is an aesthetic reading; the second step includes a thematic analysis of the motif in the Hebrew Bible, an historical-critical analysis of its source verses, and an exploration of the reception of this motif throughout the Hebrew Bible and New Testament; the third step explores the history of biblical and literary scholarships, culminating in the particular receptions of our interpretive partners and their interpretations. What this means is that we will look at what the text

---

78. Fish, 'Literature in the Reader', 86–90.
79. Alter, *Canon and Creativity*, 3.
80. Luz, *Matthew in History*, 1–4.

meant at the time of its origin, what new significances it has taken on in the course of its history, and what it means for us now. A synopsis of the history of the interpretation of the text is of course included. All interpretations from whatever age have their horizon of expectations, which reflects the fusion of horizons of the text and its interpreter in his or her context and brings a new and original element that stimulates fresh interpretations. The novelist's interpretation can therefore be checked against the history of interpretation in order to show us whether this interpretation is within its horizon of expectation, and therefore whether it is, or is not, legitimate.

Unlike Clines, Thiselton assigns significance to tradition and to a diachronic analysis of a text:

> A crucial point…is the *fundamentally a-historical viewpoint of reader-response theory*, in contrast to the genuine engagement with horizons of expectation located within an ongoing historical tradition of textual effects, as this is explored in the reception theory of Gadamer's pupil Hans Robert Jauss.[81]

Thiselton undoubtedly offers a significant temporal perspective which sees interpretations of the biblical text of different kinds throughout history joined by a line of tradition. Building on the hermeneutics of Gadamer and Jauss, his approach legitimizes artistic interpretations of a biblical text, including interpretations in the form of novels. Such a hermeneutic makes this kind of interpretation not only legitimate but even significant and supportive. Reader-response does not operate with the diachronic dimension of analysis and is therefore, in my view, deficient. It does, however, offer a useful perspective that is absent from the hermeneutics of Jauss, and that is the possibility of a negative response to the history of interpretation, as we see in critical theory. Critical theory in biblical studies builds upon the notion that the biblical text has been 'contaminated' by various ideologies, both at the time of its origin and throughout the history of its reception.[82] It employs two steps in deconstructing the text, or in Clines' words '[showing] how the text deconstructs itself';[83] both steps are strictly synchronic: 'A text typically has a thesis to defend or a point of view to espouse; but inevitably texts falter and let slip evidence against their own cause'.[84] First, we will look at whether

---

81. Thiselton, 'Communicative Action and Promise', 157.
82. Clines, *Interested Parties*, 9–25.
83. Clines, *On the Way to the Postmodern*, 41.
84. Ibid., 40.

the text deconstructs itself: whether we find contradictory elements in the immediate or larger context of our text. Secondly, we will look at the text from the perspective of our interpretive communities: are there elements which cannot be accepted by the twenty-first-century reader? As a scholar of the Hebrew Bible, Clines describes the strategy of reading the biblical text from the point of view of the contemporary reader as 'reading the text from left to right'.[85]

Thiselton employs a 'hermeneutics of suspicion'. Although he rightly attributes the authorship of this concept to Ricoeur,[86] he sees no problem in adding this step to Jauss's approach, which does not generally admit to the possibility of disagreeing with tradition. On the one hand this suits our analysis: as I have already pointed out, an artistic interpretation of a biblical text does not have to correspond to the history of interpretation of that text as it is by nature artistic, prophetic, interruptive, and most likely contrary. On the other hand, it is important to sustain the diachronic nature of the analysis as this legitimizes the importance of artistic interpretations of biblical texts. We can argue, therefore, that we should use both synchronic and diachronic analysis as they are mutually complementary.

How do we reconcile this apparent conundrum? The concept of 'paradigm shifts', brought into biblical scholarship by David Parris, sheds light on the riddle of how to bridge the gaps between different horizons of expectation. Parris's concept offers a detailed explanation of Alter's assertion that 'both continuity and discontinuity' fit within the realm of the literary reception of a biblical motif over time. Parris borrowed his concept from the philosopher Alasdair MacIntyre and appropriated it for biblical studies.[87] Parris is well aware that changes in paradigms, originally described by the natural scientist Thomas Khun, are less common in the human sciences than in the natural sciences and that in the humanities Copernican revolutions acquire a more subtle form. However, Parris usefully points out the differences between the various approaches towards the biblical text in different eras. Today, we certainly approach the biblical text with a different set of questions from those used, say,

---

85. Ibid., 3.

86. Thiselton, 'Reception Theory', 300.

87. The term paradigm shift is closely related to the concept of the horizon of expectations and describes similar features, such as changes in interpretations over time. Although the latter concept is more widely used, for our study the argumentation of paradigm shifts is more persuasive and accurate. We will nonetheless engage with the horizon of expectations when we move on to study the history of reception.

a century ago.[88] History does not follow a cumulative model of understanding: it moves in great leaps. There is a dynamic between operating
within a paradigm and a paradigm shift. Each paradigm has its own set
of questions appropriate to it – its own horizon of expectations – and
when this set is used up, 'when a tradition is no longer able to address the
questions in its core problematic in a manner that satisfies its members,
that tradition is said to enter an epistemological crisis'.[89] The crisis in turn
leads to a paradigm shift. The concept of paradigm shifts nonetheless still
allows for some degree of continuity within diversity and the possibility
of progress through learning from the past and is thus most useful for our
own approach.

88. 'While the centrality of an authoritative text, such as the Bible, is one of
the elements that constitutes the continuity of the Christian tradition, the function it
serves in this tradition has changed over time. As the tradition changes, the questions
put to the text will also change… These questions were embedded in their stage in
the narrative of the Christian tradition. The answers they received from the text in
turn contributed to the growth of the tradition and how the authoritative role of the
Bible was understood at that stage.' David Parris, *Reception Theory and Biblical
Hermeneutics*, Princeton Theological Monograph Series 107 (Eugene, OR: Pickwick,
2009), 175, 179.
89. Ibid., 188.

Chapter 2

THE CONTEXT AND RECEPTION OF THE PROMISED LAND MOTIF IN THE HEBREW BIBLE AND THE NEW TESTAMENT

In the terminology of the previous chapter, this exploration of our motif in the Hebrew Bible and the New Testament will take the 'scientific way' towards understanding.

Our thematic analysis of the motif in the Hebrew Bible will first explore its origin and its semantic background and overall significance, and then carry out a standard historical-critical analysis of the two key verses, Gen. 15.7 and Exod. 3.8,[1] which will include a translation of the texts, a syntactic-structural analysis, a synchronic literary analysis, and an analysis of the origin of the two verses. Many biblical scholars in reader-oriented approaches argue that the differences and disagreements between the various theories regarding the origins of biblical texts has damaged the reputation of diachronic analysis to such an extent that it is not worth carrying out. I do not hold this position and will seek to maintain a balance between synchronic and diachronic approaches. Following Gordon Wenham, I will progress from the *certain* or given – the text as it is in its final form, i.e. the synchronic analysis – to the *uncertain* and hypothetical – the development of the text and its possible sources, i.e. the diachronic analysis.

The second part of the chapter will explore the reception of our motif in the Hebrew Bible and the New Testament, although the extensive nature of the material will prevent us from covering all occurrences. Many other

---

1. Throughout this study, these verses will be suggested as bearers of the motif of the promised land in the Hebrew Bible. They meet the requirements for 'promised land terminology' in the Hebrew Bible and are among the earliest references. They also correspond to the promised land terminology used by John Steinbeck, more of which later.

sources have set out to do this.[2] Our aim is to follow the development of the motif and the different ways it is interpreted in the Bible. We will proceed according to the division suggested by Janzen: In the Hebrew Bible, (i) the Torah, (ii) the Deuteronomistic history, (iii) the literary Prophets to the end of the exile, and (iv) the postexilic era; in the New Testament, (i) the Gospels and Acts, (ii) the Pauline Epistles, and (iii) the non-Pauline Epistles.

A thematic analysis of the promised land in the Hebrew Bible

In a contribution to the *Anchor Bible Dictionary* entitled 'Land', Janzen relies heavily on Brueggemann's theology of the land: 'The land theme is so ubiquitous that it may have greater claim to be the central motif in the OT than any other, including "covenant"'.[3] Schmid suggests that in the biblical context, land is almost always understood in the figurative sense: 'The term *'ereṣ* acquires its specific theological usage in the context of the land promise and its appropriation in the conquest tradition'.[4] Janzen also observes: 'Parenthetically, the two common English designations "Promised Land" and "Holy Land", though correctly expressing central theological concerns, are not characteristic for the OT'.[5] The starting point for our semantic analysis of the idiom 'promised land'. The key word in the Old Testament which forms the 'promised land terminology' is 'land' (ארץ in MT, and γῆ in LXX). On the other hand, the 'promise' is verbalized in the ordinary expression for 'speech' (אמר in MT, and λαλέω or λέγω in LXX; [Gen. 12.7; 13.15, 17; 15.5, 18; 17.8; 18.19; 21.1; 28.15; 47.29, etc.). Janzen reminds us that in the Hebrew Bible, the word 'land' is rendered by the two Hebrew words ארץ and אדמה.[6] He defines 'land'

2. See Jacobus Cornelis De Vos, ed., *The Land of Israel in Bible, History, and Theology: Studies in Honour of Ed Noort* (Leiden: Brill, 2009); David Frankel, *The Land of Canaan and the Destiny of Israel: Theologies of Territory in the Hebrew Bible* (Winona Lake, IN: Eisenbrauns, 2011); Brueggemann, *The Land*; William Davies, *The Gospel and the Land: Early Christianity and Jewish Territorial Doctrine* (Berkeley, CA: University of California Press, 1974); Gary Burge, *Jesus and the Land: The New Testament Challenge to 'Holy Land' Theology* (Grand Rapids, MI: Baker Academic, 2010).

3. Waldemar Janzen, 'Land', in *The Anchor Bible Dictionary*, 6 vols (New York: Doubleday, 1992), 4:146.

4. H. H. Schmid, 'ארץ', in *Theological Lexicon of the Old Testament*, ed. Claus Westermann and Ernst Jenni, 3 vols (Peabody, MA: Hendrickson, 1997), 1:177.

5. Janzen, 'Land', 144.

6. See ibid., 143.

as follows: '"Land" is the usual translation of *'ereṣ* when it refers to (a) a specific geographical region...or (b) the territory of a specific people... In the majority of instances of type (b), the land in question is identified in some way as promised to, claimed by, or possessed by Israel or a part of Israel.'[7]

There are numerous witnesses to the promise and loss of land in the Hebrew Bible. There is of course the promise given to the patriarchs[8] and a particular reference to the land being provided by YHWH.[9] As we have already suggested, Brueggemann sees the promise and loss of land as a central theme of the Hebrew Bible and recognizes land as a *symbol* that reflects the relationship between YHWH and God's people,[10] and the corresponding dynamics of faithfulness to YHWH (the promise of land) and falling away from YHWH (the loss of land).[11] He observes:

> Biblical faith is surely about the life of a people with God as has been shown by all the current and recent emphases on covenant in a historical place. And if God has to do with Israel in a special way, as he surely does, he has to do with land as a historical place in a special way. It will no longer do to talk about Yahweh and his people, but we must speak about Yahweh and his people and his land... God is committed to this land and...his promise for his people is always his land.[12]

---

7. Ibid., 144.

8. See Gen. 12.7; 13.15; 15.7, 13, 18; 17.8; 21.23; 24.7; 26.3-4; 28.4; 35.12; 48.4; Deut. 1.8, 35; 6.10, 18, 23; 7.13; 8.1; 9.28; 10.11; 11.9, 21; 19.8; 26.3, 15; 27.3; 28.11; 31.7. Schmid, 'ארץ', 177–8.

9. See Deut. 1.8, 25, 35; 2.29; 3.20; 4.1, 21, 38; 5.31; 6.10, 23; 9.6, 28; 10.11; 11.17, 31; 12.1; 15.4, 7; 16.20; 18.2, 14; 19.10; 20.16; 21.23; 24.4; 25.19; 26.1, 3; 31.7. Ibid., 178.

10. This book will use inclusive language when referring to God and will generally seek to avoid using the pronouns he/him/his; likewise when referring to the author or redactor of the biblical text.

11. See also: 'Not only is the nation physically separated from its land when it is carried into exile, but in the prophetic denunciation of current ills and predictions of coming judgement as well, the land figures prominently as the sphere of God's punishment on a wayward people. Image clusters include pollution, blighting and drought, and we can detect an analogy in this fall from grace to the original expulsion from the Garden of Eden.' Leland Ryken, ed., 'Land', in *Dictionary of Biblical Imagery* (Downers Grove, IL: InterVarsity, 1998), 487. 'The theme of Israel's relationship to its land is clearly pivotal, holding a central place within the overall structure of the narrative of the Hebrew Bible.' Frankel, *The Land of Canaan and the Destiny of Israel*, 1.

12. Brueggemann, *The Land*, 5.

This dynamic is a golden thread throughout Brueggemann's *The Land*, which explores the links between the various narratives concerning God's dealings with the chosen people.[13] Brueggemann's argument for the centrality of land and its equal role in the triangular relationship between God, God's people and God's land in the Hebrew Bible is a bold one. Other authors recognize a strong link between the people of Israel and the land and affirm that the destiny of the people of Israel is more or less dependent on their immediate relationship to the land.[14] According to Theodore Hiebert, there were two beliefs in Israel concerning its relationship to the land and neither of these is self-evident. The first is that Israel is not indigenous to its land; the second is that the God of Israel gave it the land.[15] Skinner suggests that unlike the promise of descendants, the promise of land is bound by a covenant (Gen. 15.18),[16] an agreement between God and God's people. Ottosson observes: 'Yahweh lives in the land, in the midst of the people (Num 35:34) – thus land, people, and God belong together'.[17] Wright argues that land functions as a 'midterm in the relationship' between YHWH and God's people because it is the inheritance of both YHWH and the people of Israel.[18] Wright is persuaded that, 'Israel's behaviour on the land determines Yahweh's response to Israel in the land, and the land will "respond" to both'.[19] Hiebert notes two aspects of Israel's relationship to the land: first, the eternal relationship referred to in Gen. 17.8, Deut. 4.40, 2 Sam. 7.10, and Amos 9.15; secondly,

---

13. I will deal with Brueggemann's view of the land in detail in Chapter 4. See also: 'As a land of promise, the land of Canaan becomes an evocative image of longing of the Israelites as they journey toward it'. Ryken, 'Promised Land', 666.

14. Scholars from the field of ideology critique tend to relativize Israel's claim on the land. This is of course difficult to prove or disprove. We will encounter some of these attempts when discussing ideology critique of the motif of the promised land in Chapter 4.

15. Theodore Hiebert, 'Land', in *Eerdmans Dictionary of the Bible*, ed. David Freedman (Grand Rapids, MI: Eerdmans, 2000), 788.

16. John Skinner, *A Critical and Exegetical Commentary on Genesis*, 2nd edn (Edinburgh: T. & T. Clark, 1951), 276. See also Wolf Plaut and Annette Böckler, *Die Tora: in jüdischer Auslegung*, Dt. Erstausg., Teil. 1 (Gütersloh: Kaiser, Gütersloher Verl-Haus, 1999), 173.

17. Magnus Ottosson, 'ארץ', in *Theological Dictionary of the Old Testament*, vol. 1, ed. Helmer Ringgren (Grand Rapids, MI: Eerdmans, 1977), 402.

18. Christopher Wright, 'ארץ', in *New International Dictionary of Old Testament Theology and Exegesis*, ed. Willem Van Gemeren, 5 vols (Carlisle: Paternoster, 1997), 1:523.

19. Ibid.

that Israel's relationship to the land depends on the people's loyalty (or disloyalty) to God. The passages in Deut. 4.25-27 and 11.13-17, Jer. 7.1-15, and Amos 6.1-8 refer to such a condition.[20] Hiebert also observes:

> According to this latter view, the exile and the experience of landlessness after the fall of Samaria and Jerusalem were understood as the ultimate punishment for Israel's covenant faithlessness (2 Kgs 17:7-23; 21:1-16). Exilic prophets predicted God's new act of salvation primarily in terms of the restoration to the Israelite exiles of their preexilic lands (Isa 40:1-11; 49:19-20; 51:1-3; Ezek 20:40-44).[21]

The land is also mentioned in the context of the giving of the commandments.[22] Plaut suggests a parallel between Gen. 15.7, the promise of land given to Abraham, and Exod. 20.1, the beginning of the Decalogue.[23] Such a parallel could suggest a strong connection between the two themes: that keeping the Ten Commandments secures the people's place in the promised land; equally, a crime against YHWH is a crime against the land[24] which results in expulsion. In the exile, we find the expectation of a re-possession of the land.[25]

Kwakkel points out that references to the people of Israel and the land in the book of Hosea are difficult to distinguish and are even used interchangeably.[26] Two promises were made to Abraham: the promise of progeny and the promise of land. Schmid insists that in the patriarchal period, the latter is less important than the former: the promise in Gen. 15.18 is most likely the oldest promise and Gen. 12.7 and 28.13-15 are later additions handed down at particular holy places.[27] For Ottosson,

---

20. Hiebert, 'Land', 789.

21. Ibid.

22. See Josh. 21.43; 23.16; Judg. 2.1, 6; Jer. 32.22; Ezek. 33.24. Schmid, 'ארץ', 178.

23. Plaut and Böckler, *Die Tora*, 173.

24. Note Lev. 18.25, 27-28; Num. 35.34; Ps. 37.11, 22, 29, 34; Prov. 2.21-22; 10.30; Isa. 65.9; Jer. 2.7; 3.2; see ibid. Note also Lev. 25.23; Jer. 2.7; 16.18; Ezek. 36.20; Hos. 9.3; see Ottosson, 'ארץ', 204.

25. See Jer. 30.3; Ezek. 36.28. Schmid, 'ארץ', 178.

26. Gert Kwakkel, 'The Land in the Book of Hosea', in *The Land of Israel in Bible, History and Theology: Studies in Honour of Ed Noort*, ed. Cornelis De Vos and Jacques Van Ruiten (Leiden: Brill, 2009), 167–81.

27. Schmid, 'ארץ', 771. Gen. 15.18 could also be a later insertion, but this is immaterial from the perspective of reception history scholarship. Schmid refers to Gen. 15.18 as the place where the covenant is mentioned; the promise itself is given in v. 7. Ibid.

the central passages are Gen. 17.1-8 and Gen. 15.5, 7, 16; Genesis 12 is secondary.[28]

Regarding the attributes that accompany the notion of the promised land, Schmid refers to 'a good land',[29] and 'a land flowing with milk and honey';[30] Ottosson mentions 'a broad land',[31] and 'a land of pleasantness, a precious land'.[32] Ryken describes attributes which in combination imply abundance:

> A land that produced an abundance of milk had to be rich in pasture, so by extension a picture of successful farming enters one's imagination. Honey valued for its sweetness rather than as a necessity of life was rare enough to rank as a luxury. As images of desirability and abundance, therefore, these two images combine to form a picture of total satisfaction.[33]

One area of uncertainty is the question of who owns the promised land. Ottosson notes verses which suggest that the land belongs to YHWH: it is God's heritage,[34] which, leaving chronology aside, is indeed in tension with the verses mentioned above (Gen. 12.7; 15.7, 18; 28.13-15), where God gives (נתן) the land to Abraham and his descendants as a gift. Although the land is bound by the covenant, and the continuation of the covenant is dependent on the people's conduct, as long as the covenant is not broken the land should be theirs. Kwakkel, however, confirms the point of view that the people of Israel were tenants rather than owners:

28. Ottosson, 'ארץ', 403.

29. Schmid, 'ארץ', 177. See Deut. 1.25, 35; 3.25; 4.21, 22; 6.18, etc.; Exod. 3.8; Num. 14.7; 1 Chron. 28.18. Schmid also observes that, 'It is the "good...land" (Exod 3:8; Num 14:7; Deut 1:25 etc.), an expression that combines "fruitfulness, wealth, beauty – in short, the fullness of blessing"; "it is the abundantly blessed, glorious land".' Ibid. See also Ottosson, 'ארץ', 402–3.

30. Ibid. See Deut. 6.3; 11.9; 26.9, 15; 27.3; Exod. 3.8, 17; 13.5; 33.3; Lev. 20.24; Num. 13.27; 14.8; 16.13-14; Deut. 31.20; Josh. 5.6; Ezra 20.6, 15; Jer. 11.5; 32.33.

31. Ottosson, 'ארץ', 403. See Exod. 3.8; Judg. 18.10; 1 Chron. 4.40; Isa. 22.18; Neh. 9.35.

32. Ibid. See Ps. 106.24; Jer. 3.19.

33. Leland Ryken, ed., 'Land Flowing with Milk and Honey', in *Dictionary of Biblical Imagery*, 488. See also Hans Ausloos, '"A Land Flowing with Milk and Honey": Indicative of a Deuteronomistic Redaction?', *Ephemerides Theologicae Lovanienses. Louvain Journal of Theology and Canon Law* 75 (1999): 297–314.

34. Ottosson, 'ארץ', 402. See 1 Sam. 26.19; 2 Sam. 14.16; Pss. 68.10(9); 79.1; Jer. 2.7; 16.18; 50.11.

> The phrase ארץ יהוה occurs only here [Hos. 9.3] in the Old Testament. It testifies to the idea that Yhwh, as the rightful owner, lays down the law in the land of Israel... In Canaan, it is Yhwh who provides his people with food and drink. Therefore, he should be honoured as the giver. If the Israelites refuse to do so, he has every right to drive them out of his land.[35]

Although the term 'YHWH's land' is to be found only in Hos. 9.3,[36] we read elsewhere about 'my/your/his land – referring to YHWH'.[37] Wright and Ottosson both argue that the key witness to YHWH's ownership of the land is Lev. 25.23.[38] Schmid argues logically that, 'Because the 'ereṣ as a region is God's possession, the 'ereṣ as ground may never be sold'.[39] Hiebert goes even further and reminds us that according to Lev. 25.23, the Israelites are 'resident aliens' and 'servants'.[40] Theologically speaking, the promised land indeed belongs to God. However, grammatically speaking, when something is given to someone, it belongs not to the giver but to the recipient. This tension might be clarified a little by explaining the historical context of 'land grants'. Robert Coote sheds some light on this issue by pointing out that the practice of land distribution in the ancient Near East worked in a similar way to that presented in the Hebrew Bible. Land was never given to someone in the way we would understand it now, but rather only granted for some limited time:

> Land was held by the patriarchal household in three allocations of land use. Rights to arable land was through periodic repartition by lot. This facilitated the fencing of rotating fallow grounds for grazing and contributed to local solidarity. Proprietary allocation, comparable to freehold, was made by sale or grant and typically applied to vineyards, orchards, and private gardens, that is, property requiring long-term investment. Common allocation was applied to the use of outback for pasturage.[41]

In Coote's view, therefore, the promise of land to Abraham and the patriarchs can be understood as a territorial grant in which God is acting as grantor, even though the handover of the grant was realized

---

35. Kwakkel, 'The Land in the Book of Hosea', 179.

36. Ibid., 178. See Isa. 14.2. See also Ottosson, 'ארץ', 401.

37. Schmid, 'ארץ', 178. See Ps. 85.2; Jer. 2.7; Joel 2.18. See also 2 Chron. 7.20. Ottosson, 'ארץ', 401.

38. Wright, 'ארץ', 522; See also Ottosson, 'ארץ', 401–2.

39. Schmid, 'ארץ', 871.

40. Hiebert, 'Land', 788.

41. Robert Coote, 'Land', in *The Oxford Encyclopedia of the Bible and Theology*, vol. 2, ed. Samuel Balentine (Oxford: Oxford University Press, 2015), 27.

through conquest.[42] According to Millar, the relationship between God as the owner of the land and Israel as the people to whom the land was entrusted reflects a father–son relationship. The visible sign of this union is the inheritance, the land, but the exile prompted a reconsideration: 'Was Israel by the event of exile – the act of the removal of land from it – deprived of its Son's rights?'[43] Millar's answer to his own question is that, 'Israel seems to have concluded that their sonship remained intact, even though the outward sign of their familial relationship with God had been taken away'.[44] Numerous metaphors are used to illustrate the relationship between God and the people of Israel. God is 'father' (Ps. 68.5; Isa. 63.16; Mal. 2.10; Mt. 23.9; 1 Cor. 8.16; Eph. 4.6), 'mother' (Deut. 32.11-12, 18; Ps. 131.2; Isa. 42.14; 49.15; 66.13; Hos. 11.3-4; 13.8; Mt. 23.37; Lk. 13.34), a 'pillar of fire', 'cloud' (Exod. 13.21-22), 'king' (Pss. 47.7; 68.24; 74.12; 145.1), 'lover' (Song of Songs), and much else. Millar's statement regarding the father–son relationship is therefore an oversimplification, although the author does retroactively apply the equivalent New Testament metaphor to the context of the Hebrew Bible. Coote's discussion of inheritance and land grants suggests a relationship closer to king–subject. Coote adds that a religious dimension to territorial grants was by no means peculiar to Israel: 'Landholding was regularly sanctioned by cultic or religious practice, centred at a local level on household or clan burial sites, at a regional level on saint's tombs, and at a monarchic level on a temple and dynastic burial sites'.[45] Janzen adds that, '"Inheritance" designates the land as transferred to Israel by God without the right to sale… The emphasis falls on God as the one who has authority to dispose of land belonging to him. And on Israel's inalienable right to retain such land as God confers.'[46] Wright agrees that YHWH's ownership of the land raises a two-fold expectation: first, it is God's inheritance that God is granting to an Israelite family and it must stay within the family; secondly, it is a free gift which plays a prominent role in the history of salvation.[47] Millar sees no conflict between divine ownership of the land and the fact that God gave the land to the Israelites and it is therefore 'theirs': the idea of the gift does not disprove YHWH's ownership of the

---

42. Ibid., 27–8.

43. J. G. Millar, 'Land', in *New Dictionary of Biblical Theology*, ed. T. Desmond Alexander (Leicester: Inter-Varsity, 2003), 626.

44. Ibid.

45. Coote, 'Land', 28.

46. Janzen, 'Land', 144–5.

47. Wright, 'ארץ', 522.

land, neither are the conditionality and unconditionality of the gift incompatible.[48] He also observes:

> The land is the context of Israel's obedience, and obedience is the condition both of entering the land and of continued occupation of it... Enjoyment of life with Yahweh in the land (in fulfilment of the covenant promise) is open-ended and dynamic. To realize it, Israel must continue to obey... The gift of land was never intended to be an end in itself, but a means of developing the relationship between God and his people.[49]

The matter is more complex, however. Some verses, for example Gen. 15.19, tell us that the land belongs not to Israel, nor indeed explicitly to YHWH, but to other nations, so its being given as a free gift to the Israelites is problematic whether or not we understand God as the original owner. When Janzen touches upon this problem, he makes an important distinction between the nature of the promises given to the patriarchs and those given to Moses-Israel.[50] Although the promises have the same general content, there are important differences, not only regarding the lack or inclusion of paradisiacal attributes ('milk and honey') but other theologically significant differences:

> Nonetheless, Abraham, Isaac and Jacob live in the land as sojourners (Gen 17:8; 23:4; 26:3; 28:4; 35:27; 36:7; 37:1; Exod 6:4), until the family of Jacob/Israel, overtly driven by famine, but on a deeper level, guided by God, leaves Canaan again to settle in Egypt... The book of Exodus introduces the Israelites as a numerous people enslaved in a foreign land (Exod 1). Moses becomes God's chosen instrument to lead them out of Egypt toward the goal of the land promised to the Patriarchs (Exod 3:7-8; 6:2-8).[51]

Like Janzen, Frankel makes a distinction between the promise made to the patriarchs[52] and the promise of a 'land flowing with milk and honey' made to the whole of Israel.[53] Minear on the other hand sees a connection between the promise given to Abraham and God's call to Moses to lead

48. Millar, 'Land', 623.
49. Ibid., 624, 626.
50. Janzen, 'Land', 144. I will explore this point further when discussing Gen. 15.7 and Exod. 3.8.
51. Ibid., 147. We shall see later that Steinbeck finds a similar pattern to the two promises.
52. Frankel, *The Land of Canaan*, 2–3. See Gen. 12.7; 13.14-17; 15.7-21; 16.3; 17.8; 18.4, 13; 35.12.
53. Ibid., 3. See Exod. 3.8; Deut. 7.23.

his people from Egypt to the promised land.[54] The attributes of this land promised to the whole of Israel are described in Exod. 3.8.[55] Ausloos argues that this motif – the land flowing with milk and honey – is original to Exod. 3.8 and belongs to the pre-Deuteronomistic tradition.[56] He argues further that the promise in Exod. 3.8 is the original promise made to the Israelites: '"The land of milk and honey" is a central part of the divine promise to the Israelites. No mention is made of an oath to the patriarchs.'[57] We can see, therefore, that there are two streams of references to the promised land in the Hebrew Bible – the promises to Abraham and the patriarchs and the promises to the whole of Israel – and that they bear significant differences. We shall deal with both streams, first separately and then in tandem.

Most commentaries and lexica suggest that the promises made to Abraham and the patriarchs pre-date the promise made to the whole of Israel. We will start with the promise of land in Genesis, then proceed to Exodus. There are numerous references to the promised land in Genesis. For Ottosson and Brueggemann, and to some extent for Schmid,[58] the central passages are in chs. 15 and 17.[59] Exodus is a little more straight-forward. The final choice of verses that will be subjected to careful historical-critical analysis was made on the basis of the intersection of the results of this current section (narrowing down the spectrum of references in Genesis to chs. 15 and 17) and the verbal resemblance of Steinbeck's 'promised land vocabulary', which uses the language of the King James Bible: the first is the 'free gift of land' in Gen. 15.7 (KJV, 'And he said unto him, I am the LORD that brought thee out of Ur of the Chaldees, to give thee this land to inherit it'); the second is the 'land flowing with milk and honey' in Exod. 3.8 (KJV, 'And I am come down to deliver them out of the hand of the Egyptians, and to bring them up out of that land unto a good land and a large land, unto a land flowing with milk and honey').

---

54. Paul Minear, 'Promise', in *The Interpreter's Dictionary of the Bible*, ed. George Buttrick, 4 vols (New York: Abingdon, 1962), 3:893. Also: 'As celebrated in song and saga, this promise to Abraham and Moses was proof of God's steadfast love, his readiness to forgive, and his determination to bring them to a good end'. Ibid., 893.

55. William Johnston, *Exodus 1–19*, Smyth & Helwys Bible Commentary (Macon, GA: Smyth & Helwys, 2014), 77.

56. Ausloos, '"A Land Flowing with Milk and Honey"', 304.

57. Ibid., 305.

58. He does not specifically refer to Gen. 17. See Schmid, 'ארץ', 771.

59. Ottosson narrows the narrative down to Gen. 17.1-8. See Ottosson, 'ארץ', 403. See also Brueggemann, *The Land*, 12.

We will therefore be looking closely at these two verses, treating them in the immediate context of the chapter in which they occur, and in the broader context of the neighbouring chapters or the whole book.

An historical-critical analysis of Genesis 15.7 and Exodus 3.8

An historical-critical analysis of Genesis 15.1-21

The syntactic-structural analysis of Gen. 15.1-21 will be combined with my translation of the Hebrew text. Such a translation is clearly indispensable for a standard historical-critical analysis. A syntactic-structural analysis is less common but of great benefit to studies which rely mostly on a synchronic literary analysis of the biblical text and which seek out the grammatical and textural features of rhetorical and narrative highlights within that text.

Our analysis uses a system of Hebrew syntax suggested by Niccacci in *The Syntax of the Verb in Classical Hebrew Prose*.[60] Niccacci follows Schneider's system, which unlike previous approaches does not analyse verb forms in isolation but considers their use and function within the text: '[A] verb form needs to be studied in texts, not in isolation but in connection with all its associated linguistic markers'.[61] Niccacci also points towards the importance of 'tense shifts', which, he suggests, 'trace out a broader picture which is both structured and consistent'.[62] Whereas Niccacci's system is clear and well suited to the needs and specificities of the Hebrew language, other approaches, such as that developed by Talstra, are rather more complex.[63]

In Hebrew prose, syntax is determined by verbs and their position in a phrase. The graphic schema of the Hebrew syntax on the pages that follow will help us to understand the syntactic-structural features of Gen. 15.7 and its immediate context. The main-line verb forms (*wayyiqtols*) are on

---

60. Alviero Niccacci, *The Syntax of the Verb in Classical Hebrew Prose*, Journal for the Study of the Old Testament. Supplement Series 86 (Sheffield: JSOT, 1990).

61. Ibid., 10.

62. Ibid.

63. Talstra's system combines syntactic and grammatical features of phrases on different levels and can be confusing. The system was based on research into processes within computers and the results of his analysis do indeed resemble the products of overly complex computer-generated mathematical operations. More importantly, much of the data is of little use in biblical analysis. Eep Talstra, 'A Hierarchy of Clauses in Hebrew Bible Narrative', in *Narrative Syntax and the Hebrew Bible: Papers of the Tilburg Conference 1996*, ed. Ellen van Wolde (Leiden: Brill, 1997), 85–118.

the first level of the schema, that is, the furthest right. The background information dependent on the previous *wayyiqtol* phrase is at the same level in the schema and is marked with an arrow (↑). The antecedent information is placed further left. Direct speech is furthest left:

Main narrative

Background information ↑

Antecedent information |

Direct speech |

Gen. 15.1

↑אחר הדברים האלה היה דבר־יהוה אל־אברם במחזה לאמר

(a) After these things (these ones), the word of the LORD happened to Abram in a vision saying:

אל־תירא אברם אנכי מגן לך שכרך הרבה[64] מאד

(b) 'Do not be afraid, Abram, I am your shield, your reward shall be enormous'.

15.2

ויאמר אברם

(a) But Abram said:

אדני יהוה מה־תתן־לי

(b) 'O my LORD (Adonai), what will you give me?

הולך ערירי ואנכי

(c) I keep going childless;

ובן־משק ביתי הוא דמשק[65] אליעזר

(d) And the heir of my house is Eliezer of Damascus.'

---

64. The Samaritan Pentateuch suggests replacing this with ארבה ('I shall multiply'). There is no difference in meaning.

65. Commentators struggle with 'Eliezer of Damascus'. No consensus has yet been reached regarding the person's identity, nor have any feasible suggestions been made. The suggestion to read it as an Aramaic gloss בן־משק offers little to the solution. See Gordon Wenham, *Genesis 1–15*, ed. David Allen, Word Biblical Commentary 1 (Waco, TX: Word, 1987), 328.

15.3

ויאמר אברם

(a) And Abram said:

הן לי לא נתתה זרע

(b) 'Alas, you did not give me an offspring

והנה בן־ביתי יורש אתי

(c) and lo, a servant of my house, is to be my heir'.

15.4

והנה דבר־יהוה אליו לאמר

(a) But behold, the word of the LORD (came/happened) to him saying:

לא יירשך זה

(b) 'This one shall not inherit from you,

כי־אם אשר יצא ממעיך הוא יירשך

(c) but the one that comes from your own body shall inherit from you'.

15.5

ויוצא אתו החוצה ויאמר

(a) The LORD brought (hi.) him out and said:

הבט־נא השמימה וספר הכוכבים

(b) 'Just look (impv. hi.+ emph. particle) toward heaven and count the stars

אם־תוכל לספר אתם

(c) if you are able to count them'.

ויאמר לו

(d) And the LORD said to him:

כה יהוה זרעך

(e) 'So shall your offspring be'.

15.6

והאמן ביהוה

(a) And he believed (hi.) in the LORD,

ויחשבה לו צדקה

(b) And the LORD counted it to him for righteousness.

15.7

אלין ויאמר

(a) And the LORD said to him:

יהוה אוי

(b) 'I am the LORD / I, the LORD, am the one

אשר הוצאתיך מאור⁶⁶ כשדים

(c) who brought you out of Ur of the Chaldeans

לרשתה הזאת את־הארץ לך לתת

(d) to give you the land (this one) to inherit it'.

15.8

ויאמר

(a) But he said:

אדני יהוה במה אדע

(b) 'O my LORD (Adonai) how shall I know

כי אירשנה

(c) that I shall inherit it?'

15.9

ויאמר אליו

(a) And the LORD said to him:

קחה לי עגלה משלשת ועז משלשת ואיל משלש ותר וגוזל

(b) 'Bring me a three-year-old (part. fem. cs. pu.) heifer and a three-year-old female goat and a three-year-old ram (part. m. abs. pu.) and a turtledove and a pigeon'.

15.10

ויקח־לו את־כל־אלה

(a) And he brought him all these

ויבתר אתם בתוך

(b) and cut them in two (pi.) *in half*

---

66. For the sake of harmonization with Gen. 11.28, 32, the Septuagint suggests adding ארץ ('land of Ur')

ויתן איש־בתרו לקראת רעהו

(c) and set each half over against the other,

ואת־הצפר [67] לא בתר

(d) but he did not cut in two the birds.

15.11

וירד העיט על־הפגרים

(a) Then the fowls came down on the corpses;

וישב אתם אברם

(b) Abram drove them away.

15.12

↑ויהי השמש לבוא

(a) When the sun was going down,

↑ותרדמה נפלה על־אברם

(b) a deep sleep fell down on Abram,

והנה אימה חשכה גדלה נפלת עליו

(c) and, *alas*, a great and dreadful darkness descended upon him.

15.13

ויאמר לאברם

(a) And the LORD said to Abram:

ידע תדע

(b) 'Be sure that you know (inf. abs.+impf.)

כי־גר יהיה זרעך בארץ לא להם

(c) that your offspring will be a sojourner in a land that is not theirs (pl.!).

ועבדום

(d) they shall serve them (to the oppressors)

וענו אתם ארבע מאות שנה

(e) and they shall be oppressed (pi.) for four hundred years.

67. Many manuscripts suggest reading 'birds' in the plural rather than as a collective singular.

15.14

וגם את־הגוי אשר יעבדו

(a) But the people, whom they shall serve

דן אנכי

(b) I will judge

ואחרי־כן יצאו ברכש גדול

(c) and afterward they shall go out with a great property.

15.15

ואתה תבוא אל־אבתיך בשלום

(a) And you shall go to your fathers in peace,

תקבר בשיבה טובה

(b) you shall be buried (ni.) in a good old age.

15.16

ודור רביעי ישובו הנה

(a) And they shall return in the fourth generation,

כי לא־שלם עון האמר עד־הנה

(b) for the iniquity of the Amorites is not yet complete'.

15.17

↑ ויהי השמש באה

(a) When the sun went down

↑ ועלטה היה

(b) and it was dark,

והנה תנור עשן ולפיד אש אשר עבר בין הגזרים האלה

(c) behold, a smoking furnace and firing torch passed between the pieces (those ones).

15.18

ביום ההוא כרת יהוה את־אברם ברית לאמר

(a) On that day the LORD made a covenant with Abram saying:

לזרעך נתתי את־הארץ הזאת

(b) 'To your descendants, I will give the land (this one)

מנהר[68] מצרים עד־הנהר הגדל נהר־פרת
(c) from the river of Egypt until the great river, the river Euphrates;

15.19-21

את־הקיני ואת־הקנזי ואת הקדמני ואת־החתי ואת־הפרזי ואת־הרפאים ואת־האמרי
ואת־הכנעני ואת־הגרגשי[69] ואת־היבוסי
the land of the Kenites, the Kenizzites, the Kadmonites, the Hittites, the Perizzites, the Rephaites, the Amorites, the Canaanites, the Girgashites, and the Jebusites'.

Except for the difficult reading of 'Eliezer of Damascus', the textual criticism of Genesis 15 discussed in the footnotes does not suggest any significant content-related changes to the text.[70]

Verse 1a is a simple nominal clause. It divides ch. 15 from the previous narrative but also implies some degree of dependence. It ends with an introduction to the direct speech using the participle לאמר ('saying'). Verse 1b is a verbal clause which contains direct speech by God (a promise of blessing to Abraham[71]). It is followed by an extensive exchange between God and Abraham. Verse 2a (a verbal clause) introduces Abraham's lament, which continues from 2b to 2d. The lament is interrupted by a *wayyiqtol* phrase, but the direct speech continues immediately afterwards. The author might have used the interruption to emphasize Abraham's desperate situation and his plea to God for redress. Moreover, the message that follows is a repetition: Abraham has no heir and considers himself to be in a desperate situation. The stress is laid by two macro-syntactic signals, הן and והנה (alas! and behold!), in vv. 3b and 3c. Another והנה follows in v. 4a (a simple nominal clause) and introduces God's response to Abraham and sharp disagreement with Abraham's interpretation of his future. God comes to Abraham with a revolutionary message in vv. 4b and 4c: Abraham shall have an heir

---

68. It is possible to read נחל ('wadi') instead of נהר ('river') but no manuscript support was found in favour of this reading.

69. The Septuagint and the Samaritan Pentateuch suggest adding ואת־החוי ('the Hivites').

70. The textual criticism is based on comments in Karl Elliger and Wilhelm Rudolph, eds., *Biblia Hebraica Stuttgartensia*, 4. Aufl (Stuttgart: Deutsche Bibelgesellschaft, 1990).

71. Except when quoting Scripture, or other authors, we follow Brueggemann in always using the name Abraham, even when discussing a time, as here, when the patriarch was called Abram.

that will be his own son. A small interruption in v. 5a (a director's note) informs us that the background has changed. God and Abraham went out to see the sky. Verses 5b and 5c include direct speech from God. In v. 5b we find a construction of an imperative Hiphil + emphatic particle that suggests a negative response: Abraham's inability to count the stars. Verse 5d (a *wayyiqtol* phrase) is an interruption of God's extensive direct speech to which yet another speech follows in 5e. Verse 6 can be considered the turning point in the narrative. The author's use of a different verb form to interrupt the direct speech (*w+qatal*) suggests antecedent information. The message of v. 6 also stands out from the rest of the narrative: Abraham was not expected to confess his faith. This might also suggest the special nature of this verse.

Verse 7a (a *wayyiqtol* phrase) further interrupts the direct speech that follows in vv. 7b to 7d and contains the divine self-presentation and a promise of land to Abraham. Verse 8a interrupts the direct speech with another *wayyiqtol* phrase and introduces Abraham's answer to God's monologue. Abraham questions God's promise: he seeks some kind of guarantee. Another *wayyiqtol* phrase interrupts Abraham's speech and introduces God's surprising response in v. 9a. Instead of a simple answer, God asks Abraham to perform a ritual (v. 9b). Verses 10a to 10c form a chain of *wayyiqtol* phrases describing Abraham's ritual conduct. Verse 10d is a compound nominal clause suggesting a change in such conduct: contrary to the preceding practice, Abraham did not cut the birds in two. Verses 11a and 11b are *wayyiqtol* phrases that express two simultaneous events: the birds came, and Abraham drove them away. Verses 12a and 12b contain background information to the dreadful darkness in 12c which is introduced by והנה. Verse 13a is a *wayyiqtol* phrase that introduces God's response to Abraham in the form of a dream or vision. Verse 13b is the beginning of God's response to Abraham, which continues until the end of v. 16. Verse 13b contains an unusual construction: infinitive absolute + imperfect (*figura ethymologica*), which suggests stress laid on the verb ('be sure that you know!'). Verses 17a and 17b provide background to the divine revelation in 17c. The content of these verses is surprising as the sun had already set in v. 12. This might be a result of corruption of the text, but it has no bearing on the overall reading. The stress is laid by the macro-syntactic signal והנה in 17c. Verse 18 is a repetition of the promise of land in v. 7 but here it gains a covenantal form. Verse 18a is an introduction to the direct speech. Verses 18b and 18c contain the promise itself, and vv. 19-21 define the extent of the land that is promised to Abraham and his descendants.

Wenham suggests that Gen. 15.7 is part of a larger unit that includes Gen. 15.1-21. It is clearly divided from the previous chapter by the phrase 'after these things'. This formula, which introduces a time shift, is repeated in Gen. 22.1; 22.20; 39.7; 40.1; and 48.1, and according to Wenham suggests a cycle of 'Abraham narratives'.[72] Cotter is interested in the broader context of Genesis 15 and places it within the whole Abrahamic cycle (chs. 12–25). However, unlike other scholars such as Walsh and Dorsey, he places God rather than Abraham at the centre of the cycle.[73] The focus is not, therefore, the covenant with Abraham and the promise of land (chs. 15 and 17), or Abraham's faithfulness to God, but God's faithfulness to and conduct towards the people. The key chapter for Cotter, the centre of the cycle, is ch. 16, where God claims responsibility for Hagar, the husbandless homeless single mother, and thus a symbol for all abandoned and disadvantaged people. And such was to be, according to Cotter, the primary mission of Israel: to take care of the abandoned and the disadvantaged.[74]

We will now leave the broader context of ch. 15 and focus on its internal logic. Wenham suggests a concentric structure to the unit comprising two scenes that run in parallel. For example, v. 7 (the promise of land) is parallel to v. 1 (a promise of reward).[75] Two of Wenham's 'keywords' are mentioned in v. 7: ירש ('to inherit') and יצא ('to bring out'),[76] which highlights the importance of this verse to the rest of the chapter. The grammatical structure of the unit indicates a typical Hebrew narrative. The content on the other hand suggests that the narratives merely introduce the dialogues and it is these that form the core of the unit. The *wayyiqtols* do not imply a narrative as they do not suggest any action or movement and are mostly comprised of expressions of speech: אמר ('to say'), a verb that introduces direct speech, appears eleven

72. See Wenham, *Genesis 1–15*, 325, 327.

73. For more on this, see David Cotter, Jerome Walsh, and Chris Franke, *Genesis*, Berit Olam: Studies in Hebrew Narrative & Poetry (Collegeville, MN: Liturgical, 2003), 84.

74. See also: 'Called to be a blessing, Abraham wasn't. So God was. Central to God's way of being in the world is salvation – creating a place for Hagar, the alien, the homeless woman – for central to God's way of being in the world is justice. The God, who commanded later, whose prophets preached it and whose sages taught it, could not have acted otherwise from the very beginning.' Cotter, Walsh, and Franke, *Genesis*, 87.

75. Wenham, *Genesis 1–15*, 325.

76. Ibid., 326.

times, and indeed, aside from the narrative in vv. 10-12 which describes Abraham's cultic actions, direct speech dominates the unit. There is a notably high usage of הנה ('alas, lo, behold') in Gen. 15.3-4. In v. 3 it stresses Abraham's miserable situation and deep frustration, but in v. 4 it turns his attention to a future event, one that will contradict Abraham's statement in v. 2: his descendant will not be his servant but a child of his own. Cotter takes note of the word הנה and the effect it has of drawing the reader into the text, but he does not list all of its usage. He refers to vv. 4, 12 and 17,[77] but does not remark on the cluster of occurrences in vv. 3 and 4 (three times in two verses).

Turner is conventional in dividing ch. 15 into two parts: vv. 1-6 and 7-21. Scholars who support the theory of two sources in ch. 15 divide it in the same way, as we shall see later. Skinner sees nuances between the promise of a son and the promise of land: it is only the promise of land that is bound by a covenant. He supports the usual division of the chapter by holding to two sources,[78] but also maintains that the 'double call of Abram' and other elements make sense only if we accept that the chapter is composed of two originally independent units:

> The promise of land, Abram's request for a pledge (v. 6) and the self-introduction of Yahweh (which would be natural only at the commencement of an interview), are marks of discontinuity difficult to reconcile with the assumption of the unity of the narrative.[79]

Turner considers Abraham's act of faith in v. 6 the turning point of the story, noting that here the promise changes from progeny to land.[80] We could argue that a shift of promise alone is not sufficient reason to divide the chapter. Furthermore, Turner later admits that the internal logic of the promises suggests that they are so connected and interdependent that it makes little sense to make a division based on the change from one to the other.[81] He also observes that, 'A divine argument "I am the Lord" (15:7a; cf. 15:1b) elicits a question from Abraham, "how am I to know?" (15:8; cf. 15:2a)'.[82] This rhetorical analysis lends further support to the division mentioned above. From a syntactic-structural perspective, there is an interesting grammatical feature in v. 6 in the sudden and notable change

---

77. Cotter, Walsh, and Franke, *Genesis*, 98, 99.
78. Skinner, *A Critical and Exegetical Commentary on Genesis*, 276.
79. Ibid., 280.
80. Laurence Turner, *Genesis* (Sheffield: Sheffield Academic, 2000), 74.
81. Ibid., 76.
82. Ibid., 74.

in verb tense, which may support the prominence of this verse. Cotter also sees v. 6 as a turning point and understands Abraham's faith not as something automatic but as something into which he grows.[83] Although Wenham does not divide the chapter, he makes a similar argument to support his theory of a concentric structure.[84] Based on rhetorical analysis, Towner divides the chapter into the same two parts as Turner, arguing that a similar development exists within the two texts. Towner suggests that Gen. 15.1-6 is a vision and the first recorded dialogue between the Lord and Abraham, with a structure as follows: (i) the Lord makes a promise, (ii) Abraham objects, and (iii) the Lord reassures him; Gen. 15.7-21 on the other hand is partly a dream, but with the dialogue structured the same way: (i) promise, (ii) objection, and (iii) reassurance.[85] Wenham does not offer support for the synchronic unity of the chapter, but based on the 'unity' of the promises – the promise of a descendant and the promise of land – it is possible to argue for the unity of the fifteenth chapter.

Regarding source criticism, Wenham accepts that the fifteenth chapter is made up of J and E, and points out that it is not necessary to explain all the discrepancies by introducing a different source: the twin introduction of the deity in vv. 1 and 7 can easily be explained as Hebrew literary style rather than as evidence of an extra source. Thus, Wenham opts for the unity of the text.[86] Towner agrees with the theory of two sources of Genesis 15: he assigns vv. 13-16 to E because of their prophetic character,[87] and the rest of the chapter to the scribal circle of J; he is also convinced that vv. 13-16 could be removed with no change in the meaning of the story. To support his theory, Towner introduces the term 'Amorites' as the preferred term in E sources for the 'Canaanites' of J.[88] Skinner retains the two sources approach but suggests the possibility of redactional adjustments by an editor whom he calls R^{je}; elements of the E source are nevertheless traceable in vv. 11 and 13-16.[89] Speiser confirms this theory and points out that the E source uses 'Amorites' for all of the

83. Cotter, Walsh, and Franke, *Genesis*, 100.

84. Wenham, *Genesis 1–15*, 326.

85. Wayne Towner, *Genesis* (Louisville, KY: John Knox, 2001), 148.

86. Wenham, *Genesis 1–15*, 326.

87. Towner, *Genesis*, 148. Towner believes that the E source comes from the northern kingdom and is influenced by the prophetic ministry of Elijah, Elisha, and Micaiah ben Judah. See ibid.

88. Ibid., 153.

89. Skinner, *A Critical and Exegetical Commentary on Genesis*, 276–7. Skinner himself nonetheless admits that his theory may be too complicated to be maintained. See ibid.

pre-Israelite inhabitants of Canaan, whereas the J source would probably use 'Canaanites'.[90] This, however, only clarifies the likely formation of v. 16. Interestingly, just a few verses later, in vv. 19-21, we have an extensive list of the other inhabitants of Canaan, including both Amorites and Canaanites. Speiser is inclined to ascribe other verses where the name YHWH is used (vv. 1, 6, 7, 8, and 18) to J.[91] It should be noted that the more recent debate regarding sources of the Hebrew Bible, the so-called new redaction criticism, sees less strict boundaries between literary-source criticism and redactional-textual criticism. Lemmelijn and others[92] have urged us to rethink the traditional idea that redactors and copyists used little of their own creativity and generally resisted the temptation to insert original elements with theological or socio-political significance. Lemmelijn believes literary-source criticism and redactional-textual criticism could overlap,[93] and that the work of authors and redactors differs less than is often thought. Vervenne agrees, and argues that, 'The former contention still seems to discriminate between "authors" who are considered to be very original writers and "redactors" who rather emerge as (creative) collectors of existing and definitely neat compositions'.[94] Such a theory reinforces Gadamer's argument that new readers always bring new insights and significance to the meaning of a text.

90. Ephraim Speiser, *Genesis: Introduction, Translation, and Notes* (Garden City, NY: Doubleday, 1964), 113.

91. Ibid., 114.

92. See also Marc Vervenne, 'The "P" Tradition in the Pentateuch: Document and/or Redaction? The Sea Narrative (Ex 13,17–14,31) as a Test Case', in *Pentateuchal and Deuteronomistic Studies: Papers Read at the XIIIth IOSOT Congress Leuven 1989*, ed. C. Brekelmans and J. Lust, Bibliotheca Ephemeridum Theologicarum Lovaniensium 94 (Leuven: Peeters, 1990); Rolf Rendtorff and John Scullion, *The Problem of the Process of Transmission in the Pentateuch*, Journal for the Study of the Old Testament Supplement Series 89 (Sheffield: JSOT, 1990).

93. 'Until recently, and unfortunately sometimes even still today, the generally accepted position was indeed that textual criticism as the study of the transmission of the complete literary work began where literary criticism as the study of the history of the origin and literary formation of the text left off. In line with recent text-critical research…I am to argue…that a clear distinction between these two processes simply cannot be satisfactorily made.' Bénédicte Lemmelijn, 'Influence of a So-Called P-redaction in the "Major Expansions" of Exod 7–11? Finding Oneself at the Crossroads of Textual and Literary Criticism', in *Textual Criticism and Dead Sea Scrolls Studies in Honour of Julio Trebolle Barrera. Florilegium Complutense*, ed. Andrés Piquer Otero and Pablo Torijano Morales, Supplements to the Journal for the Study of Judaism 158 (Leiden: Brill, 2012), 204.

94. Vervenne, 'The "P" Tradition in the Pentateuch', 88.

Looking at Gen. 15.7 in its immediate and broader contexts shows us the place of the promise of land within ch. 15. Wenham and Cotter suggest that v. 7 ('I am the Lord / I, the Lord, am the one who brought you out of Ur of the Chaldeans') is parallel to Exod. 20.2 and Deut. 5.6, the so-called Exodus formula (in the latter two verses, 'Ur of the Chaldeans' is replaced by 'the land of Egypt'),[95] a correspondence that suggests the continuity of a promise initially given to a single person. As that person lived to see the promised offspring, the promise of land was broadened to the whole of Israel. In v. 7, as in Gen. 12.7, Gen. 13.15, and Lev. 25.38, God 'gives the land' but gives it to be 'inherited', which is otherwise close to Deuteronomic vocabulary (Deut. 3.18; 9.6; 21.1; 19.14).[96] Wenham notes that the word אדני usually introduces intercessory prayers (Gen. 18.3; 19.18; 20.4; 27.30-32); within the book of Genesis, it occurs only in the Abrahamic cycle. The traditional interpretation suggests the translation 'my LORD', where the suffix is understood as a plural of majesty. Based on the Ugaritic parallels, Wenham argues that the suffix could intensify the meaning of the noun and suggests the translation, 'Lord of all, sovereign'.[97] Wenham notes further that the word ירש ('to inherit') is rare in Genesis (Gen. 21.10; 22.17; 24.60; 28.4) but common in Deuteronomy, where it refers to Israel's inheritance of the land.[98] He also observes:

> This is one of only four passages in Genesis where God refers to himself as Yahweh (the Lord). Here the use of his name helps to enhance the analogy between God's call of Abram and his subsequent redemption of Israel from Egypt. This is expressly prefigured in vv. 11-18.[99]

Speiser suggests that vv. 7-21 represent a broadening of the perspective offered in vv. 1-6: 'It involves a nation to be, and its establishment in the Promised Land... The emphasis shifts thus to world history, and

---

95. Wenham, *Genesis 1–15*, 329. See also Cotter, Walsh, and Franke, *Genesis*, 101.

96. Ibid., *Genesis 1–15*, 331.

97. Ibid., 327. Also: 'We have had problems with translating the phrase יהוה אדני. It might seem to be a pleonasm when both of these words are usually translated as LORD. However, it could shed some light on the interpretive query of verse seven and the problem with the identification of the attribute. If we acknowledge יהוה to be a revelation of the divine name and not the attribute, then we read: "I, the Lord, am the one who brought you out..." Thus, we might say that Abram, in both instances (vv. 2,8) very emotional and deeply frustrated, used יהוה to call God "God's name". Or, at least to specify God himself as naming is problematic.' Ibid.

98. See ibid., 329.

99. Ibid., 331.

the importance of the episode is underscored by the conclusion of a covenant.'[100] Cotter notes an interesting concentric structure to vv. 13 and 14-16 framed by the motif of the promised land: v. 13 describes three stages of suffering – alienation from the promised land, enslavement, oppression – while vv. 14-16 describe three stages of redemption which conclude with settlement of the promised land. Cotter does not say it explicitly, but it would certainly be possible to use his analysis to argue that the life of the people of Israel at that time was focused on the promise of land.[101] It is worth noting that Cotter interprets the list of peoples in vv. 19-21 as a reminder to Abraham that he will settle a land that is not unoccupied: God wants Abraham to be aware of the fact that there are indeed inhabitants of the land that one day his descendants will possess. Regardless of whether Cotter is right or wrong, this is a fascinating observation, but he makes no more of it and we do not therefore know what he is implying. We may find the idea of God giving a land to people as a free gift even though this land is already settled difficult to reconcile with the notion of God's righteousness. Is Cotter suggesting that the possession of a land occupied by several other peoples is not in fact God's problem or responsibility as God had already explained the situation to Abraham? This would be a problematic idea to say the least: to accept Cotter's suggestion, we would have to admit that the Lord was offering a case that was far from watertight.

The promise of land is always bound to the moral conduct of the people who possess it:

> So much of the moral, didactic rhetoric of Deuteronomy is predicated on the gift of the land and on the need to follow an ethical lifestyle both in response to the gift and in order to prolong the enjoyment of it. In particular, Israel's whole economic system, including the equitable division of land to the tribes, clans, and families, the principle of inalienable family inheritance, the institutions of redemption of land and of sabbatical and jubilee years, and all the many mechanisms for the relief of poverty and restoration of the poor to participation in the blessings of the land was based on Yahweh's moral sovereignty in the economic sphere as the ultimate landlord.[102]

Genesis 15.16 tells us that it was the iniquity of the Amorites that led to their expulsion from the land. This verse not only anticipates the future handover of a land that is still in the possession of other peoples, but also reminds the Israelites that the gift of the land is not unconditional. The

100. Speiser, *Genesis*, 115.
101. Cotter, Walsh, and Franke, *Genesis*, 101.
102. Wright, 'ארץ', 523. See also, Plaut and Böckler, *Die Tora*, 173.

inheritance can be taken away from the people of Israel if they turn out to be as wicked as their predecessors in the land: the relationship between the people's moral conduct and their possession of the land never changes.

The analysis of Genesis 15 has been detailed and complex, but to be faithful to any biblical text it is important to consider its problematicity and to tussle with the different claims and propositions offered by various specialists in the field. It is legitimate to conclude that Gen. 15.4 and 15.7 form the lexical, grammatical, and theological centres of the chapter and that the main message is that Abraham will be the father of numberless descendants and heir of the land that will be given to him by the LORD.

An historical-critical analysis of Exodus 3.1-12

The analysis of Exod. 3.1-12 will again follow Niccacci's system. The exploration of the key verse (Exod. 3.8) will reflect the same structure as that followed in the previous section: we will go through the broader context of Exodus 3, then through the immediate context, and finally we will take a close look at Exod. 3.8 to elaborate on the motif of the land and its function within the chapter.[103]

Main narrative

Background information ↑

Antecedent information |

Direct speech |

Exod. 3.1

היה רעה את־צאן יתרו חתנו כהן מדין ומשה ↑

(a) When Moses was keeping the flock of Jethro, his father in law, the priest of Midian,

וינהג את־הצאן אחד המדבר

(b) he led the flock behind the wilderness,

ויבא אל־הר האלהים[104] חרבה

(c) he came to the mountain of God, Horeb.

---

103. The subject "God/the LORD" does not appear in 3.4a, 5a, 6a, 12a in the Hebrew text. By adding God/the LORD to the phrase, we substitute the usual English translation "he said" (which renders the matching Hebrew verb form) in order to maintain the use of inclusive language.

104. The Septuagint omits 'of God', possibly for the sake of harmonization. The 'mountain of God' typically refers to Mount Zion. Most commentators identify Horeb with Mount Zion.

3.2

וירא מלאך יהוה אליו בלבת־אש מתוך הסנה

(a) And the angel/messenger of God appeared (ni.) to him in the flame of the fire in the midst of the bush.

וירא והנה הסנה בער באש

(b) He looked, and behold, the bush is burning with/in fire

והסנה איננו אכל

(c) and yet it was not consumed.

3.3

ויאמר משה

(a) And Moses said:

אסרה־נא ואראה את־המראה הגדל הזה

(b) 'I will turn aside to look at the great sight (this one)

מדוע לא־יבער הסנה

(c) Why the bush does not burn up'.

3.4

וירא יהוה[105] כי סר לראות

(a) And when the LORD saw that he turned aside to see

ויקרא אליו אלהים[106] מתוך הסנה

(b) God called on him from the midst of the bush

ויאמר

(c) and God said:

משה משה

(d) 'Moses, Moses!'

ויאמר

(e) He replied

הנני

(f) 'Here I am'.

105. The Samaritan Pentateuch suggests replacing יהוה with אלהים.
106. The Septuagint renders this Κύριος and the Vulgate omits it.

3.5

ויאמר

(a) And God said:

אל־תקרב הלם

(b) 'Do not come closer here.

של־נעליך מעל רגליך

(c) Take the shoes off your feet

כי המקום

(d) for the place

אשר אתה עומד עליו

(e) upon which you are standing

אדמת־קדש הוא

(f) is sacred ground'.

3.6

ויאמר

(a) The LORD added:

אנכי אלהי אביך[107] אלהי אברהם אלהי יצחק ואלהי יעקב

(b) 'I am the God of your father, the God of Abraham, the God of Isaac, and the God of Jacob'.

ויסתר משה פניו

(c) And Moses hid his face,

↑ כי ירא מהביט אל־האלהים

(d) for he was afraid to look (hi.) on God.

3.7

ויאמר יהוה

(a) And the LORD said further:

ראה ראיתי את־עני עמי

(b) 'I have surely seen (*figura eth.*) the affliction of my people,

אשר במצרים

(c) who are in Egypt

107. The Samaritan Pentateuch and some versions of the Septuagint turn the singular אביך (of your father) into the more logical plural אבתיך (of your fathers).

ואת־צעקתם שמעתי מפני נגשיר

(d) and I have heard their cry on account of their oppressors.

יכי דעתי את־מכאביו

(e) Indeed, I know their suffering!

3.8

וארד[108] להצילו מיד מצרים

(a) And I have come down to deliver (hi.) them from the hand of Egypt

ולהעלתו מן־הארץ ההוא אל־ארץ טובה ורחבה

(b) to bring them up out of the land (that one) to a good and broad land

אל־ארץ זבת חלב ודבש

(c) a land flowing with milk and honey,

אל־מקום הכנעני והחתי והאמרי והפרזי[109] והחוי והיבוסי

(d) to the place of the Canaanites, Hittites, the Amorites, the Perizzites, the Hivites, and the Jebusites.

3.9

ועתה הנה צעקת בני־ישראל באה אלי

(a) And now, behold, the cry of the children of Israel came to me,

וגם־ראיתי את־הלחץ

(b) And I have seen the oppression

אשר מצרים לחצים אתם

(c) with which Egypt oppresses them!

3.10

ועתה לכה

(a) So, come now

אל־פרעה והוצא[110] את־עמי בני־ישראל ממצרים ואשלחך

(b) And I will send you to Pharaoh to bring (hi.) my people, the children of Israel, out of Egypt.'

108. The Samaritan Pentateuch suggests the cohortative verb form וארדה.
109. The Samaritan Pentateuch and the Septuagint add והגרגשי.
110. The Samaritan Pentateuch, the Septuagint and the Vulgate suggest the reading והוצאת ('you will bring my people') rather than the imperative והוצא ('bring').

3.11

ויאמר משה אל־האלהם

(a) And Moses said to the LORD :

מי אנכי

(b) 'Who am I,

כי אלך אל־פרעה וכי אוציא את־בני ישראל ממצרים

(c) that I should go to Pharaoh and bring the Israelites out of Egypt'.

3.12

ויאמר[111]

(a) And the LORD said:

כי־אהיה עמך

(b) 'I AM/WILL BE with you,

וזה־לך האות

(c) And this shall be a sign to you

כי אנכי שלחתיך

(d) That it was I who sent you

בהוציאך את־העם ממצרים

(e) When you bring the people out of Egypt,

תעבדון את־האלהים על ההר הזה

(f) you will serve me upon the mountain (this one).'

As with Genesis 15, the textual criticism of Exod. 3.1-12 reveals nothing of great significance except for the Septuagint omitting 'of God' in Exod. 3.1c. The redactor might have omitted it in order to avoid introducing another 'mountain of God' when Mount Zion was commonly accepted as such.

With no sharp division from the previous chapter, the nominal clause of Exod. 3.1a introduces the momentous events of ch. 3 with the news that Moses was shepherding a flock belonging to his father-in-law. We learn in v. 1b (a *wayyiqtol* phrase) that on this occasion he led the flock out a great distance, beyond the wilderness, and probably further than usual. In v. 1c (another *wayyiqtol* phrase) he reached Mount Horeb, the mountain of God, whereupon in 2a (a *wayyiqtol* phrase) the angel-messenger of

---

111. One version of the Septuagint suggests adding ὁ θεὸς (another suggests also adding Κύριος) Μωσεῖ λέγων ('God said to Moses *saying*').

God appeared to him. This is the last mention of the angel-messenger. In the narrative that follows, God speaks to Moses directly and appears to him 'in the flame of the fire in the midst of the bush'. The real miracle, however, happens only in 2c (a nominal clause). The message and grammar of this phrase emphasizes that a bush which is in flames should burn down and that if it does not then this is something remarkable. Verse 2b only repeats what we already know about the burning bush from 2a. Verse 3a is a *wayyiqtol* phrase which introduces the direct speech of Moses. It is in fact a monologue, or even just a thought, as no addressee is implied. The direct speech is registered in vv. 3b and 3c and we learn that Moses is aware of the odd nature of such a situation and that he wants to explore what is happening. However, as soon as God sees that Moses' interest has been piqued, God calls to him. Verses 4a to 4c are *wayyiqtol* phrases. Verse 4d is direct speech in which God calls Moses by name. Verse 4e is a small interruption which introduces Moses' answer in 4f. Verse 5a (a *wayyiqtol* phrase) re-introduces God's address to Moses in vv. 5b to 5f, which contains the demand that Moses take off his shoes before the real conversation can take place. Verse 6a (a *wayyiqtol* phrase) introduces God's self-revelation with its content in 6b (a nominal clause). In v. 6c (a *wayyiqtol* phrase) we read that Moses reacted to this epiphany by hiding his face. Verse 6d (a *kī*-clause) adds the reason for this conduct: he was afraid to look upon God.

Verse 7a brings us back to direct speech and introduces God's lengthy address to Moses. Verses 7b-10 are God's lament over the people's suffering in Egypt. Verse 7b contains a *figura ethymologica*, perhaps to emphasize that God has indeed seen this affliction. Verse 7e (another *kī*-clause) again stresses divine participation in the suffering of God's people. Verses 8a to 8d include God's intention to deliver the Israelites from Egypt. Verses 9a to 9c again tell of the suffering of Israel in Egypt, with yet more stress on the people's enslavement and oppression. Verses 10a and 10b complete God's speech and contain the commissioning of Moses. Verse 11a (a *wayyiqtol* phrase) is a small interruption of the direct speech and transfers our attention to Moses, who speaks next. In 11b and 11c he attempts to wriggle out of his commitment by questioning his authority to go to Pharaoh and ask him to let the people go. Verse 12a (a *wayyiqtol* phrase) re-introduces God as the speaker, and vv. 12b to 12f relate God's instructions to Moses. Interestingly, when Moses asks the question, 'Who am I?', God gives what appears to be an illogical answer: not in fact answering who Moses is, but who God is, and that God's authority shall be more than enough to convince Pharaoh to let the people go.

There is a rough consensus on the division of Exodus 3, and most commentators – including Johnston, Childs, Sarna and Dozeman – argue for the inclusion of 17 verses from ch. 4.[112] Johnston adds that the Masoretes suggest the same division of the unit.[113] Childs argues for an even longer extension, backwards and forwards, to include the whole of Exod. 2.11 to 4.23, suggesting that the unit is framed by Moses' flight from and return to Egypt.[114] One could argue that this is indeed the larger but not necessarily immediate context of Exod. 3.8. Durham opts for the shorter unit of Exod. 3.1-12.[115] Childs considers these verses the core of the call narrative, but insists they are not the whole unit: 'The present section 3:1–4:17 is a greatly expanded form of the basic call narrative. The call ends with the giving of the sign in v. 12 (perhaps with vv. 16 and 17a).'[116] Dozeman divides the larger unit of 3.1–4.18 into two smaller parts. Verses 1-15 follow the motif of Moses' commission and the revelation of the divine name. The whole unit is built upon the divine commission and Moses' resistance and intends to reveal the divine identity and Moses' authority.[117] Dozeman points out that much time has passed and much has changed since the original call of Abraham, so it is necessary for God to renew the promises, which remain valid, to his people: 'Exodus 3:1-15 addresses the problem of divine identity after the break in tradition from the time of the ancestors'.[118] Although Exod. 3.13-22 engages with the matter of the name of God – one of the key and most discussed topics in the Hebrew Bible – this is not directly related to our theme, so we will follow Durham's suggestion and focus only on the smaller unit of Exod. 3.1-12.[119]

112. See Johnston, *Exodus 1–19*, 69; Brevard Childs, *Exodus: A Commentary* (London: SCM, 1974), 52; Nahum Sarna, *Exodus: The Traditional Hebrew Text with the JPS Translation*, vol. 1 (Philadelphia, PA: Jewish Publication Society, 1991), 13; Thomas Dozeman, *Commentary on Exodus* (Grand Rapids, MI: Eerdmans, 2009), 119.

113. Johnston, *Exodus 1–19*, 69.

114. Childs, *Exodus*, 51.

115. John Durham, *Exodus*, Word Biblical Commentary 3 (Waco, TX: Word, 1987), 29.

116. Childs, *Exodus*, 54.

117. Dozeman, *Commentary on Exodus*, 119.

118. Ibid.

119. We admit nonetheless that the unit logically runs through to Exod. 4.17, where the dialogue between the Lord and Moses ends.

The structure of Exod. 3.1-12 is similar to that of Genesis 15. Although it includes numerous *wayyiqtols*, these mainly introduce direct speech (אמר eight times; קרא once). The whole passage is predominantly a dialogue in direct speech, but interestingly, in v. 8 we find a verb of movement, ארד, in a *wayyiqtol* embedded in the direct speech. The verse is therefore significant as a record of God's action. Durham divides vv. 1-12 into two sections: vv. 1-2 are narrative and introduce a long passage of direct speech; vv. 3-12 are a dialogue between the LORD and Moses.[120] The author suggests that the theme of these verses is 'theophany and call', which belong together.[121] He observes: 'Theophany describes the advent of God's presence; call describes the opportunity of response to that Presence. Theophany provides both stimulus and authority for response; response, despite choice, is virtually inevitable following theophany.'[122] Durham sees the 'presence' of God and the 'response' of God's people as a recurring pattern in the book of Exodus: the theophany to Moses and his response to it foreshadows the theophany to the whole of Israel in Egypt, in the wilderness, and at Sinai.[123] Childs agrees with the structure of the narrative as presented by Zimmerli and developed by Habel: first comes the divine confrontation (vv. 1-3, 4a); second, the introductory word (vv. 4b-9); third, the commission (v. 10); fourth, the objection (v. 11); fifth, the reassurance (v. 12a); and finally the sign (v. 12b).[124] Childs proposes a prophetic setting for the story, rather than the more usual cultic (Gressmann) or cultic and juridical setting (Plastaras).[125] Dozeman sees the central knot of the passage in vv. 10-12: v. 10 commission; v. 11 objection; v. 12a reassurance; and v. 12b sign.[126] Sarna divides the story differently, arguing that there are three units within Exod. 3.1–4.17: the theophany at the burning bush (3.1-6); the divine call (3.7-10); and the

120. As we have just mentioned, the dialogue runs to Exod. 4.17.

121. Durham, *Exodus*, 29. See also Christoph Dohmen, *Exodus 1–18* (Freiburg: Herder, 2015), 143.

122. Ibid., *Exodus*, 29.

123. 'It is at least possible that such a pattern, which is basic in the oldest traditions of Israel's relationship with God (i.e., the exodus-Sinai experience and in the patriarchal narratives), basic in the great confessions of worship preserved in the Psalms, basic in the experience and in the proclamation of the prophets, basic in the theological presuppositions of the great hagiographers, and basic even in the catechetical didacticism of the wise teachers, is the seminal point-of-origin for the call-narratives of the OT'. Ibid., 30.

124. Childs, *Exodus*, 53–4.

125. Ibid., 55.

126. Dozeman, *Commentary on Exodus*, 120. See also Victor Hamilton, *Exodus: An Exegetical Commentary* (Grand Rapids, MI: Baker Academic, 2011), 58.

extensive dialogue between Moses and God (3.11–4.17).[127] Dohmen argues that if we apply the classical division and structure of the unit (Exod 3.1–4.17), we come to the conclusion (with Durham) that the theme is 'theophany and call'. However, if we add verses in 4.18-31, we gain a broader picture which takes in the deliverance of the Israelites from Egypt.[128] Dohmen also suggests that we experiment with several different structures and divisions of the unit to see what interpretations may arise.[129]

Childs notes two significant groups of verbs in Exod. 3.1-12: the root ראה ('to see') is used seven times in vv. 2-7; and the root שלך ('to send') is used twice in vv. 10-12.[130] We have already noted that Exod. 3.1-12 is a long dialogue with a short introduction. The dialogue itself is not divided equally: God's speech is many times longer than that of Moses. Moreover, Moses' first piece of direct speech in v. 3 is not part of the dialogue as it is addressed to himself rather than to God. Apart from Moses' short הנני in v. 4 and his objection מי אנכי in v. 11, Exod. 3.1-12 is mostly, therefore, a monologue from God.

Regarding source criticism, Hamilton suggests that Exod. 3.1, 4b, and 6 belong to the E source and Exod. 3.2-3, 4a, and 5 to the J source. He argues that the name Elohim in J could refer to the angel of God as 'Elohim' refers more broadly to divine creatures.[131] Childs provides an extensive analysis of the problems surrounding the possible sources. He notes the popular theory regarding the changing names for the deity, according to which the following division of verses could be applied: Exod. 3.1ab, 2-4a, 5, 7, and 8 to J; and Exod. 3.1, 4b, 6, and 9-12 to E. However, he confirms that verse 1 is problematic as it contains material from both J and E.[132] He agrees that there is more unity to the passage than is usually recognized but also accepts that some of the tensions are too significant for the unit to be assigned to a single author.[133] Hyatt provides a coherent map of J and E sources, assigning Exod. 3.1ab, 2-4a, 5, and

127. Sarna, *Exodus*, 13.

128. Dohmen, *Exodus 1–18*, 143.

129. Ibid.

130. Childs, *Exodus*, 70. Childs uses the keywords 'to see' and 'to send' to strengthen his argument that Exod. 3.1-12 is a narrative of theophany and call. Dohmen also adds the verb הלך ('to go'). See Dohmen, *Exodus 1–18*, 143.

131. Hamilton, *Exodus*, 48.

132. Childs, *Exodus*, 53.

133. Ibid. See also: 'Today, instead of atomizing the Pentateuch into independent documents, they aim at understanding how the existing materials were consciously reworked in such a way as to meet new needs of interpretation. Redaction is conceived as editing which does not simply collect or compile but creatively transforms its traditional materials.' Vervenne, 'The "P" Tradition in the Pentateuch', 89.

7-8 to J, and Exod. 3.1c, 4b, 6, and 9-15 to E.[134] Johnston also refers to
the basic theory of dividing the sources according to the changing names
for the deity – YHWH for J and Elohim for E – and that everything was
put together and edited by a redactor (R).[135] Durham agrees with this
theory but notes two small problems: the two names for the deity occur
together in v. 4; and the name Horeb, typically attributed to E, appears
in v. 1, which is assigned to J.[136] Johnston himself, however, is far from
satisfied with the theory, which he suggests seems to imply that for some
reason the redactor suppressed most of the E material and retained the
J material. He therefore proposes that the supposed redactor brought
much more original material to the text than would be expected, and
that this person is therefore a 'new author', who produced a 'D-version'.
The changing of the deity's name poses no problem for Johnston as the
D-version addresses the deity as YHWH when the Israelites are in view
and as Elohim in the context of other nations.[137] Johnston therefore seems
to be aware of the 'authorial' element in the role of the redactor or copyist,
who 'co-creates' the meaning of the text, which Gadamer assumes is the
case for every new reading.

Before shifting our focus to Exod. 3.8 (together with Exod. 3.6-7,
which commentators agree are connected in significance and meaning),
we will take a closer look at v. 1. There is a nuance in this verse which
often goes unnoticed and it concerns the wordplay between Jethro and
Horeb: Jethro, the name of Moses' father-in-law, can be translated 'his
abundance';[138] Horeb, the mountain of God, means 'desolate, waste'.[139]
Strangely, the name of the mountain does not correspond to its attributes
and the expectations placed upon it. Horeb is understood to be identical
with Mount Sinai,[140] and Moses is commanded to take off his shoes when
standing on the 'holy ground' of the mountain. Why did God choose such

134. Philip Hyatt, *Commentary on Exodus* (London: Oliphants, 1971), 70.

135. Johnston, *Exodus 1–19*, 70.

136. Durham, *Exodus*, 29.

137. Johnston, *Exodus 1–19*, 70.

138. Durham, *Exodus*, 27.

139. Johnston, *Exodus 1–19*, 71. See also Durham, *Exodus*, 27. Johnston notes the
'inherent' sacred nature of the mountain: in many ancient cults, mountains were the
site of theophanies and thus also cultic places and places of worship. See Johnston,
Exodus 1–19, 71, 74. Sarna on the other hand suggests that, 'The pagan mythological
notion that certain areas are inherently holy does not exist in the Bible. It is solely
the theophany that temporarily imparts sanctity to the site, rendering it inaccessible
to man.' Sarna, *Exodus*, 15.

140. Durham, *Exodus*, 33. Sarna problematizes this accepted view, claiming that
Horeb may not be identical with Sinai. Sarna, *Exodus*, 14.

a place to appear to Moses and to commission him with the task that is central to the history of the salvation of the people of Israel? Dozeman suggests that, 'The Hebrew word *hōrēb* means "desolate and dry". The form of the word in this verse, with a locating ending (*hōrēbâ*) indicating direction, may signify a more general translation, in which the "mountain of God" is located in the desolate desert.'[141] Dozeman is suggesting that it is not the mountain itself that is 'desolate and dry' but the surrounding area. Interestingly, although commentators note the meanings of Jethro and Horeb, they do not generally probe any further into any meaning that may arise from their juxtaposition. They are contradictory in meaning, but they belong to the same semantic group. On the one hand, Moses' father-in-law, a Midianite priest, is called 'abundance', so we have a person in Moses' family who promises him a stable life, an occupation, and protection and comfort in 'abundance'. On the other hand, there is the God of the fathers, of the people who drove Moses away from Egypt (Exod. 2.11-15), who resides beyond the wilderness on the mountain called 'desolate, waste'. It is not so much of a stretch, therefore, to argue that the juxtaposition of these two names emphasizes Moses' decision to commit himself to the commission given him by God.

In v. 6, Moses is told the identity of the deity. Durham notes that the deity is first referred to as 'the God of your father', in the singular, and only then are the three patriarchs – Abraham, Isaac, and Jacob – listed. God is thus linked to Moses' family and to the Israelites in Egypt.[142] Johnston stresses the gradual development of the identification of the deity. The formula אנכי אלהי אביך אלהי אברהם אלהי יצחק ואלהי יעקב is repeated, with slight variations, in Exod. 3.6, 13, 15, 16, and 4.5. Continuity with the past ensures that the revelation of God's name avoids any suggestion of another deity, and the formula serves as a reaffirmation of the promises made to the patriarchs and their descendants.[143] Johnston observes: 'The Lord reaffirms all the promises made to the ancestors, above all of settlement in a land (see 1.6), and brings these promises a decisive stage closer to fulfilment'.[144] Dozeman agrees, stating that the self-identification of God already took place in 3.6-8: 'The parallels

---

141. Dozeman, *Commentary on Exodus*, 124.

142. Durham, *Exodus*, 31.

143. Johnston, *Exodus 1–19*, 74.

144. Ibid. Childs notes a significant difference between the call of Moses and the call of Abraham and the patriarchs. This difference is nevertheless constitutive of classic prophetism. Whereas Abraham was called as an individual based on his faith and conduct, Moses has no such qualification for his task. Moreover, he is to take the message to others. See Childs, *Exodus*, 56.

underscore that the Deity appearing before Moses is not only the God of the father (Gen 46:3 and Exod 3:6) but also a God who promised to be present with Jacob in Egypt, employing the imagery of migration down to Egypt and return (Gen 46:4 and Exod 3:7-8)'.[145] Dozeman cites Rendtorff and Van Seters, who both highlighted the importance of vv. 6-8 as God's self-identification but drew different conclusions:

> Rendtorff concluded that the insertion of the promise to the ancestors in the story of Moses introduced a new interpretation. The point of focus is no longer the reception of the promise by ancestors, as was the case in Genesis, but the continuity of divine revelation from the time of the patriarchs to the exodus generation of the Israelites.[146]

Dozeman is pointing out that for Rendtorff, continuity of divine revelation and not the promises to the patriarchs is the principal message of Exod. 3.6-8.[147] He suggests that for Van Seters, on the other hand, the main message is the promises to the fathers, that is, the promise of land.[148] Dozeman concludes:

> The land becomes the point of focus in the self-identification of God to Moses in 3:6-8... Verses 7-8 are a brief summary of salvation history... The exodus will become the point of focus in the commission of Moses (3:9-12). But in God's self-introduction to Moses the promise of land takes centre stage.[149]

---

145. Dozeman, *Commentary on Exodus*, 126.

146. Ibid., 127.

147. See also: 'Exodus 3–4 is concerned with a central and theologically important text at the beginning of the Moses tradition in which one is to expect basic pointers to the understanding of that whole, within which the author or redactor wants the questions to be understood. This goes together with the observation that with the information about the prolific increase of people (Exod 1:7) and with the first mention of the land into which Yhwh will lead the Israelites (3:8), there is no reference at all to the corresponding promise themes in the patriarchal stories. Hence, the inevitable conclusion: the Moses tradition has been reworked and interpreted from entirely different points of view than the patriarchal stories.' Rendtorff and Scullion, *The Problem of the Process of Transmission in the Pentateuch*, 89.

148. John Van Seters, *The Life of Moses: The Yahwist as Historian in Exodus–Numbers* (Louisville, KY: Westminster John Knox, 1994), 42. See also John Van Seters, *Abraham in History and Tradition* (London: Yale University Press, 1975), 145–7, 263–7.

149. Dozeman, *Commentary on Exodus*, 128.

For Van Seters and Dozeman, therefore, the centrality of the promise of land is clearly demonstrated in God's self-identification and revelation as the one 'who promises land to God's people'. Dohmen, who drew much from Durham's 'theophany and call' structure but eventually moved away from it, agreed with Van Seters and Dozeman that the main theme of Exod. 3.1–4.31 is, 'deliverance from Egypt and settlement in the Promised Land'. He argues further that the exodus and settlement of the land are indivisible, and that this connection is clear as early as Exodus 1. The promises to the patriarchs – the promises of numberless descendants and of land – also belong together. Whereas the promise of descendants (Gen. 12.7; 15.4) was fulfilled in Exod. 1.7, the promise of land remained unfulfilled.[150] The promise returns in Exod. 3.8, and exodus and settlement are again the key theme of Exod. 3.7-12.[151]

In vv. 7 to 9, we see what lay behind God's calling of Moses. God had seen the affliction of the people in Egypt and decided to ירד ('come down') to עלה ('bring up') the people out of the land. It is interesting that the verb ירד is used in a *wayyiqtol* that is rendered in the past tense: 'I have come down'. Rashbam sees God's 'descent' to make the revelation to Moses as the beginning of the act of liberation.[152] Hamilton stresses that in v. 8 we are dealing with 'liberation vocabulary':

> Sometimes the purpose of God toward Israel is to bring Israel out of Egypt (*yāsā*, Hiphil), but as in v. 8, sometimes his purpose is to bring Israel up to a new land (*'alâ*, Hiphil)… Taking both verbs together, one sees that God's saving/delivering work is both a saving 'from' and saving 'to', a deliverance from bondage and an old way of life, and an entry into freedom and a revolutionary new way of life.[153]

Hamilton is stressing not only that the 'bringing up' to a new land is at least as important as – if not more important than – the 'bringing out' of Egypt, but also that the one cannot exist without the other: when someone is saved 'from' something, the space cannot be left empty – an adequate alternative must be offered. Verse 8 also includes movement, both down and up, and this movement is both literal (physical) and symbolic. Durham mentions only the first of these movements: God

---

150. Dohmen, *Exodus 1–18*, 153.

151. Ibid., 143, 153.

152. Harry Freedman, ed., *Genesis*, Midrash Rabbah 1, 3rd ed. (London: Soncino, 1983), 32.

153. Hamilton, *Exodus*, 55.

'came down' from the heavens to meet with Moses and will bring God's people up from Egypt.[154] Johnston adds that geographically, going to Egypt had always been 'going down';[155] that psychologically, the downward movement referred to the abject condition in which they found themselves in Egypt and from which they needed to be 'brought up';[156] and that allegorically, for ancient Christian exegetes and interpreters who interpreted the exodus and the settlement narrative spiritually and eschatologically, Egypt was a symbol of hell and the promised land a symbol of heaven.[157] Concerning hell, the downward movement is self-evident. Johnston argues that יצא in Hiphil ('to bring out') has the specific meaning of release from slavery.[158] This dynamic of an upward and a downward movement in v. 8 is particularly important for the exodus (deliverance) and the promise (land and settlement). Johnston sees in v. 6 not only a reaffirmation of the promise of land but also a key to Moses' mission:

> The promise of land to the ancestors provides the framework within which Moses is to operate. 'Land' thus marks the beginning and end of Israel's journey: God will enable them to escape from the power of Egypt...and will bring them to 'a good and spacious land, a land flowing with milk and honey' (v. 8).[159]

He also points out that the term 'good and spacious' in v. 8 is an original depiction of the promised land found nowhere else in the Hebrew Bible.[160] Sarna suggests that, 'This depiction of the land of Israel is drawn from the mental image of an oppressed semi-nomadic people confined to the limited area of Goshen'.[161] The idyllic notion of 'flowing with milk and honey' returns in v. 17:

154. Durham, *Exodus*, 32.
155. Johnston, *Exodus 1–19*, 78.
156. Ibid.
157. Philo of Alexandria, *Quaestiones et solutiones in Exodum I et II e versione armeniaca et fragmenta graeca*, ed. Abraham Terian, Les Oeuvres de Philon d'Alexandrie 34c (Paris: Cerf, 1992). See also Origen, *Homélies sur l'Exode* (Paris: Cerf, 1947); Theodoret of Cyrus, 'Genesis, Exodus', in *The Questions on the Octateuch*, ed. John Petruccione and Robert Hill, Library of Early Christianity 1 (Washington, DC: Catholic University of America, 2007).
158. See also Exod. 7.4; 20.2; 21.2-11; Deut. 15.12-19. Johnston, *Exodus 1–19*, 78.
159. Ibid., 76.
160. Ibid.
161. Sarna, *Exodus*, 15.

The land is a new Eden (cf. Joel 3:18); the vocabulary used here does not recur in Gen 2–3, but the concepts are comparable. The abundant natural produce, such as milk and honey, has to be husbanded, as Adam tended the well-watered, naturally productive garden (Gen 2:15), but the backbreaking toil of agriculture (Gen 3:17-18) is unnecessary.[162]

According to Hyatt, the description of a 'land flowing with milk and honey' seems to have been intended to attract a nomadic people who were slaves in Egypt.[163] Sarna notes that such attributes did not appear in the promises to the patriarchs:

The phrase is never included in the divine promises made to the patriarchs, for whom famine was frequently a grim reality. Besides, their faith did not need to be reinforced by stressing the attractiveness of the land. For the demoralized, enslaved masses of Israel, however, such an enticement would carry weight. As a matter of fact, ancient Egyptian sources testify to the richness of the land.[164]

His argument is far from convincing, however; illogical even. First, if famine were 'frequently a grim reality' to the patriarchs, it would make more sense if the paradisiacal promise of an abundance of food and drink formed part of the promise to them. Secondly, it is not clear how Sarna concluded that unlike the masses of Israel the patriarchs were not demoralized. In our discussion of Gen. 15.7, we learned of Abraham's deep frustration at not having a legitimate heir. It is true we saw no sign of any lack of faith, but the attractiveness of the land would certainly have encouraged Abraham all the same.

Dozeman sees the description of the promised land in Exod. 3.8 as utopian. Sarna believes 'milk and honey' refers to the fertility of a land which promises a rich diet for those who live there.[165] Dozeman notes other references to 'flowing with milk and honey' in Deuteronomy (Deut. 6.13; 11.9; 26.9, 13; 27.3; 31.20).[166] Hyatt assigns this characteristic of the promised land to J and Dt authors,[167] and reminds us that milk and honey is the traditional food of the Greek gods.[168]

162. Johnston, *Exodus 1–19*, 77.
163. Hyatt, *Commentary on Exodus*, 73. Hamilton suggests that milk and honey are somehow alien to the biblical land of that time and that the most suitable translation of חלב ודבש is 'fat and sap'. Hamilton, *Exodus*, 56.
164. Sarna, *Exodus*, 16.
165. Ibid.
166. Dozeman, *Commentary on Exodus*, 129.
167. Hyatt, *Commentary on Exodus*, 71.
168. Dozeman, *Commentary on Exodus*, 129.

Dohmen points out the interesting fact that there is no consistent picture of the occupants of the promised land over time. At one point it is uninhabited, then it is inhabited by people with whom the Israelites must share the land, then by people whom they must drive out.[169] In this context, Dohmen argues that Exod. 3.8 tells us that the land is spacious enough to accommodate all the nations living peacefully side by side,[170] and that the list of the peoples is given in order to specify the general area covered by the land rather than the specific geographical boundaries.[171]

We have seen that although the promise of land is a single promise, certain differences exist between the promise made to Abraham and the patriarchs and the promise made to the whole of Israel, and the historical-critical analysis of Gen. 15.7 and Exod. 3.8 confirmed this. There is continuity in the promise, but there are differences in the addressees. In the first instance, the addressee, Abraham, is someone of extraordinary faith and the promise is made to him in the singular. Ottosson says: 'Yahweh's love to Abraham is specified as the ultimate reason for the possession of the land'.[172] In the second instance, the person, Moses, does not exhibit any particular quality, not even regarding faith, as he is more than likely practising the cult of Midian. He is also not the 'recipient' of the promise. He is rather God's emissary who is to deliver the promise to the people of Israel in the name of the God *Adonai*. There is also a difference in how the land is described. In the first case, stress is laid on the fact that the land is to be 'his (Abraham's, Isaac's, Jacob's) own' in contrast to Ur where he was an alien. However, this promise is never fulfilled completely as all the patriarchs who came to the promised land resided there as 'sojourners' only. If the promise made to the patriarchs had been fulfilled, there would be no need for the promise made to the whole of Israel through Moses. In this second case, ownership of the land is never mentioned. Rather, stress is laid on the quality of the land: it is to be 'good and large, flowing with milk and honey'. Having claimed continuity between the promises but insisted on there being differences, we now see the validity of the decision to analyse the two verses separately.

We have suggested that Gen. 15.7 and Exod. 3.8, and the promise of land of which they speak, play a prominent role in their immediate and extended biblical contexts. Not all commentators agree with such an interpretation, but many do. Brueggemann may overstate the centrality of the promise of land in the Hebrew Bible – more of which later – but the sheer

---

169. Dohmen, *Exodus 1–18*, 153.
170. Ibid.
171. Ibid., 154.
172. Ottosson, 'ארץ', 404.

volume of references to the promise of land throughout the Bible suggests that it is certainly a key issue. Both verses clearly underline the fact that God pursues a relationship with people through land.

Reception of the promised land in the Hebrew Bible

The theology of land in the Hebrew Bible is described from two main perspectives, the agricultural and the territorial, each of which is highly political. The perspectives overlap and each is biased in favour of the people of Israel because the issue of land is, as we have just seen, one of the key factors in the relationship between God and God's people. How this three-way relationship – God, God's people, land – is received in the Bible is the focus of the remainder of this chapter.

The books of the Bible were written in different eras by different authors with a variety of religious-political agendas. It is no surprise, then, that the depiction of the promised land also differs significantly throughout the Bible. Coote suggests, for example, a challenging dialectic between the reception of the promised land in the Torah and the Prophets:

> The Torah concept of territory is categorical, proleptic, and vague; the prophetic concept is contingent, fulfilled, and idealistic. Jerusalem goes unnoticed in the one and serves as the dazzling focal point of the other. These two dominant concepts of land, of the Torah and Prophets, created the great conceptual divide with respect to the land: the Torah constituting Israel of the land and the Prophets admonishing Israel in the land.[173]

Coote insists that the way in which God's people relate to the land is always contextual and always contingent on obedience (or otherwise) to God.

The Torah

We began with the territorial aspect of the land as this is the aspect at stake in our two source verses, Gen. 15.7 and Exod. 3.8. There is more to the concept of the promised land than the territory, however: land was the key provider for ancient Near Eastern people. Janzen highlights the stress on the relationship between human beings and the land in the Pentateuch.[174] To see this connection, it is necessary to consider another Hebrew word that English translations sometimes render as 'land', and that is אדמה. Although in the early chapters of Genesis there is no explicit

---

173. Coote, 'Land', 32.
174. Janzen, 'Land', 147.

political concern regarding land – here it is more a matter of agricultural interests – it is all but impossible to detach the political agenda from any discussion concerning 'the promised land'. Janzen rightly disagrees with Coote's claim that, 'the Bible reflects mainly non-producer politics, whether royal, priestly, or colonial, [and] represents land mainly as territory'.[175] Hiebert insists that, on the contrary, 'So central was this agricultural way of life to Israel's self-understanding that according to one of its creation accounts, the Eden narrative in Gen 2:4b-3:24, the first human was made from arable soil (Heb. *'ăḏāmâ*, 2:7) and given the task of cultivating it (2:15; 3:23)'.[176] Janzen draws examples from primeval history where land is a creation of God and is meant to provide for both plants and animals (including human beings). When the transgression of God's prohibition in Genesis 3 and the first crime in Genesis 4 take place, the land is always in view: in ch. 3 the land is cursed because of the transgression of the first couple; in ch. 4 the land opens its mouth to receive the blood of the murdered Abel, and Cain is cursed and driven from the land. It is not only the first chapters of Genesis that discuss the agricultural or producer's concern for the land. In Leviticus, a Sabbath for resting the land is examined, and this also concerns the land in the agricultural rather than the territorial sense (see Lev. 25.1-7). The relationship between the land and the people, relationships among the people, and the relationship between the people and God must all be set right. The corruption of any one of these relationships affects the other two. Thus, when there is a transgression against the land, God draws away from the people. In Lev. 18.25, we read that the land 'vomited out its inhabitants' (the Canaanites) because they worshiped heathen gods. If the Israelites joined them in this practice, they too would be vomited out of the land (Lev. 18.28; 20.22).[177] Wright adds a reference to the exile and the 'scattering of the Israelites among the nations' (Lev. 26.32-39; Deut. 18.63-64).[178] Nonetheless, any discussion of the importance of the land for the people of the ancient Near East cannot but include the perspective of husbandry. These two aspects are so connected, however, that it makes almost no sense to distinguish between them: the longing for some land of one's own to cultivate and harvest naturally develops into the longing for a real piece of land, a piece

175. Coote, 'Land', 30.

176. Hiebert, 'Land', 788. Also: 'Just as human identity was grounded in the arable land, its cultivation, and its agricultural produce, so too Israel's view of God was closely associated with this landscape'. Ibid.

177. Ottosson, 'ארץ', 402. See also Wright, 'ארץ', 524.

178. Wright, 'ארץ', 524.

of territory, to possess. Although Janzen discusses the agricultural aspect of land in the early chapters of Genesis, he fails to address the importance of the Sabbath for resting the land mentioned in Leviticus. In Leviticus 25 the land is certainly not meant in the territorial sense.

As we have already stated, Coote completely disregarded the agricultural aspect of land. Although Coote's analysis falls short in this respect, he makes a valuable contribution in his argument that God gives the land to the Israelites as a 'monarchic grant'. Coote maintains that the earliest representation of the Israelites' territory is in the J source, in the books of Genesis, Exodus, and Numbers. Further, the land of Canaan is portrayed as a mythical land flowing with milk and honey, producing an abundance of food without needing to be cultivated (see Isa. 7.14-25). In these biblical books, God is the true king of Israel, who thus gives the land as a monarchic grant sealed by an oath to Abraham, who is to build sanctuaries at Shechem and Bethel: 'The grant includes more than pasturage and thus is anticipatory, looking forward to the Israelites taking possession some time after a trek as fugitive slaves through the desert from Egypt'.[179] Indeed, in the books of the Torah, Israel never fulfils the promise of the land, but for theological reasons (see Gen. 15.15) the authors of the Pentateuch skilfully included their report of the burial of the patriarchs in Canaan. Janzen observes: 'Only a burial plot, the field and cave of Machpelah, bought by Abraham to bury Sarah, becomes their permanent possession in Canaan, and therewith a proleptic sign of the fulfilment of God's promise (Genesis 23)'.[180]

We have already discussed the emphasis upon the land as the 'inheritance' of God and what it meant for the Israelites. The land is always 'entrusted' to the Israelites; they are not to use it as they please. Neither is the inheritance permanent: successful occupation of the land is contingent on obedience to the Torah. Janzen sees the promise of land as a concrete expression of the covenant between God and God's people.[181] Millar comments on the same relationship:

> The one reliable way of gauging Israel's faithfulness and obedience in future will be their continuing occupation of the land; the primary consequence of faithlessness and disobedience will be loss of land. This is made clear in Deuteronomy 4 and 30, where the exile is predicted, and in chapters 27–28, where it is made clear that disobedience will actualize the curses of

179. Coote, 'Land', 30.
180. Janzen, 'Land', 147.
181. Ibid.

the covenant, which involve expulsion from the land and much else besides (see also Lev 26:32-39). Moses puts the issue of land at the forefront of national consciousness; land represents, in many ways, the spiritual state of the nation.[182]

The concepts of Sabbath and Jubilee (Lev. 25) show that the territorial-political notion of the land arises organically from the agricultural. For decades, the political attachment of the Israelites to 'their' land was created by their dependence on husbandry. Milgrom suggests that the Sabbatical and Jubilee laws originated in the second half of the eighth century, when money began to replace the barter system in trade and commerce. Instead of borrowing seed to sow, farmers who had suffered a crop failure had to borrow money, which they often could not repay and so fell into debt.[183] Balentine tells us the land was to rest, just like the people, every seventh day as both land and people belonged to YHWH; the land, moreover, was to lie fallow after every seventh year so that it could 'regain its strength': 'Every seventh year "the land shall observe a Sabbath for the Lord." During this time there is to be neither sowing nor pruning, for the land, like God and God's creatures, must be returned to the freedom from toil that it enjoyed on creation's first Sabbath'.[184] Note here that Balentine elevates the land to the level of 'creature', alongside people and animals: land has an equal right to rest. Although this all makes good agricultural sense, the religious justification may seem more obscure. In the context of the 'promised land theology' discussed above, however, it makes perfect sense. Milgrom notes that although the verses in Leviticus 25 make no mention of it, the Jews of the Diaspora were exempt from the law regarding a Sabbath for the land as they had to keep working to be able to pay taxes to their foreign rulers.[185] The fiftieth year, the 'Jubilee year', served as a 'general amnesty' when liberty was proclaimed throughout the land:

> The liberty is envisioned as the promise of returning home. Israelites who have been forced to mortgage their land because of economic distress are allowed to reclaim their holdings and resume their lives as free and unindentured persons who may work toward the promise of providing for themselves and their families.[186]

182. Millar, 'Land', 625.

183. Jacob Milgrom, *Leviticus 23–27: A New Translation with Introduction and Commentary,* Anchor Bible 3b (New York: Doubleday, 2001), 2243.

184. Samuel Balentine, *Leviticus* (Westminster: John Knox, 2002), 194.

185. Milgrom, *Leviticus 23–27*, 2243.

186. Balentine, *Leviticus*, 195.

The land belongs to God, so to break a law pertaining to the land is to dishonour God (Lev. 25.23). In Lev. 25.25-28 we read that if a landowner in financial trouble is to sell a property it must be sold to close kin, who will keep it until the original owner can buy it back or until the next Jubilee year.[187] This land law is similar to the law we encounter in Ruth 4.1-6, where Boaz serves as a redeemer not only to Naomi but also to Naomi's daughter-in-law Ruth, whom he also marries.

Hartley points out that the laws regarding resting the land in the Sabbatical and Jubilee years are secured by a parenesis in Lev. 25.18-19 that is similar to Leviticus 18–20: to dwell securely in the land, Israel must keep God's commandments. Another reminder of the conditional nature of God's gift of land appears in Lev. 18.28: the people of Israel are to keep God's commandments or be 'vomited out' both *from* and *by* the land.[188] The people's wellbeing in the land is therefore dependent on their moral conduct, especially their treatment of those who had to lease the land or subject themselves to servitude.[189] Hartley takes the following position: YHWH created the land and is its only true owner; YHWH delivered the people from slavery in Egypt and is their only true owner.[190] Two events are mentioned here: creation and deliverance. Although God's 'ownership' of the Israelites could have been justified by creation alone, the author-redactor clearly wanted to refer to the exodus, a key event in the history of the salvation of Israel. Likewise, in the two readings of the Decalogue (Exod. 20.8-11 and Deut. 5.13-15), both reasons are given for keeping the Sabbath, so both were clearly important enough for the author-redactor to have mentioned them.[191] Again, it is important to stress the interconnection between God, the people, and the land. The Sabbath for resting the land and the Sabbath for resting the people are equal focal points in Leviticus 25: land and people belong equally to God, so neither is to be 'enslaved'. The land shall rest every seventh year and in the fiftieth year its original owner shall buy it back; the people shall rest every seventh day and in the fiftieth year all those who have had to sell

187. Ibid., 196.

188. Note that the land here is also an agent of the execution of the punishment (see also Gen. 3.17; 4.11).

189. John Hartley et al., *Leviticus*, Word Biblical Commentary 4 (Waco, TX: Word, 1992), 424.

190. Ibid., 427.

191. The two Decalogues differ with regard to the rationale for keeping the Sabbath: Exod. 20 appeals to the people to rest on the seventh day because of the seven days of creation; Deut. 5 argues that God liberated Israel from Egypt and made a covenant with them.

themselves into servitude shall be released and returned to their families. The Jubilee year was designed to do more than secure social equality in Israel, however:

> The goal of the Jubilee was to maintain the solidarity of various clans in Israel by keeping alive the ideal of the equality of all Israelite citizens under the covenant. From another perspective, this legislation sought to prevent the rich from amassing property into large estates (cf. Isa 5:8) and reducing the poor to landless tenant farmers. Thus, it attacked head-on the dehumanizing powers of debt and landlessness.[192]

The Jubilee year was therefore meant not only to release those in servitude and allow the original owner of the land to buy it back; it was also clearly intended to prevent the accumulation of property in the hands of the wealthy and powerful. Hartley also believes that the Sabbath for the land can be read as a profoundly prophetic regulation with respect to our modern-day environmental crisis: careless cultivation, failing to adequately rest the land, and the 'latifundialization' of agriculture have led to greater exploitation of the land and the depletion of natural resources.[193] Milgrom concludes his commentary on the Jubilee law with an application to the current context:

> The Jubilee has become the rallying cry for oppressed peoples today, as was the exodus theme for their counterparts in previous decades. This time, however, they are not enslaved politically (except where colonial rulers have been replaced by their own) but shackled economically. The global market economy has generated unprecedented growth and prosperity, but not for them.[194]

Concerning the risk of latifundialization, Hartley, Bailey, and Milgrom all refer to the story of Naboth's vineyard.[195] To strengthen his argument that the story is about the violation of land laws and not simply

---

192. Hartley et al., *Leviticus*, 443. Also: 'The belief in Yahweh's ownership of the land, therefore, produced in ancient Israel a distinctive economic system based on the perpetual right of a family to its patrimony... Yahweh gave Israel the sabbatical year and the year of Jubilee to curtail the human desire to accumulate more and more by interrupting the continuous activity of sowing and harvesting.' Ibid., 443, 445.

193. Ibid., 445.

194. Milgrom, *Leviticus 23–27*, 2271.

195. Ibid. See also Lloyd Bailey, *Leviticus – Numbers*, Smyth & Helwys Bible Commentary (Macon, GA: Smyth & Helwys, 2005), 303; Milgrom, *Leviticus 23–27*, 2243.

about murder and social injustice, Bailey notes that God sends the prophet Elijah to Ahab when he is 'in the vineyard' to prevent him from confiscating it.[196] We will return to the social aspects of promised land theology and the story of Naboth's vineyard later.

Deuteronomistic History

Promised land theology is developed strongly in the book of Deuteronomy. The land as a sign of the covenant between God and God's people is never executed in the books of the Torah: full possession of the land comes only with Joshua's account of the conquest of the Canaanites. The conquest and subsequent colonization are, however, 'foretold' in Deuteronomy.[197]

In his detailed study of Deuteronomistic sources, Ausloos argues that many of the verses that deal with the motif of the promised land in the Hebrew Bible – in the Pentateuch, from Joshua to 2 Kings, and in Jeremiah – can be attributed to some sort of Deuteronomistic tradition. This tradition includes a covenantal understanding of the promise of land and attempts to determine and establish its location and borders:

> The nationalistic and patriotic attitude of Deuteronomy is recognisable in the establishment of the Promised Land. Reference can be made in addition to the conditional character of the gift of the land in the Deuteronom(ist)ic literature. It is likewise remarkable in this regard that the loss of the land is never seen as definitive.[198]

The strength of Ausloos's contribution to research on the Deuteronomistic tradition lies especially in his careful study of its sources. Ausloos argues strongly for the inclusion of Jeremiah in the Deuteronomistic tradition, referring not only to its sources but also to its theological implications, particularly the strong connection to the books from Joshua to 2 Kings with respect to land theology. Janzen sums up the promised land theology of the books of the Deuteronomistic History (Joshua, Judges, 1–2 Samuel, and 1–2 Kings) as Israel's performance in the land and God's response to it.[199] Coote adds that the theology was shaped by the politics of the

---

196. Bailey, *Leviticus–Numbers*, 303.

197. Deut. 4.1-2, 25-27; 5.29-30; 6.10-19; 11.8-9; 13–17. See Coote, 'Land', 31.

198. Hans Ausloos, *The Deuteronomist's History: The Role of the Deuteronomist in Historical-Critical Research into Genesis–Numbers*, Oudtestamentische Studiën 67 (Leiden: Brill, 2015), 296. Ausloos discusses all the possible predecessors and successors of the so-called Deuteronomist authors-redactors. See ibid., 263–4.

199. Janzen, 'Land', 148.

divided kingdom and by attempts to legitimize the sovereignty of the
Davidic dynasty after the destruction of the northern kingdom. These
books always stress, therefore (1–2 Chronicles are omitted as they do not
fully share this conviction), that the cult is to be localized in Jerusalem,
and also speak about the 'rebellious tribes' (the northern kingdom), who
are condemned for the 'sin of Jeroboam' (1 Kgs 15.30; 16.2, 19, 26):

> The revival of the Davidic claim to Israel after the fall of Samaria was likely
> reason for the plot of the DH that gave shape to the sources incorporated:
> law and covenant laid by Moses, which, unlike JE, make the political
> nation's possession of Canaan contingent on popular obedience to Yahweh.[200]

Janzen sees contradictory accounts of the settlement of Canaan in
Joshua and Judges. Whereas Joshua speaks of the total conquest of the land
in the holy wars of God, Judges refers to unconquered Canaanite enclaves
(Judg. 1.19-35; 3.1-6). Biblical scholarship no longer holds to the theory
of the total conquest of the land, but Janzen outlines the explanations
of the various schools regarding how the Israelite population achieved
its status there: Alt and Noth speak of a small but continual infiltration
by nomadic tribes; Mendenhall and Gottwald argue that the Israelites
recruited members from the Canaanites who took over some parts of
Canaan in a social revolt against the ruling class.[201] The book of Judges
offers a foretaste of the dynamic between the possession and loss of land
which is repeated throughout the Deuteronomistic History. Brueggemann
presents the interesting notion that the land is a gift but also presents a
threat:[202] if the Israelites do not keep the Torah, their possession of the
land is jeopardized. In Judges, this threat is personified in the Canaanites,
who represent a test for the Israelites. Ever since the first spies came back
from the land of Canaan, the Israelites had imagined a local population
that was bigger, wealthier, and more powerful than the people of God. A
pattern is established: the Israelites sin against God, their position in the
land is put at risk, they repent, and God raises a powerful judge who leads
a campaign against Israel's enemies and reclaims the land.

Like Deuteronomy and Judges, the books of 1–2 Samuel and 1–2 Kings
suggest that possession and loss of the land are directly dependent upon
obedience to the Torah, and present King David's obedience and loyalty
to God as a model for the people to follow. Janzen observes:

200. Coote, 'Land', 31.
201. Janzen, 'Land', 148. I will explore Gottwald's theory in more detail later.
202. Brueggemann, *The Land*, 62–5.

In his long and nuanced account, the final author of the Deuteronomistic History assesses Israel's faithfulness or unfaithfulness to Yahweh, applying especially the yardstick of David's loyalty to Yahweh to all subsequent kings. This results in a demonstration of the inevitability of the loss of land.[203]

The most oft-quoted example of the connection between land and transgression of the Torah is the story of Naboth's vineyard in 1 Kings 21.[204] Ahab's crimes were not just those of theft and murder. Together with his Canaanite seducer Jezebel, he committed a crime against the land. Two important aspects therefore come together. First, the personal and intra-Israelite: Ahab is violating the land law; YHWH's inheritance was granted to Naboth's family and it could not be sold or given to anyone outside the household. Secondly, the national: it was Jezebel the Canaanite who was behind the scheme and who convinced Ahab to commit his crime. The story therefore represents a violation of the Israelite land law by other nations, namely the Canaanites, who steal the inheritance YHWH had granted to Israel.

Gray recognizes the significance of one further aspect of the land law when he acknowledges that although the offer of compensation to Naboth was fair, Naboth refused it so that he and his family would not become servants of the king.[205] De Vries agrees that losing an ancestral inheritance would also mean losing social status and becoming a royal dependant. He admits that the reason Naboth refused to give up his inheritance lay in the land law of Leviticus 25, but does not go on to imply that violation of the land law meant transgression of the Torah and thus a crime against YHWH.[206] Nelson insists that the king's action against Naboth was indeed a crime against YHWH as it involved a 'stolen heritage' and an act of social injustice: 'Along with Isaiah 5:8 and Micah 2:2, this story is a reminder that offenses against the heritage of the defenceless are offenses against

203. Janzen, 'Land', 148.

204. Ibid. See also Hiebert, 'Land', 788; Millar, 'Land', 626.

205. John Gray, *I & II Kings: A Commentary* (London: SCM, 1964), 389. The newly allotted land granted by the king – even if it was better land – would not grant Naboth the same social status. From a freeman having the inheritance of land granted by an ancestor he would become a royal dependant with a commitment to the king. Gray observes: 'In the administrative texts from the palace of Ras Shamra we are familiar with grants of lands to certain classes and individuals at the king's discretion, usually with feudal or fiscal burdens'. Ibid., 389–90.

206. Simon De Vries et al., *I Kings*, Word Biblical Commentary 12 (Waco, TX: Word, 1985), 256.

God, not just against some abstract principle of economic justice'.[207] In
referring to Mic. 2.2, Nelson reminds us that the prohibition of sale (Lev.
25.23) is occasionally violated. He argues that it was Naboth's personal
decision to take an oath never to sell his inheritance (1 Kgs 21.3), and that
there is no mention in the text that it was Jezebel the Canaanite princess
who caused the death of Naboth and the theft of his inheritance. In
postmodern hermeneutics, this fact neither proves nor disproves anything:
Jezebel was without doubt a Canaanite princess. As we have already seen,
Westphal argues that the text carries both more and less than the author-
editor wanted to write.[208] Nelson notes that such a royal confiscation was
unknown in Israelite law, but lists an external source that suggests it could
have been common practice in the ancient Near East.[209]

Nelson does refer to the Canaanite element in another context. Ahab
wanted Naboth's vineyard for a vegetable garden (1 Kgs 21.2), which
Nelson sees as an 'ironic reference' to Deut. 11.10, where the 'vegetable
garden' of Egypt which needs to be cultivated is contrasted with the land
of promise which 'flows with milk and honey' and requires no cultivation. The vineyard under God's care, as Nelson rightfully points out,
serves as a metaphor for Israel (cf. Isa. 3.14; 5.1-7; Jer. 12.10).[210] Nelson
adds:

> Other indications in the narrative point to the theology of land as the
> theological background: Naboth's use of the loaded word 'inheritance'
> (v. 3), Jezebel's use of 'take possession' (v. 15; a Deuteronomistic code verb
> for the conquest; cf. Deut 15:4 for both words together), and the explicit
> evocation of God's gift of the land in verse 26. If the 'portion of ground'
> (*heleq*) is to be restored in the text of verse 23, as is usually done, this offers
> yet another contact to Deuteronomistic land theology (Deut 12:12; 14:27).[211]

Janzen points out that the two books of the Chronicles pay much less
attention to the land than do the books of the Deuteronomistic History.
The conquest is never mentioned, and Joshua is named just once (1 Chron.
7.27).[212] The kings of Israel and Judah are not evaluated according to their
faithfulness to God; the Chronicler sees divine justice in each of them.

---

207. Richard Nelson, *First and Second Kings*, Interpretation: A Bible Interpretation for Teaching and Preaching (Louisville, KY: John Knox, 1987), 144.

208. Westphal, *Whose Community?*, 81.

209. Nelson, *First and Second Kings*, 139.

210. Ibid., 141.

211. Ibid.

212. Janzen, 'Land', 148.

Although the books reflect the gradual accumulation of sin that resulted in the exile, Janzen argues that this is not a core theme:

> That the Chronicler does not deny the cumulative impetus of a history of sin towards the loss of the land, and that he sees the restoration under Cyrus as the effect of God's grace to an Israel that had served its time in exile 'until the land had enjoyed its sabbaths', is evidenced in his concluding words (2 Chr 36:15-23). Nevertheless, these themes seem marginal rather than central.[213]

The Chronicles indeed deviate from the mainstream interpretation that the promise and the exile are causally related to the faithfulness (or faithlessness) of the Israelites (as represented by their king) towards God. However, this voice is important from a hermeneutical standpoint in order to maintain a plurality within the Hebrew Bible which helps to prevent the silencing of minorities.

The literary prophets to the end of the exile

A concern for the land in the books of the Prophets is clear. The emphasis may change, but the main message is consistent: Israel has violated the covenant with God in numerous ways – serving heathen cults, committing social injustices – and will be punished. The triangular relationship between God, the people, and the land is still valid. Transgressions against the land, against each other, and against God directly are all considered offences against God and will be punished in the same way via the third partner in the relationship, the land: Israel has broken the covenant with God and will be exiled.

Wright observes that, 'In the prophets the great historical land-gift tradition puts Israel's oppressive and exploitative behaviour in a bad light (Amos 2:9-10; Mic 6:1-5)'.[214] What lies behind the criticism of the socio-political reality which we find in Amos, Isaiah, and Micah is the violation of the land law by powerful landowners who had taken inherited land from weak peasants so that the rich became richer and the poor poorer.[215] Janzen insists that land is of 'central theological importance' for these three prophets, and that here we see the importance of the land and its cultivation for all the people of the ancient Near East.[216]

213. Ibid., 148–9.
214. Wright, 'ארץ', 522–3.
215. Janzen, 'Land', 149. See Isa. 3.13-15; 5.9-10; 10.1-2; Amos 3.9-10; 5.11; 6.4-7; 8.4-6; Mic. 2.1-4; 3.1-3; 7.2-3.
216. Ibid.

In all three books we see a similar transgression of the Torah to that
we encountered in the story of Naboth's vineyard. YHWH's inheritance
was to be equally distributed among the people of Israel, and this was
a key feature of the land law: 'For Amos and Micah, the responsibility
[for the equitable distribution of the land] is rooted in God's expulsion of
the previous inhabitants and his gift of the land to Israel coming out of
Egypt (Amos 2:9; 9:7; Mic 6:4-5)'.[217] The event of the exile and the loss
of the land is reflected in the 'funeral song' of Amos 5.1-2 (cf. 7.11).[218] In
Amos and Micah, the faithlessness of the people of Israel results in God's
judgement in the form of exile, the loss of the land;[219] in Isaiah, consistent
with its emphasis on the righteousness and purity of Jerusalem/Zion, the
punishment is represented by the humiliation of Israel/Judah through the
Assyrian conquest.[220]

While Isaiah, Amos, and Micah stress that the people's unfaithfulness to
God is manifested in their violation of the land law, Hosea and Jeremiah,
with no less emphasis on the land, draw a direct link between unfaithfulness to God and the worship of Baal, which ironically, being a fertility
cult, also centred on the land. The nations with whom Israel shared the
land were seen as a threat, seducing them to worship other gods. Hosea
and Jeremiah therefore look back nostalgically to the time of 'wandering
in the wilderness' where there were no Canaanites to lead them astray and
into Baal worship: 'Hosea and Jeremiah, steeped in the exodus tradition,
extol an ideal time in the wilderness and indict the people for unfaithfulness in the land'.[221]

It will be instructive now to consider how Jeremiah interpreted Israel's
attitude towards the land and the impact of that attitude on the history
of the salvation of Israel and its expulsion into exile. Fretheim describes
Jeremiah 2 as a 'divine lament, accusation speech or covenant lawsuit'
(cf. Mic. 6.1-8).[222] Like Hosea, Jeremiah uses the metaphor of marriage
to emphasize the two-way commitment between God and the people of
Israel. But whereas God keeps the covenant and is faithful to the people,

217. Janzen, 'Land', 149. See also, Hiebert, 'Land', 788.
218. Wright, 'ארץ', 524.
219. Janzen, 'Land', 149. See Amos 4.1-3; 5.27; 6.7; 7.11; 9.4, 9, 15; Mic. 1.16;
2.4; 4.10; 5.2(3).
220. Ibid. See Isa. 1.7-9, 24-25; 3.18-26; 5.26-30; 7.20; 10.5-6.
221. Ibid. This dynamic between 'landlessness', when the people of Israel are
faithful to God, and 'landedness', when the people of Israel sin against the law, gains
particular emphasis in Brueggemann's work. I will explore it in more detail later.
222. Terence Fretheim, *Jeremiah*, Smyth & Helwys Bible Commentary 15
(Macon, GA: Smyth & Helwys, 2002), 61.

the Israelites stray into idol worship and thus break the covenant with their God.[223] Huey suggests that the seemingly idyllic years of wandering in the wilderness as described by Jeremiah do not correspond to the accounts in Exodus and Deuteronomy, which register repeated acts of disobedience and idolatry.[224] Craigie agrees, and adds:

> The focus of the language is not so much the evocation of the 'desert ideal'…as it is an elaboration upon the Sinai Covenant… The wilderness was not a positive ideal but a place of hardship, yet the difficulties of that early period had easily been conquered by love.[225]

The metaphor of youthful lovers, God and the people of Israel, changes on Mount Sinai. Here their love is sealed in a covenant that created Israel as a sovereign nation in the promised land. Craigie observes: 'The gift of a constitution at Sinai was matched now by the gift of a land; the youthful people were to become a mature nation'.[226]

Interestingly, Huey, Craigie, and Fretheim agree that Jeremiah 3 includes a reference to the 'divorce law' (Deut. 24.1-4):[227] Judah has abandoned her husband, prostituted herself with many lovers, and disgraced the land (cf. Lev. 18.24-28; Num. 35.34; Ezek. 23.7; Hos. 6.10).[228] Huey notes the irony in the fact that, 'although the fertility cults were supposed to ensure rainfall, Judah's participation in them was actually the cause of drought in the land'.[229] Transgression of the covenant with God therefore affected the land in the agricultural sense before it did so in the political sense through the exile.

Social justice plays a minor role in Hosea but is still important in Jeremiah, where, as in Amos and Micah, God's judgment comes with the loss of the land and exile. Interestingly, in Jeremiah, the people of Israel are exhorted to accept their status as exiles, build houses, have children, make Babylon their new home, and wait until God returns them to their homeland in 70 years' time (Jer. 29.5-10):

223. Ibid.

224. F. B. Huey, *Jeremiah, Lamentations*, The New American Commentary 16 (Nashville, TN: B&H Publishing Group, 1993), 62.

225. Peter Craigie, David Hubbard, and Page Kelley, *Jeremiah 1–25*, Word Biblical Commentary 26 (Waco, TX: Word, 1991), 24.

226. Ibid.

227. Huey, *Jeremiah, Lamentations*, 71. See also Craigie, Hubbard, and Kelley, *Jeremiah 1–25*, 51; Fretheim, *Jeremiah*, 72.

228. Huey, *Jeremiah, Lamentations*, 71.

229. Ibid.

> For Jeremiah, hope and assurance were not to rest on naïve patriotic and
> unreasoned expectations that God would swiftly put an end to the power
> of Babylon and so send the exiles back to their homes. Rather they were
> to be built upon the painful acceptance of the reality of Babylonian rule in
> the present. Consequently, they had to adapt to this situation and learn to
> endure it.[230]

For Jeremiah, the righteous are those who went into exile. In the vision
of the baskets and the figs (Jer. 24), we are told that those who accept the
exile and go to Babylon are on the side of God, but those who remain in
Judah or go to Egypt will be abandoned, as Coote explains:

> The concept of land in the book of Jeremiah as governed by its Deuterono-
> mistic composition conveys the prophet's charge that until the ruling class
> in exile recognizes the violation of the Mosaic covenant as the reason for
> their loss of land, they will not recover the land; the deportees' role now
> is to make life in Babylon a proof of this realization (e.g., Jer 24; 29; 32).[231]

Chapters 30 to 33 of Jeremiah are sometimes called the Book of
Consolation and deal with the future restoration of Israel. It is not
completely clear why these chapters are placed before the destruction
of Jerusalem (ch. 39). Fretheim suggests it could be a sign that God's
redeeming work had already begun during the time of 'judgment', and
that for Jeremiah, God's promises are still at work.[232] He supports his
argument with a list of references to the promises to Abraham and the
patriarchs and the whole of Israel in the Book of Consolation.[233] Janzen
concludes that in Amos, Micah, Hosea, and Jeremiah, in agreement with
their exposition, redemption takes place in the return of the exiles to the
land; in Isaiah, redemption comes in the purification of Jerusalem/Zion.[234]

Although it may appear that the prime concern of the Prophets is the
political aspect of the land and that the landedness/landlessness pattern
forms the core of land theology, we have also encountered, albeit implicitly, the agricultural concern. Israel's participation in heathen fertility cults
resulted in drought, and so, as we read in Lev. 18.25, the Israelites were
'vomited out' both from and by the land.

---

230. Ronald Clements, *Jeremiah*, Interpretation: A Bible Interpretation for
Teaching and Preaching (Atlanta, GA: John Knox, 1988), 172–3.

231. Coote, 'Land', 31.

232. Fretheim, *Jeremiah*, 413.

233. Ibid., 414–15. See also Fretheim's parallel of Jeremiah's purchase of a field
(Jer. 31.1-25) and Abraham's purchase of land (Gen. 23). Ibid., 415.

234. Janzen, 'Land', 149.

The postexilic era

The division between the exilic and postexilic prophetic books is far from clear cut, especially as it is commonly held that the books of Jeremiah, Isaiah, and Ezekiel were written over a long period of time, and that some of the chapters are exilic and some postexilic. A new question has arisen regarding the exilic and postexilic books that deal with the restoration of Israel and the temple: Was the promise of the recovery of the glory of Israel and the temple meant geographically and politically, or spiritually and eschatologically? The prophecies of Ezekiel and second Isaiah, which are essentially eschatological, occur at specific, locatable places in Israel-Palestine. Jeremiah's account, which also bears apocalyptic characteristics, speaks about the practical tasks necessary for surviving and flourishing during the forthcoming seventy years of exile. It is a difficult question, therefore. It is true that the question is crystalized in the New Testament, but we should bear in mind that the New Testament authors-redactors drew their argument for a spiritual and eschatological interpretation of the promised land from the Hebrew Bible, especially the 'eschatological' prophecies of the later chapters of some of the Prophets.

In Janzen's view, other postexilic writings rarely focus on the land,[235] with the exception, that is, of Ezra and Nehemiah, in which the Persian king Cyrus is seen as God's instrument for redeeming God's people, repatriating them from exile, and restoring them to their homeland. The Edict of Cyrus went even further, ordering that the centre of Israel's community life – the temple in Jerusalem – and the cult of their God YHWH should be restored. In Ezra and Nehemiah, we are clearly dealing with land in the political and territorial sense. Janzen observes:

> Jeremiah had stated in totally non-eschatological terms that 'houses and fields and vineyards shall again be bought in this land' (32:15) after the exile of 70 years (25:11-12; 29:10). Consequently, the Edict of Cyrus (Ezra 1:2-4; 6:1-5) and the subsequent return and rebuilding of a Jewish presence around Jerusalem and the temple (Ezra, Nehemiah) could at least in part be considered as fulfilment of prophecy and as a sign of God's impending universal rule.[236]

Janzen points out Ezekiel's interest in the land and the references to the promises given to Abraham and the patriarchs (Ezek. 20.5-6,

---

235. Ibid., 150. See Job, Proverbs, Ecclesiastes, Song of Songs, Esther, Jonah, Daniel.

236. Ibid.

42; 33.24).[237] Odell argues that the election of Israel is consistent with Deuteronomistic usage: election is connected to the gift of land and maintaining that election is dependent on keeping the commandments.[238] Allen observes that, 'Yahweh's promise of salvation lay at the basis of his relationship with Israel; it was reinforced by promise of subsequent blessing. The love gift of the land was the result of Yahweh's careful searching: only the best was good enough for his people'.[239] Ezekiel 33.24 mentions the promise of land to Abraham to emphasize that if it was promised to a single person, so all the more should it be acknowledged as a promise to the whole nation of his descendants. To support the settlement narrative, Ezekiel argues that Israel had its origins in foreign lands (Ezek. 16.3, 45). In Ezek. 20.7-10 and Ezekiel 23 we find a reference to Israel dwelling in Egypt and being delivered by God. The message, however, is an accusation against the people of Israel for their continual faithlessness since the time in Egypt. This could explain why references to the event of the conquest are rare (Ezek. 20.28). Blenkinsopp and Odell both suggest that ch. 20 pretends to know nothing of the promise made to the patriarchs. The promise of land comes only in Egypt (Ezek. 20.15); in fact, according to Ezekiel 20, the whole of salvation history begins in Egypt[240] but is oriented towards the promised land. Greenberg argues that, 'No other survey [Ezek. 20] makes so much of the promised land versus other lands (*ha'areṣ* – five times, *'admat yiśra'el* – two times, *'ereṣ miṣrayim* – six times, *ha'araṣot* – six times, and *'ereṣ mᵉgurehem* – once)'.[241] Unlike Hosea and Jeremiah, Ezekiel describes Israel's wandering in the desert as a time of infidelity and judgment:[242] the account of the people's deliverance from Egypt is intended as a reminder of their transgressions. Israel's unfaithfulness, Janzen continues, consists in the idolatry that results in the loss of land and exile.[243]

237. Ibid., 149. See also Margaret Odell, *Ezekiel*, Smyth & Helwys Bible Commentary 16 (Macon, GA: Smyth & Helwys, 2005), 245.

238. Odell, *Ezekiel*, 249.

239. Leslie Allen, *Ezekiel 20–48*, Word Biblical Commentary 29 (Dallas, TX: Word, 1990), 10.

240. Joseph Blenkinsopp, *Ezekiel*, Interpretation: A Bible Interpretation for Teaching and Preaching (Louisville, KY: John Knox, 1990), 88. See also Odell, *Ezekiel*, 246.

241. Mosheh Greenberg, *Ezekiel 1–20*, Anchor Bible 22 (New York: Doubleday, 1983), 382.

242. Blenkinsopp, *Ezekiel*, 88.

243. Janzen, 'Land', 149.

Social injustice, Janzen insists, plays a minor role.[244] Interestingly, Ezekiel uses a term that is rarely used elsewhere in the Hebrew Bible, namely 'the land of Israel', which we find in two forms, used interchangeably: ארץ ישראל (1 Sam. 13.19; 2 Kgs 5.2, 4; 6.23; Ezek. 27.17; 40.2; 47.18; 1 Chron. 22.2; 2 Chron. 2.16[17]; 30.25; 34.7) and אדמת ישראל (Ezek. 11.17; 12.19; 13.9, etc.).[245] In Ezek. 20.6, Janzen notes, it is described as 'the most glorious of all lands' (cf. Jer. 3.19; Dan. 8.9; 11.16, 41, 45).[246] When it comes to the question of who is better off during the exile – those who left or those who remained in Israel – Ezekiel is with Jeremiah: God is with the exiles.

> They will be 'revived' by Yahweh (37:1-14) and will return to the land (11:17-21; 20:40-44; 34:11-16; 37:15-28). In fact, Yahweh himself has taken leave of his house and his city to 'emigrate' with the exiles (chaps. 8–11) and will return with them eventually to the temple (43:1-5) in a land restored according to the elaborate blueprint laid out in chaps. 47–48.[247]

As we find in the Chronicles, Ezekiel makes little distinction between Judah and Israel. The two kingdoms who share a destiny of land loss and exile, albeit at different times, are discussed as a single concern:

> Ezekiel's priestly vision depicts a recovery of the Israelite dominion by a combined Judah and Israel under a Davidic head (Ezek 34:23-24; 37:15-28). The dominion is highly idealistic: the land from the Jordan to the Mediterranean is segmented by east–west boundaries into 13 slices, one each for the 12 tribes and one for a new temple and adjacent capital city (Ezek 47:13-21; 42:1-35).[248]

Regarding Ezekiel's account of the salvation history of Israel, Blenkinsopp's view is that 'salvation would happen despite the people of Israel'.[249]

---

244. Ibid. See Ezek. 6.1-7, 13; 8.1-18; 14.1-11; 16.15-22.

245. Ottosson, 'ארץ', 401. See also Schmid, 'ארץ', 671.

246. Janzen, 'Land', 149.

247. Ibid.

248. Coote, 'Land', 32.

249. See also: 'There will be another exodus accomplished, as of old, by the mighty hand and outstretched arm of God, in which the Israelites will be brought, in spite of themselves, from the land of exile into the "wilderness of the peoples" – the desert between Mesopotamia and Israel – and thence to the land of Israel, where they will at last acknowledge Yahweh's kingship'. Blenkinsopp, *Ezekiel*, 90.

On closer inspection, Ezekiel 20, which we have already described as a summary of Israel's salvation history, can be seen as a vision in response to the elders of Israel. Odell argues that the message of this vision is that the people of Israel had broken the covenant so many times, 'that it is absurd for the exiles to remind Yahweh of [the covenant] now'.[250] The vision could, however, promise a new beginning, a suggestion to which Allen responds:

> Both the exiles and Ezekiel assumed that territorial residence and religion went hand in hand and that Yahwistic religion required a return to Jerusalem; its assimilation to a pagan faith was not to ensue. In vehement protest, Yahweh lays claim to his people's allegiance (cf. Exod 12:12; Num 33:4).[251]

Janzen points out that second Isaiah provides an original perspective on the exodus by taking the land motif of the Pentateuch and Joshua and adding the significance of Zion. He sums up second Isaiah's view of the 'promised land' as follows:

> A new Israel redeemed from Babylon (48:20-21) will be led by God through a wilderness, turned into a Garden of Eden (40:3-5; 41:17-20; 42:14-16; 43:14-21; 48:21; 51:3) into her own land (49:14-18). Jerusalem/Zion will become the exalted center for the whole earth (49:14-18; 52:1-10) when the Lord takes up residence in it (52:8; cf. Ezek. 43:1-5).[252]

According to Throntveit, the argument of Ezra 1 is built on references to Jeremiah and Isaiah: first on Jeremiah's prophecy of the seventy-year Babylonian bondage (Jer. 29.10); and secondly on second Isaiah's reference to God's stirring up of Cyrus to overthrow Babylon and restore Israel (Isa. 41.2; 44.28; 45.1, 13).[253] The author-redactor of Ezra shares in the prophetic tradition of identifying foreign kings as agents of God's punishment of an unfaithful people. God's use of Cyrus, however, seems to be a positive gesture towards Israel's destiny:

---

250. Odell, *Ezekiel*, 246.
251. Allen, *Ezekiel 20–48*, 14.
252. Janzen, 'Land', 149.
253. Mark Throntveit, *Ezra–Nehemiah*, Interpretation: A Bible Interpretation for Teaching and Preaching (Louisville, KY: John Knox, 1992), 14. See also Jacob Myers, *Ezra, Nehemiah*, Anchor Bible 14 (New York: Doubleday, 1965), 6.

In the past, God had frequently made use of foreign nations through the agency of their kings, but God's purpose had always been to chastise Israel... But now, when he 'stirred up the spirit of King Cyrus of Persia' (1:1) with the positive intention of redemption that Israel might return to the land, God's use of the nations encompassed a new purpose.[254]

The frustration of exile led to the inevitable question of whether the people of Israel, so harshly tested, were still the chosen people. Together with the attempt to legitimize the efforts to restore Israel, the question resulted in the key emphasis of Ezra 1: continuity with the previous salvation history of Israel.[255] Stressing this continuity and the validity of God's covenant with the people of Israel, Breneman points to the prayers in Ezra 9.6-15 and Neh. 1.5-11 and 9.5-37.[256] Throntveit observes: 'By insisting that the return is interpreted as the activity of the same God who had previously raised up Israel's enemies for judgement, the overriding concern for continuity is preserved'.[257] Breneman suggests the return can be interpreted as a 'new exodus' because of the celebration of the Passover after the temple was completed (Ezra 6.19-22) and the celebration of the Feast of Tabernacles after the reading of the Law (Ezra 3.1-7). Both of these feasts, Breneman concludes, 'celebrate God's great saving acts in the exodus'.[258] Williamson interprets the return in the same

254. Throntveit, *Ezra–Nehemiah*, 13–14. Levering also argues for the significance of Cyrus in Israel's salvation history: 'Because this God who is in Jerusalem is the transcendent God of heaven, Cyrus's work of restoration of the people and the land ultimately will lead to a universal blessing... Through Cyrus, God is moving toward fulfilment of his covenant with Abraham, in which God promises that "by you [Abraham] all the families of the earth shall bless themselves" (Gen. 12:1-3; cf. 22:18). "Salvation is from the Jews" (John 4:22).' Matthew Levering, *Ezra & Nehemiah* (London: SCM, 2008), 44.

255. Mervin Breneman, *Ezra, Nehemiah, Esther* (Nashville, TN: B&H, 2009), 50.

256. Ibid., 51.

257. Throntveit, *Ezra–Nehemiah*, 15. Throntveit adds: 'Thus, these few verses proclaim nothing less than the announcement of God's gracious activity in fulfilment of the hopes and promises that the great prophets of the exile had used to ease the pain of God's judgment.' See also: 'Initially, it is clear that the experience of judgment led to the sensation of disorientation and discontinuity, a radical break with the past... In contributing his narrative of this process to the task of theological reconstruction, our author evidently felt the need to emphasize the lines of continuity between the community of his own day and the history of the nation which had preceded it.' H. G. M. Williamson, David Hubbard, and John Watts, *Ezra, Nehemiah*, Word Biblical Commentary 16 (Waco, TX: Word, 1985), 20.

258. Breneman, *Ezra, Nehemiah, Esther*, 50.

way: 'The purpose of this typological pattern (exodus – new exodus and the pertinent feasts) is to encourage the readers to interpret the return as an act of God's grace that can be compared in its significance with the very birth of the nation of Israel itself'. Van Wijk-Bos reminds us that despite the enthusiasm of Ezra 1 regarding Cyrus and God's role for him in Israel's salvation history, the land is still under foreign control. The author cites Neh. 9.36-37, which talks about political dependency on Persia and the fact that the Israelites are still 'slaves in the land that you gave to our ancestors to enjoy its fruit and its good gifts'.[259] Breneman nonetheless tries to find something positive about the people's dependence on Persia:

> In fact, this new situation under foreign rule meant that the Jewish people became again more strictly a covenant community and not a nation as in the monarchy. The community's identity did not now depend on its political institutions and identity as a nation but on its special covenant relation to God.[260]

We have seen that the postexilic prophets reflect the deep frustration of the Israelites in exile. Whereas the earlier prophets warn against the unfaithfulness that will surely end in the loss of the land, the postexilic prophets seek to bring comfort. But again, the question must be asked: Without the land, which is understood as a visible sign of its covenant with God, is Israel still God's chosen people, or have the promises been withdrawn? Ezekiel presents a salvation history in which there never was a time, not even during the wandering in the wilderness (Jeremiah, Hosea), when the people of Israel kept the covenant and were faithful to God. The whole history of salvation is thus an indictment of the Israelites, who are to be redeemed despite their conduct. There will be a new or second exodus (Ezra 6): God will reunite Israel, give it a new heart (Ezek. 36), and bring it back to the promised land.

The notion of the land in Ezekiel and Ezra–Nehemiah is predominantly political, but this political notion does not necessarily correspond fully to the territorial notion. The question of a territorial or spiritual-eschatological understanding of the promise of land is the domain of later, apocalyptic books in the Hebrew Bible and the New Testament. This matter, although important and relevant to other promised land discourses, is not as helpful here, so we mention it only in passing.

---

259. Johanna Van Wijk-Bos, *Ezra, Nehemiah, and Esther* (Louisville, KY: Westminster John Knox, 1998), 18.

260. Breneman, *Ezra, Nehemiah, Esther*, 51.

Reception of the promised land in the New Testament

The New Testament contains a rich variety of approaches towards the concept of the promised land. The usual way the New Testament renders the Hebrew term ארץ is with the Greek γῆ (248 times in 221 verses), otherwise with οἰκουμένη, κόσμος, κλίμα, or μέρος.[261] Most occurrences of γῆ carry no reference to the promise of land. In some cases, ἐπαγγελία ('promise') refers to promises such as the 'numberless descendants', and sometimes to the promise of land. There is therefore an interesting shift from 'land terminology' in the Hebrew Bible to 'promise terminology' in the New Testament. The term ἐπαγγελία is used 52 times in the New Testament, including 23 occurrences in the Pauline *homologoumena*.[262] If we consider that in the Hebrew Bible the word generally translated as 'promise' when referring to the promise of land is the everyday expression אמר ('to speak, tell'), this shift in terminology is extraordinary. According to Schniewind, the Greek word originally came with no religious overtones but was used largely in the context of financial compensation. It gained its religious meaning only later, and even then it was generally confined to promises made by people to God, and not for divine promises to people until it was taken up by Second Temple Judaism.[263] Dunn agrees that from the second century B.C.E., ἐπαγγελία gained wider use in the sense of a promise.[264] Schniewind adds that because of the frequent references to the 'promises' in the widely read and highly influential Pauline letters, we are used to considering the promised land theology of the Hebrew Bible through the lens of Paul's teaching, even though the Hebrew Bible contains no such concept of 'promise'. Sand agrees: 'In the Septuagint, the word ἐπαγγελία is used only 17 times and never in relation to Abraham or the patriarchs'.[265]

261. Johannes Louw and Eugene Nida, eds., *Greek–English Lexicon of the New Testament Based on Semantic Domains* (New York: United Bible Societies, 1989), 13–15.

262. A. Sand, 'Ἐπαγγελία', in *Exegetical Dictionary of the New Testament*, vol. 2, ed. Gerhard Schneider (Grand Rapids, MI: Eerdmans, 1990), 14. The *homologoumena* are the epistles that most scholars agree were originally written by Paul or by his scribes under his personal supervision.

263. Friedrich Schniewind, 'Ἐπαγγελία', in *Theological Dictionary of the New Testament*, vol. 2, ed. Gerhard Kittel (Grand Rapids, MI: Eerdmans, 1964), 576–9. See also Robert Jewett, *Romans: A Commentary*, ed. Roy Kotansky and Eldon Epp, Hermeneia 59 (Minneapolis, MN: Fortress, 2007), 325.

264. James Dunn, David Hubbard, and John Watts, *Romans 1–8*, Word Biblical Commentary 38a (Waco, TX: Word, 1988), 213.

265. Sand, 'Ἐπαγγελία', 14.

Davies, Burge, and some other scholars argue that the concept of the land in the New Testament, especially in light of the Roman occupation and the fall of the second temple, is always spiritualized and eschatologized.[266] Millar considers the New Testament completely 'disinterested in land' in the territorial and political sense. Referring to Isa. 56.3-7 and Ezek. 47.22, which speak of the Gentiles' share in the inheritance of Israel, he argues that, 'In God's new covenantal economy, loving fellowship (*koinōnia*) has replaced land tenure'.[267] However, Millar goes even further to interpret Ezek. 47.22-23, Zech. 2.11, and Isa. 60.3-14 as preparation for embracing the Gentiles.[268] Wright argues that as the promises of the Hebrew Bible were fulfilled in Christ, there is no place for understanding the land as a political territory, but also suggests that, 'what the land stood for in Israel's faith is certainly affirmed as a continuing reality in the Messiah. The language of "inheritance" is prominent in describing the present and future experience of those in Christ.'[269] Coote also adds:

> The New Testament sees the overthrow of the center of Zion, the Temple, and with it the territorial claims of the Davidic king – until he returns to claim a universal dominion. New Israel is based not on land but on covenant – the off-the-land concept of the Torah.[270]

But even if we admit that the concept of land in the New Testament is mostly spiritualized and eschatologized, things are not as straightforward as Coote would like to suggest. Wright is aware of this:

> The OT itself prepares the way for an ethical paradigm understanding of the relevance of the land... [G]iven the moral consistency of God [whose inheritance the whole earth is], it is legitimate to extrapolate from the

---

266. Burge, *Jesus and the Land*. See also Davies, *The Gospel and the Land*. Also: 'In Christian eschatology the promise of the Holy Land to Abraham, guaranteeing it to his posterity, together with other references to sacred space (→7:47-48), has usually been spiritualized into the promised land of life eternal (→23:8), often without consideration of the status of God's abiding covenant with the people of Israel (→3:25) and of the permanent validity of the promise in the context of the historical "economies" or dispensations of God also within this world.' Jaroslav Pelikan, *Acts*, Theological Commentary of the Bible (London: SCM, 2006), 100.

267. Millar, 'Land', 623.

268. Ibid., 626.

269. Wright, 'ארץ', 425.

270. Coote, 'Land', 32.

principles of Israel's economic values and systems to analogous objectives for social and economic justice elsewhere in the world. This will not be a matter of slavish imitation, but rather of applying a paradigm from Israel's land.[271]

Janzen is also aware that the New Testament perspective on the promised land is far from neat and uniform. He agrees that there is too much geography in the New Testament concerning the person of Jesus and the ministry of the apostles for the territorial aspect of the promised land to play no role at all, but nonetheless adheres to the 'spiritualized and eschatologized' perspective on New Testament land theology. He does, however, mention the 'Lohmeier-Lightfoot Theory' of new theological-geographical realism:

> While this 'localisation' of many of the OT's land-related realia (goal of promise, inheritance) 'in Christ' can be seen as a rejection of the theological relevance of place, it is also true that the incarnate Christ himself represents a certain realism of geographical presence associated with the places of his ministry and memories that attach to them. This realism of the incarnation then continues in the presence of the resurrected Christ in his body, the church, and its members, repeatedly referred to as a 'temple' by Paul (1 Cor 3:16-17).[272]

The geographical 'realia' could of course have been provided simply to enhance the credibility of the story. Apart from the religious and political reasons for interpreting the promise of land in the New Testament spiritually and eschatologically, there is, Hiebert suggests, another more practical and immediate reason for downplaying the territorial and political aspects of land theology, and that is the urbanization of the population. At the time the New Testament was being written, only a minority of Christians lived in the countryside and made their living from agriculture: 'With this shift, the world of agriculture, which had had such a profound influence on the definition of humanity and the understanding of divine activity in Israel, was left behind and replaced with an urban perspective'.[273] The argument appears persuasive. Another reason, Hiebert says, is the simple fact that Gentile communities did not share the 'Hebrew' view of the land, so that gradually, 'By stressing a future existence in a heavenly realm, unencumbered by the realities of earthly existence – whether

271. Wright, 'ארץ', 524.
272. Janzen, 'Land', 152.
273. Hiebert, 'Land', 789.

agricultural or political survival – Christianity diminished the role of land in its religious consciousness (John 14:1-7; 1 Cor 15:1-58; 1 Thess 4:13-18)'.[274] The promise of the land was therefore transformed in the New Testament but nonetheless survived in various forms.

The Gospels and Acts

Janzen notes several examples which suggest that even after the frustration of losing the temple, 'promised land theology' was not dead. Matthew 2.20-21 carries two references to the 'land of Israel', a term rarely used in the Hebrew Bible and which undoubtedly refers here to a piece of geopolitical territory. The context is the Holy Family's flight to Egypt after the birth of Jesus, and their return to their homeland.

> While no overt theological interpretation is offered, it seems certain that a parallelism between the journey of Israel's messiah and the earlier journey of Israel from Egypt to the promised land, now 'Israel's land', is intended (cf. 2:15, and Hos 11:1). In that case, this naming of land would appear to suggest a certain continuing validity of the OT's theological meaning of the land.[275]

Another possible reference to the political-territorial aspect of the promised land is Mt. 5.5, although here Janzen admits, and Luz agrees, that in the context of the Beatitudes, which promise citizenship in the kingdom of God, the promise is most likely spiritualized (cf. Mk 10.14; Lk. 22.28-30).[276] Luz argues further that the broadening of the promise of the land of Canaan to the promise of the whole world took place long before the Gospels were written: 'It is the earth, not only the land of Israel, that belongs to those who are kind, for the traditional promise of land had long since been transposed into the cosmic realm [cf. Ps. 37:11; Isa. 61:7; Isa. 60:21]'.[277] Witherington is also in favour of an eschatological interpretation of the promise of land in the Beatitudes, and also makes reference to Isaiah 61. Interestingly, however, Witherington leaves open the possibility of interpreting the promise of land, 'inheriting the earth', in the cosmological sense. The history of the salvation of Israel was a history of their attempts to emancipate themselves, even from

274. Ibid.

275. Janzen, 'Land', 150.

276. Ibid., 150–1. See also: '[The promises] are all to be understood eschatologically and are not anticipated by the grace of the presence of God experienced in the present'. Ulrich Luz, *Matthew 1–7: A Commentary*, rev. edn, Hermeneia (Minneapolis, MN: Augsburg Fortress, 2007), 201.

277. Luz, *Matthew 1–7*, 195.

God. Witherington therefore contrasts the 'meek' and vulnerable who are completely dependent upon God with the Israelites whom the prophets condemned for seeking to escape God's influence: 'Those who are totally dependent on God will in due course inherit the land. It would appear that Jesus did believe in an eschatological restoration of the land to those whom God had chosen, but not before the eschaton.'[278] The kingdom of heaven, replacing the land in the territorial sense, is the new promise to the faithful: no longer the land as a piece of territory or a political entity (as we see in the Hebrew Bible), but a metaphysical concept that is realized only after death. Explaining the problematic term 'meek', Hagner agrees with Witherington that the reason the meek inherit the earth/land/ world is that they are wholly dependent upon God:

> In view are not persons who are submissive, mild and unassertive, but those who are humble in the sense of being oppressed (hence, 'have been humbled'), bent over by the injustice of the ungodly, but who are soon to realize their reward. Those in such a condition have no recourse but to depend upon God.[279]

Hagner stresses further that the message of the Beatitudes is nothing revolutionary but is foreseen by the prophets, for example in Isaiah 65–66; Mt. 5.5, he suggests, is a quotation from the LXX Ps. 36(37).1.[280] Davies argues that Mt. 5.5 is an 'eschatological reversal' of Deut. 4.1. Possession of the land is an eschatological hope. The promise of land does not refer to the land of Israel but to the whole earth:

> One might argue from 8:11 and 19:28 that our evangelist looked forward to a time when the Son of Man would set up his throne within the boundaries of Israel. But 19:28 seems to promise a cosmic renewal (ἐν τῇ παλιγγενεσίᾳ), and throughout Matthew nationalistic hopes – which are otherwise absent from 5:3-12 – are undone.[281]

Janzen sees another example of New Testament 'promised land theology' in Acts 7, which deals with the history of the Jewish people and

---

278. Ben Witherington, *Matthew*, Smyth & Helwys Bible Commentary 19 (Macon, GA: Smyth & Helwys, 2006), 121.

279. Donald Hagner, David Hubbard, and John Watts, *Matthew 1–13*, Word Biblical Commentary 33a (Waco, TX: Word, 1993), 92.

280. Ibid., 92–3.

281. William Davies and Dale Allison, *A Critical and Exegetical Commentary on the Gospel According to Saint Matthew*, International Critical Commentary (Edinburgh: T. & T. Clark, 1997), 450.

their journeys between Mesopotamia and Egypt. However, although the promise of land made to Abraham and the patriarchs and the conquest are both recognized and affirmed in Stephen's speech (vv. 3, 17, and 45), the apostle is critical of the current Jewish claim on the land and continues in the tradition of Hosea and Jeremiah: Israel was closest to God while wandering in the wilderness (vv. 44-45). Janzen concludes: 'Their stay in the land was marked by idolatry leading to exile, and the building of the temple by Solomon seems an ill-considered, if not rebellious act of confining the Lord of the universe (vv. 47-51)'.[282] Chance argues that in the book of Acts, God is presented as the one who is not bound to a particular place or piece of land.[283] God called Abraham when he was in Mesopotamia but Abraham never received the land as an inheritance – he was a man without the land.[284] Other patriarchs were 'aliens in a land belonging to others': Joseph was sold to Egypt, and yet God was there with him, and Joseph's family went to Egypt because of the famine in Canaan. Chance uses all these examples to show that God acts whenever God pleases,[285] and argues that the Babylonian exile was punishment for Israel's disobedience and unfaithfulness to God. The author-redactor of Acts follows a similar trajectory to that which we saw in Ezekiel 20: Israel's salvation history is a history of a falling away from God which resulted in exile. Keener and Barrett both point out that this perspective is shared by Flavius Josephus, who states that the very same behaviour of the people of Israel resulted in the Jewish war. Wright observes: 'Josephus presents his War as the fulfilment of biblical prophecy, comparable to Luke–Acts'.[286] Although the people of Israel are no longer held in exile, as in Ezra and Nehemiah, their frustration is constantly being fed by the facts of political dependence and foreign dominion and so remains vivid in the

282. Janzen, 'Land', 151.

283. J. Bradley Chance, *Acts*, Smyth & Helwys Bible Commentary 20 (Macon, GA: Smyth & Helwys, 2007), 111. See also Joseph Fitzmyer, *The Acts of the Apostles: A New Translation with Introduction and Commentary*, Anchor Bible 31 (New York: Doubleday, 1998), 366.

284. Fitzmyer, *The Acts of the Apostles*, 364.

285. Chance, *Acts*, 111–12.

286. Craig Keener, *Acts: An Exegetical Commentary. 1. Introduction and 1:1–2:47* (Grand Rapids, MI: Baker Academic, 2012), 484. See also: 'Josephus… is akin to Stephen in that he uses his view of history to make a point with reference to the present: whenever the Israelites took up arms they were defeated; when they put their trust in God alone they were delivered'. Charles Barrett, *A Critical and Exegetical Commentary on the Acts of the Apostles: In Two Volumes. Preliminary Introduction and Commentary on Acts I–XIV*, International Critical Commentary 1 (Edinburgh: T. & T. Clark, 1994), 336.

people's minds.[287] Therefore, according to Chance, the author-redactor of Acts goes further than other New Testament authors-redactors, is not content with a 'simple' spiritualization and eschatologization of the promises, and seeks to prove that the promise of land was already spiritual and eschatological at the time it was given. Finally, Keener suggests that the book of Acts functions according to the scheme of promise and fulfilment: the fulfilment is understood to be the Messiah, Jesus of Nazareth.[288]

The Pauline Epistles

It is notable that despite his Jewish background, the Apostle Paul does not appear to recognize the national claims of the Jews, among which the claim for land plays a key role. Paul refers to Scripture often, using countless quotations and paraphrases, but rarely uses 'land terminology'.[289] There are only six occurrences of γῆ in the Pauline *homologoumena*, but 23 occurrences of ἐπαγγελία (out of 52 in the entire New Testament). The promises to Abraham and the patriarchs are implied in the Pauline letters but the context is never completely clear. Paul often refers to 'promises' but with no addressee. More importantly, he never identifies the promises, so we can never be sure which he is referring to. The 'promises' usually imply the promise of the blessing of land and descendants,[290] so the promise of land is naturally assumed to be among Paul's 'promises', although it is unlikely to be understood in its territorial and political sense. We have seen that this is arguably true of much of the Hebrew Bible, although in some exilic and particularly postexilic books, the question of whether to understand the promise of land territorially or spiritually remains open.

The promise of land and its being conditioned by the law could be understood as the one Jewish national attribute that is a stumbling block for the inclusion of the Gentiles. Paul's discussion around the law and circumcision presenting an obstacle to non-Jewish Christians (Gal. 3 and 4; Phil. 3) is often quoted, but the law and circumcision are only one part of the covenant between God and the people of Israel; the promises to Abraham and the patriarchs are the other. As a rabbi and accomplished interpreter of the Scriptures, Paul uses this argument for his own purposes but turns it upside down:

---

287. Chance, *Acts*, 115.
288. Keener, *Acts*, 485.
289. Burge, *Jesus and the Land*, 74.
290. Sand, 'Επαγγελία', 14; cf. Louw and Nida, *Greek–English Lexicon of the New Testament Based on Semantic Domains*, 421.

The idea of 'inheritance' was a fundamental part of Jewish understanding of their relationship with God, above all, indeed almost exclusively, in connection with the land... [T]he land is theirs by inheritance as promised to Abraham... Already, before Paul, the concept had been broadened out from Canaan to embrace the whole earth.[291]

Wright adds that, 'In fact, Paul uses land inheritance language to speak of the inclusion through Christ of those who formerly, by not having a share in the ownership of the land, were excluded from the covenant people, i.e., aliens or 'Gentiles' (Eph 2:11-22; 3:6)'.[292] The basis of the argument is Gen. 15.6. The promises were not made because of Abraham's righteousness, that is, through the 'law', Dunn argues, but because of his faith: so the promises are dependent not on ethnicity but on faith.[293] Cranfield highlights the revolutionary nature of Paul's interpretation of the promises by pointing out that the common understanding among the rabbis of Paul's day was that Abraham was given the promises on the basis of fulfilment of a law that he knew intuitively. According to Dunn, the act of faith itself in Gen. 15.6 was understood as a meritorious work of keeping the law.[294] Fitzmyer agrees:

Paul is implicitly assailing the Jewish view that all blessing came to Abraham because of his merit in keeping the law, which he was supposed to have known in advance... For Paul, the heirs of the promise of inheriting the world are not the observers of the Mosaic law, but the people of faith; for him law and promise have not been interrelated.[295]

To clarify the Jewish assumption of inheriting the world, Fitzmyer adds: 'The embellishment was based on the universality mentioned in Gen. 12:3, "all the families of the earth shall be blessed in you." This universality came to be associated with the "inheritance"...that Abraham and his offspring were to expect'.[296] Jewett concludes that Paul erases the conditionality of the promises by declaring that they are no longer

291. Dunn, Hubbard, and Watts, *Romans 1–8*, 213.

292. Wright, 'ארץ', 425.

293. Dunn, Hubbard, and Watts, *Romans 1–8*, 233.

294. Charles Cranfield, *A Critical and Exegetical Commentary on The Epistle to the Romans: In Two Volumes*, International Critical Commentary (Edinburgh: T. & T. Clark), 239.

295. Joseph Fitzmyer, *Romans: A New Translation with Introduction and Commentary*, Anchor Bible 33 (New York: Doubleday, 1993), 384.

296. Ibid.

dependent on keeping the law.[297] Janzen points out that Gal. 3.15-18 and 2.9–4.7 and Rom. 4.16, which deal with the promises in the Hebrew Bible, are notable for an absence of geographical terminology. The promise made to Abraham is narrowed down to the promise of a single descendant: Christ.[298] Hiebert agrees and says that 'it is noteworthy that Paul, who makes so much of Abraham's role in salvation history, does not discuss God's promise to him of land (Gal 3:6-18; Rom 4:1-25)'.[299]

The four main places in the Pauline *homologoumena* that refer to the promises to Abraham and the patriarchs are Romans 4 and 9 and Galatians 3 and 4.[300] Romans 4.13 is a unique case within the Pauline letters as it combines both 'promise terminology' and 'land terminology', using the terms ἐπαγγελία and κόσμος.[301] Whereas some scholars, Talbert for example,[302] treat κόσμος in Rom. 4.13 like any other term that may refer to 'land/earth', Sasse points out that it cannot be used in an eschatological way: it refers, rather, to a world alienated from its Creator,[303] a fact which leads to the following observation: Paul's use of κόσμος instead of γῆ was probably not unintentional. Κόσμος ('world') may be understood as a broadening of the inheritance, which would be parallel to a broadening of the heirs of Abraham (Gal. 3.29). For it cannot be understood in the eschatological way; we have to understand it in a territorial and socio-political way. Such an observation challenges the simple conclusion that the promise of land in the New Testament is always meant eschatologically and spiritually. It is true that the promise of land in Rom. 4.13 does not refer to a particular territory, namely the land of Canaan, but neither does it refer to the 'heavenly kingdom' or the 'kingdom of God'. One possible solution is that it refers to the broadening of the inheritance of land to the whole earth, meaning that Christianity will spread all over the

297. Jewett, *Romans*, 325.

298. Janzen, 'Land', 152.

299. Hiebert, 'Land', 789.

300. Brueggemann, *The Land*, 177; Davies, *The Gospel and the Land*, 166–82; Burge, *Jesus and the Land*, 75–88.

301. Hermann Sasse, 'Κόσμος', in *Theological Dictionary of the New Testament*, 3:867–8, 885, 888; cf. Burge, *Jesus and the Land*, 86. According to Fitzmyer, although the inheritance of the world is not expressed explicitly in Genesis, the Jewish tradition reflects this as a promise to Abraham. Fitzmyer, *Romans*, 384; cf. Jewett, *Romans*, 338.

302. Talbert interprets the term κόσμος eschatologically: 'In this context, the promise to inherit the world refers not to taking possession of the land of Israel but to gaining life in the New World beyond the resurrection'. Charles Talbert, *Romans*, Smyth & Helwys Bible Commentary 24 (Macon, GA: Smyth & Helwys, 2002), 119.

303. Sasse, 'Κόσμος', 885.

world. This would be nothing new: both Dunn and Fitzmyer argue that although there is no indication in the book of Genesis that the Jewish people will inherit the whole world, this was a commonly held belief in Jewish tradition. Paul probably shares in this tradition but shifts it into the Christian discourse.[304] So, how does the Pauline promised land theology of Rom. 4.3 differ from that suggested in the Gospels and Acts? In Rom. 4.3, faithful Christians will inherit not 'only' the earth as the eschatological and spiritual (metaphysical) concept of the kingdom of heaven; they are heirs of the whole earth. In other words, if the New Covenant people of God remain faithful, they will increase in number and cover the face of the earth. The 'land' here is not a concrete territory, but neither is it an eschatological concept. Rather it stands for the fullness of people who are faithful to God and serve the Lord on the earth.

The Non-Pauline Epistles

Like Acts, the book of Hebrews describes Abraham's status in the promised land as an 'alien' – a status which never changed to 'possessor' – and this becomes one of the main arguments against a political and territorial understanding of the land.[305] For Wright, Hebrews suggests that the promise of land to the Israelites had always been provisional and imperfect: 'Hebrews tells Jewish Christians that Christ has granted them the "rest" that even Joshua's conquest of the land had not fully achieved – another use of terminology with strong association with the land (Heb 4:1-11)'.[306] Koester adds that, 'Many understood Canaan to be Abraham's inheritance (Ps 105.11), but Hebrews maintains that Abraham receives his true inheritance in God's heavenly city'.[307] Commenting on Heb. 11.9, Janzen suggests that when it was pronounced to Abraham, the promise of land was already spiritualized. This argument for a spiritualized and eschatologized promise of land is in line with the approach taken in Acts. Attridge agrees with this view:

---

304. Dunn, Hubbard, and Watts, *Romans 1–8*, 233; Fitzmyer, *Romans*, 384.

305. Robert Gordon, *Hebrews* (Sheffield: Sheffield Academic, 2000), 133.

306. Wright, 'ארץ', 524.

307. Craig Koester, *Hebrews: A New Translation with Introduction and Commentary*, Anchor Bible 36 (New York: Doubleday, 2001), 484–95. Koester (*Hebrews*, 497) adds: 'Hebrews poignantly comments that Israel's ancestors died without having received what was promised (11:13a)... Hebrews affirms that death is real, but not final, for God calls people to a destination that lies beyond it.'

The references to the promise have up to now been allusive and there has been no explicit designation of the land of Canaan as the goal of Abraham's wandering. The silence is deliberate, for just as entry into the land did not afford true rest (4:8), so too Israelite possession of the land did not fulfil the promise to Abraham.[308]

Gordon claims that Acts pushes the agenda further: 'The alien status of Abraham is put more starkly in Stephen's speech before the Sanhedrin'.[309] Koester, however, is persuaded that Hebrews is very clear in pointing out the vulnerability of the 'resident alien' who does not share the same rights as a citizen. The status of 'resident alien' could be seen as an insult to those who are supposed to be 'heirs'.[310] He therefore redefines and spiritualizes the term to include everyone who answers God's call by faith and thereby becomes a citizen of the heavenly kingdom:

Hebrews seeks to reverse the stigma of foreignness by declaring that Abraham did not merely accept foreign status but confess it (11:13c). Confessing oneself to be a foreigner on earth is the counterpart to confessing faith in God's promise... In a cosmological sense, those whose citizenship is in heaven are foreigners upon earth.[311]

The promises in Hebrews, Koester argues, are simply meant as an affirmation of God's commitment to and affection for all people and a reminder that God will never leave them.[312] According to Lane, the real promise to Abraham was the promise of an inheritance he would have to wait for, namely citizenship in the heavenly city:

According to the writer of Hebrews, Abraham's status as an immigrant and alien in the land had the positive effect of indicating that Canaan was not, in the final sense, the promised inheritance. It served to direct his attention beyond Canaan to the established city of God as the ultimate goal of his pilgrimage.[313]

308. Harold Attridge, *The Epistle to the Hebrews: A Commentary on the Epistle to the Hebrews*, Hermeneia (Minneapolis, MN: Fortress, 1989), 323–4.

309. Gordon, *Hebrews*, 133.

310. Koester, *Hebrews*, 485. See also William Lane et al., *Hebrews 9–13*, Word Biblical Commentary 47b (Waco, TX: Word, 1991), 349.

311. Koester, *Hebrews*, 497.

312. Ibid., 110–11.

313. Lane et al., *Hebrews 9–13*, 351.

The patriarchs were strangers in the land. A better country, the promised
land, was waiting for them in heaven.[314] Thus, Janzen concludes, the
author-redactor of Hebrews went one step further in spiritualizing the
promise than did other New Testament authors-redactors, and made the
spiritualization retrospective, that is, made it seem that the promise was
already meant spiritually when it was pronounced to Abraham: 'Strangers
and exiles does not mean here long-term guests in God's land (cf. Lev
25:23), but geographically footloose wanderers toward eternity'.[315] As in
the Gospels and Acts, faithfulness to God is rewarded not on earth but in
heaven. Arguably, therefore, Hebrews presents the agent between God
and God's people as the metaphysical concept of the kingdom of God.

Unlike the discussion of promised land theology in the Hebrew
Bible, where the discourse was rich with nuance, the debate in the New
Testament concerns whether the promise of land was meant territorially
and politically or spiritually and eschatologically. This development is
understandable given the uneasy relationship between the Jews and the
newly established communities of the first Christians and the tension
created by the concept of the land. The spiritual and eschatological interpretation of the promised land influenced later discussions in the early
Christian era when it transformed further into the concepts of heaven and
hell.

314. Janzen, 'Land', 151.
315. Ibid., 152.

Chapter 3

THE EXTRA-BIBLICAL AND POST-BIBLICAL HISTORY OF THE PROMISED LAND MOTIF

Gadamer and other reception history scholars insist that everyone and everything belongs to some kind of tradition, or traditions, and that to understand the present we must study the past. This chapter will therefore ask diachronic questions such as: Did interpretations differ from era to era? Were some interpretations similar to those in other eras? If so, which?

Robert Wilken, a prominent researcher into the reception of the promised land motif, observes that, 'Christians…from Oliver Cromwell in seventeenth-century England to Martin Luther King in the twentieth century invoked the Exodus as the paradigmatic story of redemption'.[1] This remark does not bring anything particularly new, but reflects the importance of the exodus and the motif of settlement in the Christian milieu, and confirms something we discovered in the previous chapter: the motif of the promised land is of greater concern to the writers of the Hebrew Bible than it is to those of the New Testament. Wilken's remark also reminds us that the question of temporality plays a key role in reception history.

To establish Steinbeck as a legitimate and respectable interpreter of the biblical text, and to be true both to biblical studies and to literature, I will situate him within his interpretive community.[2] An interpretive community is made up of those who share the same strategies for interpreting particular texts, such as the Bible, and serves as a means of establishing the influences on our author and legitimizing his interpretation. I will be using interpretive communities that view Steinbeck as: (i) a representative of a religious tradition that makes his claims about the biblical text plausible; and (ii) a creative author, a novelist, and a

1. Robert Wilken, *The Land Called Holy: Palestine in Christian History and Thought* (New Haven, CT: Yale University Press, 1992), 3.
2. See Fish, 'Literature in the Reader', 13–14.

member of a literary tradition which interprets the Bible within the sphere of quality literature. The religious interpretive community will be the early twentieth-century American Episcopal Church,[3] and I will use the Episcopalian prayer book, hymn book, and lectionary to establish the sources of influence and the biblical texts which lie behind Steinbeck's interest in 'the land'. The literary interpretive community will be Jefferson agrarianism.[4] Although Steinbeck can be located within these two traditions, I should add that he stands in a critical position towards both of them, questioning and revising them. To be faithful to both the scientific and the artistic ways of understanding, I will also trace the influence of the interpretive partner I have chosen for Steinbeck from the field of biblical criticism, namely Walter Brueggemann.

The chapter will explore the histories of biblical and literary scholarship and the history of the religious influences on Steinbeck and Brueggemann, which together will form a history of reception and contribute to the interpretation of the promised land motif. The diachronic line of the three histories will lead into the synchronic line of interpretive communities and to a better understanding of both Steinbeck and Brueggemann.

The history of biblical scholarship

The interpretation of the promised land has changed significantly from era to era. In certain periods it acquires significant socio-political overtones in the territorial and national sense; in others it is oriented towards personal longing for a promised land of one's own. This section will set out the exegetical history of the motif of the promised land from the conception of the biblical canon to the present day, concluding with Brueggemann's interpretation.

3. Although a largely secular author, Steinbeck was raised in the strict Episcopal tradition, especially by the family of his mother Olive Hamilton. Steinbeck could be assigned to another religiously (or rather spiritually) defined interpretive community, namely Darwinism, but this community would add little to the analysis as it is not interested in 'land'. See Joseph Fontenrose, *John Steinbeck: An Introduction and Interpretation* (New York: Holt, Rinehart & Winston, 1963), 2–3.

4. 'Behind the hunger for the land expressed in both the narrator's and the characters' words lies Jefferson Agrarianism, a quintessential element in the American Dream, but Jefferson Agrarianism that is questioned and revised in the course of the novel.' Louis Owens, *The Grapes of Wrath: Trouble in the Promised Land* (New York: Twayne, 1989), 8. Another literary stream Steinbeck could be associated with is American Transcendentalism, but again, this stream would help us little with the theme of land in his novels.

Antiquity

Philo of Alexandria

Tracing the history of reception of the promised land in Antiquity requires a different type of analysis from that we are used to conducting in biblical scholarship. The commentators of Antiquity approached the biblical text in novel ways and wrote commentaries that are unlike most others. The authors do not address the origin or composition of the text; nor do they address its literary features. Such commentaries are written in the form of question-and-answer, a genre we know from catechisms; in this era they are called *Quaestiones*. The commentaries deal mainly with the content and theological concerns of the biblical text.

One of the most influential figures in biblical hermeneutics is Philo of Alexandria. Although Jewish, Philo had a huge impact on the early church fathers, particularly Origen. Philo's *Quaestiones in Genesim*, *Quaestiones in Exodum*, and *De Abrahamo* all contain allegorical reflections on the promised land. Wilken suggests that the reason Philo did not promote a national and territorial interpretation of the promised land is that he did not live in Palestine. His approach is therefore more typical of exiles.[5] Some of Philo's allegorical commentary broke through the history of reception, has been maintained until the present day, and is even embedded in Steinbeck's novels.

We do not have access to the originals of Philo's *Quaestiones in Genesim* and *Quaestiones in Exodum*, only to an Armenian translation which can be compared with fragments of the Greek version.[6] Regarding the main topics in the *Quaestiones in Exodum*, Abraham Terian, the editor of a French edition of Philo's work, observes: 'The allegorical nuances in the *Quaestiones in Exodum*, which concern the topic of Exodus and the visible sanctuary of the Jewish cult, concern the sanctuary of the soul and the sanctuary of the cosmos'.[7] The main point of Philo's interpretation of the promised land motif is that to enter the promised land is to achieve union with God, which is also an entrance into philosophy. The promised land therefore signifies philosophy, and as philosophy signifies union with God, the promised land also signifies union with God.[8]

---

5. Wilken, *The Land Called Holy*, 3.

6. Abraham Terian, 'Introduction', in *Quaestiones et solutiones in Exodum I et II E versione Armeniaca et fragmenta Graeca*, Les Oeuvres de Philon d'Alexandrie 34c (Paris: Cerf, 1992), 19.

7. Ibid., 25.

8. Philo, *Quaestiones in Exodum*, 127.

In *De Abrahamo*, Philo describes Abraham's journey to the promised land – leaving his family and homeland and setting off on a journey towards the unknown – as an act of piety.[9] What Philo considers the act of righteousness, Wilkens points out, is not the act of journeying itself but that of abandoning his comfortable life in his father's house in Ur of the Chaldeans.[10] In the *Quaestiones in Genesim* (15.7), Philo deals with the symbolic meaning of the land of Chaldea: 'Chaldea' means mathematics, astronomy, the logical principles of the universe.[11] For the Chaldeans, everything is countable, and everything can be explained using the movement of the stars and the laws of the universe. Later, however, 'They celebrated the visible beings and had no idea about those that are invisibles and yet intelligible...not without impiety, they assimilated creation to its author'.[12] Purely logical and intellectual astronomy slipped into astrology: the principles of the universe became their god. YHWH, the true God, therefore had to cut astrology out of the salvation history of God's beloved nation: Chaldea was no longer suitable for his chosen servant Abraham, so he was sent away to a different land.[13] Nevertheless, in Philo's view, wisdom, the original principle of the Chaldeans, remains of the highest value in God's sight.[14] Philo interprets Abraham's journey towards the promised land as an allegory of the soul's journey towards God. The soul, led by her senses, knows that she longs for wisdom and desires to journey towards God.[15] The promised land, where Abraham was sent, is the symbol of wisdom, or philosophy.[16] This allegory is slightly modified in the medieval visions of heaven and hell depicted by, for example, Dante Alighieri.

9. Philo of Alexandria, *De Abrahamo*, ed. Jean Gorez, Les Oeuvres de Philon d'Alexandrie 20 (Paris: Cerf, 1966), 49, 51.

10. Wilken, *The Land Called Holy*, 35.

11. Philo of Alexandria, *Quaestiones et solutiones in Genesim III-IV-V-VI: e versione Armeniaca*, ed. Charles Mercier, Les Oeuvres de Philon d'Alexandrie 34b (Paris: Cerf, 1984), 471.

12. Philo, *De Abrahamo*, 53.

13. 'Well then, give up the explorers of the sky and the whole Chaldean teaching. Leave the largest of cities, our world, and go to a smaller one, which will help you better understand the sovereign of the Universe. This is why it is said that he emigrated for the first time from the Chaldean land to that of Harran.' Ibid., 55.

14. 'The ancients have very well said that wealth, nobility of lineage, affections, glory, and all external good of the same kind are at the service of the body, while health, strength and vigour of the senses are at the service of the soul, and the soul of the intellect'. Philo, *Quaestiones in Genesim*, 471.

15. Philo, *De Abrahamo*, 55.

16. Philo, *Quaestiones in Genesim*, 15.

In his commentary on Gen. 15.13, Philo develops his allegory of the soul wandering towards God and describes it as belonging to 'the ether, or universe', and being sent to the mortal body. The body is, in fact, alien to it. Philo sees this as similar to Abraham's being sent to a land which is not his. The soul is pure intellect, and the distance between the soul and the body is immense. The soul undergoes numerous afflictions as if it were a human person in slavery. The soul is saved when God calls her to judgment to condemn the sinful body and save the soul, the intellect.[17] The soul that dwells in and endures affliction in the body is strengthened; it is called to reflection and intellectual thinking.[18]

If we set aside the allegorical realm and focus on the land as a terrestrial entity, we find the seemingly paradoxical issue of inheritance. The land as something deeply earthly is always subject to corruption. How can something which in the vocabulary of the judeo-christian tradition is destined to corrupt the soul with every thinkable temptation then be given to human beings as an inheritance? The true inheritance, according to Philo, is the soul's God-given dominion over the body. The soul is tested and purified, but if it endures to the end all earthly afflictions, it enters the promised land of eternal dwelling with God: just as the land is put under the dominion of Abraham and his descendants, so the body is ultimately subordinated to the soul.[19]

Philo attempts to shed light on the incongruity of a land that is given to one people as a free gift but inhabited by another people who are obviously disinclined to welcome an invasion. His exposition of this issue

17. Ibid., 41, 43.

18. Ibid., 43. In his commentary on *Quaestiones in Exodum*, Charles Mercier explores the body-soul dichotomy through the example of the Passover meal. 'In the 15th question in the *Quaestiones in Exodum*, Philo explains the meaning of the Paschal meal. In the literal sense, the unleavened bread signifies the haste with which the Israelites set up their exodus from Egypt. The bitter herbs signify the "bitter life" of the Israelites as slaves in Egypt. There are two types of bread: a leavened and an unleavened. These two types of bread signify two types of souls: an arrogant soul and a *leavened* proud soul and a moderate and modest soul which is able to avoid extremes. The bitter herbs signify the migration of a soul. The soul is on a journey from passions to avoiding passions and from indulgence to virtue. The repenting soul is moving from passions and indulgence to virtue and wisdom. Thus, the soul is on a path towards wisdom and wisdom together with happiness, fullness and immortality are the highest possible goals that the soul can possibly reach. The journey is in fact repentance. Those who repent eat the unleavened bread and the bitter herbs in order to acknowledge our former life and its problematic nature.' Philo, *Quaestiones in Exodum*, 419.

19. Philo, *Quaestiones in Genesim*, 105.

is neither original nor unexpected but is nonetheless worth mentioning. In the allegorical sense, God gives to Abraham and his descendants everything earthly and corporeal as a free gift so that they have no need to collect taxes or similar. Taxes, Philo explains, stimulate greed, which is undesirable. The ruler of the Israelites, as opposed to the rulers of the neighbouring nations, is therefore truly sovereign and independent of any external influence, material stipulations, gifts or taxes.[20] In his commentary on Gen. 15.19-21, Philo deals with the issue of the native inhabitants and nations being determined to cause trouble for the Israelites. The Canaanites are top of a list of ten undesired nations. Ten is the number of fullness or completeness: in this case, Philo warns, the fullness of evil.[21] Philo goes on to develop the distinction between 'good invaders' and 'bad natives' and, in a reference to Exod. 23.28, introduces the idea of wasps chasing the native inhabitants away, which signifies God chasing away the 'unwilling'.[22]

Philo's apologetic against the native inhabitants of Canaan is of course highly problematic, indefensible even. It nonetheless bears valuable witness to the creation of the dichotomy between the oppressors and the oppressed, the 'superior' colonizers and the victimized, and encourages hatred of the inhabitants of Canaan and indeed of any adversary of the 'chosen nation', whether that be the Israelites in the Hebrew Bible or Christians in the Middle Ages or modern European history. Such hatred, as is now common knowledge, influenced the hatred of all colonized 'natives', including, as we will encounter in the work of John Steinbeck, Native Americans.

Origen

Origen is undoubtedly one of the most important biblical interpreters from among the church fathers, and although widely influenced by Philo, he stays firmly within the Christian tradition. Origen saw the earthly and heavenly promised lands as counterparts,[23] but connects his views more with New Testament images such as the kingdom of heaven than with philosophy.[24] According to Jaubert, Origen's interpretation of the promised land is spiritual: his concern is the holiness, justice, and love

20. Ibid., 417.

21. Ibid., 53.

22. Philo, *Quaestiones in Exodum*, 141, 143.

23. Annie Jaubert, 'Introduction', in *Homélies sur Josué*, by Origen, Sources Chrétiennes 71 (Paris: Cerf, 1960), 24.

24. Origen, *Homélies sur les Nombres*, Sources Chrétiennes 29 (Paris: Cerf, 1951), 501, 502.

in the land, not its location or terrestrial attributes.[25] As we saw when discussing the New Testament, for Christians, the promised land merges into one with the kingdom of God: 'The Promised Land is acquired after death in the Kingdom of Heaven; it is a pre-existing celestial land of which the earthly Palestine was an archetype and foreshadowing'.[26]

As is typical of ancient hermeneutics, Origen's commentaries are full of typology and allegory. Looking first at his typological approach, in his homily 'Seconde promesse faite a Abram', Origen juxtaposes the first promise given to Abraham, the promise of land, and the second promise, which becomes the promise of heaven;[27] the second promise naturally supersedes the first. Based on a paraphrase of 1 Cor. 15.47 ('The first man was from the earth, a man of dust; the second man is from heaven'), Origen develops the juxtaposition of Adam and Christ,[28] which is supported by the fact that in Hebrew, 'Adam' and 'land' have the same root, אדם. The first man (Adam) inherited the land and the second man (Christ) inherited heaven;[29] the first man is superseded by the second. Clearly, by replacing Adam with Christ, Origen replaced not only land with heaven but Judaism with Christianity. Origen develops a further level of typology in his homily 'La part de Caleb', in which he juxtaposes the names Joshua-Jesus, emphasizing the same Hebrew root, יהושע. It is Jesus who conquers and distributes the land,[30] and it is only Christians who are the heirs; Ruben, Gad, and Manasseh, who refused to cross the Jordan, represent the Jewish people and are heirs not of Joshua-Jesus but of Moses.[31] As a foreshadowing of what was to come, Joshua parcelled out the land beyond the Jordan; Jesus did the same with the holy and good land[32] that will be inherited by the true Israel, the spiritual Israel: the church.[33] Typologically, Origen identifies the promised land directly with

25. '… the main thing was the holy character of the land, not its location.' Jaubert, 'Introduction', 18.

26. Ibid., 22.

27. Origen, *Homélies sur la Genèse*, Sources Chrétiennes 7 (Paris: Cerf, 1944), 175.

28. This typology is already suggested in the homilies on Numbers. See Origen, *Homélies sur les Nombres*, 506.

29. Origen, *Homélies sur la Genèse*, 176.

30. Origen, *Homélies sur les Nombres*, 502–4.

31. Ibid., 503, 507.

32. Elsewhere, still referring to Exod. 3.8, Origen speaks about the land of the living, which must be spiritual. Origen, *Homélies sur Josué*, 405. See also Origen, *Homélies sur les Nombres*, 507.

33. Here Origen is referring explicitly to Exod. 3.8. See Origen, *Homélies sur Josué*, 385.

the figure of Christ, not only Christ in his human nature but Christ within all Christians. Thus, all faithful Christians who fulfil the will of God make up the promised land.[34]

Origen also develops a typology between the formless void[35] and the land,[36] both of which he identifies with the earth.[37] According to the creation narrative in Genesis 1, through being cultivated and cared for by God, the formless void of the very beginning gradually developed into a land.[38] This caring process, the cultivation of the land, is a process of perfection similar to that experienced by human beings on their way towards God.[39] The soul in the earthly body is a sinful soul, a formless void in need of perfection: pious, just, and chaste behaviour elevate the formless void to a cultivated land. Jesus has already begun the conquest of the promised land, showing us the way of perfection and purification that we must travel ourselves, every day, if we are to reconquer the land. The promised land can also, therefore, be lost: to lose our faith is to lose the land. The soul is always in danger of returning to Egypt, making the cultivated and fertile land once more a formless void. This dynamic between the promise and loss of land becomes paradigmatic for the whole reception of the motif of the promised land and will be repeated throughout its history.

The leading idea in Origen's allegorical treatment of the motif of the promised land sees it as the deliverance of the soul from the bondage of the earthly body. This allegory is taken from his teacher Philo of Alexandria and adopts Philo's understanding and interpretation. The promised land is a symbol of science, wisdom, virtue, and perfection. Like Philo, Origen explains this deliverance as the process of the perfection of the soul.[40] Jaubert explores Origen's eschatological perspective and explains how the promised land motif affects and places demands on the spiritual life of every Christian. The promised land was first conquered by Jesus, but it must be reconquered every day by every Christian: 'What is emphasized here is not the eschatological character of the promised land

34. 'It is interesting to discover here the spontaneous flourishing of Christian interpretations around the central christological theme: the promised land is Christ. Thus, the land is the church, the land is Christians.' Jaubert, 'Introduction', 32.

35. See Gen. 1.2. Méhat translates Origen's original ἀόρατος [καὶ ἀκατασκεύαστος] as *l'aride*; in Hebrew we read תהו ובהו.

36. Origen, *Homélies sur les Nombres*, 505–6.

37. Jaubert, 'Introduction', 22.

38. Origen, *Homélies sur la Genèse*, 67–8.

39. Origen, *Homélies sur les Nombres*, 505–6.

40. Ibid., 509.

but what happens in the present'.[41] This idea of reconquering the promised land, of laying claim to an inheritance, is suggested in the New Testament in Gal. 4.26 and Heb. 12.22 (where the land is now Zion, the heavenly Jerusalem), and 1 Pet. 1.4.[42]

We cannot speak about Origen and the promised land without mentioning his attitude towards the Canaanites. They are 'les ennemis cananéens': the unfriendly, hostile, antagonistic Canaanites, demons who attempt to seduce the soul on its way to the promised land.[43] They are not real people, therefore. In Origen's typology they are a hostile principle, 'Evil Spirits'[44] which we must chase from our hearts.[45] In the *Homélies sur l'Exode*, the Canaanites acquire human form: they have lost their courage and are afraid of Joshua-Jesus. For Origen, to fear Jesus is to be ruled by demons.[46] In *Homélies sur Josué* the Canaanites are a demonic race and a symbol of the powers against which a military campaign must be led. They are called 'native inhabitants' of the land but have no right to what is ostensibly theirs; their raison d'être is simply to be chased away and annihilated.[47] Furthermore, because for Origen this is an allegory of the soul's battle against evil powers, we are to fight these powers just as the Israelites fought the Canaanites.[48] The Canaanites inhabit us in the guise of our evil inclinations and we must conquer them. Just as God gave the land to the Israelites as a free gift (e.g. Gen. 15.7), but one they must still fight for, so Jesus has conquered the devil but we must confirm his victory in us every day.[49]

To sum up, in Philo and Origen, two of the most prominent biblical hermeneutists and interpreters of Antiquity, the motif of the promised land was largely allegorized and spiritualized. The leading idea, which has survived centuries of interpretation and influenced our Western

41. Jaubert, 'Introduction', 38.

42. Ibid., 26.

43. 'The Canaanite enemies are the demonic powers who seek to rule the soul and rob it of its Land.' Jaubert, 'Introduction', 16.

44. *Les Esprits du Mal* in the French translation.

45. See Origen, *Homélies sur les Nombres*, 148.

46. Origen, *Homélies sur l'Exode*, 156–7.

47. Origen, *Homélies sur Josué*, 109.

48. Ibid., 111.

49. See also: 'This seems to me a great thing, indeed, that man, prisoner of the flesh, fragile and tottering, armed only with faith in Christ and his teaching, triumphs over the Giants, over "legions" of demons. Although it is [Christ] who triumphs in us, he says that it is better to conquer the demons together, Him and us, than to conquer them by Himself.' Origen, *Homélies sur les Nombres*, 151–2.

understanding of the relationship between the body and the soul (spirit), is the soul's journey from its earthly body (Egypt) to the kingdom of heaven (the promised land); the Canaanites, the native inhabitants of the promised land, are an evil principle (attacking from both within and without) which seduces the soul on its journey towards God.

Reformation

The hermeneutics of the Reformation offer something of a conundrum: on the one hand they reject allegorical interpretations and insist on a literal understanding of the biblical text; on the other they arrive at similar conclusions to some of those we see in Antiquity. The Reformation proudly leans towards the *sui ipsius interpres* paradigm of the Bible: 'the Bible is its own interpreter';[50] to understand the biblical text, there is no need for tradition. An interpreter approaches the matter of biblical interpretation 'critically' but only regarding the 'doctrinal sediment' of the tradition. The authority of the Bible is inherent. A 'critical reading of the Bible' in the days of the Reformation therefore meant something different from what it means today.[51] The more the Reformers turn their backs on allegory, the more they dwell in typology, interpreting the books of the Hebrew Bible christologically. For the Reformers, Bray explains, 'the Bible is the Word of God in written form, which points to the Word of God incarnate in Jesus Christ'.[52]

John Calvin

Known for both his interpretation of the Bible and his doctrinal teaching, Calvin is one of the most prominent commentators of the Reformation and a leading figure in Protestant church circles.[53] He wrote commentaries on several books of the Hebrew Bible and the New Testament, was influenced by the Renaissance and the humanist movement, and studied the biblical languages.[54] His arguments are always logical and well structured and his preference is for detailed and systematic verse-by-verse commentary.[55] From the perspective of modern academy, Calvin's commentaries are nonetheless pre-critical: he retains Mosaic authorship and reads the

50. Gerald Bray, *Biblical Interpretation: Past and Present* (Leicester: Apollos, 1996), 192.

51. Ibid., 189–200.

52. Ibid., 198.

53. Ibid., 201.

54. William Bouwsma, 'John Calvin', *Britannica Academic*, http://academic. eb.com/EBchecked/topic/90247/John-Calvin.

55. Bray, *Biblical Interpretation*, 201.

Hebrew Bible purely typologically, through a christological lens.[56] Calvin insists on a three-step approach to biblical interpretation: biblical exegesis (commentary), dogmatics (doctrinal teaching), and homiletics (preaching).[57] The internal logic of Calvin's approach therefore resembles Gadamer's 'three readings' of understanding, interpretation, and application. Calvin's commentaries provide interesting historical comments that testify to the life and struggles of the Swiss Reformation, although many of these comments are strongly anti-Jewish and anti-Catholic.

Calvin appears little concerned with questions of the Canaanites or the land. Like the patristic authors, he sees the Canaanites as an evil principle, the sum of all the wickedness in both the biblical context and his own. Regarding the origin of this wickedness, Calvin notes that Noah's cursing of Canaan rather than of Ham – Canaan's father, the person who had shamed Noah – is not logical, and he also therefore allows for Noah's cursing of Ham. Calvin fails to provide any explanation for Noah's cursing of Canaan, stating only that it was God's providence. He summarizes his view of the Canaanites as follows: 'It is not without reason that the Canaanites are spoken of as…evil, *disloyal and inhuman*'.[58] We saw that in the patristic era the Canaanites were often identified with evil spirits and demonic powers. Calvin's term 'disloyal', on the other hand, seems unusual and it is difficult to see why he chose it.[59] His doctrine of determinism undoubtedly influenced his interpretation: the whole nation is evil and shall therefore be destroyed; the Canaanites symbolize the inhabitants of this world, who are equally evil; therefore, the whole world is evil.[60]

The role of the land as physical earth is to bear people and provide for them. There is a strong connection, therefore, between human beings and the land. The land is cursed as a result of the 'fall' (which Calvin holds to), that is, as a result of the actions of people. The land may have been cursed, but the consequences fall fully on the people.[61] This is not to suggest

56. The typology of the Hebrew Bible is built on the bipolarity of type-antitype. The typology works well within the Hebrew Bible, but the New Testament opened a new space for the extension of such a typology. See Gerhard von Rad, 'Typological Interpretation of the Old Testament', in *Essays on Old Testament Interpretation*, ed. Claus Westermann (London: SCM, 1963), 19–21.

57. Bray, *Biblical Interpretation*, 203.

58. John Calvin, *Commentaires de Jean Calvin sur l'Ancien Testament*, ed. André Malet (Geneva: Labor et Fides, 1961), 199.

59. Ibid., 356.

60. Ibid., 209–10.

61. Ibid., 84.

any 'proto-ecological' attitude towards the land; it simply means that the land depends fully on people and has no meaning or rights on its own. For Calvin, the promised land is an inimical environment full of hostile inhabitants: the Canaanites. At the moment of our birth, we are sent by God to the promised land, to an earthly life, to suffer the afflictions of the 'evil, disloyal and inhuman' Canaanites. When we humbly and patiently endure the afflictions, we are purified and converted to God. Since we were suffering in the promised land at the time of our sojourning, we do not enjoy mastery over it even after our enemies are crushed: we look to heaven and hope that God has prepared something better for us.[62] Unlike the church fathers, Calvin sees human life as a unity; he does not separate the body and the soul and set one off against the other. As we have seen in the book of Hebrews, we should not, according to Calvin, understand the promised land spiritually only after the Christ event but from the time the promise was given. Calvin believed that even Moses understood the true meaning of the promise of the land, which is that the true inheritance will come only after the promise made to the patriarchs is surpassed by Jesus. For Calvin, the true inheritance is heaven: 'So then, what was the earthly and temporal promise worth for eternal salvation? I answer that this belief that Moses mentions is not restricted to a single member but includes all those mentioned in the promise.'[63] Calvin attempts to redeem Moses even though he could not confess Jesus as his Messiah. Earlier, in his interpretation of Gen. 12.3, Calvin suggests a classic christological interpretation of the promised land:

> However, I extend it further, because I think that [Moses] will repeat this promise more clearly in Gen 22:18. This also leads me to the authority of St Paul (Gal 3:17), who says that the Promise, four hundred and thirty years before the Law, was made to the seed of Abraham, that is, Christ.[64]

Here Calvin is referring to the Pauline theology of substitution: God's covenant with the Jewish people is valid until Christ comes and fulfils the promises, after which the true heirs of Abraham are all those who confess Jesus of Nazareth as their Messiah; the promises to the heirs of Abraham are transferred to Christians. This interpretation was dominant until well into the twentieth century.

---

62. Ibid., 197–8.

63. Ibid., 232.

64. Ibid., 195. Also: 'This portion of the land was promised to the ancient people until the renewal brought by Jesus Christ. Now, since the Lord has dedicated the whole world to his people, we enjoy this heritage yet more fully.' Ibid., 617.

Matthew Henry

Trained in the classical languages, particularly in Hebrew, Matthew Henry was a Welsh theologian and non-conformist minister whose life spanned the turn of the seventeenth and eighteenth centuries. Henry's best-known exegetical work is his six-volume *Exposition of the Old and New Testaments*, although the sixth volume, 'Acts to Revelation', was completed by others after his death. Like most commentaries of the pre-critical era, Henry's is largely typological.[65]

From a hermeneutical point of view, it is interesting that Henry anticipated certain matters discussed in modern biblical criticism. He assumes, for example, that the book of Genesis was later than many of the accounts of the settlement motif. He even suggests that the account of the cursing of Canaan might have been added to bolster the Israelites in their wars against the Canaanites, a finding which is generally credited to the ideology critique of the second half of the twentieth century, but which may explain why unlike many of his predecessors Henry does not see the Canaanites as ontologically inferior or evil. Their role in the history of Israel is fixed at the time of Noah's curse. Henry does not seek to explain why the curse was laid upon Canaan rather than on any of Ham's other sons or even on Ham himself. He does not question the fact that Canaan is cursed, nor does he explain it as being a result of his evil nature.[66] He observes that, 'though the Canaanites were a *formidable* people, yet they were of old an accursed people, and doomed to ruin'.[67] It seems that for Henry, the Canaanites were simply an unfortunate people who were in the wrong place at the wrong time and had inherited a land that would one day be given to others. This observation influenced Jonathan Edwards, a missionary to the Native Americans in the second half of the eighteenth century, who roots his missionary work and sermons in the commentaries of Matthew Henry: the Native Americans were not 'ontologically' inferior to the European settlers – they were inferior because they were uneducated and had been exposed to the Gospel for a shorter period. This is at least a more sympathetic view of native inhabitants than earlier views of the Canaanites as demonic powers and the incarnation of evil. It is no longer the Canaanites themselves who are irredeemable but rather their culture,

---

65. David Wykes, 'Henry, Matthew 1662–1714)', in *Oxford Dictionary of National Biography*, http://www.oxforddnb.com/view/article/12975.

66. Matthew Henry and Thomas Scott, *A Commentary upon the Holy Bible: With Numerous Observations and Notes from Other Writers, Also Maps of the Countries Mentioned in Scripture and Various Useful Tables* (London: Religious Tract Society, 1834), 36.

67. Ibid.

religion, and way of life. The negative side effect of such a view is that it urges missionaries to evangelize Native Americans and 'save' them.[68]

Henry's attitude towards the land is cautious: there is a bond between the land and people, but the land is certainly not, hermeneutically speaking, an equal partner in the relationship. The land is cursed because of human sin, not only 'because' of humanity but also 'instead' of humanity. Henry suggests that this 'substitution' takes place because land is not as precious as a human being. The people's condition is affected by the curse of the land:

> God gave the earth to the children of men to be a comfortable dwelling to them: but sin altered the property of it; it is now cursed for man's sin. It is not what it was in the day it was created. But observe mercy in this sentence: Adam is not himself cursed, as the serpent was, but *only the ground for his sake*. This curse upon the earth, which cut off all expectations of a happiness in things below, might direct and quicken him to look for bliss and satisfaction only in things above.[69]

Declaring human beings responsible for the cursed land does not imply environmental concern, but that we should all the more direct our expectations towards the promised land that is in heaven. For Henry, the land of Canaan is spiritualized and eschatologized. It is the heavenly Canaan that we shall inherit after death: 'Doubtless the Lord did not promise Canaan to Abraham merely as a temporal inheritance. Canaan was not as other lands, a mere outward possession, but a type of heaven, and in that respect the patriarchs so earnestly prized it.'[70] Henry describes the promised land

---

68. Wheeler observes: 'In the Calvinist doctrine of human depravity, Edwards found grounds to affirm the equality of Indian and English... Thus, it was the universalizing core of Christianity that in Edwards' hands both promised equality and sponsored colonialism. On the latter point, Edwards was very much a man of his times, fully sharing in the conviction of English cultural superiority and the necessity of extinguishing Indian "savagery" in order to make room for English "civility" and Christianity.' Rachel Wheeler, 'Edwards as Missionary', in *The Cambridge Companion to Jonathan Edwards* (Cambridge: Cambridge University Press, 2007), 207.

69. Henry and Scott, *A Commentary upon the Holy Bible*, 15.

70. Ibid., 43. Also: 'The prospects of an eye of faith are much more rich and beautiful than those of an eye of sense. Those for whom the heavenly Canaan is designed in the other world, have sometimes by faith a comfortable prospect of it in their present state...God bade him walk through the land, that is, Do not think of fixing it, but expect to be always unsettled, and walk through it to a better Canaan.' Ibid., 47.

as a vineyard that is small in area but rich in fruitfulness. The land is tiny because those who believe in God have a larger share in heaven.[71]

The interpretation of the motif of the promised land by these two Reformers is similar, but we have seen a development in the hermeneutics. Unlike Calvin, Henry does not imply an explicit substitution of the territorial and 'Jewish' promise of land by the spiritual and eschatological 'Christian' inheritance of the kingdom of heaven. Similarly, whereas for Calvin the Canaanites are 'incarnated evil' (just like his many opponents, the Catholics, Turks, Muslims, and Jews), for Henry they are 'unfortunate creatures' who happened to be born in a land which by divine order was intended for others. The application of Henry's more sympathetic view of native inhabitants inspired missionaries to the New World to work hard to convert Native Americans: those who are not ontologically evil can be 'saved' more easily than those who were lost from their very conception.

Late tradition and application

In the modern school of biblical studies, the major themes of the Hebrew Bible once more became a focus of Christian biblical scholars. Although the three scholars I have chosen as representatives of this period are all from the twentieth century, we will nonetheless see a dramatic development of views on the promised land. Gerhard von Rad and Claus Westermann are members of the German school of biblical criticism from the beginning to the middle of the twentieth century, a period dominated by biblical archaeology, form criticism, and particularly source criticism. The American scholar Norman K. Gottwald, a politically active Marxist, is a pioneer of the sociological analysis of the Bible.[72] It was this sociological approach that prompted Brueggemann to turn towards the kind of postcolonial criticism that viewed the issue of the land in a more complex but problematic way.

Gerhard von Rad

In his early essay 'Promised Land and Yahweh's Land in the Hexateuch' (1943), von Rad suggests that the motif of the promised land has a

---

71. Also: 'This was the vineyard of the Lord, the garden enclosed; but as it is with gardens and vineyards, the narrowness of the extent was abundantly compensated by the extraordinary fruitfulness of the soil: see here then how small a part of the world God has for himself. Though the earth is his, and the fullness thereof, yet few know him, and serve him; but those few are happy, very happy, because fruitful to God.' Ibid., 358.

72. Norman K. Gottwald, *The Tribes of Yahweh: A Sociology of the Religion of Liberated Israel 1250–1050 B.C.E.* (London: SCM, 1980).

prominent place in the Hebrew Bible: 'In the whole Hexateuch there is probably no more important idea than that expressed regarding the land promised and later granted by Yahweh, an idea found in all the sources, and indeed in every part of each of them'.[73] In his later *Old Testament Theology*,[74] however, the account of the land is less prominent.

Von Rad states that in primeval history, the land is constitutive in the relationship between God and human beings. People also have a fundamental need to relate to the land: 'What is basic for man's existence is his relationship to the fertile soil (אדמה)'.[75] The relationship between God, human beings and the land is therefore a triangle in which each side (each bi-party relationship) must remain intact. If Westermann sees Genesis 1–11 (primeval history) as an account of crime and punishment,[76] for von Rad, the visible result of this crime is the violation of the relationship between people and the land.[77] Unlike Brueggemann, however, who sees the land as an equal partner in the triangle, von Rad appears to see it merely as an agent of the bipolar relationship between people and God. It is possible nonetheless to trace a kind of proto-environmental concern here. It is not the land itself that is precious, but we do at least anticipate a bond between human beings and the land: people's wellbeing is directly bound up with the state of the land.

The problematic relationship between human beings and the land continues with the patriarchs. When God called Abraham (Gen. 12), three commands were given: the command to abandon the land comes first, followed by the command to give up the clan, and finally the command

73. Gerhard von Rad, 'The Promised Land and Yahweh's Land in the Hexateuch', in *The Problem of the Hexateuch* (Edinburgh: Oliver & Boyd, 1966), 79.

74. First published in 1957 (volume 1) and 1967 (volume 2): *Theologie des Alten Testaments, Band 1: Die Theologie der geschichtlichen Überlieferung Israels* (Munich: Chr. Kaiser, 1957); *Theologie des Alten Testaments, Band 2: Die Theologie der prophetischen Überlieferung Israels* (Munich: Chr. Kaiser, 1967).

75. See also: 'It was of course from the soil that he was taken (Gen II. 7) and so with its gifts the soil is the motherly basis of his whole life. But the relationship has been broken, resulting in an estrangement which is expressed in a silent combat between man and the soil. For man's sake a curse lies upon the soil, and it now refuses to let him win its produce easily (Gen III. 17-19).' Gerhard von Rad, *Old Testament Theology* (New York: Harper & Row, 1962), 159.

76. Claus Westermann, *Genesis 1–11: A Continental Commentary* (Minneapolis, MN: Fortress, 1994), 494.

77. Von Rad, *Old Testament Theology*, 163. Also: 'The son of [this] first couple slew his brother, because he was envious that God took pleasure in him. But God heard the wailing of the spilt blood and *cursed* the murderer *away from the fertile land*. So Cain went away "from the presence of Jahweh".' Ibid., 155.

to leave the family. Von Rad suggests that the commands go from the general to the particular, and that it was easier for Abraham to obey the command to leave the land than to obey the other two. Nonetheless, leaving all three things behind is a major step. For von Rad, this event is the 'beginning of the saving history, the call of Abraham and Jahweh's plan for history indicated therein, to bless "all the families of the earth through Abraham"'.[78] Unlike the primeval history, the call of Abraham, 'through whom all the families of the earth shall be blessed', is very particular. In the primeval history, the whole of humanity is in view; in the stories of the patriarchs, focus is placed on a single nation growing from a single couple. We can also see that the land is being narrowed down to a particular part of the earth that will witness the salvation of the nation: the promised land. In the New Testament, we saw the opposite tendency: a broadening of the blessing to encompass all people and a broadening of the inheritance to encompass the whole world.

Von Rad notes the inconsistency in Scripture regarding 'ownership' of the land: the land is promised as an 'inheritance', but equally it is said to be God's.[79] All of the 'cultic' prescriptions in the Hexateuch, von Rad suggests, testify to God's ownership of the land: 'It is now quite clear that this notion is of a totally different order from that of the promise of the land to the early patriarchs. It is a wholly cultic notion, as compared with the other which may be characterized as the historical conception'.[80] The fact that ownership of the land is described in two ways became crucial for later environmental-ecological interpretive concerns: postcolonial criticism builds on the notion of the land as God's and the need to treat it with care and respect. Von Rad suggests that the passages which imply divine ownership of the land were undoubtedly influenced, at least in part, by Baalism, and that the passages which refer to the paradisiacal character of the promised land are borrowed from the Canaanite cult of natural religion.[81] This is an interesting starting point for postcolonial criticism and suggests that Canaanite religion was more conscious of the need to

78. Ibid., 164.
79. Ibid., 82–4.
80. Ibid., 88.
81. Ibid., 89. Also: 'Inter alia, it is to be found in the emphatic portrayals of Yahweh's blessing on the land. Even the saying that the land "flows with milk and honey" may be of this kind. Above all, however, there are the descriptions of an almost paradisal blessing on human progeny, on the offspring of the cattle, on basket and kneading-trough, the fruit of the fields, rain for the earth, peace, deliverance from wild animals and so on; these descriptions would surely seem to have been composed under the influence of Canaanite nature-religion.' Ibid.

care for and respect the land. Today, we would be tempted to give the Canaanites credit for this sense of thoughtfulness, but we should always be mindful of the complexity of the ancient context.

The eschatological-spiritual dimension of the promise of land is also present in von Rad's work. The spiritual promise continues, he suggests, even after the earthly promise has been fulfilled:

> Here we come face to face with one of the most interesting problems of Old Testament theology: promises which have been fulfilled in history are not thereby exhausted of their content, but remain as promises on a different level, although they are to some extent metamorphosed in the process. The promise of the land itself was proclaimed ever anew, even after its fulfilment, as a future benefit of God's redemptive activity.[82]

One could argue that von Rad's remark comes rather from the realm of pastoral ministry than from Hebrew Bible scholarship. However, his spiritual-eschatological interpretation of the promise of land differs from the interpreters of the pre-critical era, who argue that the promise was fulfilled in Jesus of Nazareth. For von Rad, the eschatological dimension of the promise lies in its eternal postponement, a vision which resonates with the allegorical interpretation of Antiquity to the extent that Jesus of Nazareth is not a condition sine qua non for the fulfilment of the promise.

Claus Westermann

Westermann believes that people's relationship to the land has always been based on pragmatism. The land may not be a prominent issue in his work but it is a notable one and he does offer it space when expounding on the curse on the land in Genesis 3 and Gen. 4.2-16 and on the patriarchal narratives in Genesis 12–50. Westermann describes the narratives in Genesis 3 and 4 as aetiological myths. He does not believe the land is cursed in the strict sense of the word. Rather, he holds that the relationship between people and the land is cursed: people must now work hard to earn their daily bread. Unlike Gunkel, however, who sees the curse creating 'an extremely pessimistic view of human life and agriculture',[83] Westermann believes it is simply a matter of reality: there never was an ideal state that preceded a cursed life of sweat and toil.[84]

---

82. Von Rad, 'The Promised Land and Yahweh's Land', 93.
83. Westermann, *Genesis 1–11*, 265.
84. Ibid., 263–5.

In *The Promises to the Fathers*, Westermann follows Noth and others in distinguishing two basic realms of promise: the promise of posterity and the promise of land; the latter is the more important.[85] Different promises were addressed to different groups of people: the promise of descendants was made to a nomadic people with no interest in the land; the promise of land was made to settlers.[86] What is noteworthy about Westermann's interpretation, which in other respects tends to be over-theoretical, is that he seeks to join up the narratives that deal with the promise of the land, pointing out, for example, that the end of the story of Joseph (Gen. 50.24) links the exodus with the patriarch narratives:

> Here is a direct statement that the promise of the land to the patriarchs has as its actual goal the deliverance of Israel from Egypt and the entrance of Israel to Canaan… In the entrance into Canaan, it is only the ancient promise of the land that finds fulfilment.[87]

Here, therefore, is a direct link between the promise of deliverance from Egypt and the gift of the land in Exod. 3.7-8, and the promise of land to the patriarchs: 'In [Gen. 50.24] we are told that the fulfilment of the promise given to the fathers Abraham, Isaac, and Jacob is seen in the gift of the land of Canaan to Israel as it comes up out of Egypt'.[88] The key text that deals with the promise of the land and the one that is likely to be the most original is Gen. 15.7-21.[89]

Westermann's exposition of the promise of land is useful in connecting what often remains separate: the promise of land given to the patriarchs and the promise of land granted to Israel as a nation. However, although *Promises to the Fathers* contains a section entitled 'The Theological Significance of the Promises', theological and content-related remarks are scarce and we never fully discover Westermann's position on the matter. He acknowledges this lacuna and argues for the need for further elaboration, but his exposition remains in bondage to form critical, source critical, and lexical analysis.

---

85. Claus Westermann, *The Promises to the Fathers* (Philadelphia, PA: Fortress, 1980), 7. See also Martin Noth and Bernhard Anderson, *A History of Pentateuchal Traditions* (Englewood Cliffs, NJ: Prentice Hall, 1972), 55.

86. Westermann, *The Promises to the Fathers*, 6.

87. Ibid., 21–2.

88. Ibid., 148.

89. Ibid., 144.

Like von Rad and others, Westermann sees the curse of Canaan (Gen. 9.25) as another aetiological myth.[90] However, unlike von Rad and the greater part of the history of interpretation of this text, Westermann refuses to consider the political dimension. He notes the hypotheses of his predecessors such as Gunkel and Herrmann, in which Shem, a forefather of the Israelites, is justified in having dominion over the Canaanites, but he rejects them one by one.[91] He concludes that the whole story of Noah and his sons (Gen. 9.20-27) is about the individuals Ham, Canaan, Shem, and Japheth, and not about the nations: the curse and blessings alike are directed towards individuals. Westermann therefore rejects the interpretations of this text which have served to condemn the Canaanites as a whole nation[92] and opens a space for seeing the Canaanites in a different light.

Norman K. Gottwald

Gottwald places himself within traditional historical-critical scholarship but develops its findings by offering a sociological interpretation which considers that like any other texts, biblical texts witness to the sociological structures that controlled public life at the time.[93] The texts do not retell what actually happened but are an account of what the leading authorities wanted to be said.[94] Gottwald promotes the revolutionary hypothesis that, 'the Israelites were confederated tribes bonded together in a sacral league dedicated to the cult of the god Yahweh, and the hypothesis that Israelites were Canaanite peasants in a revolt against the political economy in which they were exploited participants'.[95] His suggestion opens a raft of possibilities regarding the relationship between the Israelites and the Canaanites, and explains, quite plausibly, the origins of the rivalry and animosity between the two nations.

---

90. Westermann, *Genesis 1–11*, 482–94.

91. See ibid., 490–2.

92. 'The curse decrees that the son who has dishonoured his father is to live in disgrace; it is in the context of a family event... The curse can certainly have its effects in the political era; but it is here a pre-political, social matter.' Ibid., 492.

93. 'Sociological exegesis tries to situate a biblical book or subsection in its proper social setting – taking into account the literary and historical relations between the parts and the whole. It further attempts to illuminate the text according to its explicit or implied social referents, in a manner similar to historical-critical method's clarification of the political and religious reference points of texts.' Norman K. Gottwald, *The Hebrew Bible: A Socio-Literary Introduction* (Philadelphia, PA: Fortress, 1985), 28–9.

94. Ibid., 26.

95. Gottwald, *The Tribes of Yahweh*, xxii. See also 192–203.

It is widely accepted that the patriarchal and Mosaic narratives are not a credible account of history.[96] Their core message nonetheless remains valid: YHWH is 'the deliverer of the oppressed peoples from imperial-feudal thralldom into an autonomous egalitarian "tribal" existence. According to our best calculations, the Moses group was the bearer of the experience of the god Yahweh as a deliverer from *political* oppression.'[97] According to this hypothesis, the god YHWH was the uniting element for all the oppressed groups of people who met on the way to Canaan, regardless of their origin: 'Israel was in fact composed in considerable part of native Canaanites who revolted against their overlords and joined forces with a nuclear group of invaders and/or infiltrators from the desert'.[98] According to Gottwald, it is entirely possible that these 'desert infiltrators' were groups of slaves who escaped from Egypt under the ideological rule of the cult of the god YHWH – the so-called exodus Israelites. However, in Gottwald's view, the larger group recruited from the lower-class Canaanites who were exploited first during the Egyptian dominion and later by their Canaanite lords. This group of subordinated Canaanite peasants was attracted to YHWH – God the liberator – and the group of rebels gathered in this name.[99]

According to Gottwald, the apparent Israelite–Canaanite polarization and animosity are caused by a shift in terminology: 'As soon as the Canaanite lower classes converted and left Baalism, they were no longer seen as Canaanites. Henceforth, the term "Canaanite" referred to the city-state hierarchical structure, with its ideologically supportive Baal religion.'[100] The hypothesis that the term 'Canaanite' refers not to an ethnic group but rather to a socio-political and cultural group is a milestone in the history of the perception of the Canaanites as an inferior, evil and devilish nation. The Canaanites are now the enemies of liberation, freedom, and independence, rather than of one particular nation, Israel. However, as well as throwing light on the identity of the Canaanites as

96. Ibid., 32.

97. Ibid., 38.

98. Ibid., 210.

99. '[T]hese Israelite tribes [became] immediate allies of the Canaanite lower classes. Both groups shared a lower-class identity. The former slaves from Egypt, now autonomous, presented an immediate appeal to the restive serfs and the peasants of Canaan. The attraction of Israelite Yahwism for these oppressed Canaanites may be readily located in the central feature of the religion of the entering tribes: Yahwism celebrated the actuality of deliverance from socio-political bondage, and it promised continuing deliverance whenever Yahweh's autonomous people were threatened.' Ibid., 214.

100. Ibid., 216. For a more detailed and extended argument, see ibid., 237–660.

adversaries, it also explains much about what is meant by 'Israel' in the motif of the promised land.[101] Israel is now understood as a symbol of deliverance from socio-political oppression. Similarly, the conquest of the land is a symbol of the 'strivings for autonomous existence amongst several converging proto-Israelite social sectors [that] were realized by their unification as segments in an intertribal system'.[102] This understanding of the exodus and the settlement motif is indeed highly symbolic.

Given that Gottwald is carrying out a sociological analysis, it is not surprising that he has a limited interest in the land as a physical entity or territory and does not appear to acknowledge the importance of the promised land in either its territorial or its symbolic (eschatological-spiritual) sense:

> Yahweh was not in bond with a land, a region, or a city. Although there are a few traces in tradition that some Israelites felt they could not worship Yahweh if they were removed from the land occupied by Israel in Canaan…
> it is striking that Israel's god is never called 'the God of Canaan', or 'the God of the land of Israel'.[103]

Gottwald's suggestion that the Israelites 'recruited' from the Canaanite nation is a keystone in the later development of postcolonial studies. Moreover, such a sociological argument based on biblical sources is more plausible than a mere reference to the 'lawlessness' and 'violence' of the Bible itself. At the end of his book, Gottwald invites questions regarding the legitimacy of the relationship between the Canaanites and the Israelites in the reception history of the promised land motif.[104] He does not address the topics himself, however, and does not ask how 'God the Liberator' in the ancient biblical context became 'God the Oppressor' in the history of reception of this narrative.[105]

101. 'The intent of biblical theology to characterize the distinctiveness of early Israel is better served by depicting the religion of Yahweh as the symbolic boxing dimension of a synthetic egalitarian, intertribal counter-society, originating within and breaking off from hierarchic, stratified Canaanite history… "Yahweh" is the historically concretized, primordial power to establish and sustain social equality in the face of counter-oppression from without and against provincial and nonegalitarian tendencies from within the society. "The chosen people" is the distinctive self-consciousness of a society of equals created in the intertribal order and demarcated from a primarily centralized and stratified surrounding world.' Ibid., 692.

102. Ibid., 698.

103. Ibid., 688.

104. Ibid., 692–9.

105. Robert Warrior, 'Canaanites, Cowboys, and Indians', *Union Seminary Quarterly Review* 59, no. 1–2 (2005): 1–8.

The history of literary scholarship

This section will explore the impact of the motif of the promised land on culture, and literature in particular. I will divide the history into two: (i) Antiquity, the Middle Ages, and the Reformation, and (ii) late reception and application. Just as the previous section built up a picture of the potential exegetical influences on Walter Brueggemann, here I will sketch a brief history of literary scholarship to see what may be among the influences on his interpretive partner, John Steinbeck.

The aim is not to offer a systematic interpretation of the work of the authors presented. Distinguished literary scholars have already dealt with this issue in numerous monographs. My focus is on elements that may serve to illuminate the central concept of our study, the motif of the promised land, and how the authors perceive the question of the land both as a political territory and as a physical patch of earth. I will also look at how 'native inhabitants' have been perceived and how this perception has developed over time.

Antiquity, the Middle Ages, and the Reformation

The natural place to begin our tour of sixteen-hundred years of literary scholarship is with a contemporary of Philo of Alexandria, the historiographer Flavius Josephus, who offers us both temporal and spatial proximity to the biblical text. His *History of the Jewish War* and *Antiquities of the Jews* were accepted with some hesitation into the Western historiography of the Jewish religion but are still valid, nonetheless. For his immense impact on the development of Western literature, Dante Alighieri could hardly be left out of any history of literary scholarship. Finally, with respect to the subject of the promised land, John Milton is undoubtedly one of the most influential figures for the American context and is one of a group of authors who resurrected political notions of the promised land.

Flavius Josephus

Although as a Pharisee Josephus took his religion seriously, he had no great fondness for Jewish nationalism.[106] The theme of the promised land in its territorial and political sense belonged to the nationalist discourse and the realm of political upheaval, so it is no surprise that references to the promise of land are rare in Josephus's writings. Poole observes: 'Politically...the Pharisees had no sympathy with the intense

---

106. Gary Poole, 'Josephus Flavius', *Britannica Academic*, http://academic. eb.com/EBchecked/topic/306479/Flavius-Josephus/3765/Josephus-as-historian? anchor=ref72691

Jewish nationalism of such sects as the military patriotic Zealots and were willing to submit to Roman rule if only the Jews could maintain their religious independence'.[107] Cornfeld adds: 'It is noteworthy also that Josephus scarcely mentions the part played by the contemporary messianic movements that preceded and accompanied the political upheaval, apparently regarding them as so many aspects of Zealotry'.[108] Others, such as William Farmer, understand the Law of Moses and the 'covenant' (the promises to Abraham and the patriarchs) as an indivisible unity. Observance of the Torah is fulfilled with the promises and the promises are granted when the Torah is kept: 'A cardinal tenet of the postexilic community was that the promises of the covenant were conditional upon strict obedience on the part of Israel to every detail of the Law as it is written down in the Five Books of Moses'.[109] Arguably, however, although Josephus condemned the Jewish leaders for fighting for 'one of their promises', he failed to point out that they could hardly do otherwise as they were seeking to obey the Torah. For Farmer, the emphasis in Jewish nationalism on the covenant, namely the promise of land, is deeply rooted in rural areas and among farming people, and it is these people who have the greatest longing for the land, on the personal, social, and political levels.[110]

Josephus's *Jewish War* (75–79 C.E.) and *Antiquities of the Jews* (93 C.E.) are two books that narrate a single history, although the earlier work follows on chronologically from the later.[111] The original Aramaic

---

107. Ibid.

108. Flavius Josephus, *The Jewish War: Newly Translated with Extensive Commentary and Archaeological Commentary and Archaeological Background Illustrations*, ed. Gaalyah Cornfeld, Benjamin Mazar, and Paul Maier (Grand Rapids, MI: Zondervan, 1982), 7.

109. William Farmer, *Maccabees, Zealots, and Josephus: An Inquiry into Jewish Nationalism in the Greco-Roman Period* (New York: Greenwood, 1973), 49.

110. Ibid., 176.

111. Josephus, *Jewish War*, 6. See also: 'And indeed I did formerly intend, when I wrote of the war, to explain who the Jews originally were – what fortunes they had been subject to – and by what legislature they had been instructed in piety, and the exercise of other virtues – what wars also they had made in remote ages, till they were unwillingly engaged in this last with the Romans: but because this work would take up a great compass, I separated it into a set treatise by itself, with a beginning of its own, and its own conclusion; but in process of time, as usually happens to such as undertake great things, I grew weary and went on slowly, it being a large subject, and a difficult thing to translate our history into a foreign, and to us unaccustomed language.' Flavius Josephus, 'Antiquities of the Jews', http://www.gutenberg.org/files/2848/2848-h/2848-h.htm#linkpre2H_PREF

version of *Jewish War* has been lost but a Greek translation prepared under Josephus's supervision survived. According to Poole, the book was written to persuade the Mesopotamian Jews of the foolishness of the Jewish revolt.[112] The book's style and narrative brilliance have led scholars to suggest the influence of Josephus's Greek assistants.[113] Josephus was a great admirer of the Romans and probably lost favour in the eyes of Jewish officials for his endless apologia for Roman sophistication in contrast to what he described as Jewish barbarity. Although Josephus sought to clarify that his message concerned only Jewish nationalists and the leaders of the revolt – not the Jewish people as a whole, whom he held in high esteem – the balance was certainly in favour of the Romans:

> The fact that it was being ruined by civil strife, that the tyrannical Jewish leaders were those who drew the might of the unwilling Roman army to the holy sanctuary, and the flames that subsequently consumed it, is attested to by Titus Caesar himself, who ravaged the city. Throughout the hostilities he pitied the people who were left to the mercy of the rebellious parties and delayed the capture of the city time and again; for by prolonging the siege he gave the guilty a chance to repent.[114]

Farmer stresses the unity of the Jewish nationalism that was driving the Maccabees' revolt against the Seleucids and the Jewish war against the Romans. For Josephus, though, the two national upheavals were about entirely different matters.[115] Whereas the Maccabees are seen as pious keepers of the Law conducting a just revolt, the leaders of the war against the Romans are sinners carrying out an act of inexplicable wilfulness. Farmer summarizes Josephus's position as follows: 'The dual role as apologist for both the Romans and the Jews would have encouraged him to praise the Maccabees, who had been allies of Rome, while simultaneously blaming those Jews who had brought catastrophe upon his people by their revolt against Rome'.[116]

---

112. Poole, 'Josephus Flavius', *Britannica Academic*. Also: '[I] therefore considered it altogether inexcusable for the truth to be misrepresented and disregarded when such momentous issues were involved. The Parthians, the Babylonians, and the remote people of Arabia, as well as our countrymen beyond Eufrates and the people of Adiabene, were accurately informed through my diligent work of the origin of the war, the chain of calamities brought in its wake, and its tragic end.' Josephus, *Jewish War*, 8–9.

113. Ibid.

114. Josephus, *Jewish War*, 9.

115. Ibid., 11.

116. Farmer, *Maccabees, Zealots, and Josephus*, 20.

In his *Antiquities of the Jews*, Josephus offers a description of Jewish religion and culture to the Greeks and Romans,[117] explaining that the balance between the Law and the promises is definitely towards the former. Josephus favoured quiet and peaceful observance of the Law 'within the borders defined for it by the Roman occupants'. Introducing his readers to the history of the Jewish nation, Josephus chooses Moses rather than Abraham or another patriarch as the most significant figure in that history. He also emphasizes Moses as lawgiver, not Moses as fulfiller of the promises to the patriarchs.[118] Religion and philosophy were more important to Josephus than was politics: his attitude towards the territorial and political aspect of the promise of land is of course very much in harmony with his rejection of Jewish nationalism. If *Jewish War* is an apology for the Romans, who were 'driven into the war' and 'destroyed Jerusalem and the temple...unwillingly', *Antiquities of the Jews* represents an apology for the Jews and an attempt to present them in the best possible light, stressing their piety and devotion to the patriarchs.[119] Josephus differs from Philo in many respects – Josephus was an insider, Philo an exile; Josephus's account is that of a historian, Philo's of a philosopher; where Philo offers a systematic interpretation of the biblical text, Josephus follows the biblical line more freely, recounting the history but leaving out the prophetic books entirely – but their understanding of the promised land bears certain similarities: neither author, for example, viewed the promised land in the territorial or political sense.

Dante Alighieri

Dante's colourful life was clearly imprinted on his masterpiece *Divine Comedy*, especially his experience of exile and his death sentence, but also his love for Beatrice, who became his guide through Paradise; being written in Italian rather than Latin undoubtedly boosted its reach and popularity and made a decisive argument in favour of the vernacular. Ricardo Quinones describes the work – an allegory of a journey through hell, purgatory, and heaven – as a medieval 'vision of men's temporal and eternal destiny'.[120] It is a literary adaptation of the popular religious leitmotif of the soul wandering from slavery in Egypt to the promised land in heaven, a motif drawn from Philo and Origen, and which clearly survived, with some modification, across time.

117. Josephus, 'Antiquities of the Jews'.

118. Ibid.

119. Ibid.

120. Ricardo Quinones, 'Dante', *Encyclopedia Britannica Online*, http://www.britannica.com/biography/Dante-Alighieri#toc22149

One of the crucial themes in *Divine Comedy* which connects to the motif of the promised land is the concept of hierarchy, which Mazzeo suggests is deeply rooted in medieval thinking, has both a philosophical and a theological impact on the poem, and reflects the feudal (monarchical) and religious (Jewish and Christian) arrangement of medieval ecclesial society.[121] The greatest philosophical-theological influence on *Divine Comedy*, Mazzeo argues, is Pseudo-Dionysius the Areopagite, and particularly Pseudo-Dionysius's understanding of the Plotinian principle of emanation, which he filled out with the notion of divine creation. There is also, however, a movement in the opposite direction, back towards God, which Mazzeo describes in terms of Philo's ascent towards knowledge:

> The system is thus simultaneously a system of creation and exaltation, an outgoing and a return... Thus hierarchy has the purpose of drawing its members towards the divine, providing them with a ladder, so to speak, as well as the function of distributing all divine powers through creation.[122]

This ascent towards knowledge appeared in Philo's interpretation of the narratives of exodus and settlement, which Philo saw as an allegory of the soul's enslavement in the earthly body (Egypt), its longing for union with God, and its journey towards the promised land (Canaan). Philo's allegorical interpretation was followed by Origen and the Alexandrian school and by much of the scholarship of the Middle Ages, only coming to a halt at the Reformation. The Reformers' rejection of allegory was far from complete, however. They may have opposed it in principle, but in practice their interpretation of the promised land was broadly similar. The change of orientation from territorial-horizontal (a journey from one particular place on earth to another) to spiritual-vertical (a pilgrim or a soul on his or her spiritual journey towards God) can in fact already be seen in Philo's interpretation. Mazzeo suggests that *Divine Comedy* may represent, or at least include, an allegorical interpretation of the motif of the promised land: 'It is also a ladder, Jacob's ladder and its ascent in the Exodus of the Hebrews from Egypt to the promised land'.[123] However, Dante's work introduces a new element into the allegorical interpretation, namely the concept of purgatory. The idea was not fully developed in Antiquity, but it is not so much of a stretch to see Philo's

121. Joseph Mazzeo, *Medieval Cultural Tradition in Dante's Comedy* (Westport, CT: Greenwood, 1968), 24.
122. Ibid., 15, 21.
123. Ibid., 37.

description of the soul's pilgrimage through an earthly life filled with the temptation to worldly delights in the experience of purgatory as narrated in *Divine Comedy*. The motif of the promised land was therefore strong enough to endure even the advanced allegorical reading of the Middle Ages.

In Dante's vision of a pilgrim journeying through hell, purgatory, and heaven, we can detect a further spiritual interpretation of the pilgrimage to the promised land as developed by Philo. The hierarchical structure of hell, purgatory, and heaven corresponds to the medieval concept of the human ascent to God and the divine emanation towards the world. It also develops Philo's description of the attempt of every pilgrim (soul) that is thrown into life to return to the promised land of proximity to God (heaven). The original element of purgatory illuminates the state of the 'errand into the wilderness', which I will elaborate on when we come to the Puritans.

Finally, we should note one passage in the epic that hints at the dichotomy in our culture between white Europeans and people of colour. Dante's description of Satan symbolically places hell in Egypt. He refers to the devil as having three faces:

> And oh, my astonishment when, on his head
> I saw no fewer than three faces! One
> in front and that was vermilion-red;
> to this face two others were joined on
> Just midway above 'twixt where begins and ends
> each shoulder and all three joined at the crown.
> The right was coloured of the tint which blends
> yellow with white; the left, of that we find
> *in such as come from whence the Nile descends*.[124]

In Dante's mind, 'in such as come from whence the Nile descends' could simply be a description of a colour – a black colour – but it is striking that whereas the other colours are described by their names alone, this last colour is connected to the Nile, a symbol of Africa and specifically of Egypt, and not just to the Nile itself but to the people of the Nile. Such stereotypes, ingrained even in the popular culture of the Middle Ages, undoubtedly have an impact on the stereotypes that continue to influence our lives today.

124. Inferno, Canto 34. Dante Alighieri, *Divine Comedy* (London: Bibliophile, 1988), 249 (italics mine).

John Milton

In her socio-political study of *Paradise Lost*, Lydia Schulman suggests that John Milton's poetry and political influence impact American political life in equal measure.[125] The formation of the first colonies in America and the formation of the American republic itself were strongly influenced by the seventeenth-century English revolt against the monarchy, the English Civil War, and the formation of the English Commonwealth, historical events which would become embedded in Milton's great epic. The key factor, Schulman argues, in both the English Commonwealth and the push for American independence was the interplay between politics and religion.[126] Milton was therefore a natural champion for Americans in their struggle for independence:

> Indeed, the inclination of Americans of that time [was] to see their struggle against a corrupt Britain apotheosized in Milton's depiction of the cosmic battle between God and Satan... It is an example, moreover, that illustrates key points of intersection of the English libertarian and Puritan traditions, such as their shared emphasis on individual liberty and their concern over its degeneration into satanic license.[127]

The blending of politics and religion that Schulman sees in *Paradise Lost* was indeed a prominent feature of events on both sides of the Atlantic.[128] The departure from old monarchic systems was seen as an indispensable condition for commercial expansion and the establishment of a free market, and for the overall welfare of the state. The other side of the coin is that republican systems are more demanding on the political responsibility of citizens: 'Both individuals and society were freer to achieve but also to fall – like Adam and Eve in *Paradise Lost*'.[129]

The political dimension of Milton's work also includes the idea of the significance of land in the process of people's emancipation into a new and

125. Lydia Schulman, *Paradise Lost and the Rise of the American Republic* (Boston, MA: Northeastern University, 1992), ix. Also: 'The influence of *Paradise Lost* in late eighteenth-century America is a striking example of the active role poetry can play in shaping political culture'. Ibid., 13.

126. Ibid., ix–x.

127. Ibid., x.

128. Ibid., 11. Also: 'Each of these contexts in which the Fall theme proved compelling – seventeenth-century England and Holland and eighteenth-century America – featured a national agenda of independence, republicanism, and commercial expansion, whose success required the curbing of market society's propensity to corruption'. Ibid., 4.

129. Ibid., 5.

better system. In Schulman's view, Milton stresses that in order to plead for higher ethical standards it was first necessary to focus on people's living conditions, and if most seventeenth-century English people were dependent on agriculture for their living, that meant improving the standards of husbandry. Farms were often oversized, which led to high rents for land, and the land itself was overworked.[130] Milton was clearly concerned for the land and aware that the people's wellbeing required it to be well looked after. The British Isles was a group of densely populated islands and Milton knew that concern for the land and for its condition and wellbeing was paramount.

Although the strength of Milton's legacy concerning the promised land lies in the political realm, we need to consider the poet's attitude towards the land on a more personal level. The verses below stand out from the natural flow of the first book of *Paradise Lost* (which addresses the 'fall' of humankind and the expulsion from paradise) and direct our attention as modern readers towards Milton's concern for the land.

> Men also, and by his suggestion thought,
> Ransacked the centre, and with impious hands
> Rifled the bowls of their *mother earth*
> For treasures better hid. Soon had his crew
> *Opened into the hill a spacious wound*
> And digged out ribs of gold. Let none admire
> That riches from hell; *that soil may best*
> *Deserve the precious name.*[131]

Fowler, a careful editor of this version of *Paradise Lost*, provides here a wealth of allusions to the impure and rapacious mining industry and, perhaps surprisingly, to the formation of Eve, who according to Gen. 2.21 was created from one of Adam's ribs and became 'mother earth', the universal mother of all human beings.[132] The warning against mining implies a concern for the land and a plea for careful industry: mother earth, represented by Eve, must not be 'raped' by careless mining; it is the soil that 'may best deserve the precious name'. Milton's concern for the land – its current and future states – is clear and indisputable, and he offers an equally consistent account of God's selection of the beloved people, the peculiar nation:

130. Ibid., 115.
131. John Milton, *Paradise Lost*, ed. Alastair Fowler, 2nd edn (Harlow: Pearson & Longman, 2007), 102 (italics mine).
132. For more discussion, see ibid.

And *one peculiar nation* to select
From all the rest, of whom to be invoked,
A nation from one faithful man to spring:…
For gods! Yet him God the most high vouchsafes
To call by vision from his father's house,
His kindred and false gods, *into a land*
Which he will show him, and *from him will raise*
A mighty nation, and upon him shower
His *benediction so,* that in his seed
All the nations shall be blest; he straight observes
Not knowing to what land, yet firm believes:
I see him, but thou canst not, with what faith
He leaves his gods, his friends, and native soil…
With God, who called him, *in a land unknown*.[133]

These verses are especially remarkable for the consistent biblical vocabulary. Here Milton retells part of the story of God's choosing of Abraham in order to emphasize that it is always the individual who is elected and through this election comes the election of the descendants. However, according to Milton's account, there were other individuals – Adam and Noah – who preceded the election of Abraham, but the succeeding generations of these elect failed, just like the seed of Abraham. Fowler distinguishes between individual election and the election of the nation: personal election for salvation is still possible for Fowler.[134] The new elect of God comprises those who believe that Jesus of Nazareth is the Christ. They are the new Israel. It was the English people who were the first to overthrow their monarch to form the English Commonwealth and make God their only king. They, the English people, are therefore the new Israel, God's new elect. This notion of the English as the new Israel is implied throughout Milton's work.

Although Milton was no supporter of the Church of England, its national and political legacy was clearly imprinted in his epic. And although Milton dealt more with the political dimension of the promised land than with a concern for nature, we can also find traces of his legacy in this latter regard. Milton maintained that a person's wellbeing was dependent on their conditions at work and at home. The theme of Milton's epic – the fall of humanity and the loss of paradise – cannot have been arbitrary, just as the decision to narrate the history of the Jewish nation to the English people at a time of national upheaval was not arbitrary.

133. Milton, *Paradise Lost*, 652–3 (italics mine).
134. Ibid., 652.

Late reception and application

The literary scholars discussed in this section agree that the most prominent stream with respect to the theme of the land was Jefferson agrarianism, a stream, as the name suggests, with its roots in the politics of Thomas Jefferson and which became a popular theme in the works of American authors, particularly those from the southern states.[135] In twentieth-century literature, however, it was received more critically, and its 'naïve' perspective was widely reconsidered, so that 'thoughtless' cultivation of the land was now seen as 'rape'.[136] The following pages will be devoted to Steinbeck's eighteenth-, nineteenth-, and twentieth-century predecessors from American literature, whose influence on Steinbeck's work will become increasingly apparent as we progress; the accounts of the authors will also become more detailed.

The idea of the rich and bountiful land of America is embodied in the work of one of the country's most famous presidents, Thomas Jefferson. In *Notes on the State of Virginia* Jefferson revealed a clear preference for agriculture over manufacturing and insisted that because American soil was rich and exceptional the American people were designed to work on and with the land. Ralph Waldo Emerson and Walt Whitman will introduce us to the reception of the motif of the promised land in the nineteenth century. Emerson's essay *Nature: Addresses and Lectures* (1849) captured the idea of transcendentalism. The idea of the universal, transcendental, and all-embracing soul which replaced the personal God of Christianity became popular during Emerson's time and influenced the great American poets such as Whitman. Although Whitman did not work with the idea in any systematic way, he supplemented it with the national tone: America was a great country with a bountiful land and wild nature; it was a land of promise. F. Scott Fitzgerald, our representative from the twentieth century, is sceptical of the so-called American dream and the idea of the elect people. The characters in his ground-breaking novel *The Great Gatsby* are archetypal protagonists of the unfulfilled promises of America.

Thomas Jefferson

Jefferson outlined his view of the promised land most clearly in his *Notes on the State of Virginia*. The notes are based on Jefferson's initial response to a questionnaire sent to him (and to twelve other state

135. Annette Kolodny, *The Lay of the Land: Metaphor as Experience and History in American Life and Letters* (Chapel Hill, NC: University of North Carolina Press, 1975), 27, 138–9.
136. Ibid., 144–7.

governors) by his friend François Marbois, a consul-general of France who was living in Philadelphia. The *Notes* provide us with a thought-provoking picture of America in the late eighteenth and early nineteenth century and its attitude towards both the land and its native inhabitants.

Fohlen identifies three main themes in Jefferson's work: the natural resources, political organization, and 'aborigines' of the state of Virginia.[137] The treatise on the Native Americans, or Indians as Jefferson calls them,[138] is thorough and detailed, although according to Fohlen far from 'scientific'.[139] Jefferson writes as an ethnologist, providing an account of the territory of each Native American tribe, its history and language, and even its possible origin.[140] He acknowledges the variety and riches of Native American culture, the many tribes and their various languages, and appears well informed about their living conditions. Native Americans are seen as an interesting ethnographic object which makes the socio-cultural diversity of the United States more unique. Jefferson saw no special or respectable place for them in American society at the time, but regretted what he saw as a lack of cultural curiosity:

> It is to be lamented then, very much to be lamented, that we have suffered so many Indian tribes already to extinguish; without our having previously collected and deposited in the records of literature, the general rudiments at least of the languages they spoke.[141]

He is nonetheless a typical representative of the Age of Enlightenment. He has little understanding of the primitive socio-political organization of Native Americans and criticizes them for not being organized into any constructive unit, such as a government: 'Their only controls are their manners, and the moral sense of right and wrong, which, like the sense of tasting and feeling, in every man makes a part of his nature... It will be said that great societies cannot exist without government. The savages, therefore, break them into small ones.'[142] It is clear, then, that despite his appreciation of the cultural diversity that the Native Americans bring to the country, they are inferior to the settlers from Europe. Jefferson also denies that the colonial conquest of the Native

137. Claude Fohlen, *Thomas Jefferson* (Nancy: Presses universitaires, 1992), 39.

138. I will continue to refer to the indigenous people of North America by the politically neutral term Native Americans.

139. Fohlen, *Thomas Jefferson*, 39.

140. Ibid.

141. Thomas Jefferson, *Notes on the State of Virginia* (Boston, MA: Lilly & Wait, 1832), 104.

142. Ibid., 96–7.

American people is the main reason for their unfortunate state of affairs. Some of the reasons he does list, however, such as illness and alcoholism, were undoubtedly imported by Europeans.[143] Jefferson maintains that Native American territory was purchased for a good sum and that fertile lands were granted in return.[144] There is certainly a difference between taking someone's land by military conquest and taking it by exchange or purchase, but Jefferson's attempt to play down settler accountability is hardly convincing.[145]

The key passage on what later became known as Jefferson agrarianism is 'Query number XIX'. Here Jefferson argues that the true vocation of every American is in husbandry – to work on and with the land:

> But we have an immensity of land courting the industry of the husbandman. Is it best then that all our citizens should be employed in its improvement, or that one half should be called off from that to exercise manufactures and handicraft arts for the other? Those who labour in the earth are the chosen people of God, if he ever had a chosen people, whose breasts he has made his peculiar deposit for substantial and genuine virtue. It is the focus in which he keeps alive the sacred fire, which otherwise might escape from the face of the land.[146]

This could be a manifesto for Jefferson agrarianism, a vision of the paradisiacal land where all would be farmers, working the soil. America is a bountiful and fertile land, the promised land, and those who cultivate it are God's chosen people. The land is clearly rich enough to provide for everyone and it would be a 'sin' to waste time and energy on manufacturing.

Jefferson's ideal was to divide the land into small portions on which farmers could earn their living in freedom and democracy and he planned to put this ideal into practice. The dream was to have been realized in the 'Empire for Liberty', an extensive territory along the Mississippi River

143. 'What would be the melancholy sequel of their history, may however be argued from the census of 1669; by which we discover that the tribes therein enumerated were, in the space of 62 years, reduced to about one-third of their former numbers. Spirituous liquors, the small pox, war and an abridgment of territory, to a people who lived principally on the spontaneous production of Nature, had committed terrible havoc among them, which generation, under the obstacles opposed to it among them, was not likely to make good. That the lands of this country were taken from them by conquest, is not so general a truth as is supposed.' Ibid., 97–8.
144. Ibid., 98.
145. Ibid., 97–8.
146. Ibid., 172.

which he purchased from Napoleon in 1803,[147] but despite acquiring an enormous plot of arable land for the American settlers, the plan did not turn out well. Historians still debate how much of the blame for the failure of the project should fall on Jefferson's shoulders.[148]

Two problems with the realization of Jefferson's dream are relevant to our discussion. First, the territory was inhabited by Native Americans. Jefferson believed that they should be allowed to stay only if they learned to farm in the same way as their white neighbours. Naturally, the Native Americans were not in favour of changing their way of life and were forced to leave their land and move westwards. Secondly, the soil along the Mississippi soon proved suitable for planting cotton. Huge cotton plantations appeared, closely followed by the introduction of slavery. Jefferson was not strictly speaking in favour of slavery, but neither did he voice any strong condemnation of it.[149]

Jefferson's 'Empire for Liberty' failed not only because the Native Americans were expelled and slaves were dragged in, but because the land was exploited by both latifundialization and cotton planting. There was plenty of land available in eighteenth-century America, but Jefferson's treatise still appears naive and simplistic. It might seem that before the huge increases in population and the development of fertilizers, pesticides, herbicides and genetic modification, concern for the land was not on the agenda, but as we have seen, care for the land was already grounded in the Bible, in the Sabbath for resting the land in Lev. 25.2-6. Instead, Jefferson sees the potential in the American countryside and the fertility of its land and decides to make the best possible use of it.

As we have said, Jefferson appreciated the Native Americans for their ethnographic and cultural value – they enriched America's socio-cultural palette and added to its colourful history; they gave their aboriginal names to rivers, mountains, and other natural features, and so made America more 'interesting' – but regarding their destiny, no attempt was made to help them out of their desperate situation, only to defend the attitudes and actions of the settlers from Europe.

So far, I have put forward Jefferson's view of the land as physical earth and his attitude towards the Native Americans, but during the formation of the American republic the idea of America as the promised land also took a more civic shape, and this was enshrined in another document to which Jefferson put his name, *The Declaration of Independence*, written in 1776:

147. The 'Louisiana Purchase'.
148. Bernard Sheehan, 'Jefferson's "Empire for Liberty"', *Indiana Magazine of History* 100, no. 4 (2004): 346–63.
149. Ibid.

> We hold these truths to be sacred & undeniable; that all men are created
> equal & independent, that from that equal creation they derive rights
> inherent & inalienable, among which are the preservation of life, & liberty,
> & the pursuit of happiness.[150]

These words became influential for much of the developed world, beginning with the French Revolution and subsequently other Enlightenment
movements in Western and Central Europe. The idea of equality, liberty,
and happiness (or success) develops organically from the original view
of America being the new promised land. Support for this conviction
appears in a recent foreword to the Declaration by the director of the U.S.
Citizenship and Immigration Services:

> The Declaration of Independence and the Constitution of the United States
> are the two most important and enduring documents in our Nation's history.
> It has been said that 'the Declaration of Independence was the promise; the
> Constitution was the fulfilment'.[151]

The biblical language of promise and fulfilment emphasizes the conviction
that America is the new promised land and its people are the new people
of God.

Ralph Waldo Emerson and Walt Whitman

Before exploring Whitman's *Leaves of Grass*, one of the most
influential poems in American literary history, I will briefly discuss the
transcendental philosophy of Ralph Waldo Emerson which inspired the
literary output of both Whitman and Steinbeck. The roots of Emerson's
transcendentalism lie in Unitarianism, which reacted against the rigid
doctrines of Calvinism which still governed public debate in eighteenth-
century America. Emerson had himself been a Unitarian minister before
leaving to explore what he saw as more open-minded worldviews.
Transcendentalism is deeply rooted in human respect for and love of
nature – neither of which requires any 'revelation' – and seeks to rid
itself of Christian tradition, which it sees as holding people back from
true emancipation:

---

150. Thomas Jefferson, *Jefferson's 'Original Rough Draft' of the Declaration of
Independence*, available at https://jeffersonpapers.princeton.edu.

151. Thomas Jefferson, 'The Declaration of Independence', in *The Declaration
of Independence and the Constitution of the United States* (U.S. Citizenship and
Immigration Services).

Our age is retrospective. It builds the sepulchres of the fathers. It writes biographies, histories, and criticism. The foregoing generation beheld God and nature face to face; we through their eyes. Why should not we also enjoy an original relation to the universe? Why should not we have a poetry and philosophy of insight and not of tradition, and a religion by revelation to us, and not the history of theirs?[152]

Emerson is suggesting a clean break from a Christian tradition that was so deeply rooted in American history and culture that it had become a part of American identity. He does not want to venerate God as a Supreme Being, something beyond human beings and nature. Human beings and the natural world are an inseparable unity: people are a part of nature, and nature carries, cares for and provides for people: 'Philosophically considered, the universe is composed of Nature and the Soul. Strictly speaking, therefore, all that is separate from us, all which Philosophy distinguishes as the NOT ME, that is, both nature and art, all other men and my own body, must be ranked under this name NATURE.'[153] Emerson rejects the notion of a Supreme Being distinct from human beings and nature. Rather, a spirit, which he later called the *Over-soul*, connects Nature and people; this spirit is not separate from either of them but arises from them both.[154] Emerson uses the example of the landscape and the horizon: although we can see various farms and fields which can be distinguished from each other and have different owners, they nonetheless compose a horizon that is indivisible and a landscape that belongs to no one: the landscape cannot be owned; the horizon cannot be divided.[155] Here Emerson seems to be suggesting something similar to postmodern hermeneutics, the philosophy of Edmund Husserl, and the fight against subject–object dualism, namely a universal and remarkable unity of all creation connected by the spirit:

We learn that the highest is present to the soul of man, that the dread universal essence, which is not wisdom, or love, or beauty, or power, but all in one, and each entirely, is that for which all things exist, and by which they are; that the spirit creates; that behind nature, throughout nature, spirit is present; one and not compound, it does not act upon us from without, that

152. Ralph Waldo Emerson, 'Nature', in *Nature, the Conduct of Life and Other Essays*, ed. Sherman Paul (London: Dent, 1970), 1.

153. Ibid., 2.

154. 'I become a transparent eye-ball; I am nothing; I see all; the currents of the Universal Being circulate through me; I am part or particle of God.' Ibid., 4.

155. Ibid., 31.

is, in space and time, but spiritually, or through ourselves: therefore, that
spirit, that is, the Supreme Being, does not build up nature around us, but
puts it forth through us, as the life of the tree puts forth branches and leaves
through the pores of the old.[156]

Whitman shares Emerson's faith in the human being,[157] but his view of the
soul is more complex and differs from poem to poem. For both Whitman
and Emerson, the soul integrates human life and connects it to the outer
world; it is a channel for communication that transcends all boundaries.[158]
Whitman supplements Emerson's transcendentalism with a national note:
America is a unique country, the most democratic in the world, the land
of promise. Pelzer sums up this myth of America's superiority over
other nations, the dominant idea in the public debate in nineteenth- and
twentieth-century America, in the following way:

> The central facet of this myth [of the American dream] is the belief in
> Edenic possibilities, the hope that Paradise could be re-created not in the
> next world and not out of time, but in the here and now of a new continent,
> a New World. Europeans, from the time of its first settlement, saw America
> as a land of hope and opportunity, a place where men and women could
> escape centuries of poverty, misery, and corruption and start anew in a land
> undefiled. Here, in this New World, human beings could satisfy their mythic
> yearnings for a New Eden. They could re-create a paradise on earth.[159]

Jefferson, Emerson, and Whitman represent the line of thinking that
presents America as the promised land, and of all the naivety and exaggerated uncritical self-confidence that goes with it. They neglect the
unfortunate side-effects of the American dream: the impact on the land
and its native inhabitants. The early reception of Whitman's work shared
this uncritical view. For earlier Whitman scholars, Whitman is the
preacher of democracy and equality,[160] and *Leaves of Grass* is the 'Bible

156. Ibid.
157. Jimmie Killingsworth, *Walt Whitman and the Earth: A Study in Ecopoetics*,
The Iowa Whitman Series (Iowa, IA: University of Iowa Press, 2004), 31.
158. Ibid., 31–2.
159. Linda Pelzer, *Student Companion to F. Scott Fitzgerald*, Student Companions to Classic Writers (Westport, CT: Greenwood, 2000), 100.
160. According to Holloway, Henry David Thoreau wrote that 'Whitman is apparently the greatest democrat the world has seen'. See Emory Holloway, 'Introduction',
in *Leaves of Grass* (London: Everyman's Library, 1971), vii. Holloway also suggests
that Whitman is fully devoted to his country and is a passionate preacher of 'the
democratic virtues of liberty, fraternity, and equality'. Ibid.

of democracy'; Whitman himself wanted it to be the 'new Bible'.[161] Later in the twentieth century, studies began to look at his work from a more critical and detailed perspective and demonstrated that Whitman's work contains not only numerous statements in support of slavery but also the view that people of colour are inferior to white people.[162]

Whitman's view of Native Americans in *Leaves of Grass* appears ambiguous. On the surface it can seem sympathetic, but on closer inspection there is no space for Native Americans in his vision of a New America. One poem from *Leaves of Grass* which neatly illustrates Whitman's attitude towards the land and to Native Americans is 'Song of the Redwood-Tree', which portrays the end of the American wilderness and its succumbing to cultivation and industrialization.[163]

In the poem, Whitman provides the sequoia tree with a human voice so that it can hold a dialogue with the poet. Whitman and the spirits – the dryads and hamadryads – of the great sequoia are discussing the future of America. The sequoia, or redwood as it is called in the poem, represents the wild and virgin landscape of North America and its native inhabitants. The poem therefore depicts the fading away not only of American nature but also, implicitly, of its inhabitants. Killingsworth observes: 'The great tree is made to submit willingly, and even gladly, to the superior "race" of human beings marching westwards'.[164] Killingworth asks whether the personification of the sequoia makes the relationship between nature and human beings more equal or is rather a device for establishing nature as even more subordinate, an active participant, complicit in its own extinction.[165] Such a conclusion is easy to draw from the tree's cry in the second stanza:

> A California song,
> A prophecy and indirection, a thought impalpable to breathe as air,
> A chorus of dryads, fading, departing, or hamadryads departing,
> A murmuring, fateful, giant voice, out of the earth and sky,
> Voice of a mighty dying tree in the redwood forest dense.

161. Ibid.

162. Martin Klammer, *Whitman, Slavery, and the Emergence of Leaves of Grass* (University Park, PA: The Pennsylvania State University Press, 1996), 1–2. See also Killingsworth, *Walt Whitman and the Earth*.

163. A draft of this poem goes back to 1874. Whitman, *Leaves of Grass*, 178.

164. Killingsworth, *Walt Whitman and the Earth*, 66.

165. Ibid.

Farewell my brethren,
Farewell O earth and sky, farewell ye neighboring waters,
My time has ended, my term has come.

Along the northern coast,
Just back from the rock-bound shore and the caves,
In the saline air from the sea in the Mendocino country,
With the surge base and accompaniment low and hoarse,
With crackling blows of axes sounding musically driven by strong arms,
Riven deep by the sharp tongues of axes, there in the redwood forest dense,
I heard the mighty tree its death-chant chanting.
…
Murmuring out its myriad leaves,
Down from its lofty top rising two hundred feet high,
Out of its stalwart trunk and limbs, out of its foot-thick bark,
That chant of the seasons and time, chant not of the past only but the future.[166]

Reading the lyrics from the perspective of modern-day environmental consciousness, I have to call the idea that nature might agree to its own destruction deeply perverse and only adding to its humiliation. Killingsworth continues: 'Whitman's tree appears as an abstraction, a non-being, an idea that the poet inhabits in order to justify the ways of humans to nature'.[167] The abstraction of the tree is not all that serves to justify the maltreatment of nature. In the following lines, it is possible to read the sequoia prophesying – even welcoming – its own destruction.

Nor yield we mournfully majestic brothers,
We who have grandly fill'd our time;
With Nature's calm content, with tacit huge delight,
We welcome what we wrought for through the past,
And leave the field for them.
For them predicted long,
For a superber race, they too to grandly fill their time,
For them we abdicate, in them ourselves ye forest kings!
In them these skies and airs, these mountains peaks, Shasta, Nevadas,

---

166. Whitman, *Leaves of Grass*, 175. The voice of the tree is in italics. See also: 'From an ecopoetical perspective, the troubles with the poem begin in its reliance on not only old mythological conventions but also traditional poetic language – "myriad leaves", "stalwart trunk and limbs" and "lofty top" – to portray the disappearance of one of the most distinctive natural features of North America'. Killingsworth, *Walt Whitman and the Earth*, 69.
167. Killingsworth, *Walt Whitman and the Earth*, 69.

These huge precipitous cliffs, this amplitude, these valleys, far Yosemite,
To be in them absorb'd, assimilated.

...
Not wan from Asia's fetiches,
Nor red from Europe's old dynastic slaughter-house,
(Area of murder-plots of thrones, with scent left yet of wars and scaffolds
everywhere,)
But come from Nature's long and harmless throes, peacefully builded thence,
Those virgin lands, lands of the Western shore,
To the new culminating man, to you, the empire new,
You promis'd long, we pledge, we dedicate.[168]

In focusing on Whitman's idea of nature's enthusiastic agreement to its own destruction, we should not ignore the even more disturbing element of the 'superber' race:

> Worse yet, the language of the poem – the mention of superior race and assimilation, for example – nods toward the darker side of the manifest destiny, the racist logic that at the time Whitman wrote the poem was used to uproot indigenous peoples from their land so that white settlements could grow and dominate the western United States.[169]

To Killingsworth, the parallel between the redwood tree and (red) Native Americans is plain to see, although it is not clear that Whitman intended such a link. Moreover, Killingsworth argues, the rhetoric of ghostly figures fading from the scene to make room for the 'real people' is a pattern applied repeatedly to native peoples.[170]

In the more critical era of the later twentieth century, the collection of poems that make up *Leaves of Grass*, once venerated for its democratic and egalitarian ideas, were shown to be highly problematic. Native Americans are treated with false sympathy, and instead of being granted their rights and sovereignty they are encouraged to 'melt' into the new culture and allow themselves to be dominated by the 'new race'. The land, or more broadly nature, is portrayed as bountiful, virgin, and wild: the land of promise. It should nonetheless welcome the development of industry, its prospective rapist. What Whitman's poetry does, therefore, is implicitly glorify American progress and mistreatment of both the land and the Native American people. It appears to be a softer, kinder, ostensibly

---

168. Whitman, *Leaves of Grass*, 176.
169. Killingsworth, *Walt Whitman and the Earth*, 69.
170. Ibid., 70–1.

more sympathetic vision of 'managing' the land and the (native) people. Such management is presented as legitimate, even natural, and is accompanied by fine-sounding sentiments which evoke the feeling that it is for the good of both land and people. But it is indeed a dangerous vision. A careful reading, especially where the poetry is at its most fluent, reveals the absence of any true sense of egalitarianism.

F. Scott Fitzgerald

Fitzgerald followed in the wake of a group of authors who had begun to describe the failure of the American dream,[171] a dream which developed naturally from the Puritan heritage of an American elect. Pelzer sums up Fitzgerald's literary vision:

> Fitzgerald responded to the promise inherent in the national myth and lived its contradictions, and his fiction reflects his understanding of it... America, with its vast promise; America, with its high idealism; America, with its bounty and richness; America, a concept defeated before it is begun by the forces of time and human nature; America is Fitzgerald's overarching subject, his greatest theme.[172]

Critics still disagree as to whether Fitzgerald promoted or discredited the American dream. Bloom is persuaded that Fitzgerald could do both in a single novel.[173] It is true that the author's view of his country can appear somewhat ambivalent. Sharp criticism of America and its consumerist society, its carelessness and hypocrisy, stand side by side with huge doses of nostalgia and unconscious adoration of the American project. It would be bold, therefore, to suggest that *The Great Gatsby* is only critical. Reading the novel, we sense that Fitzgerald was both an admirer and a critic of the American dream. In the closing pages, the narrator Nick

---

171. Stephen Matterson, *The Great Gatsby: An Introduction to the Variety of Criticism*, The Critics Debate (London: Macmillan Education, 1990), 2; F. Scott Fitzgerald, *The Great Gatsby*, Wordsworth Editions, Wordsworth Classics 18 (Ware: Wordsworth, 1993), viii. See also: 'The American dream is the ideal of opportunity for all, of an advancement in a career or science without regard to one's origin. The ideal was embodied in Jefferson's "Declaration of Independence" as "Life, Liberty, and the Pursuit of Happiness".' Jackson Bryer, Alan Margolies, and Ruth Prigozy, eds, *F. Scott Fitzgerald: New Perspectives* (Athens, GA: University of Georgia Press, 2000), 25.

172. Pelzer, *Student Companion to F. Scott Fitzgerald*, 33.

173. Harold Bloom, *F. Scott Fitzgerald's The Great Gatsby* (New York: Infobase, 2010), 9.

Carraway reflects upon this ambiguity: 'And as the moon rose higher the inessential houses began to melt away until gradually I became aware of the old island here that flowered once for Dutch sailors' eyes – a fresh, green breast of the new world'.[174] Fitzgerald's narrator is not the only American to slip into such an emotional account of their homeland – here describing the fascination of the first settlers to see the American shore. It is the same for other American writers, and numerous sentimental passages in Steinbeck's novels are far from reflecting a stance of critical distance.

Such distance is nevertheless apparent in other parts of *The Great Gatsby*. It is likely that when writing the novel, Fitzgerald had in mind T. S. Eliot's *The Waste Land*,[175] a poem whose mythical and philosophical background touches upon the theme of the land and its relationship to human beings and which was influential for many twentieth-century American authors.[176]

Eliot's writings were influenced by the social anthropology of James Frazer.[177] Frazer highlighted the narrative of the dying king or dying god which repeats every year as a magical ritual in many animistic religions. The king dies to regenerate the barren land and give rise to the new seedling, a ritual which suggests a close relationship between the land and human beings, whose wellbeing is dependent upon the land. The king must return to the land and re-unite with it. In other words, if the barren land is to be healed, the king must die.[178] The land is healed when the king returns to it because he was first taken from it.[179] In transcendence, therefore, people and the land once again become one and nature is healed. In *The Waste Land*, the king is called the 'son of man', a clear reference to the christological title Son of Man, who 'must undergo great suffering, and be rejected by the elders, the chief priests, and the scribes,

---

174. Fitzgerald, *The Great Gatsby*, 115.

175. Bryer, Margolies, and Prigozy, eds, *F. Scott Fitzgerald*, 3.

176. Matterson, *The Great Gatsby: An Introduction to the Variety of Criticism*.

177. T. S. Eliot, *The Waste Land and Other Poems* (London: Faber & Faber, 1971), 44.

178. Jewel Brooker and Joseph Bentley, *Reading 'The Waste Land': Modernism and the Limits of Interpretation* (Amherst, MA: University of Massachusetts Press, 1990), 66. Also: 'Frazer's dying god is one type of figure referred to; Perceval the questor who must prepare the god or king to die is another type, clearly distinguished from the first because he is only an enabling adjunct to the savior whose death will regenerate the barren land'. Ibid., 58.

179. Gen. 2.7; 3.19.

and be killed, and after three days rise again' (Mk 8.31; Lk. 9.22). The son of man in *The Waste Land* is also destined to die, but unlike the original magical rituals of the dying king and the Christian 'good news of Easter Sunday', the son of man dies and the dream remains unfulfilled.

Eliot's rich symbolism of the land prompted Fitzgerald to address aspects of the American 'waste' land, such as the failure of the institution of marriage. In *The Great Gatsby*, marriage has clearly lost all meaning. All of the characters are unfaithful and even appear proud of their actions. Either that or they have ceased to care as they no longer try to hide anything. The husband of Daisy, the main female character, has a mistress who is also married. To stress the fact of two ruined marriages, Fitzgerald uses a reference to the waste land when the narrator goes to see the mistress:

> I followed [the husband] over a low whitewashed railroad fence, and we walked back a hundred yards along the road under Doctor Eckleburg's persistent stare. The only building in sight was a small block of yellow brick sitting on the edge of the waste land, a sort of compact Main Street ministering to it, and contiguous to absolutely nothing.[180]

One symbolic way to describe the failure of the American dream or the American elect is 'movement eastwards'. The American pioneers, as we saw in Walt Whitman, moved naively and enthusiastically westwards. In *The Great Gatsby*, to highlight the perversion of the dream rooted deeply in the American psyche, it is the East that represents the 'land of enchantment, mystery, and beauty'.[181] Pelzer observes: 'Instead of making their way west to the land of opportunity and promise, the traditional American journey, these Midwesterners go east, seduced by its constant motion that suggests possibility'.[182] Bryer argues that Dan Cody – whose protégé is Gatsby – is a composite of the two great pioneers Daniel Boone and Bill Cody, who stood for freedom, exploration and opportunity, but is actually a negation of them both, a figure of decline: 'Carraway hints that Cody is an unattractive, violent, drunken character, an anachronism, the "pioneer debauchee" who brought back to the Eastern seaboard the savage violence of the frontier brothel and saloon'.[183]

---

180. Fitzgerald, *The Great Gatsby*, 17.
181. Pelzer, *Student Companion to F. Scott Fitzgerald*, 91.
182. Ibid.
183. Bryer, Margolies, and Prigozy, eds, *F. Scott Fitzgerald*, 6.

Fitzgerald's view of America as the land of promise is ambivalent and not unlike that of many of his peers. He undoubtedly criticizes the American dream on every page of *The Great Gatsby*: all the characters, especially Gatsby himself, testify to its failure. But only Gatsby and perhaps Nick Carraway admit that the dream is also a possibility. The other figures, especially Daisy and Jordan and all those who attended Gatsby's parties but did not attend his funeral, were extremely superficial: a harsh caricature of the American dream. This caricature in fact suggests that from the very beginning the dream was either unfulfilled or corrupted and empty – like the characters. Bryer suggests that the American dream failed because it was infected by a lust for success and money. This lust might, however, have been there all along. Fitzgerald does not entirely abandon his sentiments towards his country. The idea of the American elect appears from time to time and lays bear the author's difficulty in overcoming a legacy rooted so deeply in American hearts.

The history of religious communities in the American Episcopal Church

The community of New England Puritans

If one era were to be singled out within the trajectory of the interpretation of the promised land motif from biblical times to John Steinbeck and Walter Brueggemann it is undoubtedly the seventeenth-century settlement of America by the English Puritans.[184] The Puritans left the 'Old Continent' for the New World when their struggle to purify and reform the Church of England from within was ultimately defeated by church officialdom and the rebels were expelled.

The general millennial mood that preceded the English revolt and the formation of the Commonwealth had been shaking both England and the continent ever since the effects of the Reformation had begun to be felt around Europe.[185] As with the rise of national churches during the

---

184. 'Puritanism as a name had first emerged in the 1560s to designate those who wished to purify the practices within the Church of England beyond the degree of reform attained by the bishops, and the name was first attached to those who opposed the retention of ecclesiastical vestments, reminiscent of Rome, and insisted upon the suitability of the plain Geneva gown for the ministry... Puritans would sincerely insist that they were reformers within the Church of England and not a separate group outside of it.' Larzer Ziff, *Puritanism in America: New Culture in a New World* (New York: Viking, 1973), 32.

185. Schulman, *Paradise Lost*, 131–2.

Reformation, so the politics of the English Commonwealth and New England in America began to gain redemptive-historical significance. Politics and religion began to merge,[186] and the settlers from England saw America, specifically New England, as the 'new promised land'.[187]

One of the first English explorers to sail to North America was John Smith, and it was Smith who gave the name New England to what had previously been known as North Virginia. To legitimize the colonization of North America and the cultivation of its natural riches, Smith appealed to the Bible. In the conclusion to his 'A Description of New England', Smith traced the history of human efforts to cultivate the land from Adam and Eve, to Christ, and on to his contemporaries. Although his account was intended to encourage further colonization and to attract more settlers, he did not shy away from describing the hard grind of everyday life in the colony.[188] The territory of New England was far from being a land that promised 'milk and honey'. The harsh climate and difficult soil, the solitude of the farms and the hostile attitude of the native inhabitants made for a far from joyful life.[189] The first settlers called their mission an 'errand into the wilderness' and expected a struggle before the kingdom of God would come down on the earth, to New England. Browne suggests that the word 'wilderness' is neutral: it can be understood as a place of hardship or a place of abundance.[190] It is ultimately a place of challenge which is detached from the world around it; it is a sacred place. In my analysis of Exodus 3, I translated the Hebrew word המדבר as 'wilderness'; the King James Bible translates it 'desert'. 'Wilderness' indeed signifies

186. Sacvan Bercovitch, *The American Jeremiad* (Madison, WI: University of Wisconsin Press, 1978), xiv.

187. '"America", Cotton explained, 'was the new promised land, reserved by God for his new chosen people as the site for a new heaven and a new earth.' Ibid., 8–9.

188. John Smith, 'A Description of New England' (AMS, 1986).

189. According to Ziff, the climate was so harsh and the soil so barren that one of the largest supporters of New England, Lord Saye and Sele, wanted to transfer his colonial interests and monetary support to the more fruitful islands of the West Indies. Ziff, *Puritanism in America*, 82–4.

190. 'The wilderness can be a place of material hardship, hunger, and despair; it can, too, represent a world of natural abundance, fecundity, well-being. And, of course, the colonial Puritans understood these competing senses better than their Old World counterparts – they lived the wilderness, so to speak, and when we refer to the symbolic force of its imagery, we ought in no sense to diminish its material impact on Puritan life. But the wilderness was above all the sacred place, the new Canaan, where God had invited His people to build and hence to transform the world anew.' Stephen Browne, 'Samuel Danforth's Errand into the Wilderness and the Discourse of Arrival in Early American Culture', *Communication Quarterly* 40, no. 2 (1992): 97.

detachment and sacrality, and a challenge, but also a promise of something
new to come. The Puritans used the concept of the wilderness to make
their mission appear new and special but also to ground it in something
with the greatest possible relevance: the biblical model of the ancient
Israelites on their way from slavery in Egypt to the fulfilment of the
promise in Canaan.[191] Thus, Browne explains: 'This process of making
sacred new space is definitive of the Puritan experience: as they transformed the wilderness of America into a new Canaan, they literally and
symbolically put behind them the profane, the Old, England'.[192]

In *The Province of Piety*, an exploration of the historical novels of
Nathaniel Hawthorne, Michael Colacurcio rightly points out the differences between the various groups and generations of settlers in New
England, distinguishing between the first generation Pilgrim Fathers and
the Puritans of the second and subsequent generations. While the pioneers
emphasized faith in God's grace, later generations began to reckon more
on good works. Colacurcio describes this slow progress from grace to
law[193] and the gradual 'institutionalization' of what had begun as the
theoretical Bible-based laws of the newly established theocratic state of
New England:

> From the very beginning of his treatment of the Puritans, then, Hawthorne
> goes straight to one of the most important problems of New England's
> history: the problem of discovering and enforcing the will of God with
> instruments that are invincingly natural; and more largely, the relation
> between nature and grace.[194]

191. 'The new phenomenon of colonization is to be seen as God making a way.'
Ziff, *Puritanism in America*, 37.

192. Browne, 'Samuel Danforth's Errand into the Wilderness', 93. See also:
'The most typical Puritan colonial appeal spoke centrally of the probability of the
settler's improving himself materially, and surrounded this attractive proposition with
a justification of the legality of migration. The justification went first to the Bible.'
Ziff, *Puritanism in America*, 41. And: 'The Old Testament character of Puritanism in
New England, frequently noted and commented upon, stems from its emergence out
of the sect ideal into one of the holy commonwealth. Apologists who lived through
the shift were to rely on a rhetoric of analogy between their migration and that of
Abraham. What had been described in propaganda addressed to would-be settlers as
a removal for the sake of liberty of ordinances, economic improvement, and national
welfare, came in such apologetics to be described as the calling forth of a chosen
people.' Ibid., 80.

193. Michael Colacurcio, *The Province of Piety: Moral History in Hawthorne's
Early Tales* (Durham, NC: Duke University Press, 1995).

194. Ibid., 62.

The gradual institutionalization of the Puritans' idealistic and largely naive view of the 'Kingdom of Heaven on Earth' in New England went hand in hand with the religious fundamentalism and mass hysteria that resulted in the dark episode of the Salem witch trials (1692–1693). Today, the trials are generally regarded as signifying the failure of the principles of the new theocracy. We described a similar process of 'unhealthy institutionalization' in the discussion on Deuteronomistic theology and its view of the corruption of the monarchy. The institutionalized and legally enforced religious fundamentalism of the later Puritans does not immediately appear to resemble the idolatry of the Israelites under the monarchy, but the two communities were equally guilty of acts of 'faithlessness'. A late reaction to the New England Puritans' journey 'from grace to law' came in the shape of the Great Awakening, which broke out almost a century later in 1720 and lasted until 1742. One of the chief protagonists was the intellectually gifted Puritan minister, philosopher, theologian, and missionary Jonathan Edwards. In November 1734, Edwards delivered a series of sermons entitled 'Justification on Faith Alone' in which he condemned the 'terror of the law' from which no one could ever be redeemed by their good works; redemption was to be found only in the endless grace of God.[195]

We should keep in mind that Puritan hermeneutics were those of 'literal parallelism' or a 'typology' between biblical and contemporary events,[196] and represented a continuation of the hermeneutics and theology of John Calvin.[197] The name New England is used interchangeably with new Canaan, the promised land, or even the new Eden. The term 'errand into the wilderness' refers of course to the wandering of the Israelites on their way from Egypt to Canaan, but also to the voice of the prophet Elijah 'calling in the wilderness'. It could also refer to Moses' 'errand *beyond* the wilderness' to Mount Horeb (Exod 3:1), the place of theophany. In the language of Dante's medieval visions, wandering in the wilderness is also a time of purification, a time when the human soul dwells in purgatory. Samuel Danforth adapted the same concept for the seventeenth-century Puritan discourse and spoke of John the Baptist 'calling in the wilderness' for people to repent.[198]

195. Jonathan Edwards, *Sermons and Discourses, 1720–1723*, ed. Wilson H. Kimnach, The Works of Jonathan Edwards 10 (New Haven, CT: Yale University Press, 1992).

196. Browne, 'Samuel Danforth's Errand into the Wilderness', 99.

197. Ziff, *Puritanism in America*, 27.

198. Samuel Danforth, 'A Brief Recognition of New-England's Errand into the Wilderness: Made in the Audience of the General Assembly of the Massachusetts

Referring to New England as the new Canaan made the people who crossed the ocean to settle there the new Israelites, God's chosen people: the 'elect'.[199] Schulman suggests that the idea of the 'elect' American (i.e. English) settlers as God's chosen people dates back to Tudor England[200] and the formation of the Church of England as an offshoot of the Reformation in Europe. The English millennials who advocated the Commonwealth believed their system to be the only progressive step forward. To follow the model of the ancient Israelites – before they became corrupted and demanded that a king rule over them – it was necessary to overthrow the monarch and have God the only true king as ruler. They would then be the true heirs of the Israelites; the New Englanders, Schulman argues, believed themselves the true heirs of the English 'elect'.[201] The English had lost this claim after the suppression of the Commonwealth movement and the return of the monarchy. Sacvan Bercovitch, a researcher in American literature and specifically the Puritan legacy, agrees with Schulman that the Puritans in America saw their fellows in England as pitiful apostates from the true path to the kingdom of God.[202]

The Puritan minister John Winthrop sailed for New England in 1630. While still on board the *Arbella* (or *Arabella*), he preached about the election of the settlers of New England. In his well-known sermon 'A Model of Christian Charity', Winthrop transfers the biblical concept of a 'city upon a hill' to the New England context and adopts all aspects of the Jewish election for the New Englanders:

> For we must consider that we shall be as a 'city upon a hill'. The eyes of all people are upon us, so that if we shall deal falsely with our God in this work we have undertaken, and so cause Him to withdraw His present help from us, we shall be made a story and a byword through the world; we shall open the mouths of enemies to speak evil of the ways of God and all professors

Colony at Boston in N.E. on the 11th of the Third Month, 1670, Being the Day of Election There by Samuel Danforth' (printed by S.G. and M.J. in Cambridge, Massachusetts, 1671).

199. Ziff, *Puritanism in America*, 28.

200. Schulman, *Paradise Lost*, 132.

201. 'Milton showed a similar sense of millennial optimism and national election in his view of the special role of England in the continuing reformation of the church. The motif of the chosen nation, which had its roots in the Tudor period, was epitomized in Milton's patriotic declaration that it was God's manner to reveal himself "first to his Englishmen".' Ibid., 132.

202. 'Puritans in New England saw themselves to be on the better way towards the better England; after the re-establishment of the monarchy, they were isolated and abandoned.' Bercovitch, *The American Jeremiad*, 5.

> for God's sake; we shall shame the faces of many of God's worthy servants,
> and cause their prayers to be turned into curses upon us till we be consumed
> out of the good land whither we are going.[203]

The election of the New Englanders is therefore twofold: they are God's special people and all merits arising from God's election are included in their blessing; but they have a difficult task to fulfil, having been sent by God to convert the people and prepare for the arrival of the kingdom of God.[204] In addition, the typological comparison between the settlement of the New World and the history of salvation began to include comparisons between the people involved in the two narratives. Jeremiah, Nehemiah, and Ezra – the prophets of exile and return – play a key role in the sermons of the New Englanders. Like Jeremiah, John the Baptist is a prophet used typologically for the call to repentance and was also a core figure in the Puritan legacy in New England.[205] Winthrop himself, Schulman suggests, began to merge with the figure of Nehemiah, 'the prophet of return'.[206]

Jeremiah, the prophet of exile, return, and the call to repentance and conversion, gave his name to the political and apocalyptic-millennial 'Jeremiad' sermons that became popular in Puritan America. Jeremiads had their predecessors in English sermons from the fifteenth and sixteenth centuries and were common in the Middle Ages.[207] The New England

---

203. John Winthrop, 'A Model of Christian Charity. Reader's Edition', ed. John Uebersax (2014), http://www.john-uebersax.com/pdf/John%20Winthrop%20-%20 Model%20of%20Christian%20Charity%20v1.01.pdf

204. 'Experience later modified the theory, but this implicit yoking together of social identity and the claim to election became a cornerstone of the American jeremiad. One of its most remarkable aspects is the expansion of Cotton's and Winthrop's ambiguities into a cultural commonplace. Over and again the colonial Jeremiahs portray the settlers as a people of God in terms of election, the body politic, and the advancing army of Christ.' Bercovitch, *The American Jeremiad*, 46.

205. Ibid., 14.

206. 'The rhetoric of the New England Puritans, like Milton's, was pervaded by such typological habits of thought, through which historical individuals and events were related to the scheme of redemptive history. Thus, Winthrop's biographer Cotton Mather represented the first governor of Massachusetts as a type of Nehemiah, the prophet of the return, who led the Israelites back from Babylon to the Promised Land.' Schulman, *Paradise Lost*, 133.

207. Bercovitch, *The American Jeremiad*, 6, 33–4. Also: 'It is precisely this effort to fuse sacred and profane that shapes the American jeremiads. Their threats of doom, derived from Christian tradition, imply a distinction between the two realms; their language itself, expressing their special sense of mission, incorporates the threats within the broader framework of the absolute.' Ibid., 29.

minister Increase Mather used the title *Jeremiads* for one of his collections of exhortations.[208]

According to Bercovitch, there are two aspects to jeremiads: theology espouses politics; and the country's politics is directed towards the establishment of the kingdom of God.[209] Despite these similarities between the American jeremiads and the political sermons of the Middle Ages, there are also certain differences. Where the sermons of the Middle Ages ended in a dark hopeless apocalypse and the torments of hell, the American jeremiads saw the promised kingdom of God coming down from heaven to New England:

> In explicit opposition to the traditional mode, it inverts the doctrine of vengeance into a promise of ultimate success, affirming to the world, and despite the world, the inviolability of the colonial cause... Theirs was a peculiar mission, they explained, for they were 'peculiar people', a company of Christians not only called but chosen, and chosen not only for heaven but as instruments of a sacred historical design. Their church-state was to be at once a model to the world of Reformed Christianity and a prefiguration of the New Jerusalem to come. To this end, they revised the message of the jeremiad.[210]

The Puritans were not of course settling a wilderness – the land was inhabited. To the typological comparisons between New England and Canaan and the New Englanders and the Israelites must therefore be added the unfortunate comparison between the Canaanites and the Native Americans,[211] a comparison which caused the bloodshed of the 'Indian Wars' and continues to heap stigma on Native Americans to this day. Despite the 'inferior state' of the Native Americans in the eyes of the New Englanders, they were initially approached in a less openly hostile manner,[212] but were still nonetheless treated as 'not other human beings' and 'not people',[213] whose culture and religion were completely dismissed. The settlers did not respect the Native Americans and regarded them as wild and pitiful creatures who deserved sympathy because they

208. Increase Mather, *Jeremiads*, ed. Sacvan Bercovitch, Library of American Puritan Writings 20 (New York: AMS, 1984).
209. Ibid., xiv.
210. Ibid., 7–8.
211. Increase Mather, 'An Earnest Exhortation to the Inhabitants of New England (1676)', ed. Reiner Smolinski, *Electronic Texts in American Studies*, no. 31 (1676): 15.
212. Ziff, *Puritanism in America*, 42.
213. Mather, 'An Earnest Exhortation', 3.

did not know the only God and the Messiah Jesus Christ. In a show of apparent good will, the settlers sought to convert them to save them from the torments of hell, but as time passed and it became clear that not all the Native Americans would convert to Christianity (and serve the settlers), things began to turn ugly. According to God's plan for the new Israelites, these 'new Canaanites' must be annihilated.[214] In his description of the Pequot War, Ziff is at pains to stress the true intention of the Puritans: to exterminate the whole tribe.[215] The Puritans hit on a winning strategy which involved all the settlements in New England uniting against the Native American tribes, which were, on the contrary, to remain divided.[216] Here, Ziff describes the war with the Mohegans:

> But English war, the Mohegans learned that day, was not symbolic and exemplary of the superior art of the victor; it was massive and aimed at annihilation. The English imagination pictured the Indian as bloodthirsty because he fought by stealth and cut down the weaker at the perimeter while attempting to avoid direct confrontation with the full military power of his enemy. The Indians now came to see the English as incredibly furious, bent on the kill at the expense of all else.[217]

Prominent among the early settlers was the Puritan minister and author John Cotton, who fled England to avoid persecution for his progressive ideas about the Church of England, which he saw as being too close to the Catholic Church. One of Cotton's most important works was the treatise 'An Abstract of the Lawes of New England', which reveals the New Englanders' ambition to build a colony based on the legal code of the nomadic community of ancient Israel. Cotton's numerous literary

214. Ibid.

215. 'The Pequot War had called forth in its most vigorous form the Puritan culture's sense of itself as an armed band of the Lord... For the Puritans the war came very rapidly to be a matter not of capturing and executing the Pequots who had committed criminal acts, but of exterminating the tribe altogether... The Puritan colonists, however, wanted the very lives of the entire tribe... More than a hundred men, women and children were killed. An entire tribe was obliterated.' Ziff, *Puritanism in America*, 90–1.

216. 'The slaughter that took place on that day in May 1637 taught the Puritans that a united policy...would succeed not only because of the superior force it could bring to a war but also because it prevented the various settlements from working at cross purposes in allying with certain tribes in order to discipline the others. With their economic value sinking into insignificance, the Indians were now to be considered primarily in terms of their military value, and the Puritans must keep them divided in order to procure their aid, on one hand, and to defeat them, on the other.' Ibid.

217. Ibid., 92.

works gained such a reputation that he started to be called the 'patriarch of New England'.[218] The 'Abstract' was written to give legal order to the 'theocratic state' of New England, whose only head was God.[219] The treatise was practical, however, and dealt with questions of everyday life. All of the orders and requirements were footnoted and referenced to specific verses from the Bible.[220] There is a clear resemblance between Cotton's legal system and the biblical model. Everything was to be created according to the model of ancient Israel, including the orders regarding war, which were as important for the English settlers as they had been for the ancient Israelites. Now, the 'Canaanites' of New England were standing in the way of God's plan for a new Israel to create a new Canaan.

The American Episcopal community of later centuries

The idea of the 'elect' is firmly set in the minds of many twentieth-century Americans, if only unconsciously. It is no surprise, therefore, that such a mindset had a huge influence on the community in which both Steinbeck and Brueggemann grew up, the American Episcopal Church of the nineteenth and twentieth centuries. Loughlin observes that it is the symbols, archetypes, and stories from the Bible which appeal most to any community of believers.[221] The interest of non-theologians, whether novelists or their readers, is thus oriented not towards one particular Bible verse but towards the motif or narrative that is influenced by it. Keeping Steinbeck and Brueggemann in mind, this section will seek out the motif of the promised land as it appears in the prayers, hymns, pericopes, and lectionary of the American Episcopal Church, thereby tracing any possible influences on their respective works.

The Book of Common Prayer

The *Book of Common Prayer for the Use of the American Episcopal Church* includes prayers that clearly resonate with the idea of America as the promised land, a special land given to the fathers of the American nation. We find an emphasis on the 'free gift' and the 'inheritance' of the land in the sense of Gen. 15.7, and on the 'fruitfulness' and 'bounty' of

---

218. John Davenport and Samuel Whiting, 'The Life of Mr. John Cotton', in *The New England Way*, ed. John Cotton, Library of American Puritan Writings 12 (New York: AMS), 3–6.

219. The final lines of the 'Abstract' read: 'The Lord is our Judge, The Lord is our Law-Giver, The Lord is our King, He will save us. Isay 33.22'. John Cotton, 'An Abstract of the Lawes of New England', in Cotton, ed., *The New England Way*, 17.

220. Ibid.

221. Gerard Loughlin, *Telling God's Story: Bible, Church and Narrative Theology* (Cambridge: Cambridge University Press, 1996), 19.

the land referred to in Exod. 3.8. America was understood as the promised
land both in the territorial-political sense and in the sense of a piece of
'one's own promised land' and the longing that goes with it. The new
promised land in America was the rightful heritage of the settlers as the
true heirs of the promises made to the ancient Israelites.

The prayer entitled 'A Prayer for the President of the United States,
and All in Civil Authority' reflects the political and legal realm of the
promised land in America and emphasizes the 'theocratic' legacy of the
American republic.

> ALMIGHTY God, whose kingdom is everlasting and power infinite, Have
> mercy upon this whole land; and so rule the hearts of thy servants THE
> PRESIDENT OF THE UNITED STATES, the Governor of this state, and all
> others in authority, that they, knowing whose ministers they are, may above
> all things seek thy honour and glory; and that we and all the People, duly
> considering whose authority they bear... Amen.[222]

The prayer, written not for official state ceremonies but for the liturgy
of the church, suggests a special bond between God and the land of the
United States, whose officials, the presidents and state governors, were
called to be God's servants and ministers, directly subordinated to God,
as befitted the 'theocratic colony' of New England.[223]

The 'Prayer for Our Country' blends the political and legal realm with
the paradisiacal vision of a 'good land' 'flowing with milk and honey'.

> ALMIGHTY God, who hast given us this good land for our heritage; We
> humbly beseech thee that we may always prove ourselves a people mindful
> of thy favour and glad to thy will. Bless our land with honourable industry,
> sound learning, and pure manners... Amen.[224]

The prayer includes allusions to verses in the Bible that refer to the
promise of land: the giving of the land;[225] a good land;[226] the land as an

---

222. *The Book of Common Prayer and Administration of the Sacraments and
Other Rites and Ceremonies of the Church according to the Use of the Protestant
Episcopal Church in the United States of America Together with the Psalter or
Psalms of David* (New York: James Pott, 1892), 27–8.

223. Cotton, 'An Abstract of the Lawes of New England', 17.

224. *Book of Common Prayer* 1929, 36.

225. Schmid, 'ארץ', 177–8. See Gen. 12.7; 13.15; 15.7, 13, 18; 17.8; 21.23; 24.7;
26.3-4; 28.4; 35.12; 48.4; Deut. 1.8, 35; 6.10, 18, 23; 7.13; 8.1; 9.28; 10.11; 11.9, 21;
19.8; 26.3, 15; 27.3; 28.11; 31.7.

226. Ibid., 177. See Deut. 1.25, 35; 3.25; 4.21, 22; 6.18, etc.; Exod. 3.8; Num.
14.7; 1 Chron. 28.18.

inheritance.[227] The agreement between God and the people is bilateral, and the people know they are expected to act in accordance with God's will.

The bidding prayer below represents the sense of the 'new elect' of the American people. Many Americans, consciously or unconsciously, believed themselves special people living in a special land and in receipt of special promises from God.

> GOOD Christian People, I bid your prayers for Christ's holy Catholic Church, the blessed company of faithful people; that it may please God to confirm and strengthen it in purity of faith, in holiness of life, and in perfectness of love, and to restore to it the witness of visible unity; and more specially for that branch of the same planted by God in this land, whereof we are members; that in all things it may work accordingly to God's will, serve him faithfully, and worship him acceptably... Amen.[228]

The prayer suggests God's special treatment of the people of the United States. American Christians of the nineteenth and twentieth centuries continued in their Puritan fathers' belief that they had a closer relationship to God and a more prominent place in the worldwide church than did Christians from other parts of the world; that God had a special agreement with them, one of the most significant elements of which was the land; that they were God's new elect, God's new Israel.[229] The expression 'planted by God in this land' references their unquestioning faith in the legitimacy of their dwelling in the land: the land is theirs, and the land is sacred. The prayer again reflects an awareness of the bilateral nature of the agreement. God asks from his people something in return: those who enjoy God's promises are bound to obey his laws.

Like the prayer above, the 'Collect for Independence Day' alludes to God's new elect, the new Israelites in the new promised land of America:

> O ETERNAL God, through whose mighty power our fathers won their liberties of old; Grant, we beseech thee, that we and all the people of this land may have grace to maintain these liberties in righteousness and peace; through Jesus Christ our Lord. Amen.[230]

227. Ottoson, 'ארץ', 401. See Gen. 15.7; 1 Sam. 26.19; 2 Sam. 14.16; Pss. 68.10(9); 79.1; Jer. 2.7; 16.18; 50.11.
228. *Book of Common Prayer* 1929, 47.
229. Ziff, *Puritanism in America*, 28.
230. *Book of Common Prayer* 1929, 263.

The prayer carries a clear allusion to the events of the exodus.[231] The 'liberties of old' could refer to the promises to Abraham and the patriarchs and to Moses:[232] God took the people out of oppression and slavery in Egypt and brought them to Canaan, the promised land. Explicitly, the liberties of old refer to the Puritan fathers who built the colonies in the New World, and to the founders of the American republic who won independence from Britain: God took the settlers out of oppression and political and religious insecurity in England and brought them to America, the new Canaan, the new promised land. Later, with independence, came the completion of God's redemptive work with the new Israel. The prayer bears a sense of the special status of the settlers. The reference to 'all the people of this land' does not necessarily include the Native Americans.

The Hymnal

Many of the hymns and songs in the Episcopalian hymnal are similar in tone to the prayers in the *Book of Common Prayer*. The hymn 'For Missions to the New Settlements in the United States' refers to the 'wandering fathers' and, by allusion, to Danforth's 'errand into the wilderness', which as we have seen is suggestive of the opportunities but also the challenges and hardships that faced the settlers in the New World. As with the Puritans, however, the tone of later interpretations in the hymns demonstrates the people's positive attitude to the challenges and their faith that the opportunities would outweigh the hardships.

> 1. WHEN, Lord, to this our western land,
> Led by thy providential hand,
> Our wandering fathers came.
> Their ancient homes, their friends in youth,
> Sent forth the herald of thy truth,
> To keep them in thy name.
>
> 2. Then through our solitary coast,
> The desert features soon were lost;
> Thy temples there arose;
> Our shores, as culture made them fair,
> Were hallowed by their rites, by prayer,
> And blossomed as the rose.

---

231. See Exod. 3.7-8.
232. Gen. 12.7; 13.15, 17; 15.5, 18; 17.8; 18.19; 21.1; 24.7; 26.3-4; 28.15; 35.12; 47.49; 48.4; 50.24; Exod. 3.8, etc.

3. And O may we repay this debt
To regions solitary yet
Within our spreading land:
There, brethren, from our common home,
Still westward, like our fathers, roam;
Still guided by thy hand.[233]

The first and the third verses of this hymn allude to the settlement both of North America by the Puritans and of the promised land by the Israelites; the author assumes that both of these events were led by the powerful hand of God.[234] The reference to the 'wandering fathers' again alludes both to the first settlers in the New World and to the Israelites on their way to the promised land. The song suggests great enthusiasm regarding the new explorations and urges a continuation westward to settle and cultivate what was seen as virgin, uninhabited land.

The hymn 'Blessed is the Nation Whose God is the Lord' refers to the Americans' identity as inhabitants of a unique land.

1. GOD bless our native land!
Firm may she ever stand,
Through storm and night;
When the wild tempests rave,
Ruler of winds and wave,
Do thou our country save
By thy great might.

2. For her our prayer shall rise
To God, above the skies;
On him we wait;
Thou who art ever nigh
Guarding with watchful eye,
To thee aloud we cry,
God save the state![235]

The hymn is dedicated to a particular kind of people: to the people of 'this' (American) land for whom 'God is the Lord', and to whom belongs a special blessing. The hymn also highlights the connection between the

---

233. *Hymnal According to the Use of the Protestant Episcopal Church in the United States of America* (New York: James Pott, 1874), 231–2.

234. See Gen. 12; 15; 17; Exod. 3; 6.

235. *Hymnal*, 244.

legacies of Gen. 15.7 and Exod. 3.8, which becomes clear at the end of
the second verse where 'land' is replaced by 'state'.

The 'Peace Hymn of the Republic' is not in the Episcopal hymn
book. It was written by the famous American poet Henry Van Dyke and
combines socio-political aspects with a utopian, paradisiacal view of the
land.

> Lord, our God, Thy mighty hand
> Hath made our country free;
> From all her broad and happy land
> May praise arise to Thee.
> Fulfil the promise of her youth,
> Her liberty defend;
> By law and order, love and truth,
> America befriend![236]

The hymn celebrates the new republic and its independence from
Britain. It assumes the roots of the United States lie in God's leading
the forefathers out of the land of oppression and into the land of promise
that he gave to them. It is another allusion, therefore, to the parallel
between the settlement of North America by the English Puritans and
the settlement of Canaan by the Israelites. The phrase 'promise of her
youth' refers to the young American nation.

The Lectionary

The lectionary of the American Episcopal Church shows which biblical
books were especially read in the given time horizon. It is an important
source of influence for both John Steinbeck and Walter Brueggemann and
any of their predecessors who were members of their religious interpretive
community and the tradition of the American Episcopal Church.

The prescribed pericopes of the lectionary include all the verses we
have found significant for our theme: Gen. 15.1-19 is a set reading for
the Second Sunday after Trinity;[237] Gen. 17.1-15, a verse of particular
significance for Brueggemann, is set for the Feast of the Circumcision
of Jesus.[238] Exodus 3 is mentioned as a parallel text for the main texts of

---

236. M. Durham, *Methodist Hymn Book*, http://www.ccel.org/ccel/walker/harmony2.H51.html?

237. *Book of Common Prayer* 1892, ix. See also First Friday after Epiphany in the 1929 edition: *Book of Common Prayer* 1929, xii.

238. *Book of Common Prayer* 1892, x. See also Second Monday after Epiphany in the 1929 edition: *Book of Common Prayer* 1929, xiii.

Genesis 15 and Genesis 17. However, as a text which refers to the bounty of the promised land, it is a possible source of influence for the prayers and hymns which refer to the bounty of America. The text is prescribed for the Sixth Sunday after Trinity.[239]

239. *Book of Common Prayer* 1892, ix. See also Second Sunday after Epiphany in the 1929 edition: *Book of Common Prayer* 1929, xiii.

Chapter 4

INTERPRETATIONS OF THE PROMISED LAND MOTIF
BY WALTER BRUEGGEMANN
AND JOHN STEINBECK

The American Protestant scholar and church minister Walter Brueggemann has made the promise and loss of land the backbone of his theology:
'Land is a central, if not the central theme of biblical faith'.[1] Author of the
ground-breaking *The Land* which triggered a flood of other writings on
the subject,[2] Brueggemann is a natural successor to Gottwald and a fitting
endpoint to the trajectory of the reception of the promised land.

The promise and loss of land is no less significant a theme for John
Steinbeck,[3] heir to and passionate critic of the American dream, and
the novelist whose works I will present as artistic interpretations of our
biblical theme. Such interpretations offer biblical scholars a broader and
brighter insight into biblical themes and narratives and are worthy of
much closer attention. Steinbeck is a representative of the political and
literary stream of Jefferson agrarianism, which fused the political sphere
with the religious identity of American Protestantism, including the
American Episcopal Church, and which illustrates the central role played
by the motif of the promised land in American culture.[4] It is essential to

1. Brueggemann, *The Land*, 3.
2. Norman Habel and Walter Brueggemann, *The Land Is Mine: Six Biblical
Land Ideologies*, Overtures to Biblical Theology (Minneapolis, MN: Fortress, 1995);
Frankel, *The Land of Canaan and the Destiny of Israel*; Burge, *Jesus and the Land*.
3. 'The newcomers were of peasant stock, and they had their roots in a Europe
where they had been landless... In America they found beautiful and boundless land
for the taking – and they took it... They cut and burned the forests to make room for
crops; they abandoned their knowledge of kindness to the land in order to maintain its
usefulness.' John Steinbeck, *America and Americans* (New York: Bantam, 1968), 146.
4. 'In short, the place America had long promised to be, ever since the first
explorers declared themselves virtually "ravish with the pleasant land" and described

stress at this point that although Steinbeck was certainly influenced by popular national tradition, he always had his Bible to hand when writing his novels.[5]

Steinbeck and Brueggemann approach the promised land motif in ways that correspond to their respective occupations – Steinbeck the novelist and Brueggemann the Hebrew Bible scholar and minister of the church – but their interpretations bear striking similarities. Brueggemann often confesses the influence on him of Steinbeck's novels:

> It may be that John Steinbeck has put the issue most eloquently. He has presented two stories of the dispossessed. In *Of Mice and Men*, Lennie holds to a vision which keeps him functioning. 'We could live offa the fatta the lan'. He lives while he holds to that hope. When that hope is gone, he is a despairing exile. More fully, *Grapes of Wrath* is a story, as true today, about dispossessed exiles. Two lines can serve as our conclusion. First, as they set off from Oklahoma, Pa is sick atop the truck which holds all their belongings. (Exiles travel light.) Pa cannot bear to leave the land because 'Pa is the land'… Second, when they arrive in California, they seek a place to settle. Like Israelites come to Canaan they find that all the land is occupied… The Steinbeck picture parallels the tractored land of Pharaoh and Solomon in which there is enormous prosperity but the dispossessed never enter history and never share in the prosperity. They die and they disappear.[6]

the new continent as a Paradise with all her Virgin Beauties.' Kolodny, *The Lay of the Land*, 4. Also: 'Eden, Paradise, the Golden Age, and the idyllic garden, in short all the backdrops for European literary pastoral, were subsumed in the image of an America promising material ease without labor or hardship, as opposed to the grinding poverty of previous European existence; a frank, free affectional life in which all might share in a primal and non-competitive fraternity; a resurrection of the lost state of innocence that the adult abandons when he joins the world of competitive self-assertion; and all this is possible because, at the deepest psychological level, the move to America was experienced as the daily reality of what has become its single dominating metaphor: regression from the cares of adult life and return to the primal warmth of womb or breast in a feminine landscape.' Ibid., 6.

5. 'The imagery and implications of Pilgrim's Progress were very real to him, and the image of stern grandfather (a memory he could not have possibly had) reading solemnly and with all finality from the Bible came back periodically to haunt him.' Benson, *The True Adventures of John Steinbeck, Writer*, 20. See also: 'The boy became an avid reader, especially of the Bible, Milton's *Paradise Lost*, Dostoevsky, Flaubert, George Eliot, and Thomas Hardy'. Warren French, *John Steinbeck* (Boston, MA: Twayne, 1975), 21.

6. Brueggemann, *The Land*, 207–8.

Brueggemann quotes the two novels which he sees as offering insightful interpretations of the motif of the promised land. The question is, does Steinbeck bring not only an innovative approach to interpreting the Scriptures but also new themes for interpretation and new insights worthy of discussion?

Brueggemann's interpretation of the promised land motif

Brueggemann entered the discussion on the promised land with the key work *The Land* (1977). Placing the land at the very centre of theological interest undoubtedly provoked much discussion around possession and ownership of land and in more recent times a rethinking of these concepts in postcolonial and liberation theologies in all corners of the world.[7] Brueggemann had indeed released the genie from the bottle, not knowing what would follow. Brueggemann's original need to come to terms with the issue of the land was of course motivated by his American heritage. Observing the development of 'land research' as the years progressed, he pushed himself to revise *The Land*, republishing it in 2003 with an extensive preface in which he acknowledges liberation and postcolonial studies of this issue. Two of Brueggemann's more recent articles, 'The God of Joshua... Give or Take the Land' (2012) and 'Reading the Bible amid the Israeli–Palestinian Conflict' (2016), demonstrate his consuming passion to free himself from dangerous ideologies. Brueggemann's work is influential and thought-provoking in many respects. In this chapter, I will explore his fascination with land, his concept of landlessness and landedness, and his critique of the ideologies that tend to infuse and infect promised land ideology.

The land as symbol and fascinans

Brueggemann claims that a longing for land has always been, and probably always will be, a natural and constitutional phenomenon among human beings. In centuries past, land was the people's immediate provider and people were only too conscious of their dependence upon it. Although we remain dependent on the land, we are now less aware of this dependence as it has become less immediate. Brueggemann suggests

---

7. Norman Habel in Australia, Gary Burge in Israel/Palestine, Sugirtharajah in India. Although the fields of ideology critique, liberation theology, and postcolonialism share many common aims and goals, and the champions of one enter debates with their colleagues and counterparts from the other two, I will nonetheless stick to the basic terminological differentiation that I present later in this chapter.

our current longing for land is motivated by the failure of the great urban project: '[A] sense of place is a human hunger which the urban promise has not met'.[8] Land also has a prominent place in the Bible. For Brueggemann, the promise of land is the primary category of faith: 'It is land that provides the central assurance to Israel of its historicality, that it will be and always must be concerned with actual rootage in a place which is a repository for commitment and therefore identity'.[9] In his review of the original edition of *The Land*, Thomas Mann appreciates Brueggemann's attention to both the physical and the symbolic dimensions of the land, but criticizes him for not making enough of the distinction between the two. Mann also disagrees with Brueggemann's intertwining of the garden of Eden and the Land of Canaan,[10] but we have seen such a conflation during the whole history of the reception of the promised land motif, whether discussing the Puritans, twentieth-century American authors, or earlier authors such as Dante and the Reformers.

A fascination with the land and a tendency to see a close connection between the American attitude towards both the physical earth and the symbolic dimension is prominent throughout Brueggemann's work. This fascination also shines a light on his need to reconcile his conscience with America's colonial history, a history written with the promise of a land flowing with milk and honey, but a land for the elect only.

With one eye on remaining accessible to his readers, Brueggemann occasionally presents the parallel between the settlement of Canaan and the settlement of North America and the challenges the latter brought to his fellow countrymen: 'The identity questions must all be addressed again. And we are only beginning that task in the newly landed America. As Israel, we take our new identity vis-à-vis the land.'[11] For Brueggemann, the leading argument in promised land theology is the tension between landlessness and landedness, which both have the potential to be

---

8. Brueggemann, *The Land*, 4.

9. Ibid., 5. See also: 'Land is a defining theme in Old Testament tradition. For that reason, one cannot consider the faith of the Old Testament or the God of the Old Testament without at the same time being concerned with socioeconomic analysis, for land is not just a "good idea," but actual real estate that evokes and hosts profound hope, imaginative social policy, deep moral conflict, savage acts of violence, and acute communal disappointment.' Walter Brueggemann, *Reverberations of Faith: A Theological Handbook of Old Testament Themes* (Louisville, KY: Westminster John Knox, 2002), 120.

10. Thomas Mann, review of *The Land: Place as Gift, Promise, and Challenge in Biblical Faith*, by Walter Brueggemann, *Theology Today* 35, no. 2 (1978): 218.

11. Brueggemann, *The Land*, 45.

transformed into the other: 'The central learning about the land motif which has come out of this study [*The Land*] is that grasping for home leads to homelessness and risking homelessness yields the gift of home'.[12] Landed people, Brueggemann argues, must always remember to treat the land as a gift, not as a given; the land must serve as an arena for freedom and justice and not be misused by officials, sovereigns, or any other deputies.

Brueggemann in fact recognizes the land as a symbol that reflects the relationship between YHWH and YHWH's people and corresponds to the dynamics of faithfulness (the promise of land) and falling away from YHWH (the loss of land).[13] This dynamic runs as a golden thread throughout *The Land*, linking the various narratives concerning God's dealing with the people of Israel:

> The dialectic in Israel's fortunes between landlessness (wilderness, exile) and landedness, the latter either as possession of the land, as anticipation of the land, or as grief about loss of the land; it was on that basis that my argument in the book took shape, all aspects of land being referred to the God of covenant Torah.[14]

Mann criticizes Brueggemann for using 'land' as a catch-all term for matters of different kinds and different values, which suggests that Mann is either unable or unwilling to accept Brueggemann's rhetoric and to see the land as a symbol; Brueggemann clearly devotes ample space to arguing why he brings the land, human beings, and the relationship between the two under the same umbrella.

Brueggemann narrates an ongoing dynamic between the promise and loss of land: between being in the land, controlling it, celebrating it, and exploiting it, and being landless, enslaved, exploited, and in mourning. The former state is attributed fully to God's faithfulness to and care for the chosen people; the latter state is the fault of no one but an unfaithful

---

12. Ibid., 202.

13. 'Not only is the nation physically separated from its land when it is carried into exile, but in the prophetic denunciation of current ills and predictions of coming judgement as well, the land figures prominently as the sphere of God's punishment on a wayward people. Image clusters include pollution, blighting and drought, and we can detect an analogy in this fall from grace to the original expulsion from the Garden of Eden.' Ryken, ed., 'Land', 487. See also: 'The theme of Israel's relationship to its land is clearly pivotal, holding a central place within the overall structure of the narrative of the Hebrew Bible'. Frankel, *The Land of Canaan and the Destiny of Israel*, 1.

14. Brueggemann, *The Land*, xi–xii. See also: 'As a land of promise, the land of Canaan becomes an evocative image of the longing of the Israelites as they journey toward it'. Leland Ryken, 'Promised Land', in *Dictionary of Biblical Imagery*, 666.

people.[15] For Brueggemann, the immediate continuation of this dynamic between the promise and loss of land is slavery in Egypt and the deliverance rhetoric of the book of Exodus in Exod. 3.7-8.

> Time after time, Israel saw the land of promise became the land of problem... But Israel's experience is of being in and belonging to a land never fully given, never quite secured. And its destiny vis-à-vis the land is always on the move toward fulfilment from promise to the security of slavery.[16]

The dynamic between the promise and loss of land, or, as Brueggemann puts it, the promise of land which ends in enslavement, also operates on the general level. According to Brueggemann, people who are safely 'landed' begin to manage things, such as the land, and are unable to treat it with the respect appropriate for a gift, and unable to keep the land law and the 'Sabbath' for resting the land and resting the people: land and people both have to be 'managed'.

> The link between Torah and land is central. It seems so obvious but so radical. In a coercive society, exactly the opposite is true. The ones who have made it, the ones who control the land and the machinery of governance are the ones who need not so vigorously obey... It is the landless poor and disadvantaged who are subject to exact legal claims of careful devotion to all social jots and tittles, not only last hired and first fired, but first suspected, last acquitted.[17]

Mann also criticizes Brueggemann for implying that 'land management' is a pejorative concept.[18] It is true that Brueggemann uses the term 'to manage' in the negative sense, and that a brief note explaining exactly what he means would not have gone amiss, but he uses it in this way consistently enough throughout the book, often in opposition to 'careful cultivation', for there to be no danger of confusion.

---

15. Brueggemann, *The Land*, 7–10.

16. Ibid., 10, 12. Also: 'But of course the story of Israel [in Egypt] is that being in the land soon led to slavery. Its prosperity (Exod 1:7) soon resulted in oppression (Exod 1:8-9)'. Ibid., 8.

17. Ibid., 57. Also: 'Landed people are accustomed to managing things. And as we manage things, we would manage people. We manage them by taxation and interest rates, by debts and mortgages, and soon everyone is either owner of others or part of the owned. When we forget our history, we think that is the way it has always been and is supposed to be.' Ibid., 60.

18. Mann, review of *The Land*, 218.

Faithful to his dialectical interpretation, Brueggemann structures his land theology into alternating phases of landlessness and landedness, three of each. The phases of landlessness are: (i) the wandering Fathers: Abraham, Isaac and Jacob, sojourners and resident aliens in the land; (ii) Israel's wandering in the wilderness on the way to the promised land; and (iii) the exile. The interposed phases of landedness are: (i) settlement in Egypt under Joseph; (ii) the monarchy; and (iii) the small community around Jerusalem in the times of Ezra and Nehemiah. The dialectical relationship between landlessness and landedness can be traced throughout the Bible and its inner logic provides a key to the interpretation of the salvation history of Israel: 'Land as locus of slavery posed for Israel an enormous choice which it had to make again and again, between expulsion to the desert or continuation in slavery... Israel was left to wonder if land always led to slavery.'[19]

Mann insists that Brueggemann's dialectic between landlessness and landedness is overstated and that his grouping of the landed and landless states of Israel is inadequate.[20] Brueggemann's use of the settlement in Egypt under Joseph does indeed appear a little weak. One cannot help thinking that he used this example as he needed a landless phase to maintain the alternating sequence and failed to find a better one. Equally, his vision of a faithful Israel during the time of landlessness does not correspond to the account in Exodus of the wandering fathers and mothers who never truly left the ideal of the 'Egyptian fleshpots' and were far from faithful to God.

Brueggemann's land symbolism: between landlessness and landedness

Landlessness

Brueggemann's view is that landlessness always involves an openness towards being landed, and that being landed always includes the risk of losing the land:

> Our lives are set between expulsion and anticipation of losing and expecting, of being uprooted and re-rooted, of being dislocated because of impertinence and being relocated in trust. Clearly these stories are not remote from the contemporary experience of Western culture.[21]

The Israelites generally enjoyed a higher ethical state when landless rather than landed. People are often more faithful when they are uprooted

19. Brueggemann, *The Land*, 9.
20. Mann, review of *The Land*, 220.
21. Brueggemann, *The Land*, 15–16.

and feel fragile and this was the case with the wandering fathers and the exiles. As we have seen, perspectives on the era of the wandering fathers and mothers differ throughout the Hebrew Bible and depend on the ideological outlook of the author: Exodus presents the wandering in the wilderness as a time of murmuring and idolatry; Hosea and Jeremiah paint the landless Israelites as a model of faithfulness.

The first experience of landlessness in Brueggemann's exposition is the experience of the patriarchs, Abraham, Isaac, and Jacob, to whom the promise of land was given, but who never experienced it. Brueggemann argues that the patriarchal narratives are founded on the expectation of the promised land: 'The narrative [of the book of Genesis] concerns the promise God has made to Israel to give it land and to be their peculiar God. Promise weaves in and out of the narrative.'[22] The promise is constitutive not only in the patriarchal stories but also in the whole salvation history of Israel: 'This ancestral promise of land – in a sure oath from God – is defining for all events that follow in the Bible'.[23]

For Brueggemann, the turning point between the 'old history' that leads to the expulsion and the 'new history' that leads to the promise is Gen. 15.7-21, which represents the oldest, most primitive and probably most original narrative of the encounter between God and Abraham: 'It is a new history moving toward a radical promise – land!'[24] Brueggemann stresses the importance of Abraham's confession which initiates the turn towards the promise.[25] Genesis 15.6 is quoted much in the New Testament, by Paul and by the author of Hebrews, usually to commend Abraham for his faith.[26] The two promises given here to Abraham – the promise of land and the promise of an heir – are interrelated. The promise of land, Brueggemann suggests, is the primary promise, but the land cannot be given to a single generation, so Abraham needs an heir.[27]

Brueggemann sees Genesis 17 as noteworthy for its narration of two divine promises given to Abraham: the promise of land, and the promise of YHWH's faithfulness to the people, and since the latter promise overshadows the former, ch. 15 rather than ch. 17 serves as the pivotal text for the motif of the promised land in the Hebrew Bible. Nevertheless,

---

22. Walter Brueggemann, *Genesis*, Interpretation (Atlanta, GA: John Knox, 1983), 2.

23. Brueggemann, *Reverberations of Faith*, 120.

24. Brueggemann, *The Land*, 20.

25. See Brueggemann, *Genesis*, 140, 143.

26. Ibid., 140.

27. Ibid., 142.

we also find in ch. 17 a unique pre-Sinaitic covenant between God and God's people, the key component of which, for Brueggemann, is clearly the land:

> Closely related to promise, perhaps even an alternative version of it, is covenant (vv. 2-7). In the entire Abraham narrative, only 15:18 elsewhere refers to covenant... Nevertheless, as the tradition now stands the covenant is the primary metaphor for understanding Israel's life with God.[28]

Brueggemann sees the promise of land as a constant presence in the patriarchal narratives. The promise of land given to Abraham in Gen. 15.7 is God's response to Abraham's confession of faith, which in Brueggemann's view is the point at which the narrative turns from the history of expulsion towards the history of promise. Brueggemann sees the patriarchal narratives as model stories of the faithful people of God. In this instance, landlessness is a metaphor for proximity to God.

According to Exodus, the era of wandering in the wilderness, unlike the era of the patriarchs, was a time of constant falling away from YHWH: 'In the Genesis narrative it drives Israel to radical faith. But in the wilderness tradition, Israel's experience of landlessness nearly destroys both Israel and its faith.'[29] Interestingly, Brueggemann draws a parallel between the barren women of the patriarchs – the greatest challenge to their relationship with God and to God's promises, but a challenge they met with faith – and the barren land through which the Israelites wandered on their way to the promised land – a test they largely failed:

> This is Israel's dominant memory of landlessness, to be at the disposal of an environment totally without life supports and without any visible hint that there is an opening to the future. This is the central struggle of both the patriarchs with barren women (Gen 11:30; 25:21; 29:31) and Israel in the barren land (Exod 16–18).[30]

The experience of exile was arguably even more challenging than the time of wandering. The Israelites were taken into exile after a time of political independence and relative security. Moreover, the prophets made a point of reminding the Israelites that their plight was of their own making. The experience of wandering in the wilderness came after the mighty deeds of their God YHWH, who brought the people out of Egypt.

28. Ibid., 154.
29. Brueggemann, *The Land*, 27.
30. Ibid., 28.

They were then supposed to be faithful to their God, who had delivered them from slavery. The wilderness stories are full of God's immanent presence and direct care for the people: 'Wilderness, landlessness for Israel, is a place without resources, but it is also the place where Yahweh is present with and to his people'.[31] But it seems that the more God's leading of the people is stressed, the more the unfaithfulness of the Israelites comes to the fore.

Wilderness is a key hermeneutical tool for interpreting the promised land motif. It always offers traffic in both directions, to the land of promise and the land of slavery, and thus captures the tension between the promised land of Canaan and the slavery of Egypt and the fragility of being 'on the way' to the promised land: 'Two more antithetical views of landlessness cannot be imagined. The wilderness is the route of promise on the way to land, or the wilderness is unbearable abandonment to be avoided by return to slavery.'[32]

In Brueggemann's view, the crux of the journey towards the promised land and the point at which the risk of backsliding to Egypt is finally overcome is the experience of crossing the Jordan: 'Nothing is more radical than this, that the sojourner becomes a possessor'.[33] Brueggemann points out that being oppressed is not an ontological given: the oppressed can become the oppressors. Burge misinterprets Brueggemann's description of the tension between marching towards the promise land and sliding back to the land of slavery and understands it as a choice between accepting the land as a gift and usurping it as a possessor:

> Brueggemann finds in the land a timeless paradigm for our theological understanding of God's participation in history. Two choices confront us: there are those who await the gift and those who grasp. There are those who live with contingency, who embrace faith, and those who seek to seize history aggressively, grasping what they think is theirs.[34]

Burge's interpretation is puzzling. He is able to acknowledge Brueggemann's exposition of a 'timeless paradigm' but fails to recognize this dialectic as a symbolic concept that concerns all people regardless of origin or socio-political and religious-cultural context. The story of

31. Ibid., 40.
32. Ibid., 35.
33. Ibid., 43.
34. Gary Burge, review of *The Land: Place as Gift, Promise and Challenge in Biblical Faith*, by Walter Brueggemann, *Books & Culture* 9, no. 4 (2003): 40.

the exodus and the settlement of the promised land is a prime witness to the fact that given a change of context the oppressed can become the oppressors (and vice versa). Burge's interpretation manifests the same problem that we see in some liberation theology scholars who believe that 'the poor' are ontologically 'better'.[35] Tim Noble argues that we are called to care for the poor because God comes to us 'through' the poor other. The poor are the 'icons' of God, but there is always a risk of turning them into 'idols', an 'object of worship' rather than a 'window' towards God.[36] Noble is convinced that 'the danger of idolizing the poor has not been sufficiently or adequately addressed, either by liberation theology or its critics, and nor has it been shown what tools liberation theology itself has to avoid its danger'.[37]

The third and most frustrating state of landlessness is exile. In Lev. 18.25-28, Israel is reminded that if they break the covenant with God they will be 'vomited out' of the land, just like the Canaanites before them. Leviticus presents many ways in which the Israelites were not to break the covenant with God, such as holding to a socio-ethical law and a law of religious praxis, but Brueggemann sees the breaking of the land law as one of Israel's most significant transgressions. For the Israelites, exile meant being pulled up from their roots and separated from the temple in Jerusalem and the cult associated with it. It is still, however, Brueggemann argues, one of the most crucial theological events in the salvation history of Israel: 'These three factors, historical experience, paradigmatic power, and inventive literary imagination, are crucial for recognizing the context of the Exile as decisive for shaping Old Testament faith'.[38]

The trajectory of the salvation history of Israel is always from land-lessness to landedness: land is always the final goal. Exile must therefore have seemed like the end of their history. The two preceding phases of landlessness were survived because of the promise of land, but now the land had been taken away from Israel, by God, because of its wretched-ness. In Jer. 25.8-9 and 27.6, God sends Israel's arch enemy the king of Babylon to destroy Jerusalem. As if that were not enough, the king is actually executing God's will: 'The one who will take the land away from

35. Tim Noble, *The Poor in Liberation Theology: Pathway to God or Ideological Construct?* Cross Cultural Theologies (Sheffield: Equinox, 2013), 149.

36. Ibid., 16.

37. Ibid., 99.

38. Walter Brueggemann and Patrick Miller, *Like Fire in the Bones: Listening for the Prophetic Word in Jeremiah* (Minneapolis, MN: Fortress, 2006), 118.

Israel is not some alien power, but it is the Holy One who gave the land... Nebuchadnezzar the land-grabber, the quintessence of imperial expansionism which threatened Israel, is doing the work of Yahweh.'[39]

Brueggemann holds that the most satisfactory discussion on the theme of the exile takes place in the book of Jeremiah: 'None saw the alternative picture more clearly than Jeremiah. And none expressed it more poignantly. In the Old Testament he is the poet of the land par excellence... Jeremiah knew, long before the others could face it, that history in land moves to exile.'[40] For Jeremiah, the exile is a direct result of Israel having a king, and things could not have ended otherwise.[41] The context of Jeremiah, as far as we can deduce from the text, is the royal priestly ideology of the Jerusalem establishment: 'The text offers imaginative alternatives to established ideology in the conviction that God is at work to create a new community'.[42]

Jeremiah 22.29-30 connects the exile to the preceding phases of landlessness. Here, Jeremiah is seeking to remind the Israelites of the desperate state in which the patriarchs found themselves, that is, without an heir. To the parallel between barren wives and a barren land, he now adds the exile: Israel is barren and without a land: 'The language recalls the state of Abraham and Sarah without heir, without promise, and ultimately without land. Israel without land is no people. A king without a throne is no king. Land without Israel is no place.'[43]

Land-loss as the natural end of the history of Israel is emphasized throughout Brueggemann's writings. God nevertheless remains faithful to Israel and continues to open new beginnings and new opportunities for overcoming their problems; God's patience with Israel appears limitless.[44] Brueggemann observes: 'The exile is the moment in the history of Israel and in the life of God when an irreversibly new theological datum is introduced in the horizon of faith'.[45] Thus, what seemed to be the final breakup between God and the people of Israel is interpreted in the later prophetic books – 'second' and 'third' Isaiah, 'second' Jeremiah,

---

39. Brueggemann, *The Land*, 106–7.

40. Ibid., 101, 103.

41. See Walter Brueggemann and Rebecca Kruger Gaudino, *Theology of the Old Testament: Testimony, Dispute, Advocacy* (Minneapolis, MN: Fortress, 1997), 615.

42. Walter Brueggemann, *A Commentary on Jeremiah: Exile and Homecoming* (Grand Rapids, MI: Eerdmans, 1998), 14.

43. Brueggemann, *The Land*, 111.

44. Ibid., 104–5.

45. Brueggemann and Miller, *Like Fire in the Bones*, 129.

and Ezekiel – as an opportunity for a new beginning and on a different foundation. Since Israel is incapable of keeping the covenant, YHWH offers the people a new covenant – one that is not conditioned on Israel's faithfulness and obedience.[46] The key formula of this new covenant is, 'You shall be my people and I will be your God' (Jer. 30.22; 32.38; Ezek. 37.27). Ezekiel speaks of God giving the people a new heart and a new spirit to convert them:

> Exile is the way to new life in new land. One can scarcely imagine a more radical, less likely understanding of history. In covenantal categories, embrace of curse is the root to blessing. In New Testament categories the embrace of death is the way to life (Luke 9:23-27; Rom. 6:1-11). Thus, in the movement among images, exile = death and restoration of land = life.[47]

Jeremiah voices another paradox of the exile: those who went into exile, the landless, are blessed; those who stayed in Judah, the landed, are cursed. Accustomed as we now are to Brueggemann's rhetoric, this statement will not surprise us, but for the Israelites it remained perplexing. The paradox is both implicitly and explicitly described in the parable of the Two Baskets of Figs in Jeremiah 24. Brueggemann notes that this parable was written between the years 598 and 587,[48] between the two drafts into exile, and in the context of the rivalry, perhaps even conflict, between the community in exile and the community at home:

46. Brueggemann, *The Land*, 115–22. See also, Walter Brueggemann, *To Pluck Up, to Tear Down: A Commentary on the Book of Jeremiah 1–25*, International Theological Commentary (Grand Rapids, MI: Eerdmans, 1988), 211. Brueggemann does not suggest that the exile is a direct sanction for not keeping the covenant: 'That moral, theological fracture generated two primary responses. On the one hand, the paradigm of exile/restoration is concerned with the moral failure of Israel, so that exile is punishment and judgment from God… On the other hand, however, it is clear that the crisis of exile cannot be contained in the categories of covenantal sanctions.' Brueggemann and Miller, *Like Fire in the Bones*, 117.

47. Brueggemann, *The Land*, 115.

48. 'In other words, [the Deuteronomistic tradition] was shaped and written during the period of the dynamism of the Jeremian tradition. It was written, according to common interpretation, to trace the failed history of Israel from the moment it entered the land (Joshua 1–4) until the final destruction of 587 BCE at the hands of the Babylonians – one long tale of disobedience that led inexorably to destruction.' Walter Brueggemann, *The Theology of the Book of Jeremiah*, Old Testament Theology (New York: Cambridge University Press, 2007), 144.

> The Lord of history gives history to the landless who should have no history. He takes the barren as the mother of promise. He takes the slaves as bearers of freedom. He takes the desperately hungry as heirs of the new land. And now he takes hopeless exiles as his new people.[49]

Typically, the Jews in exile concluded that those left behind in Judah were spared by God and those led into exile were forsaken. The opposite is true, however. The good figs are the exiles. Even though those taken into exile were considered to be among Israel's elite, this does not mean that those left behind are ontologically worse as people. Brueggemann takes us back to Deuteronomy:

> [The exiles'] goodness does not rest in themselves but in the sovereign assertions of Yahweh, who announces them to be good (cf. Deut 9:6). The freedom of Yahweh in making such a dramatic assertion parallels that of Gen 15:6, in which Yahweh 'reckons' (*hashab*) Abraham to be righteous.[50]

Brueggemann outlines two ways of explaining this apparent discrepancy. That the exiles are 'the good ones' could be propaganda, or at best an ideologically biased interpretation by the prophet. As one of the first to be taken into exile, Jeremiah would naturally favour those who had been exiled with him. It could on the other hand be a consolation to the exiles who felt forsaken by God. Whereas the exiles are comforted, those who remained in Judah or escaped to Egypt are cursed (Jer. 24.8-10), and this was no ordinary curse: 'The sentence pronounced against the Jewish communities in Jerusalem and in Egypt includes language out of the old curse tradition (cf. Deut 28:37)'.[51]

Brueggemann favours the consolation explanation and appeals to Jeremiah 29, which has a close affinity to Jeremiah 24.[52] Chapter 29 offers advice, comfort and 'pastoral care' to the desperate exiles:

---

49. Brueggemann, *The Land*, 118. See also: 'The exiles devalued by the world are here identified as the bearers of God's future. This revaluation of the world's rejects is the surprise of the gospel echoed in so many places. This God seems indeed to make the future with those whom the world judges to be without a future.' Brueggemann, *To Pluck Up, to Tear Down*, 212.

50. Brueggemann, *To Pluck Up, to Tear Down*, 210.

51. Ibid., 211.

52. See Walter Brueggemann, *To Build, to Plant: A Commentary on Jeremiah 26–52*, International Theological Commentary (Grand Rapids, MI: Eerdmans, 1991), 30.

[This] pastoral care is expressed around two convictions: (a) there must be a realistic and intentional embrace of the Exile as a place where Jews must now be and where God has summoned them to obedience (29:5-7), and (b) there is a long-term hope for return and restoration that can be affirmed and accepted (vv. 10-14).[53]

Brueggemann's interpretation of exile confirms his exposition of the tension between landlessness and landedness. However, we saw that some phases of landlessness, such as the sojourn in Canaan and the exile in Babylon, are more persuasive than the wandering in the wilderness: we should certainly not conclude from the accounts of Hosea–Jeremiah that the wilderness era bears witness to the faithfulness of a landless Israel.

Landedness

Brueggemann believes that for the Israelites, land has been variously a gift, a temptation, a task, and a threat, depending on which phase in the history of salvation is in view. The era of landedness is typically represented by a falling away from the God YHWH: when they feel settled and safe, the Israelites are prone to forget who secured their landedness.

Israel has memories to treasure, vows to honour, choices to make, loyalties to affirm. The tradition from the boundary believed such things were possible even in the land. But the land has done something to Israel. The ones warned about forgetting (Deut 8:11) remember nothing. Land has caused amnesia (Deut 32:15-18). Israel has forgotten everything about from whence it came, who gave the land, the demands that come with it.[54]

Brueggemann stresses the role of the 'land factor' in the forgetting and falling away from YHWH. It is clearly not some 'earthly magic' that causes this forgetting, but rather the tendency we encountered with the Puritans in America: a striving to secure wellbeing in the land and *through* the land. Landed people tend to *manage* the land as if it were not their partner. They do not treat it as a free gift sealed by a covenant but take it for granted as something they are free to exploit. The threat of being settled 'was in the beginning, is now, and ever shall be'.[55] When people are successful in their husbandry or business, they tend to leave God out of their lives. Brueggemann reminds us about the importance of a Sabbath for the land in maintaining the idea of the land as a gift:

53. Ibid.
54. Brueggemann, *The Land*, 99.
55. See ibid., 50–1.

> Land Sabbath is a reminder that (a) land is not from us but is a gift to us, and (b) land is not fully given over to our saturation. Land has its own rights over against us and even its own existence. It is in covenant with us but not totally at our disposal. Sabbath is for honouring land.[56]

During 'landed times', the relationship between God, the people, and the land becomes corrupted, leading to a series of unanswered warnings which end with the land being taken away from the Israelites by their God YHWH. Brueggemann understands it in this way: 'Israel's involvement is always with land and with Yahweh, never only with Yahweh, as though to live only in intense obedience, never only in land, as though simply to possess and manage'.[57]

During the era of landedness, social differences between the people become more evident than during the sojourning or wandering. Those who inherit a portion of land must therefore take care of those who do not: the poor (Exod. 23.6; Deut. 15.7-11), the stranger (Exod. 21.21-24; 23.9), the sojourner (Deut. 10.19), the widow and the orphan (Deut. 24.19-22), the Levite (Deut. 14.27). The poor are due special care (Lev. 25.35-38). They must be provided with shelter and a living and must not be asked for rent: 'Land is for sharing with all the heirs of the covenant, even those who have no power to claim it'.[58] This of course has always been a challenge, which is why the land became a 'task', especially during the period of the monarchy when the opportunity to pervert justice was most apparent.

But as we have seen, the land also brings a threat to the Israelites in the form of the Canaanites, the indigenous inhabitants,[59] whose cult and way of life always tempted the people of Israel away from their God YHWH: 'The land of promise is never an eagerly waiting vacuum anticipating Israel. Nor is it an unambiguous arena for faith. It is always filled with Canaanites. That is how the promise comes. And Israel knew that Canaanites are always more impressive than Israelites.'[60]

The first period of landedness for Israel is the settlement in Egypt under Joseph. This, Brueggemann argues, is a special instance that cannot be regarded as proper landedness: 'This is not the land for this turf belongs finally to Pharaoh, and not to Joseph. This is not the land because it is

---

56. Ibid., 59.
57. Ibid., 49.
58. Ibid., 62.
59. See ibid., 62–5.
60. Ibid., 63.

imperial and is attained by management and not as gift.'[61] One could
also argue that this cannot be understood as 'their' landedness as no one
really wanted to stay there. Joseph assured his brothers that when the time
came, God would deliver them from Egypt. It is also clearly stated that
the patriarchs must be buried in Canaan, in the land that had already been
promised to Abraham and his descendants. Jacob is buried in the cave at
Machpelah near Mamre in Canaan, and in his final wish, Joseph beseeches
his brothers to take his bones with them when they leave Egypt and to lay
them in Canaan.

The first true landed period for the Israelites is therefore under the
monarchy, in the promised land itself. From the time they first entered
the land, the Israelites had striven for a king so that they might be 'like
the other nations', but a monarchy was not an effective socio-political
system for Israel: 'At the center of Israel's self-awareness is the debacle
of 587 BCE, when king, temple, and city all failed'.[62] Samuel seeks to
persuade the Israelites that the only true and righteous king is their God
YHWH. If the people are successful in appointing a king, the king will
take the land away from them: 'He will take the best of your fields and
vineyards and olive orchards and give them to his courtiers' (1 Sam. 8.7).
Under a king, the land will be managed just as it is in the surrounding
nations: it will be taken away from the rightful heirs – the people of
Israel – and concentrated in the hands of the royal court, thus violating
the land law. The kings would see the land as their possession, not as
their inheritance.[63]

But the people did not listen to Samuel. Brueggemann stresses that if
a monarchy was to be established, the kings must be told that they must
still submit to the land law. They must not keep the wealth of the land
in their own hands. The land is an inheritance, not a possession: 'Other
kings incline to control the land as a possession. This [Israelite] king is to

61. Ibid., 25.

62. Brueggemann and Gaudino, *Theology of the Old Testament*, 514.

63. Brueggemann also observes: 'As tribal society with its discrete, independent
units experienced political and economic fusion, new patterns of power, wealth, and
land control emerged. In this view, monarchy is the culmination of a drive toward
centralization, monopoly, kingship, and absolutism, accompanied by the emergence
of an enormous economic surplus. The extreme forms of these aspects of monarchy
do not appear in Israel until the regime of Solomon and are not present in the books
of Samuel.' Walter Brueggemann, *First and Second Samuel*, Interpretation: A Bible
Commentary for Teaching and Preaching: O.T. (Louisville, KY: John Knox, 1990),
58.

manage the land as a gift entrusted to him but never possessed by him.'[64] In order to secure this arrangement, the king must be an Israelite because he knows the nation's history and thus also understands its meaning: 'If the land is not to be wrongly handled, the king must remember barrenness and birth, slavery and freedom, hunger and manna, and above all the speeches at the boundary'.[65] But Israel forgot, Solomon misused his royal state, the people fell back into what amounted to a state of slavery, and the kingdom was divided.[66] Brueggemann describes the four-stage decline that ended in exile: (i) the king confiscates land, (ii) Israel is reduced to slavery, (iii) Israel is cut off from YHWH, (iv) the land is lost; 'The royal apparatus designed to keep and enhance the land will cause Israel to lose it'.[67] The complementary institution of the prophets was established to raise a voice against the monarch whenever he overstepped his authority: 'The prophet is intended precisely for speech (a) in the land, (b) in the face of the king, (c) against idolatrous forms of self-securing'.[68]

Elijah raised his voice against King Ahab when he confiscated Naboth's vineyard: 'The history of Israel in its classical period is presented as a tension between royally secured land and covenanted precarious land. The narrative of 1 Kings 21 presents the clearest embodiment of that tension.'[69] Brueggemann does not doubt that the story of Naboth's vineyard is about a 'clash over land'. He admits that the story appears to present a dispute between a defenceless man and the king, and therefore merely a social issue (cf. David and Uriah the Hittite in 2 Sam. 11.2-17), but argues that the conflict is in fact between contradicting approaches to the land. Naboth represents the Yahwist approach in which the land is the inheritance of YHWH granted to the people of Israel. Such an inheritance is handed down from one generation to another, is indivisibly bound to the family, and cannot under any circumstances be traded. The other approach is represented by Jezebel. From her perspective as a princess in the line of a strong and well-rooted royal history in Canaan, land is a commodity as any other: it can be traded, and the king has the right to claim it if he so desires. Ahab's

64. Brueggemann, *The Land*, 70.
65. Ibid., 71.
66. See also: 'The God who had given land and intended it to be handled as gift is now made patron of the king who now has the land. In the Solomonic period even God now apparently has no claim on the land. He is guest and not host.' Ibid., 81.
67. Ibid., 74.
68. Ibid., 87.
69. Ibid., 94.

position is ambiguous: on the one hand, he yields when Naboth refuses to trade the land and gives his reasons, and on the other he submits to Jezebel and claims Naboth's land after his death.[70] Jezebel thought she was going to give the land to Ahab but she had no authority: it is only YHWH who can give land or take it away.[71]

Brueggemann clearly recognizes the alien Canaanite influence of Jezebel and her 'elitist' view of land as the sign of the king's dominance over the Israelites. She wants to see Ahab as a 'true king' who executes his will, so naturally wants to replace the Israelite model of monarchy according to which the true king is YHWH to whom the earthly king must submit with the Canaanite model in which the king has absolute power. By depriving Naboth of his inheritance, Jezebel steals YHWH's inheritance and makes it Ahab's, thus replacing YHWH with Ahab, who is now to be the true king of Israel. The Canaanite element in the story therefore represents a force that seeks to strip the Israelites of their land and steal its only true king YHWH.

Interestingly, Brueggemann refers to Steinbeck's observation of America's careless management of the land and draws a parallel with the mistreatment of the land during the time of the monarchy when the Israelites were safely settled and their bureaucracy managed things and people by 'writing things down'.

> John Steinbeck has shrewdly presented the power of writing as a means of confiscation when it is controlled by the bureaucracy in the service of established interests: 'Owners no longer worked their farms. They farmed on paper and they forgot the land.' The Okies learned to avoid anyone with writing equipment for writing meant land-loss.[72]

In Brueggemann's understanding, Steinbeck was using writing as a symbol of the undesirable form of 'management' that leads to oppression.

Brueggemann is far from equivocal on the monarchy and favours the attitude formed by the Deuteronomistic tradition that sees kingship as only negative and the land as conditional rather than a free gift.[73] His selection of biblical books confirms this conviction: the Chronicles, classically

---

70. See also Walter Brueggemann, *1 & 2 Kings*, Smyth & Helwys Bible Commentary (Macon, GA: Smyth & Helwys, 2000), 257.

71. Brueggemann, *The Land*, 92.

72. Ibid., 75. 'Okies' is slang for the people of Oklahoma.

73. For a discussion of these two concepts in Brueggemann's work, see Walter Brueggemann, 'The God of Joshua… Give or Take the Land', *Interpretation: A Journal of Bible and Theology* 66, no. 2 (2012): 164–75.

regarded as being positive towards royalty, are not mentioned at all in *The Land*. Mann suggests that here Brueggemann is overly influenced by Gottwald and his negative attitude towards the kings of Israel.[74]

The final period of Israelite landedness is the resettlement of Jerusalem following the edict of Cyrus in 539 B.C.E. The community was established on the basis of the religious purity of the cult of YHWH, which in the view of the authors-redactors of Ezra and Nehemiah was the only thing capable of holding the Israelites together.[75]

Brueggemann stresses that YHWH had always been presented as a jealous God, but in the times of Ezra and Nehemiah, God becomes jealous for Zion and the significance of Jerusalem enters a completely different dimension. This jealousy applies not only to YHWH. The people who returned from exile are also to be jealous:

> The land fully under covenant requires his people to be as jealous for the covenant as is Yahweh himself ([Zech] 7:9-10; Mal 3:10-12). The purists had a vivid memory and an urgent mission. They were driven to law and order by their passion for the land. And they knew, as the kings had failed to learn, that the land is covenantal and will be had in no other terms.[76]

The motivation of the returnees was twofold. First, they longed for the (relative) political freedom promised to them as a result of the change from Babylonian to Persian rule. Nonetheless, despite the euphoria of being delivered from political oppression they were aware that the new 'freedom' was limited. Nehemiah 9.36-37 clearly states that the people knew the land was not truly theirs. Secondly, they wanted to re-establish the cult of YHWH in the temple. The community relied on the zeal and purity of this cult. Interestingly, and in contrast to what we read in second and third Isaiah, second Jeremiah, and Ezekiel, that the gift of land should have been unconditional, the community of Israelite returnees saw the restitution of their city and temple as being dependent on loyalty to God and faithfulness to the covenant: 'The land, if it was to be retained would need to be understood, as monarchic Israel had not, in terms of the urgency, precariousness, and graciousness of the covenant'.[77]

74. Mann, review of *The Land*, 218.

75. See Brueggemann, *The Land*, 143–4. Also: 'The God who leads his people back to Jerusalem and the beginning in the land is disciplined and single-minded, wanting Jerusalem kept and claimed for his exclusive purposes. There is no ambition here beyond the claim of this single, symbolic place (Zech 1:14-17; 8:2-3).' Ibid.

76. Ibid., 144.

77. Ibid.

With respect to land theology in Ezra and Nehemiah, Brueggemann
notes that several major conditions must be kept if the new and fragile
community in Jerusalem is to be fully protected: the land must be purged,
which meant that no inter-religious marriages would be permitted (Ezra
10.10–11.44); the returnees should not mix with the people who stayed
in Judah during the Babylonian exile (Ezra 9.12) – the bad figs in the
parable of the Two Baskets of Figs in Jeremiah 24; the people were to
keep the Sabbath (Neh. 13.15-18); and land must be distributed fairly
(Neh. 5.3-5a).[78]

We need to bear in mind that during the time of the resettlement of
Jerusalem and its environs, the Near East was being rapidly Hellenized and
that this had a significant effect on promised land theology: 'Hellenization
was essentially an urban phenomenon, which focused in the cities and
claimed them as vehicles for and expressions of the new vision of
universal humanity'.[79] We have already seen that the process of urbanization tended to decrease people's interest in the land, but the books of
Ezra and Nehemiah are exceptional in having a clear focus on promised
land theology.[80] Whereas the later prophets, especially the apocalyptic
passages, and the New Testament tend towards a spiritual-eschatological
view of the land, Ezra and Nehemiah clearly refer to the promised land
in the territorial and political sense: 'The anticipated conclusion of the
intervention and triumph of Yahweh is restoration of an idyllic land of
security, well-being, and fertility. Israel has no other imagery. The good
future is the landed one.'[81]

Brueggemann concludes his discussion on the tension between landlessness and landedness with an exposition of the promised land motif in
the New Testament. Unlike some other New Testament scholars, such as
William Davies and Gary Burge, who argue that the promise of land lost
its original appeal and became fully spiritualized and eschatologized,[82]
Brueggemann sees the promise of land as a key symbol of the Christian
Scriptures.[83] The existential battle between landlessness and landedness
is of course symbolic. It takes place within the Jewish community 'in the
land', between the rulers and those on the margins. For Brueggemann,

78. See ibid., 146–50.

79. Ibid., 150.

80. 'The double focus of land as earth and land as "safe place" is evident. The
question of theodicy, which dominates much of the late literature, comes precisely
from the disinherited who were betrayed by the new urban arrangements.' Ibid., 154.

81. Ibid., 156.

82. Davies, *The Gospel and the Land*, 166, 178; Burge, *Jesus and the Land*, 88.

83. Brueggemann, *The Land*, 160.

the person of Jesus and his passion, crucifixion, and resurrection is the prism through which we are to understand the promised land motif in the New Testament. Jesus is the homeless one who finally reached home. The history of landedness leads to crucifixion; landlessness leads to resurrection. The equation remains valid throughout the New Testament but with changes in vocabulary: 'the kingdom of God' in the Synoptic Gospels; 'eternal life' in John; 'inheritance' in Paul; 'homeland' in Hebrews.[84] In the New Testament, therefore, landlessness and landedness is interpreted in the social realm. The hermeneutical key to this tension is the marginalized, particularly the poor (Lk. 6.20, 'Blessed are you who are poor, for yours is the kingdom of God') and the meek (Mt. 5.5, 'Blessed are the meek, for they will inherit the earth'). The orientation towards the marginalized and the oppressed is decisive for Brueggemann's ideology critique.

Philo of Alexandria viewed wandering Israel as the human soul on its way to God. Brueggemann also clearly sees the struggle between landlessness and landedness as concerning the individual. 'Crossing the Jordan' is a decisive moment for all of us: are we going to enter the promised land, or return to the land of slavery? This is not a matter of choice, but rather of our current socio-political status. The oppressor can become the oppressed, and vice versa. The oppressed are not ontologically 'better' than their oppressors. If their status improves, they may become oppressors of another socially disadvantaged group. Brueggemann's concept points towards the timeless idea he articulates in his tension between landed and landless people. Belief in the corrupt nature of the human soul, the legacy of Puritanism, seduces people into using their power against those who cannot defend themselves.

Curing one's conscience but what comes next? Brueggemann and liberation theology

The fields of liberation theology and postcolonialism naturally relate to one another and have many common features and aims, but I will point out two important differences which keep me from using the terms interchangeably. First, although liberation theology focuses on the margins, it is nevertheless viewed from the 'centre'. Liberation theologians use standard historical-critical procedures and engage almost exclusively with their colleagues from European and American academia. Postcolonial criticism, on the other hand, resists this 'centrist' agenda by engaging with subaltern scholars who did not study in the West and by finding its own appropriate hermeneutic. Secondly, because of its unconditional 'bias to

84. Ibid., 169.

the poor', liberation theology often creates false dichotomies and inverted ideologies which can lead to secondary victimization of the oppressed. Postcolonial critics, whose thinking is not formed by dialectics, see their target group in a more complex and less romanticized way. From this perspective, I tend to see Brueggemann's criticism of land ideology as a 'liberation theology' and to bring in postcolonial criticism when a corrective to Brueggemann's view is required. The term ideology critique refers simply to a recognition or renunciation of various ideologies which lie behind the writing and interpretation of the biblical text.

In the later stages of his academic career, Brueggemann discovered the dangerous nature of his land theology, based as it was on the idea of the 'elect', and embraced the perspective of the margins.[85] In the second edition of *The Land*, under pressure from the newly arising postcolonial and ideology critique in biblical studies, Brueggemann largely revises his previously unproblematic relationship with those who settled the land.[86] Influenced by Gottwald's breakthrough sociological approach[87] and the ideology critique of Michael Prior[88] and Jon Levenson,[89] he wrote an

---

85. Brueggemann refers to Michael Prior. See Michael Prior, 'The Bible and the Redeeming Idea of Colonialism', *Studies in World Christianity* 5, no. 2 (1999): 129–55.

86. 'From this fundamental recognition of "creation" that was only inchoate in the Old Testament Studies at the time of my book [the 1st ed. of *The Land*], several other important lines of interpretation are now to be noted. Among them is the recognition that the claim of "promised land" in the Old Testament is not an innocent theological claim, but is *a vigorous ideological assertion* on an important political scale. This insight is a subject of ideology critique in the field that has emerged as a major enterprise in the last decades.' Brueggemann, *The Land*, xiii–xiv.

87. Gottwald, *The Tribes of Yahweh*; Gottwald, *The Hebrew Bible*.

88. See Michael Prior, *A Land Flowing with Milk, Honey and People*, Lattey Lecture 1997 (Cambridge: Von Hügel Institute, 1997).

89. See Jon Levenson, 'Is There a Counterpart in the Hebrew Bible to New Testament Antisemitism?', *Journal of Ecumenical Studies* 22, no. 2 (1985): 242–60. As the title suggests, Levenson's article focuses on signs in the Hebrew Bible of hatred towards other nations and religions that can be compared with anti-Semitism in the New Testament. Levenson picks out the hatred directed towards the Canaanites, who are the greatest challenge to the Israelites, just as Jews are to Christian faith in the New Testament: 'Like the Jews in some New Testament and much patristic literature, the Canaanites in the Hebrew Bible are, without exception, wicked in the worst of ways. It is their wickedness, inter alia, which justifies their loss of the land to Israel and which condemns them eternally in the sight of God, who has graciously and mysteriously (Deut 7:6-8) chosen Israel to supplant them.' Ibid., 250.

extensive preface in which he comes to terms with the fact that land was indeed a huge *politicum* and that he had dealt naively with this barrel of gunpowder in the first edition of his book,[90] ignoring the political line of interpretation and the environmental impact of land theology: 'Land entitlement leads to earth occupation... Thus land as a theological theme is never to be taken as innocent and surely not as innocently as I had done in my book.'[91] In his theological dictionary *Reverberations of Faith*, he explains the twofold political agenda of the land:

> Taken negatively, this tradition stands as an important critique of the massive enterprise of colonialism in the modern world whereby imperial powers have occupied and confiscated lands not their own. Taken positively, the land promises of the Bible are a generic affirmation of liberation movements whereby disadvantaged landless people receive back (take back) their own lands too long denied them.[92]

Norman Habel comes to a similar conclusion:

> 'The land is mine!' This claim, once voiced by YHWH in the Hebrew Scriptures (Lev 25:23), has been made by individuals, social groups, and nations across the centuries. More recently, this claim has been voiced strongly by indigenous peoples of our contemporary world who have been dispossessed by colonial and corporate powers. Land claims and communal identity are often inextricably interrelated.[93]

These two observations helpfully sum up the development of postcolonial and liberation theology of the promised land. Interestingly, the former colonizing nations and the nations and ethnic groups that were once colonized (or still are) both take Bibles in their hands and in the name of the exodus and settlement narrative dismantle ideologies one by one.

Some postcolonial and ideology critics work on the synchronic level, either allowing the text to deconstruct itself (Clines) or disproving the historicity of the events (Brueggemann, Habel, Warrior). Robert Warrior is a Native American biblical scholar who promotes Gottwald's idea that the whole exodus and settlement narrative was the invention of a Yahwistic author-redactor who was seeking to promote the cult of YHWH,

---

90. See Brueggemann, *The Land*, xi–xii.
91. Ibid., xv, xvi.
92. Brueggemann, *Reverberations of Faith*, 123.
93. Habel and Brueggemann, *The Land Is Mine*, xi.

God the liberator, and that the Israelites were a subset from within the Canaanites.[94] Brueggemann also doubts that the settlement narrative reflects events as they happened, seeing it rather as a later, ideologically biased narrative of a community struggling to survive in the midst of its neighbours.[95] Brueggemann does not stop at deconstructing the settlement narrative. He also questions the historicity of the exile and plays with the idea that it could have been an ideological construct, an interpretive metaphor of the salvation history of Israel.[96]

Brueggemann's discussion of the ideology critique of the promised land motif points out that the biblical narrative disregards the fact that the God YHWH must first force the Canaanites to leave their native land. Psalm 145.9 states that YHWH is 'good to all'. Land theology suggests that this statement is not true. Brueggemann claims that God is an agent of violence, who must be subjected to ideology critique.[97] Whereas 'the Lord' sees the affliction of the Israelites in Egypt and comes down to deliver them from the hand of the Egyptians,[98] the same God seemingly fails to see any problem in violating the rights of the Canaanites in their own land. Brueggemann offers three possible explanations. First, YHWH is especially committed to Israel and disregards the needs of other nations. In other words, YHWH is a typical ancient Near Eastern tribal God who

94. Warrior, 'Canaanites, Cowboys, and Indians'.

95. 'It will now be generally agreed that the traditions of land promise and land violence (twin claims that are decisive for the tradition and cannot be separated out) are not given us in the final form of the text as reportage. Rather, the final form of the text is completely removed from what may have been the "happening" of the land, and now function as a belated rationale for the subsequent community of Israel. Thus, even though the land promises in the tradition are in purportedly old traditions, they are now to be completely understood in terms of subsequent ideological claims of important use to a later interpretive community.' Ibid., xiv. See also Prior, 'The Bible and the Redeeming Idea of Colonialism'.

96. See Brueggemann, *The Land*, xviii.

97. 'The narratives are read as they are, we must take them seriously in all of their problematic. It stands in the text, after our critical work, that YHWH is exhibited as an agent of violence. It is attested in the narrative that there was a time when YHWH acted in this way.' Brueggemann, 'The God of Joshua... Give or Take the Land', 171.

98. 'These two verses together [Exod. 3.7-8] in the very mouth of God portray the God of the Bible as vigorous against social hurt (vv. 7-8a) and powerfully resolved to work a public hope of land and well-being for the marginalized of the empire (v. 8b).' Walter Brueggemann and Patrick Miller, *Old Testament Theology: Essays on Structure, Theme and Text* (Minneapolis, MN: Fortress, 1992), 73.

cares nought for the welfare of other nations.[99] Secondly, land-by-violence is tied up with Israel's political claims to the land. The promised land motif is then an ideologically misinterpreted account given by authors-redactors who were members of the Israelite community. Thirdly, the violence over the land has a deeper socio-political meaning. It is oriented against the strong (the landed) for the sake of the weak (the landless):

> This testimony, saturated with passion and ideology, permeates Israel's sense of land, perhaps in a way that not only feeds the militarism of the Christian West, but also is evident in contemporary Israel. No doubt much nativism in the United States receives some of its theological justification from this tradition... It may be, in the long sweep, that the violence of Yahweh can be answered for, but it can hardly be justified.[100]

In the revised edition of *The Land*, Brueggemann admits that it is no longer possible to arrogate the land on the basis of the biblical story of the exodus and the settlement of the promised land and that nations living side by side need to acknowledge the rights of the other and live in peace and mutual respect.[101] However, even in this edition, Brueggemann adheres to the Marxist roots of liberation theologies and plays with the romantic notion of the ontological superiority of the poor. He is indeed right that God is on the side of the poor, oppressed and landless, but he misses Gottwald's argument that the cult of YHWH originated among the oppressed Israelites. When discussing Gottwald, I posed the question: When did 'God the liberator' become 'God the oppressor'? For Brueggemann, this is obviously an important issue, but he seems to forget, even though it is within the logic of the tension between landedness and landlessness, that as YHWH changed from 'God the liberator' into 'God the oppressor' there is a high possibility that God would change back into 'God the liberator'. In other words, if the oppressed Israelites who

---

99. 'The God "revealed" in the Book of Joshua is tribally committed and monarchically dispossessed. And without challenge, that God will continue the course of self-justifying violence.' Brueggemann, 'The God of Joshua... Give or Take the Land', 173.

100. Brueggemann and Gaudino, *Theology of the Old Testament*, 383. Also: 'Israel's testimony to Yahweh as deliverer enunciates Yahweh's resolved capacity to intervene decisively against every oppressive, alienating circumstance and force that precludes a life of well-being. Yahweh is more than a match for the powers of oppression, whether socio-political or cosmic.' Ibid., 174.

101. Brueggemann, *The Land*, 205.

worshipped YHWH as 'God the liberator' became the oppressing Israelites in whose cult YHWH became 'God the oppressor', they can just as easily become oppressed once again.

For Brueggemann, the key to the misuse of promised land theology is the idea of the unconditional gift of the land, which has its roots in the book of Genesis (Gen. 12.7; 15.7, 18; 17.8) and has always been referenced by religious-political oppressors (the modern-day Israeli government in particular).[102] There are no stipulations, commandments or conditions: the land once given to the patriarchs and thus to the whole of Israel will forever remain in their tenancy. However, Brueggemann argues, there is also the gift of land promised to Israel under the condition of strict observance of the Torah (Exod. 3.8; 19.6; Deut. 30.15-20).[103] A genuine promised land theology that does not lead to oppression must consider both the unconditional gift of land to the patriarchs and the conditional gift to the whole of Israel:

> Thus, we are in my judgment required to continue to struggle with the condi-tional–unconditional and the exclusory–welcoming hospitality trajectories without assuming an absolute resolve that disregards the capaciousness of the tradition.[104]

However, if Brueggemann wants to maintain the desired tension between the two rival socio-economic and religious groups in order to create a decent postcolonial promised land theology, he would, in addition to the conditional–unconditional nature of the gift of land, also have to consider the claim that is unpopular among liberation and postcolonial theologians that the Canaanites were driven out of the land *because of their wickedness* (Gen. 15.16; Lev. 18.25). Taking these references into account and thus maintaining the conditionality of tenancy of the land for everyone – not only for those currently oppressed – may be considered a genuine and honest attempt to free oneself from the ideological biases on both, or possibly all, sides.

Like Warrior, Brueggemann draws a parallel between the consequences of the Israelite settlement narrative and the European settlement of North America: 'There is no doubt that such land entitlement has functioned as a warrant for European seizure of what became the United States with a brutalizing dismissal of Native Americans, who are regarded as an

---

102. Walter Brueggemann, 'Reading the Bible amid the Israeli–Palestinian Conflict', *Theology Today* 73, no. 1 (2016): 38.

103. Ibid., 37.

104. Ibid., 38.

inconvenience for the arriving entitled Europeans'.[105] Brueggemann criticizes the American exclusivity that he believes has always led to ignoring the needs and wishes of other nations:

> There is no doubt that in the orbit of US exceptionalism the United States understands itself to be God's most recently chosen people or, as Abraham Lincoln termed it, 'almost chosen'. Nor is there any doubt that US chosenness readily evolved into imperial ambition and aggression.[106]

In addition to the 'Canaanite stigma', promised land theology must also be criticized for its ideological bias from the perspective of the land. Biblical scholarship has been increasingly interested in environmental-ecological interpretations, especially of the books of Leviticus and Kings, in which 'land' is not seen as a mere agent of the relationship between God and God's people but as one part of a three-way relationship:

> Given the right of the monarch to exploit the land as a source of wealth, it is logical that this ideology offers no hint of rights or concerns for the land itself. The function of the land is apparently to produce riches rather than to reflect an empathy with God's feelings or Israel's attitudes.[107]

As we saw when discussing the land law in the context of the monarchy, the land is a free gift from God to the people of Israel and is not to be re-sold. However, when Israel appoints an earthly king in place of YHWH, the land becomes just another commodity and the king claims his right over it, as we saw in the story of Naboth's vineyard. The king will naturally then wish to accumulate more and more pieces of land from small farmers and so create a latifundia.

In his most recent articles 'The Book of Joshua... Give or Take the Land' (2012) and 'Reading the Bible amid the Israeli–Palestinian Conflict' (2016), Brueggemann becomes more vocal, speaking out on current political developments in the Middle East. Although he does not go as far as Burge, his interpretation is nonetheless black and white, with a clear idea of who is who with respect to oppressor and oppressed:

---

105. Brueggemann, *The Land*, xv.

106. Brueggemann, 'Reading the Bible amid the Israeli–Palestinian Conflict', 39.

107. Habel and Brueggemann, *The Land Is Mine*, 22. See also Jonathan Morgan, 'Transgressing, Puking, Covenanting: The Character of Land in Leviticus', *Theology* 112 (2009): 172–80; Ellen Davis, *Scripture, Culture, and Agriculture: An Agrarian Reading of the Bible* (New York: Cambridge University Press, 2009); Brueggemann, *1 & 2 Kings*.

And now that violence of the chosen toward the unchosen is being acted
out with reference to the Palestinians, the current non-chosen who suffer at
the hands of the chosen who have reduced the tradition to an unconditional
promise and who have reduced the practice of "the other" to exclusion. Of
course, the Palestinians also commit unacceptable violence; but the subject
here is the role played by appeal to the biblical tradition of chosen-ness as
a justification for violence.[108]

In 'Postcolonial Biblical Hermeneutics: Interpreting with a Genuine
Attunement to Otherness', Daniel Martino suggests that to avoid roman-
ticizing the poor, biblical interpreters should 'see the other' in their own
reading of the Bible rather than 'reading with' the oppressed.[109] Martino
fears that 'reading with' the oppressed (liberation theology) only 'gives
the weapon' to the other side. However, such an approach can lead
to the kind of 'liberation' in which the former oppressors become the
oppressed. By pointing towards the context which provoked the original
injustice, true postcolonialism seeks to put the historical injustice right
without producing another injustice. In the context of the promised land,
it is the very promise and the desire it incites that brings the temptation.
Brueggemann fails to stress the temporality of the Israelite–Canaanite
relationship and the fact that it is reversible at any point in history: if
YHWH was at one time 'God the Liberator', there must have been a time
when the Israelites were oppressed by the Canaanites. The temporality of
the relationship between oppressed and oppressor is skilfully described by
Scott Langston,[110] who refers to social rather than ethnic groups and points
out that the context of the former can change quickly. Likewise, Gottwald
and Warrior insist that the Israelite–Canaanite conflict was carried out in a
social rather than ethnic context. The context of the current state of Israel
is, of course, more complex, and involves the stigmatization of communities on racial or 'national' grounds, which is of course untenable.

Brueggemann's earlier admirable symbolic interpretation and the
universal applicability of the concept of landlessness and landedness is
not applied in the later, essentially political interpretations. In the face
of actual events, Brueggemann seems to forget his own conviction that
being oppressed is not an ontological identity and not a matter of choice

108. Brueggemann, 'Reading the Bible amid the Israeli–Palestinian Conflict', 40.
109. Daniel Martino, 'Postcolonial Biblical Hermeneutics: Interpreting with a
Genuine Attunement to Otherness', *Analecta Hermeneutica*, no. 4 (2012): 14–15.
110. Scott Langston, 'Exodus in Early Twentieth-Century America: Charles
Reynolds Brown and Lawrence Langner', in Lieb and Mason, eds, *The Oxford
Handbook of Reception History of the Bible*, 433–47.

but of context: '"Chosen-ness" that does not take seriously the legitimate claims of the other is likely to be a myopic self-serving ideology'.[111] In order to problematize Brueggemann's view, we must stress that poverty is not a virtue but something God calls us to fight while protecting the poor themselves (Exod. 23.6; Deut. 15.7-11). But if we see the poor as unquestionable idols rather than as icons (windows on God), we run the risk of creating a dangerous ideology. In addition to emphasizing the conditional nature of the gift of land and therefore the possibility of losing it, Brueggemann should also stress that there is always a way back and that the risk of losing the land applies to everyone regardless of ethnicity.

It sometimes seems as though Brueggemann's liberation theology is all about salving a guilty conscience:

> It would be better – and easier – if we could just all agree on a liberal, romantic god who is all-merciful, all-compassionate, and all-forgiving... But that, of course, is not the God we meet in the middle of the night when we revisit old wounds and are revisited by old demons. That is not the God we get in our intimate battlefield when we aggressively ask with Joshua, 'are you one of us, or one of our adversaries?' (5:13)[112]

Should Brueggemann not be asking if his ideology critique does not in fact create another ideological bias? Perhaps his identity as a white male Westerner with a history of colonialism prevents a clear vision of the past. There is no doubt that an easy and ideological promised land theology which has caused oppression, violence, and the theft of land in the name of 'the elect' who hold the Bible in their hands must be crushed and condemned. But is it not also necessary to look to the future and be careful in our attempts to 'redress' in case they too plant the seeds of oppression, violence, and ideology? Are the poor in need of such unconditional protection? What if our new route to liberation causes secondary victimization? Noble argues: 'In as much as liberation theology really wants to claim to be a new way of doing theology, it must always be open to recognizing the danger of creating an ideology'.[113] Postcolonialism can function as a corrective to liberation theology because it does not perceive the problem of the margins through the lens of dialectics (i.e. in opposition to the 'centre') but focuses exclusively on the margins in their own context and their problems in all their complexity.

---

111. Brueggemann, 'Reading the Bible amid the Israeli–Palestinian Conflict', 41.
112. Brueggemann, 'The God of Joshua... Give or Take the Land', 174.
113. Noble, *The Poor in Liberation Theology*, 70.

John Steinbeck's interpretation of the promised land motif

Jackson Benson suggests that much of what influenced Steinbeck's life was imprinted on him by his parents. From his father came a respect for the land, and from his mother a sense for mysticism and philosophy:

> So, out of his diverse parental influences, there developed a deep split reflected in both John Steinbeck's personality and his work. On the one hand, there developed the biological, the strong ecological perspective that he alone of major writers of his lifetime had; on the other there was the mystical, the philosophical, which became associated with myth and legend.[114]

Although Steinbeck's mother was probably the more intellectually gifted of his parents, or at least had more opportunities to study, it was his father who encouraged the young John to follow his dream and become a writer. Decades later, after both his parents had died, Steinbeck noted in his diary:

> In my struggle to be a writer, it was [my father] who supported and backed me and explained me – not my mother. She wanted me desperately to be something decent like a banker. She would have liked me to be a successful writer like Tarkington but this she didn't believe I could do. But my father wanted me to be myself... Mother always thought I would get over it and come to my senses. And the failure of all [my mother's family] might be that they came to their senses.[115]

John Ernst Steinbeck was born to a middle-class family on February 27, 1902, in Salinas, Monterey County, California. His father John Ernst and mother Olive Hamilton Steinbeck had four children: three daughters and one son – John Ernst junior.[116] Steinbeck's grandfather, John Adolph, had come to the United States from Germany as a Lutheran missionary and settled in California. The Hamilton family had come from Northern Ireland and bought a ranch east of King City in Monterey County.[117]

114. Jackson Benson, 'An Introduction to John Steinbeck', in *A John Steinbeck Encyclopedia*, ed. Brian Railsback and Michael Meyer (Westport, CT: Greenwood, 2006), xlii.

115. John Steinbeck, *Journal of a Novel: East of Eden Letters* (New York: Viking, 1969), 103.

116. Fontenrose, *John Steinbeck*, 2. See also Robert DeMott, 'Introduction', in *The Grapes of Wrath*, ed. Robert DeMott, Penguin Twentieth-Century Classics (London: Penguin, 1992), xv; Benson, 'An Introduction to John Steinbeck', xli.

117. Fontenrose, *John Steinbeck*, 1.

John Steinbeck junior grew up in Salinas and made trips with his family to San Francisco, Monterey, Pacific Grove, Carmel, and the Hamilton ranch near King City. These places had an enormous impact on Steinbeck, and all found their way into his novels.

A gifted student with a passion for literature, Steinbeck graduated from Salinas High School in 1919. The family adopted the Hamilton's church, so Steinbeck acquired an Episcopal upbringing and attended the Episcopal Sunday school.[118] Between 1920 and 1925, Steinbeck attended Stanford University, majoring in English journalism.[119]

Between school semesters he had various manual jobs on ranches and in sugar mills where he learned something about the life of socially disadvantaged people, another influence which would become clear in his writings.[120] He took classes in story-writing, a year-long course in classical literature, and an introductory course in zoology, but never graduated.[121] Steinbeck's early manuscripts, which he sent to various magazines, were almost always rejected. The first promising piece, 'Fingers of Clouds', was published in the *Stanford Spectator*.[122] In 1925 Steinbeck moved to New York City, earning his living as a construction worker on the Madison Square Garden project before becoming a reporter on the *New York American*. He was not a successful journalist, however, and was 'released' soon afterwards. He stayed on in New York as a freelance writer but became disillusioned and returned to California. He did a series of odd jobs for three years, moving around California alternating writing and working, but no publisher would buy his stories.[123]

Steinbeck's income was therefore modest until *Tortilla Flat* was published in 1935. His first novel *The Cup of Gold* was published in 1929 but was not a great success. *Pastures of Heaven* and *To a God Unknown* were published in 1932 and 1933 respectively but they also sold poorly. In 1930 he married Carol Henning and acquired a small monthly allowance and a house in Pacific Grove.[124] The same year he met Edward Ricketts, who stimulated his interest in and passion for zoology, an influence that can be seen in novels such as *In Dubious Battle*, *Cannery Row*, and *Sweet Thursday*.[125] Steinbeck's most famous novel, *The Grapes of Wrath*, was

---

118. Ibid., 3.
119. DeMott, 'Introduction', 1992, xv.
120. Fontenrose, *John Steinbeck*, 3.
121. DeMott, 'Introduction', 1992, xv.
122. Fontenrose, *John Steinbeck*, 3.
123. Ibid., 4.
124. DeMott, 'Introduction', 1992, xvi.
125. Fontenrose, *John Steinbeck*, 4.

published in 1939, and a luminous literary career was capped in 1962 with the Nobel Prize in Literature. Steinbeck died in 1968.[126]

Steinbeck's attitude towards the land, clear throughout his novels, is summed up in the following much-quoted passage from the non-fiction work *America and Americans*:

> It is customary (indeed, at high-school graduations it is a requirement) for speakers to refer to America as a 'precious inheritance' – our heritage, a gift proffered like a sandwich wrapped in plastic on a plastic tray. Our ancestors, so it is implied, gathered to the invitation of a golden land and accepted the sacrament of milk and honey. This is not so.[127]

Steinbeck's hesitation between faith in the American dream of a new promised land and a critical distance informed by its consequences could not have been better expressed.[128] The language alludes to both the biblical roots of the promised land and the subsequent tradition: Exod. 3.8 (the 'golden land' and 'sacrament of milk and honey') and Gen. 15.7 (the 'precious heritage' and a 'gift proffered like a sandwich wrapped in plastic on a plastic tray'; in other words 'a free gift'). Here, Steinbeck testifies to the popular picture of America as the promised land, a conviction so deeply rooted in American minds that Steinbeck's hyperbole regarding graduation speeches is entirely believable. The tradition was part of the fabric of American society in Steinbeck's day and continues to be so.

It was Steinbeck's novels, however, rather than his non-fiction, which brought scholars to acknowledge his exceptional interest in the motif of the promised land,[129] conspicuous in *To a God Unknown* (1933), *The Grapes of Wrath* (1939), and *East of Eden* (1952),[130] and less

126. Benson, 'An Introduction to John Steinbeck', xlvii.

127. Steinbeck, *America and Americans*, 12.

128. See also: 'In nearly every story or novel he wrote, Steinbeck strove to hold the failed myth up to the light of everyday reality and to stress the necessity for commitment to place and to man as a way out of the waste-land defined by writers of the twenties'. Louis Owens, *John Steinbeck's Revision of America* (Athens, GA: University of Georgia Press, 1985), 3–4.

129. 'No one has yet recognized clearly, however, that behind Steinbeck's holistic philosophy, his "phalanx" theory, his non-teleological thinking, his agrarianism, his mixture of Christianity and paganism, lies a profound fascination with and acute sensitivity to California's place in the American consciousness – an awareness of California as the literal and symbolic terminus of the American Eden myth.' Ibid., 5.

130. John Steinbeck is, of course, an author of many more novels, short stories, and other writings. We have chosen those works considered significant for the

so in *The Pastures of Heaven* (1932) and *Of Mice and Men* (1937). Brueggemann references *Of Mice and Men*, *The Grapes of Wrath* and *East of Eden* in his biblical commentaries.

Steinbeck as a biblical interpreter

During the Enlightenment search for 'the objective' and 'the scientific', art was largely lost as a hermeneutical tool. The struggles of the philosophers, literary theorists, and biblical scholars who sought to point out the importance of art and restore its role in the hermeneutical process have been dealt with by many authors and also on the pages of this book. Steinbeck's own observation on the role of art in hermeneutics is worth noting:

> Not long ago, after my trip to Russia, I had a conversation with an American very eminent in the field of politics. I asked him what he read, and he replied that he studied history, sociology, economics, and law. 'How about fiction – novels, plays, poetry?' I asked. 'No', he said, 'I have never had time for them. There is so much else I have to read.' I said, 'Sir, I have recently visited Russia for the third time. I don't know how well I understand Russians; but I do know that if I had only read Russian history I could not have had the access to Russian thinking I have had from reading Dostoevski, Tolstoi, Chekhov, Pushkin... History only recounts, with some inaccuracy, what they did. The fiction tells, or tries to tell, why they did it and what they felt and were like when they did it.' My friend nodded gravely. 'I hadn't thought of that', he said. 'Yes, it might be so; I had always thought of fiction as opposed to fact'.[131]

Steinbeck is suggesting that the knowledge we obtain from reading novels can often be more profound than that obtained from reading non-fiction. 'Why?' is a basic hermeneutical question because it ultimately leads us to a better understanding of a problem. Only when we know the reason can we truly assess a problem in all its depth. Steinbeck argues that we can gain such knowledge by reading novels; Brueggemann agrees.

Steinbeck adheres to a dialogical hermeneutic between author, text, and reader, as DeMott explains: 'Steinbeck's participatory aesthetic was based on a circle of complicity that linked "the trinity" of writer, text and reader [that ensures] maximum affective impact'.[132] I would agree, and add

promised land motif by Steinbeck scholars. Works such as *In Dubious Battle*, *Sea of Cortez*, *Cannery Row*, and *Sweet Thursday* deal with Steinbeck's other passion, biology.

131. Steinbeck, *America and Americans*, 163–4.
132. DeMott, 'Introduction', 1992, xiv.

confidently that Steinbeck is a biblical interpreter,[133] a rightful 'player' in the Gadamerian sense. His co-player, as two players are always required, is the biblical text: Steinbeck plays with the biblical text and the biblical text plays with Steinbeck. This is how the 're-creation', the artistic interpretation of the biblical text in the form of his novels, arises. A transaction between the two essential elements in the reading process, the reader and the text, gives rise to a 'response'. As we have already discussed, this re-creation participates in knowledge regarding the biblical text, and by 're-presenting' it from a different perspective helps us to grasp its essence.

Steinbeck was clearly influenced by more than the biblical text. He was also informed by the popular national tradition of identifying North America with the promised land, as diachronic scholarship suggests. However, such a way of interpreting the American tradition relies too heavily on the supposed continuity within the tradition and overlooks any hiatuses. A noticeable break from tradition came in the shape of twentieth-century authors such as T. S. Eliot and F. Scott Fitzgerald, who on occasion call America's promised land heritage into question. Both authors are nevertheless formed by the religious-cultural context of promised land America and on closer inspection both fail to overcome their roots. Steinbeck, a younger compatriot of Fitzgerald, who lived through both world wars and the Great Depression, operates with a more critical distance from tradition, as Owens suggests:

> The 'new seeing' Steinbeck proposed would exchange the myth of an American Eden, with its dangerous flaws, for the ideal of commitment – commitment to what Steinbeck called 'the one inseparable unit man plus his environment'.[134]

The three most important streams of thought which formed that tradition, Puritanism, Jefferson agrarianism, and transcendentalism, can all be detected in Steinbeck's novels, but the last of these led the discussion regarding the biblical symbolism in Steinbeck's work. Frederic Carpenter kicked off the transcendental note of the debate by describing

---

133. McEntyre argues that in some of Steinbeck's novels, 'the underlying biblical material provides, through the transforming medium of fiction, a way of understanding in radically biblical, loosely Christian terms not only human history (in which there seems to be a recurrent compulsion to re-enact the dramas of Genesis, Exodus, and the Gospels) but also, more specifically, American history and culture'. Marilyn McEntyre, 'Bible', in Railsback and Meyer, eds, *A John Steinbeck Encyclopedia*, 28.

134. Owens, *John Steinbeck's Revision of America*, 3.

Steinbeck's novels as moving from Waldo's 'individual over-soul' to Whitman's 'collective over-soul'.[135] It is the other two streams, however, to which I turn for an exploration of the motif of the promised land.

Puritanism was unjustly driven from the discussion as something fundamentalist which had been overcome decades or even centuries before, but it is undoubtedly the Puritan legacy that brings Steinbeck to the idea that if there ever was a promised land, it could not be reached by failing human beings. One could also argue that the same Puritan legacy brings Brueggemann to conclude that we are either approaching the promised land or losing it and that our trajectory depends not on our choice but on our socio-economic context (determinism). In her exploration of *The Grapes of Wrath*, Agnes Donohue argues that, 'The Puritan tradition of man's corrupted will is implicit in Steinbeck's Okies, but he sees them ruefully and compassionately'.[136]

Jefferson agrarianism is another stream that tends to be neglected in discussions on Steinbeck, even though Jefferson had a clearer emphasis on the land than did Emerson or Whitman:

> Basic to [Jefferson agrarianism] is the belief that landed property held in freehold must be available to everyone… To [Jefferson], equalitarian democracy meant a country made up of small farmers… Although Jefferson himself never went so far, many Jeffersonians agreed that if a man could not get legal title to landed property, he could claim ownership to land he occupied and tilled by virtue of a natural right to it.[137]

As we shall see when discussing Steinbeck's novels, Jefferson agrarianism is probably the most important element in Steinbeck's understanding of landed property and democracy; land is certainly more important to

---

135. 'Transcendentalism sought to save the individual but not the group… Whitman sympathized more deeply with the common people and loved them abstractly, but trusted God and democracy would save them. The pragmatic philosophers first sought to implement American idealism by making thought itself instrumental. And now Steinbeck quotes scripture to urge popular action for the realization of the old ideals.' Frederic Carpenter, 'The Philosophical Joads', in *A Case Book on The Grapes of Wrath*, ed. Agnes McNeill Donohue (New York: Thomas Y. Crowell, 1970), 86.

136. Agnes McNeill Donohue, "'The Endless Journey to No End': Journey and Eden Symbolism in Hawthorne and Steinbeck', in Donohue, ed., *A Casebook on The Grapes of Wrath*, 259.

137. Chester Eisinger, 'Jefferson Agrarianism in *The Grapes of Wrath*', in Donohue, ed., *A Case Book on The Grapes of Wrath*, 145.

Steinbeck than it is to, say, Fitzgerald. Regardless of where he lived, Steinbeck was an avid gardener:

> We can only guess the full implications of what having a garden meant to him, but since the most commonly used mythic/symbolic structure in his work was the Garden of Eden, we can surmise that there was in his own gardening some sense of connection with the history of man and the processes of nature.[138]

Industrialization and the 'rape' of the land in the first half of the twentieth century prompted a small revival of Jefferson agrarianism. Deeply affected by the deaths of millions in two world wars, Steinbeck saw some hope in the 'return to the land' which was once our main provider. In Jefferson's day, agrarianism had been a thoroughly democratic stream that secured a living for middle-class people: 'Steinbeck was concerned with democracy, and looked upon agrarianism as a way of life that would enable us to realize the full potentialities of the creed. Jefferson, of course, held the same belief.'[139]

America and Americans helps us to understand Steinbeck's complicated and seemingly ambivalent attitude towards the land.[140] We have seen that different topics within the promised land motif have come to the fore in different eras, depending on the 'horizon of expectations'.[141] What was important during the patristic period was not so important in the modern era and vice versa. Steinbeck and Brueggemann face similar problems, struggles, and questions and deal with similar topics. Like Brueggemann, Steinbeck addresses attitudes to the indigenous population of the promised land, and attitudes towards the land itself.

138. Benson, 'An Introduction to John Steinbeck', xlii.

139. Eisinger, 'Jefferson Agrarianism in *The Grapes of Wrath*', 144.

140. Nancy Zane sees the two sides of the American paradise in a similar way: 'The end result is the awareness that America is a paradox – it embodies the hope and the futility of the American Dream; it offers both assurance and despair. In the midst of financial security is moral decay; coexistent with the majestic, stunning landscape is environmental abuse.' Nancy Zane, 'America and Americans', in Railsback and Meyer, eds, *A John Steinbeck Encyclopedia*, 9.

141. A horizon of expectation mediates between an 'individual experience' and a 'methodological understanding'. It contains both subjective and objective elements. The individual experience takes place during the reading process and is oriented synchronically; the methodological understanding mediates between the work and its historical setting. Both the individual experience from reading and the historical setting of the writings of John Steinbeck and Walter Brueggemann suggest that the works of these two authors will be closer to each other than the works of John Steinbeck and, for example, Flavius Josephus.

Steinbeck describes the hostile attitude of the settlers to the Native Americans, an attitude we saw outlined in Brueggemann's ideology critique of the settlement narrative. The Native Americans in their own land are compared to the Canaanites in the promised land, and their lives are likewise threatened with extinction:

> In some cases they seem to have tried to get along with their guests, and when it became apparent that this was impossible – it is difficult to be friendly with someone who wants to take everything you have – the Indians not only defended themselves but inflicted telling losses on the settlers... The Indians survived our open intention of wiping them out.[142]

Steinbeck also addresses the environmental-ecological problems created by exploitation of the land. The settlers behaved as if there were no limits to nature's ability to restore itself: 'Perhaps they felt that it was limitless and could never be exhausted and that a man could move on to new wonders endlessly.'[143] This idea is closely linked to the concept of *owning*, which inevitably leads to *managing*, and thus also to *misusing*. Like Brueggemann, Steinbeck refers to both managing the land[144] and managing the people;[145] the two forms of management are inherently related.

In our analysis of Steinbeck's novels, we will see how the author struggled with Puritanism, agrarianism, and transcendentalism throughout his life and his literary work, and will see how each of these elements

142. Steinbeck, *America and Americans*, 18, 19.

143. Ibid., 144.

144. 'They cut and burnt the forests to make room for crops; they abandoned their knowledge of kindness to the land in order to maintain its usefulness... There has always been more than enough desert in America; the new settlers, like overindulged children, created even more... The railroads brought new hordes of land-crazy people, and the new Americans moved like locusts across the continent until the western sea put a boundary to their movements. Coal and copper and gold drew them on; they savaged the land, gold dragged the rivers to skeletons of pebbles and debris.' Ibid., 146.

145. 'Later, with the development of farm machinery it became possible for very few men to farm very large tracts. The only difficulty lay in increasing taxes, the cost of machinery and fertilizer, and that new thing in the world – overproduction: too much food, with a resulting drop in prices, came to haunt large farmers. The need to borrow and the advantages of corporate organizations made the huge farms into factories, owned mostly by banks and or stock companies. Great holdings owned by one man or family became fewer and fewer, so that where once there were many estates as large as provinces, at the present there are very few; and the ones that do survive are almost museum pieces.' Ibid., 84–5.

touches on the motif of the promised land. The table below recalls the two
biblical verses that most influenced the biblical and subsequent tradition
of the promised land motif (Exod. 3.8 and Gen. 15.7);[146] the two verses
can also be traced in the five novels that we will be analysing.

Exod. 3.8	And I am come down to deliver them out of the hand of the Egyptians, and to bring them up out of that land unto *a good land and a large land*, unto a *land flowing of milk and honey*; unto the place of the Canaanites, and the Hittites, and the Amorites, and the Perizzites, and the Hivites, and the Jebusites.
Gen. 15.7	And he said unto him, I am the Lᴏʀᴅ that brought thee out of Ur of the Chaldees, to *give thee this land to inherit it*.
Pastures of Heaven	In a few minutes he arrived at the top of the ridge, and there he stopped, stricken with wonder at what he saw – a long valley floored with *green pasturage* on which a herd of deer browsed. Perfect oak trees grew in the meadow of the lovely place, and the hills hugged it jealously against the fog and the wind... 'Holy Mother!' he whispered. 'Here are the *green pastures of Heaven to which our Lord leadeth us*.'
To a God Unknown	'And I have a hunger for *land of my own*, sir. I have been reading about the West and *the good cheap land* there'... 'But they're homesteading the western land, sir. You have only a year to live on the land and build a house and plough a little bit and *the land is yours*. No one can ever take it away.'
Of Mice and Men	'We could live offa the *fatta the lan'*... 'All kin's a vegetables in the garden,... We'd belong there'... 'An' *it'd be our own, an' nobody could can us*'.
The Grapes of Wrath	Maybe we can start again, in the *new rich land* – in California, *where the fruit grows*. We'll start over.
East of Eden	'It's nice in California', he said. 'It's nice in the winter. And you can *raise anything there*... They raise a lot of wheat in California'... 'Look, Charles, things grow so fast in California they say *you have to plant and step back quick or you'll get knocked down*.'

146. 'Beginning with *To a God Unknown* in 1933, Steinbeck rejects the Eden
myth and the formal religion upon which it is based, offering in its place an ideal of
commitment to "the whole thing".' Owens, *John Steinbeck's Revision of America*, 6.

Four of the five novels have a title that alludes to familiar biblical verses: *Pastures of Heaven* to Ps. 23.1-2;[147] *To a God Unknown* to Acts 17.23;[148] *The Grapes of Wrath* to Jer. 31.29,[149] Ezek. 18.2, and Rev. 14.19;[150] and *East of Eden* to Gen. 4.16.[151] The five quotations illustrate Steinbeck's vision of the 'promised land' of California. The words in italics point towards the attributes of the promised land: its virginity, bounty, fertility, and, of course, its ripeness for being settled and farmed. They are all notably influenced by the twin emphases of Exod. 3.8 and Gen. 15.7, a rich land, a free gift,[152] although we will see as our analysis progresses how the idea of a land of promise gradually transforms into a land of slavery.[153]

A foretaste of paradise: The Pastures of Heaven *and* Of Mice and Men

We begin by sketching out expositions from *The Pastures of Heaven* and *Of Mice and Men* in which Steinbeck presents his notion of California as the promised land, and equally of the way the promised land slips away from the very people who eagerly seek it.

147. 'The LORD is my shepherd; I shall not want. He maketh me to lie down in green pastures: he leadeth me beside the still waters' (KJV).

148. 'For as I passed by, and beheld your devotions, I found an altar with this inscription, TO THE UNKNOWN GOD. Whom therefore ye ignorantly worship, him declare I unto you' (KJV). Steinbeck himself attributes the title of the book to Rig Veda 10:121, which was even printed in the book, immediately before the title page.

149. 'In those days they shall say no more, "The fathers have eaten a sour grape, and the children's teeth are set on edge"' (KJV; Ezek. 18.2 provides a parallel to this verse from Jeremiah).

150. 'And the angel thrust in his sickle into the earth, and gathered the vine of the earth, and cast it into the great winepress of the wrath of God' (KJV).

151. 'And Cain went out from the presence of the LORD, and dwelt in the land of Nod, on the east of Eden' (KJV).

152. Some of the allusions arguably refer more easily to other biblical verses, specifically 'the *green pastures of Heaven to which our Lord leadeth us*', to Ps. 23.2. The verses mentioned, however, relate to reception of the promised land motif with a source in Gen. 15.7 and Exod. 3.8.

153. 'There are no Edens in Steinbeck's writings, only illusions of Eden, and in the fallen world of the Salinas Valley – which Steinbeck would later place "east of Eden" – the Promised land is an illusory and painful dream.' Louis Owens, '*Of Mice and Men*: The Dream of Commitment', in *John Steinbeck*, Bloom's Modern Critical Views (New York: Infobase, 2008), 17.

The Pastures of Heaven is a collection of short stories set in the Corral de Tierra in the Santa Lucia Mountains of California;[154] in the stories, the valley is called *Las Pasturas del Cielo* (the Pastures of Heaven). The quotation in the table describes how the valley was discovered by a Spanish missionary. Steinbeck imagines the event: 'We can only reconstruct his holy emotion of discovery, but the name he gave to the sweet valley in the hills remains there. It is known to this day as *Las Pasturas del Cielo*.'[155] Only a few paragraphs later, however, we discover that this Edenic scenery hides serious problems, as Owens explains: '[This] small valley in California is a microcosm for America and the people of that valley, with their fatal insistence upon a kind of illusory innocence, microcosmic Americans'.[156] The first short story provides us with Steinbeck's idea of the promised land and functions as the basic setting for the stories that follow, stories which develop a basic narrative about the promise and loss of land. Steinbeck describes the paradisiacal scenery in the valley:

> [B]y some regal accident, the section came under no great land grant. No Spanish nobleman became its possessor through the loan of his money or his wife. For a long time it lay forgotten in its embracing hills… After a long time a few families of squatters moved into the Pastures of Heaven and built fences and planted fruit trees. Since no one owned the land, they squabbled a great deal over its possession. After a hundred years…the families at last lived prosperously and at peace. Their land was rich and easy to work. The fruits of their gardens were the finest produced in central California.[157]

The valley is described as the best possible place for farming, and as having the advantage of escaping attention for some years. But there is a threat in the middle of this paradise in the form of a cursed farm which is full of potential but always fails and is eventually deserted:

> Good land although it was, well watered and fertile, no one in the valley coveted the place, no one would live in the house, for land and houses that have been tended, loved and laboured with and finally deserted, seem always sodden with gloom and with threatening… The deserted farm was situated not far from the middle of the narrow valley. On both sides it was bounded by the best and most prosperous farms in the Pastures of Heaven… The people of the valley considered it a place of curious evil.[158]

---

154. Fontenrose, *John Steinbeck*, 20.
155. John Steinbeck, *The Pastures of Heaven* (London: Duality, 1946), 6.
156. Owens, *The Grapes of Wrath*, 50.
157. Steinbeck, *The Pastures of Heaven*, 6.
158. Ibid., 6–7.

Steinbeck plays further with the paradisiacal allusion: if there is evil in paradise, there must be a woman and a serpent close by. The first farmer to till the land is called Battle, and he marries a woman with 'a mild tendency to epilepsy, a disease then called "fits", and generally ascribed to animosity on the part of the deity'.[159] She has a son, John, and the chance of a happy life on the farm, but her illness gets the better of her. After making two attempts to set fire to the farm, she is sent to a 'little private prison'. The serpent comes into view after the death of Battle. One night, John, who has inherited his mother's disease and the militant religious fundamentalism that goes with it, has a fight with evil spirits. The serpent appears, bites John three times, and he dies. The people have failed in their struggle against the serpent and from that day forward the land is cursed (Gen. 3.17):

> One day in the deepening twilight John crept carefully upon a lilac bush in his own yard. He knew the bush sheltered a secret gathering of friends. When he was so close that they could not escape, he jumped to his feet and lunged towards the lilac, flailing his stick and screaming. Aroused by the slashing blows, a snake rattled sleepily and raised its flat, hard head. John dropped his stick and shuddered, for the dry sharp warning of a snake is a terrifying sound. He fell upon his knees and prayed for the moment. Suddenly he shouted, 'This is the damned serpent. Out, devil', and sprang forward with clutching fingers. The snake struck him three times in the throat where there were no crosses to protect him. He struggled very little, and died in a few minutes.[160]

The curse of the land is said to be removed when a new family comes to the Pastures of Heaven. Interestingly, the farmer overcomes the curse because he believes he is himself cursed and that the two curses cancel each other out. All is not well, however, as Steinbeck explains through some words spoken to the new farmer: 'Maybe your curse and the farm's curse has mated and gone into a gopher hole like a pair of rattlesnakes. Maybe there'll be a lot of baby curses crawling around the Pastures the first thing we know.'[161]

The stories that follow tell of the 'cursed family' living on the 'cursed farm' in the middle of the Pastures of Heaven. The paradisiacal backdrops contrast sharply with the lives of the people affected by the curse, which avoids the family itself but has an impact on all the other families living

159. Ibid., 8.
160. Ibid., 9.
161. Ibid., 17.

in the neighbourhood. Fontenrose suggests that the promised land in the valley had always been an illusion,[162] but this is not true. The promised land is never an illusion. It simply slips away from people when they believe they have reached it.

In *Of Mice and Men*, George and his 'backward' friend Lennie are migrant workers who wander from post to post. They can never hold down a job as Lennie's disability causes them constant trouble and they are always having to move on. At their final place of work, Lennie accidentally kills a girl, setting off a course of events that ends in George shooting Lennie out of mercy.

Fontenrose argues that the concern for the land that we find in this novel is replicated in all of Steinbeck's writings:

> Man's longing for the land, a favourite Steinbeck theme, appearing in some way in nearly every novel, is here expressed in the farmhand's and bindle stiff's desire for a few acres of his own, so that he can be his own boss.[163]

Eisinger suggests that *Of Mice and Men* is a classical product of the agrarian legacy. The novel's protagonist longs to own a piece of land: '[George] wants the independence that ownership can give him. Nobody could fire him if the farm was his.'[164] 'Ownership' here is not the same concept as that described by Brueggemann. It refers rather to the idea of inheritance according to both an agrarian and a biblical understanding. If the owner fails to care properly for the land and the people, ownership can result in the enslavement of both. This does not apply to the original idea of agrarianism, which like the land law in the Hebrew Bible was built on individual ownership and individual husbandry.

The hired agricultural workers in California are referred to as 'migratory', but to earn a living such migration was usually a necessity:

> George and Lennie were not migratory from choice – at any rate, they talked about settling down. They shared a dream of independence, of owning a little farm of their own. George, of course, had invented the content of the dream, and Lennie loved to hear him tell about what they would have on the farm, particularly about the rabbits which Lennie would tend – provided he kept out of trouble.[165]

---

162. Fontenrose, *John Steinbeck*, 28.
163. Ibid., 56.
164. Eisinger, 'Jefferson Agrarianism in *The Grapes of Wrath*', 146.
165. Fontenrose, *John Steinbeck*, 54.

Steinbeck's attitude towards the promised land was far from straight-forward. The story of George and Lennie suggests that the dream of owning a piece of land in order to secure freedom and independence must ultimately fail; the promised land will always slip away. Crooks, another migrant worker, describes this pattern of dreaming and failing:

> I seen hundreds of men come by on the road an' on the ranches, with their bindles on their back an' that same damn thing in their heads. Hundreds of them. They come an' they quit an' go on; an every damn one of 'em's got a little piece of land in his head. An' never a God damn one of 'em ever gets it. Just like heaven... Nobody never gets to heaven and nobody gets no land. It's just in their head.[166]

On the face of it, George and Lennie's dream appears to fail because of Lennie's inability to stay out of trouble, but Steinbeck helpfully points out through Crooks that failure is inevitable:

> It is part of the American dream, finding expression in such nineteenth-century visions as 'the garden of the west' and 'the garden of the world'. It is a vision of Eden, a land of peace, harmony, prosperity; it includes both individual independence and fellowship. And in Steinbeck's world you aren't likely to get there; as Crooks said, 'Nobody never gets to heaven'.[167]

It is always human weakness that causes the search for the promised land to fail. When George shoots his fellow and friend Lennie in an apparent act of mercy – to prevent others from doing it – he gives up on his dream of owning a small piece of land of his own and spends his entire monthly wage on drink, gambling, and prostitutes, although now of course, without Lennie, it would be much easier to make the dream a reality. Nonetheless, here Steinbeck is illustrating the futility of human attempts to reach paradise:

> From loneliness, from blowing our money in barrooms and eat houses, from jails, good Lord deliver us – and grant us the blessing of fellowship on the land. It is a religion of cooperation, but as in other religions, deprecated evils are powerful to keep man from paradise. The individual's desire for carefree enjoyment of pleasures is the serpent in the garden.[168]

---

166. John Steinbeck, *Of Mice and Men* (London: Penguin, 2000), 73.
167. Fontenrose, *John Steinbeck*, 59. Also: 'The land hunger of impoverished farm workers, a dream of independence, usually remains a dream; and when it becomes a real plan, the plan is defeated'. Ibid., 56.
168. Ibid., 59.

If Fontenrose is right, Steinbeck seems to be offering a critique of the individualism inherent in agrarianism, which ultimately prevents a person from securing the land because their very hopes and desires will always get in the way. The land of promise becomes a land of slavery because people fail to search for God, preferring immediate satisfaction rather than investing in a search that demands sweat, toil, and self-denial.

Passion to possess: To a God Unknown

Each of Steinbeck's novels deals with the American legacy of the promised land from a unique point of view. *To a God Unknown* explores the tension between landlessness and landedness which results in an exaggerated, even heathen passion to possess the land.

The novel was one of Steinbeck's early works and was little appreciated by its first readers. In a letter written in 1933 to his former Stanford classmate Carl Wilhelmson, Steinbeck jokes that his book was rejected numerous times but ended up with four publishers wanting to print it at once.[169] Steinbeck intended to write it as a play (he believed the content better suited the stage) but it did not work out well. He even complained to the publisher and his literary agent Mavis McIntosh that he lacked the skill to do it.[170] In a letter to Edith Wagner, his friend and first 'writing teacher', he bemoans the lack of appreciation for the book and suggests the critics had failed to pay enough attention to it and were not doing their jobs properly.[171]

The story begins in 1903 in the American state of Vermont, on a farm run by an old man who has four sons. The main character, with the biblical name Joseph (Wayne), receives a special blessing from his father and leaves for California. When the father dies, Joseph invites his brothers and their families to California to join him in farming. Joseph believes that the spirit of his father has entered the giant old oak growing close to his house. Nearby, Joseph and his brother Thomas discover a rock with a natural spring and Joseph begins to practise the cult of the oak and the rock. Joseph marries Elizabeth McGregor, a schoolteacher from the village, and has a son whom he initiates into his cult. An important element of the story is the presence of Native Americans and a Catholic

---

169. See John Steinbeck, Elaine Steinbeck, and Robert Wallsten, *Steinbeck: A Life in Letters* (New York: Viking, 1975), 86.

170. See ibid., 42.

171. 'I'm glad you like the book. The overthrow of personal individual character and the use of the Homeric generalized symbolic character seems to bother critics although a little study of the Bible or any of the writers of antiquity would show that it is not very revolutionary.' Ibid., 89.

priest with a penchant for a heathen mother-earth cult. Together with the Wayne family, they hold a 'fiesta' full of pagan rituals. Joseph's brother Burton, a staunch evangelical Christian, becomes increasingly offended by the fertility cult and decides to leave, but before doing so, he cuts down the oak tree. Elizabeth dies soon afterwards, and years of drought follow. The remaining family leave the farm and take Joseph's son John with them. The drought becomes unbearable. There is no harvest, no more cows, and no sign of rain to come. Joseph decides that he must die so that the land can recover. He cuts his wrists at the top of the mountain and the rain comes.[172] John Clark Pratt sums up the narrative thread of the novel as follows:

> What Steinbeck has done in this novel is to invert and combine many biblical legends and referents; his characters have been called rather than led by a patriarchal God/Christ/Moses/Joshua/Aaron figure to a land where, after their arrival, they suffer the same adversities (deaths, droughts, dying animals, adultery, lack of water) as did their migrating biblical predecessors, who were en route to their 'promised' land.[173]

The novel recalls God's promise to Abraham of an heir and descendants. As we have seen, this promise is only secondary to the promise of land, but its role in the 'double promise' is an important one. An ability to reproduce was paramount in the tribal society of ancient Israel, but significant, too, in the agricultural communities of early twentieth-century America:

> As [Joseph] watched the community of cabins spring up on the land, as he looked down unto the cradle of the first-born – Thomas' new child – as he notched the ears of the first young calves, he felt the joy that Abraham must have felt when the huge promise bore fruit, when his tribesmen and his goats began to increase. Joseph's passion for fertility grew strong.[174]

Brueggemann pointed out that barrenness is an important motif in the patriarchal narratives.[175] The barrenness of Joseph Wayne in contrast to the fertility of everything around him plays a significant role in the novel. The initial barrenness of the patriarchs' wives, Sarah, Rebecca,

172. John Steinbeck, *To a God Unknown* (New York: Bantam, 1955). See also Fontenrose, *John Steinbeck.*

173. John Clark Pratt, 'To a God Unknown', in Railsback and Meyer, eds, *A John Steinbeck Encyclopedia*, 380.

174. Steinbeck, *To a God Unknown*, 22.

175. Brueggemann, *The Land*, 28, 111, 118.

and Rachel, a barrenness that was nonetheless assigned to the men in the male-dominated society, is represented in the novel by the fact that Joseph is single but his brothers are all married. At first Joseph did not even think of marrying. He was married to the land – 'For a moment the land had been his wife'[176] – and for some time understood all the produce around him to be his progeny. Nevertheless, after some time he began to long for an heir: 'The hopeless sin was barrenness, a sin intolerable and unforgivable… Everything on the land is producing. I am the only sterile thing. I need a wife.'[177]

There are clear connections between *To a God Unknown* and the story of the biblical Joseph: the main characters share a name, and both have a brother called Benjamin whom everyone loved for no apparent reason. Joseph and Benjamin were the two youngest sons of Jacob-Israel, born to Jacob's beloved and long-barren wife Rachel. Before he leaves for California, Joseph receives a blessing from his father, an allusion to Jacob's blessing of Joseph, Ephraim, and Manasseh in Gen. 48.15-16. In the novel, we read:

> 'Come to me, Joseph. Put your hand here – no, here. My father did it this way. A custom so old cannot be wrong. Now leave your hand there!' He bowed his white head, 'May the blessing of God and my blessing rest on this child. May he live in the light of the Face. May he love his life.'[178]

Before the biblical blessing, Jacob has Joseph swear not to bury him in Egypt. In the novel, we read that even though Joseph's father died in Vermont, Joseph believed that his spirit came to California and entered the oak tree, a clear reference to the patriarchs' wish to be buried in the promised land. The blessings of the patriarchs differ in some respects: the blessing of Jacob in Gen. 27.28-29 includes a blessing on his work in husbandry, his personal prestige, and his position as a patriarch. Jacob's blessing of Joseph recalls the names of the patriarchs in order to ground them in the posterity of the forefathers of Israel. John Wayne appeals to posterity by referring to the blessing of God and of himself. The blessing comes to Joseph even though he is not the oldest son. To further recall the story of the biblical Joseph, Steinbeck even suggests a quarrel between the brothers before Joseph leaves.[179] In contrast to

176. Steinbeck, *To a God Unknown*, 8.
177. Ibid., 22, 23.
178. Ibid., 3.
179. See ibid., 2. See also Fontenrose, *John Steinbeck*, 14. There are many more biblical allusions. Some are discussed in works provided in the bibliography. Here, however, we will focus on the motif of the promised land.

his biblical namesake, however, Steinbeck's Joseph fails to be a good steward. He does not protect the land and is not prudent. Although he is warned that years of fertility are often followed by years of drought, he does not listen:

> Joseph is a Frazerian divine king who must die because he lost his divine potency. Joseph is therefore the dying king whose death renews the land rather than the dying god whose resurrection restores life (though the god may be derived from the king).[180]

When Joseph sacrifices himself so the land may live, he dies the death of a king-god in the ancient mysteries, a theme we touched upon when discussing T. S. Eliot's *The Waste Land*. Donohue stresses the parallels between Eliot's *Waste Land* and references to waste land in the novels of Steinbeck and believes the former was a huge influence on the latter.[181]

To a God Unknown captures Joseph's longing for land: 'I have a hunger for land of my own, sir. I have been reading about the West and the good cheap land there.'[182] Steinbeck brings to the fore the idea we encountered in Whitman – that because the eastern shore was industrialized and had lost its Edenic attributes, California (the West) was the ultimate promised land: 'Nuestra Señora, the long valley of Our Lady in central California, was green and gold and yellow and blue when Joseph came into it'.[183] There were even 'Canaanites' there to pose a threat to the settlers of this land of promise:

> The huts of Indians clustered about the mud walls of the church, and although the church was often vacant now and its saints were worn and part of its tile roof lay in a shattered heap on the ground and although the bells were broken, the Mexican Indians still lived near about and held their festivals, danced La Jota on the packed earth and slept in the sun.[184]

When Joseph holds his heathen fiesta with the Native Americans, his life begins its downward slide into misery. This is not to say that he previously held no heathen inclinations, but that any predisposition is promoted and multiplied by his heathen surroundings: the 'threat' posed by the Native Americans comes in the shape of their cultic practice and their praise of life and fertility.

180. Fontenrose, *John Steinbeck*, 16.
181. See Donohue, 'The Endless Journey to No End'.
182. Steinbeck, *To a God Unknown*, 2.
183. Ibid., 3.
184. Ibid., 4.

However, Joseph is not ready to submit to the cycles of nature: he wants to be in charge of them. Brueggemann describes the danger in the 'passion to possess' as a tendency to 'manage' things, and this is the passion we see in *To a God Unknown*. The land is no longer understood as a free gift: it is taken for granted and can be 'managed' and exploited. In the novel, we see Brueggemann's tension between landlessness and landedness worked out by this shift from gift to given and in the reminder that is nonetheless disregarded.

At first, Steinbeck presents the land, the virgin land of California, as a free gift: 'But they are homesteading the western land, sir. You have only to live a year on the land and build a house and plough a bit and the land is yours. No one can ever take it away.'[185] The land was still something promised: it was not at hand but in the horizon of the future. When Joseph sets out on his journey and enters California, he stands in awe before all its natural life and fertility. This sense of awe passes, however, and is replaced by a strange and animalistic urge to possess, a force which originates in the ever-present heathen mother-earth religion and threatens a hostile takeover of Joseph's life: 'This land might possess all of him if he weren't careful... His possession once became a passion.'[186] As Brueggemann observes, land changes people. The feeling of being securely settled helps us forget that there was a time without land, but we must always remember that we are to treat the land with proper respect as a free gift from God: '"[The land is] mine", he said again, "and I must take care of it"'.[187] Joseph's sense of 'possessing' the land may nevertheless be the very thing that prevents him from caring for it.

We have seen Brueggemann describe this change of attitude which happens when landless people become landed and begin 'managing' their affairs. In monarchic Israel, the kings forgot that the land was once not theirs, that they had been given it as a free gift, and that they had violated the land law, trading and managing land as if it were their own property rather than an inheritance from God. Such behaviour is criticized by the prophets, who warn the king that he must right the wrong. If he does not, the land will be taken away.

Steinbeck eventually presents an awareness that the land is to be treated as a partner rather than taken for granted. The indigenous people – the Native Americans – are able to fulfil such a requirement, and Joseph's syncretistic view of religion allows him some reflection on the synergy

185. Ibid., 2.
186. Ibid., 5, 8.
187. Ibid., 7.

between people and the land. He inherited this ability from his father, and it was passed on to him in the blessing.[188] Joseph believes that the spirit of his father has crossed the country and merged with the new land in California: 'His father and this new land were one'.[189] Before Joseph marries Elizabeth, Steinbeck has him feeling as though he were married to the land,[190] and there are signs of him attempting to live with respect towards it.

Nevertheless, his passion to manage what he possessed – his land in a Californian valley – prevents Joseph from taking seriously the warnings issued by the Native Americans. The valley where they settle, the valley of Nuestra Señora, is peculiar: it is both the promised land and Egypt, a land of promise which becomes a land of slavery. Steinbeck warns Joseph about this through Romas, a Native American:

> 'Why, all the land dried up, and the wells, went dry and the cattle died.' He chuckled. 'It was dry enough, I tell you. Half of the people who lived here then had to move away. Those who could, drove the cattle inland to San Joaquin, where there was grass along the river. The cows died along the road, too. I was younger then, but I remember the dead cows with swelled-up guts.' 'But the rain came again', Joseph said quickly. 'The ground is full of water now'. 'Oh, yes, the rain came after ten years. Floods of it came.'[191]

The drought, the swollen cows and the flood are all clear allusions to Egypt. Although there was no suggestion that dry years come regularly and follow a pattern, it is clear that no one understands why Joseph pays no attention to it. He does not behave prudently and store up for the dry years as might have been expected of a man called Joseph. Landedness in the promised land lulled the Israelites into such a false sense of security that they did not expect the exile. Joseph's possession of his own land, his farm and his fields, leads him to think that nothing in his prosperous life will ever change: 'I heard about it, Tom. But it's all over now. Something was wrong. I tell you. It won't come again, ever. The hills are full of water.'[192] Joseph cannot believe that dry years will come but eventually they do.

188. On the old farm in Vermont, his father had merged with the land until he became the living symbol of the unit formed by the land and its inhabitants. That authority passed to Joseph. Ibid., 22.
189. Ibid., 5.
190. Ibid., 8.
191. Ibid., 12.
192. Ibid., 26.

The tension between landlessness and landedness in *To a God Unknown* is presented with great skill. The violation of the land law is presented in the novel as the desire or passion to possess the land. Once the land is possessed, the land and the people working on it become managed; possession lulls the people into a false sense of security and they are no longer able to recognize the coming danger, not even when they are warned. When disaster hits, the landed become landless once more. Canaan becomes Egypt: '"Christ, let's get moving, then!" Thomas cried. "Let's get out of this bastard valley, this double-crossing son-of-a-bitch. I do not want to come back to it! I can't trust it anymore!"'[193]

Killing the land and marching further west: The Grapes of Wrath

'*The Grapes of Wrath* is arguably the most significant indictment ever made of the myth of California as a Promised Land.'[194] So says the prominent Steinbeck scholar Robert DeMott in his introduction to this worldwide bestseller. The inspiration for the novel is the life of the migrant workers in the Californian Hoovervilles[195] in the 1930s during the time of the Great Depression.[196] Steinbeck visited the migrant camps of Visalia and Nipomo, California, in February and March 1938.[197]

---

193. Ibid., 140.

194. DeMott, 'Introduction', 1992, xlviii.

195. Hoovervilles were small improvised towns for homeless people and migrant workers built in the United States during the time of the Great Depression, taking their name from the serving US president Herbert Hoover, who was also blamed for the woeful state of the country under his administration. The concept behind the towns was seen as deeply problematic and they were heavily criticized. The inhabitants suffered a life of filth and hunger and had little chance of finding a job and increasing their standard of living. For more, see 'Great Depression and World War II (1929–1945)', Library of Congress, http://www.loc.gov/teachers/classroommaterials/presentationsandactivities/presentations/timeline/depwwii/depress/hoovers.html.

196. Fontenrose suggests that Steinbeck travelled with the migrant workers all the way from Oklahoma to California and used his own experiences as inspiration for his articles. Fontenrose, *John Steinbeck*, 68. DeMott refutes this, and claims rather that Steinbeck's articles for the *San Francisco News* were influenced by Tom Collins who made such a journey and wrote about it in his journal, then discussed his reports with Steinbeck and gave him permission to use the material in his own works. Robert DeMott, 'Introduction', in *Working Days: The Journal of The Grapes of Wrath 1938–1941*, ed. John Steinbeck and Robert DeMott (New York: Viking, 1989), xxviii.

197. John Steinbeck, *Working Days: The Journals of the Grapes of Wrath 1938–1941*, ed. Robert DeMott (New York: Viking, 1989), 6.

DeMott summarizes Steinbeck's experience: 'His growing sense of anger about the plight of Visalia's starving migrants colored nearly everything in his life, including, temporarily, his will to write'.[198] The series of articles based on the journals of Steinbeck's friend Tom Collins, who travelled and worked with the migrants, and Steinbeck's own experience from the camps was called 'The Harvest Gipsies', first published in 1936 and re-published in 1938 as the pamphlet 'Their Blood is Strong'.[199] Steinbeck took some of the material and inserted it into *The Grapes of Wrath* in the form of 'inter-chapters', which offer valuable insights into the experience of the poorest of the poor during the Great Depression. It was not only poverty that forced people to leave their homes and live and work in the inhuman conditions of the camps. The environmental-ecological catastrophe of the dust bowl and the resulting air pollution blighted many states in the American Midwest, including Oklahoma, Arkansas, Kansas, and Texas.[200] Owens considers this ecological disaster to be a clear result of America's mistreatment of the land, which was in turn an outcome of the clash between two irreconcilable components of the American dream: individual freedom and self-belief, and the discovery and 'maintenance' of the earthly paradise:

> *The Grapes of Wrath* is the story of a people growing through ignorance and failure and isolation toward a commitment to something larger than the isolated self. The ignorance includes a failure of responsibility toward the land – the earth has been misused, cropped out, greedily exploited – and toward one's fellow man... [The protagonists] are para-gons of American individualism; they embody the pioneer spirit which has driven out and killed the Indian and claimed the land in the same name of despoilment.[201]

The simple narrative of *The Grapes of Wrath* describes the journey of the Joad family from Oklahoma to California. Although it is clearly a story about a single family, DeMott suggests its message is universal.[202] The family are forced off their farm – which passes to the bank – because, like many of their neighbours, they are no longer able to keep up the

198. Ibid., 3.

199. Fontenrose, *John Steinbeck*, 67. See also Owens, *The Grapes of Wrath*, 3.

200. According to Owens, 300–400,000 people travelled to California, one of the very few states that remained unaffected. Owens, *The Grapes of Wrath*, 1.

201. Ibid., 44.

202. DeMott, 'Introduction', 1992, xv.

payments. The family sells what they still own of the farm but because
everyone is selling up at the same time, they receive precious little for it.
The journey takes several days and is exhausting. When they reach
California, the 'promised land', they experience worse hardships than
they had suffered back home in Oklahoma and the hostility of the locals
is worse than the indifference of the bankers who had driven them off
their land.[203]

The biblical allusions in *The Grapes of Wrath* are even more numerous
than in *To a God Unknown*. The clearest parallels were outlined by literary
scholars such as Martin Shockley in the early 1950s. In his rebuttal of
Shockley's view, Eric Carlson argues that:

> In *The Grapes of Wrath* a few loose Biblical analogies may be identified,
> but these are not primary to the structure and the theme of the novel,
> and to contend that they give it an 'essentially and thoroughly Christian'
> meaning is to distort Steinbeck's intention and its primary framework of
> non-Christian symbolism.[204]

Carlson is a little harsh on Shockley, who was certainly not claiming
that *The Grapes of Wrath* represents a simple re-narration of the story of
the exodus.[205] Shockley actually suggests that on the basis of that story,
Steinbeck is building something new, based on Emersonian transcendentalism, as George de Schweinitz explains:

> 'Christian' can be used as a denotative word and as a connotative word...
> Mr. Carlson's paper, following Mr. Shockley's, did not seem to me to take
> into account sufficient consideration of the particular force or degree of
> unliteralness Mr. Shockley was permitting himself in his discussion.[206]

203. See also Fontenrose, *John Steinbeck*, 68; Keith Ferrell, *John Steinbeck: The
Voice of the Land* (Lanham, MD: Rowman & Littlefield, 2015), 40.

204. Eric Carlson, 'Symbolism in *The Grapes of Wrath*', in Donohue, ed., *A Case
Book on The Grapes of Wrath*, 97.

205. 'It is at least as old as the Biblical tale of the Exodus and as the Odyssey;
a spiritualized version provides the framework for the *Pilgrim's Progress*. Since
Steinbeck is known to follow classical models (Arthurian legends in Tortilla Flat,
the Genesis story in *East of Eden*), he might have been more likely to turn to Moses
than to Emerson Hough if he needed a model for a tale about man's attempt to win
the promised land.' Warren French, ed., *A Companion to The Grapes of Wrath* (New
York: Viking, 1963), 218.

206. George de Schweinitz, 'Steinbeck and Christianity', in Donohue, ed., *A Case
Book on The Grapes of Wrath*, 103.

From the many biblical parallels identified and analysed by Steinbeck scholarship, I will discuss only those that relate to Steinbeck's interpretation of the motif of the promised land.[207] Peter Lisca argues that the threefold division of the novel corresponds to the biblical event of the exodus: Chapters 1–11 correspond to the Israelites in slavery in Egypt; Chapters 12–18 relate to the wandering in the wilderness, and Chapters 19–30 narrate the arrival in the promised land.[208] This is indeed a helpful division, and it argues for the centrality of the promised land motif in *The Grapes of Wrath*.

The first striking parallel with the promised land motif is the number of wandering Joads, as Crockett explains: 'Plainly, Steinbeck has made the Joads representative of the American pioneer and by investing them and their story with biblical elements, has made their characters more universal than they could otherwise have been'.[209] The Joad family, together with Connie Rivers (the husband of the Joad girl Rose of Sharon) and Jim Casy (a former evangelical preacher), number twelve plus one, which Fontenrose interprets as the twelve disciples plus Jesus.[210] Despite indicating that the main narrative parallels the story of the exodus,[211] Fontenrose and Owens both fail to associate the family with the 'twelve plus one' tribes of Israel who entered and settled the promised land (Joseph's portion was divided between his sons Ephraim and Manasseh). They do, however, connect the family name Joad to Judah, the tribe that remains faithful to the Davidic dynasty after the division of the kingdom. Carlson is almost alone in failing to recognize the narrative line as the exodus story.[212] It is hard to believe that he could have been ignorant of the fact that the American dream is bound almost inseparably to the

207. For more on the biblical symbolism in *The Grapes of Wrath*, see Fontenrose, *John Steinbeck*; French, *John Steinbeck*; Martin Shockley, 'Christian Symbolism in *The Grapes of Wrath*', in Donohue, ed., *A Case Book on The Grapes of Wrath*, 90–5; Carlson, 'Symbolism in *The Grapes of Wrath*'; Peter Lisca, *John Steinbeck: Nature and Myth* (New York: Thomas Y. Crowell, 1987).

208. Lisca, *John Steinbeck: Nature and Myth*, 106–7.

209. H. Kelly Crockett, 'The Bible and *The Grapes of Wrath*', in Donohue, ed., *A Case Book on The Grapes of Wrath*, 106.

210. Fontenrose, *John Steinbeck*, 78; Owens, *The Grapes of Wrath*, 41.

211. See Charles Dougherty, 'The Christ-Figure in *The Grapes of Wrath*', in Donohue, ed., *A Case Book on The Grapes of Wrath*, 115; Shockley, 'Christian Symbolism in *The Grapes of Wrath*', 91; Crockett, 'The Bible and *The Grapes of Wrath*', 106.

212. 'For example, to speak of the Joads and other migrants as wandering, like the Israelites, in a wilderness of hardships while they seek the Promised Land is

Bible and its contextual outworking in the United States, something
Brueggemann confesses quite openly. Warren French parallels the story of
the journeying Joads with the exodus and is aware of Steinbeck's stinging
critique of the American dream. He quotes a book review from *The Times
of London* of September 1939 which suggests that real American authors
are critical of the American dream:

> While lesser American writers complacently recall their country's past, Mr.
> Steinbeck is anxiously in touch with its present. He, too, describes an exodus
> to the West, but this is made in ramshackle motor-cars instead of lumbering
> wagons. Here there are no battles to bring glory, and at the end the land of
> promise is a bitter disappointment. There, sure enough, are the farms and
> orchards and well-watched lands, but others are in possession of them.[213]

The other parallel is the death of the Joad grandparents, representatives
of the 'old generation'. On the way to the promised land of California,
both of the grandparents travelling with the Joad family die. They were
too connected to the old life and to the old land and could not let it go,
just like the murmuring Israelites who kept longing for the 'comfortable
life' in Egypt (cf. Exod. 17.3):

> 'Ain't nothin' the matter with me', he said. 'I jus' ain't a-goin''... 'I ain't
> sayin' for you to stay', said Grampa. 'You go right along. Me – I'm stayin'.
> I give her a goin'-over all night mos'ly. This here is my country. I b'long
> here. An' I don't give a goddamn if they's oranges an' grapes crowdin' a fella
> outa bed even'.[214]

Disembodiment is but one step from slavery

The tension between landlessness and landedness in *The Grapes
of Wrath* is suggested in the title of this section: 'Killing the land and
marching further west'. Slavery was never truly left behind and the
promised land always slips away from people just as they think they have
it in their hands: 'Israel's being in the land was never fully given, never

but to point up by conventional metaphor the general emotional pattern of the trek
westward and the long-awaited sight of California.' Carlson, 'Symbolism in *The
Grapes of Wrath*', 97.

213. French, *A Companion to The Grapes of Wrath*, 222.

214. Steinbeck, *The Grapes of Wrath*, 143. Crockett recalls the murmuring Israelites who ultimately were not allowed to enter the promised land and died on the way:
'However, there are among the family those who "hanker after the fleshpots" and
do not wish to enter or remain in the Promised Land'. Crockett, 'The Bible and *The
Grapes of Wrath*', 111.

quite secured'.[215] The Joad family experience slavery both in Oklahoma (assumed to be Egypt, but which to their ancestors was once the promised land) and in California, which had to be the promised land as there was nowhere further west to march. The endless series of crop failures plunges the Okies into debt.[216] The mortgage payments are high and eventually become unpayable, so they sell up for a pittance, leave their homes, and set off on their journey to the promised land of California.

The slavers in the novel are represented by the banks, a disembodied entity with no interest in real people and with limitless power over them. Their delegates, the tractor drivers, adopt the philosophy of depersonalization and act fully in accordance with the will of their superiors:

> The bank is something else than men. It happens that every man in a bank hates what the bank does, and yet the bank does it. The bank is something more than men, I tell you. It's the monster. Men made it, but they can't control it... No. The bank, the monster owns it. You'll have to go... Well – first the sheriff, and then the troops. You'll be stealing if you try to stay, you'll be murderous if you kill to stay. The monster isn't men, but it can make men do what it wants... We're sorry, said the owner men. The bank, the fifty-thousand-acre owner can't be responsible.[217]

The depersonalization of the banks, which men made but cannot control, can also be found in the monarchs of ancient Israel. The elevation of the king and his separation from the rest of Israel led to a serious violation of the land law. In the course of time, someone is promoted above the others, someone who then adopts the idea that he is indeed something more than other people. Brueggemann pointed towards the need to elect someone who remembered the history of the salvation of Israel, someone with knowledge of the slavery, liberation, wandering, homecoming, landedness, and exile. Nevertheless, a state with a king detached from his people, sitting in his ivory tower, tends to treat the people as mere nameless servants and the land as mere acreage on a cadastral map which can easily be bought up when the strings are pulled the right way.

Fontenrose's description of the latifundialization of agriculture in Oklahoma is helpful. Large-scale owners buy up acres of land from smallholders and combine them into one great plantation. This leads

---

215. Brueggemann, *The Land*, 12.

216. 'We can't take less share of the crop – we're half starved now. The kids are hungry all the time. We got no clothes, torn an' ragged. If all the neighbors weren't the same, we'd be ashamed to go to meeting.' Steinbeck, *The Grapes of Wrath*, 42.

217. Ibid.

to the exploitation of both the people – no competition means lower
wages – and the land – larger plantations are more susceptible to
erosion, and industrialization of the cultivated soil is less caring of the
environment.[218] Steinbeck describes a similar violation of the land law
to that presented in 1 Kings 21. When discussing *To a God Unknown*,
we saw that during the times of settlement, the land was granted to
newcomers free of charge: 'The Okies argue...that occupying the land
and devoting one's labor to it are the criteria of ownership, and that
these transcend the legal right to the land represented by the title'.[219]
We saw that Jefferson agrarianism, to which Steinbeck adhered, made
possible the ownership of small lots of land by small-scale farmers,
thus securing freedom and democracy for most of the population. The
only condition for obtaining the land was to live and work on it. When
discussing the reception of the promised land in the Bible, we saw that
the land is YHWH's inheritance: the people to whom it was entrusted
were temporary tenants who were not permitted to trade it. One of the
main arguments against establishing a monarchy in Israel was that the
king would take away the land which was rightfully distributed among
ordinary Israelites. The first king to transgress this law and enslave his
own people was Solomon, whose conduct led to the division of the
kingdom. Solomon was followed by Ahab and Jezebel, who also failed
to see the land as an inheritance that was not to be traded and wanted
to buy Naboth's land.

The main narrative line of *The Grapes of Wrath* can easily be interpreted, and in most cases is interpreted,[220] as the classical exodus pattern
where the Okies are the Israelites, first oppressed in Oklahoma and then
in California. Shockley observes: 'Like the Israelites the Joads are a
homeless and persecuted people. They too flee from oppression, wander
through a wilderness of hardship, seeking their own promised land.
Unlike the Israelites, however, the Joads never find it.'[221] This is a bold
assertion. One could argue that the Israelites' entry into the promised land
was quite similar. They, too, experienced hostility from the indigenous
inhabitants. Crockett's suggestion feels more accurate:

218. 'The banks and the agricultural corporations (creatures of the banks) found
it more profitable to foreclose mortgages and terminate tenancies, combine many
farms into one plantation, and put it all to cotton. One man with a tractor could work
an entire plantation for wages of three dollars a day.' Fontenrose, *John Steinbeck*, 67.
219. Eisinger, 'Jefferson Agrarianism in *The Grapes of Wrath*', 147.
220. Ibid., 67–83. See also Lisca, *John Steinbeck: Nature and Myth*; Shockley,
'Christian Symbolism in *The Grapes of Wrath*'.
221. Shockley, 'Christian Symbolism in *The Grapes of Wrath*', 91.

> The flight of the Okies from the parched Southwest to California [is similar] to that of the children of Israel from Egypt to Canaan. The Okies likewise come to a land flowing with milk and honey, but the modern Canaanites destroy their surplus of pigs, oranges, and potatoes while Okie children sicken of malnutrition. California thus becomes the wilderness through which the Okies must wander indefinitely, the land of promise still a mirage.[222]

DeMott also suggests:

> In their ironic exodus from home to homelessness…Steinbeck's cast of unsuspecting characters – Ma Joad, Tom Joad, Jim Casy and Rose of Sharon – have become permanently etched in our sensibility and serve constantly to remind us that heroism is as much a matter of choice as it is of being chosen.[223]

Owens pushes the discussion further. On closer analysis, he asks, is Steinbeck clearly suggesting that the Okies have their share in the oppression of the Native Americans as well as in the mistreatment of the land?[224] French confirms: 'The book [is not] based upon any concept of the innate superiority of the migrants. They were largely responsible for their troubles, both at home and on the road.'[225] Landedness led them to oppress both the land and the people. Steinbeck verbalized such a conviction in the Okies' protest against the bank's delegates who want to drive them off the land. Initially, they want to negotiate, and show no respect for the land:

> Can't we just hang on? Maybe the next year will be a good year. God knows how much cotton next year. And with all the wars – God knows what price cotton will bring. Don't they make explosives out of cotton? And uniforms? Get enough of wars and cotton'll hit the ceiling.[226]

Steinbeck reminds us that cotton exhausts the land and eventually makes it unsuitable for agriculture, but the Okies are prepared to continue

222. Crockett, 'The Bible and *The Grapes of Wrath*', 110.
223. DeMott, 'Introduction', 1992, xii–xiii.
224. 'The process became one of despoiling the Garden in the search for the Garden until, finally, Americans stood at the edge of the Pacific, having slaughtered and driven from their lands the original inhabitants, having deforested enormous portions of the continent, and having fought and gouged with all other claimants on the continent in order to reach the western shore'. Owens, *The Grapes of Wrath*, 47–8.
225. French, *A Companion to The Grapes of Wrath*, 220.
226. Steinbeck, *The Grapes of Wrath*, 42.

exploiting the land as long as they can stay on it, even at the cost of keeping the war going. Only after it becomes clear that they will not be part of the future do they begin to appeal to the sustainability of the land: 'But you'll kill the land with cotton'.[227] Steinbeck has the Okies turn their point of view upside down, although their motivation is more selfish than it is guided by a concern for the land: 'But what'll happen to us? How'll we eat?'[228] Owens observes: 'While the reader is likely to sympathize with the powerless tenant farmers, the tenants' willingness to accept war and death as the price for a chance to remain on their farms and thus further "cotton out" the land is difficult to admire on any level'.[229] When it becomes evident that not even further exploitation of the land will secure the Okies' safe residence on their farms, they bring up the history of their oppression of the Native Americans. 'Grampa killed Indians, Pa killed snakes for the land. Maybe we can kill banks – they're worse than Indians and snakes. Maybe we got to fight to keep our land, like Pa and Grampa did.'[230] The Puritans believed they were the wandering fathers in the wilderness. Owens recalls this history and the Puritans' struggles with the Native Americans, the personification of evil: 'Almost at once, in their battle to wrest a continent away from wilderness and from the inhabitants of that wilderness, the colonists imagined themselves embroiled in a desperate struggle with Satan'.[231]

We have seen that a Sabbath for resting the land (Lev. 25.3-6) is a key concept in promised land theology, but like the Israelites before them, the Okies failed to respect the land. They drove the indigenous people off the land, and once it was 'theirs', they managed the land not as a gift from God but as something granted to them. The land does not die, however. When it is mistreated, it can still vomit the people out (Lev. 18.25-28). In the language of Steinbeck, the oppressors must go:

> To believe, as the croppers and land owners in this novel do, that one can 'kill the land' is to see only part of the picture; they commit the error Joseph Wayne commits in Steinbeck's early novel *To a God Unknown* – that of believing that the land can die.[232]

---

227. Steinbeck, *The Grapes of Wrath*, 42.

228. Ibid., 43.

229. Owens, *The Grapes of Wrath*, 52.

230. Steinbeck, *The Grapes of Wrath*, 43. Also: 'The Joads describe themselves,' French argues, 'as immediate descendants of the pioneers who made the original conquest'; French, *A Companion to The Grapes of Wrath*, 221.

231. Owens, *The Grapes of Wrath*, 47.

232. Ibid., 24.

Steinbeck's suggesting that the land cannot die does not stop him blaming the people for its desperate condition: he was almost certainly persuaded that the ecological catastrophe of the dust bowl had human origins.

When the novel begins, the tenants are already being displaced from their farms. Thus, we may hardly speak about landedness. But the Joads speak about the times when they were landed, when increasing the harvest at any cost was the first priority, and when they gladly oppressed the Native Americans. Landedness in Oklahoma was first replaced by landlessness in Oklahoma, a state represented by the sale of farm property at bargain prices.[233] There was something worse, something more powerful, coming to their farms in the shape of the banks, but they were also aware that the banks would leave the land when it no longer bore fruit and then the land would be resold. Steinbeck observes through the words of one of the bank delegates: 'We've got to take cotton quick before the land dies. Then we'll sell the land. Lots of families in the East would like to own a piece of land.'[234] This does not suggest that Steinbeck would defend the position of the banks and farm holders, but it means that despite the extensive damage cotton cultivation does to the land, people would still like to buy it and have a land of their own, and after some time it will finally recover and bear fruit again.

After their experience of landlessness and oppression, the Joads set out on their journey to California. Their recent experiences prompt them to help others who like them are 'on the way'. When they meet the Wilson family, they share their food and money with them and help them repair their car.

New Canaan or new Egypt? No promised land in America
Thousands of displaced families moved west and trusted their lives to the promise of a land flowing with milk and honey: 'Maybe we can start again, in the new rich land – in California, where the fruit grows. We'll start over.'[235] The same movement, prompted by the same dream, was also

233. See also: 'And the men in the seat were tired and angry and sad, for they had got eighteen dollars for every movable thing from the farm: the horses, the wagon, the implements, and all the furniture from the house. Eighteen dollars. They had assailed the buyer, argued; but they were routed when his interest seemed to flag and he told them he didn't want the stuff at any price. Then they were beaten, believed him, and took two dollars less than he had first offered.' Steinbeck, *The Grapes of Wrath*, 125.
234. Ibid., 42.
235. Steinbeck, *The Grapes of Wrath*, 113. See also, 'Both Grampa's dream of grapes and the owner's vague visions of plenty underscore the crucial association between California and the biblical Canaan'. Owens, *The Grapes of Wrath*, 48. Also:

described by Whitman.[236] Steinbeck had deep roots in the legacy of the American dream but was one of its most vocal critics. His words in one of the inter-chapters of *The Grapes of Wrath* recall Brueggemann's warning against possessing and managing the land and the people:

> Once California belonged to Mexico and its land to Mexicans; and a horde of tattered feverish Americans poured in. And such was their hunger for land that they took the land – stole Sutter's land, Guerro's land, took the grants and broke them up and growled and quarrelled over them, those frantic hungry men, and they guarded with guns the land they had stolen. They put up houses and barns, they turned the earth and planted crops. And these things were possession, and possession was ownership.[237]

Eisinger apparently fails to interpret Steinbeck's account as a criticism of human nature and the desire to possess, own and manage, and inevitably to mistreat. He sees these failings in how the settlers behaved in California, but not in Oklahoma where exactly the same thing happened: 'Unfortunately, the California land has all been "stolen" by the early American settlers who took it from the Mexicans'.[238] We saw, however, that this same 'theft of the land' from its original inhabitants also happened in Oklahoma, but Eisinger's somewhat simplistic reading of the book seems to overlook this. Donohue feels that formed by the Puritan legacy, Steinbeck is more critical of human nature than many of his interpreters would have him be: 'The Eden imagery confirms Steinbeck's complex, not simplistic view of man. The Joad journey to California–Eden–Hell is not a simple allegory but a multileveled excursion of the human heart.'[239] Although this image is implicit in the spiritual interpretations of

'They drove through Tehachapi in the morning glow, and the sun came up behind them, and then – suddenly they saw the great valley below them. Al jammed on the brake and stopped in the middle of the road, and "Jesus Christ! Look!" he said. The vineyards, the orchards, the great flat valley, green and beautiful, the trees set in rows, and the farm houses. And Pa said, "God Almighty!" The distant cities, the little towns in the orchard land, and the morning sun, golden on the valley...' Steinbeck, *The Grapes of Wrath*, 292.

236. See also: 'The settlement of America may be seen as a process of ever westward expansion in search of that Eden which seemed to recede always before the eyes of the colonists... Surely, if there were ever to be a Garden it must be at the western shore. And the beauty and fecundity of California seemed to fulfil that promise.' Owens, *The Grapes of Wrath*, 47–8.

237. Steinbeck, *The Grapes of Wrath*, 296.

238. Eisinger, 'Jefferson Agrarianism in *The Grapes of Wrath*', 148.

239. Donohue, 'The Endless Journey to No End', 259.

the promised land which we have seen in many authors, Brueggemann included, Donohue explicitly recalls Philo's allegorical interpretation.

In his thought-provoking article 'The Philosophical Joads', Frederic Carpenter opens up the question of the 'philosophical background' of *The Grapes of Wrath* and argues, as we have seen, that it should be described as a change from Emerson's 'individual over-soul' to Whitman's 'collective over-soul'. The subsequent discussion among literary scholars who disagree as to whether *The Grapes of Wrath* uses Christian symbolism[240] has drawn on this transcendentalist aspect. It was Eisinger, however, who suggested that to see transcendentalism as the only influence on the novel is to miss the point. Eisinger is persuaded that only a combination of Emerson's transcendentalism, Whitman's democracy, James and Dewey's pragmatic instrumentalism, and Jefferson's agrarianism can convey the colourful mix of sources that influenced Steinbeck's work. Eisinger's conviction is true not only for *The Grapes of Wrath* but also for his other novels:

> [The agrarianism] emanates from the Joads and other dispossessed farmers, from the people. It is theirs and Steinbeck's, and it is a noble, traditionally popular ideal, standing as an anachronism in the midst of the machine-made culture of twentieth-century America – a culture sick and foundering in depression when Steinbeck wrote this novel.[241]

As the novel progresses, Steinbeck continues his exposition of the settlement and management of the land, which inevitably ends in oppression of both the land and the people, something that had already become a reality in Oklahoma. Now, as the people move west in search of their promised land, history repeats itself in California. First had come the pioneers, who drove out the Mexicans, combined the farms into huge plantations, cultivated the land on an industrial scale, and when drought and erosion set in, imported labourers from Mexico, China, Japan, and the Philippines. As latifundialization gained momentum, husbandry became increasingly 'disembodied'. Brueggemann quotes Eisinger's comment about landowners farming 'on paper' only and adds, 'The Okies learned to avoid anyone with writing equipment for writing meant land-loss'.[242]

---

240. Shockley, 'Christian Symbolism in *The Grapes of Wrath*', 90–5; Carlson, 'Symbolism in *The Grapes of Wrath*', 96–102; Schweinitz, 'Steinbeck and Christianity', 103–4; Crockett, 'The Bible and *The Grapes of Wrath*', 105–14.

241. Eisinger, 'Jefferson Agrarianism in *The Grapes of Wrath*', 143.

242. Brueggemann, *The Land*, 75. Also: 'No. Like I said, they wasn't people to write. Pa could write, but he wouldn'. Didn't like to.' Steinbeck, *The Grapes of Wrath*, 54.

One could argue that Brueggemann missed the main point of Eisinger's comment, even though it perfectly fitted his argument. There is no doubt that poor management is in Eisinger's mind, but claiming that Pa Joad never wanted to write and that the Okies tried to avoid anyone who wrote things down because writing led to land-loss seems a step too far. We may recall again the story of the Naboth's vineyard in 1 Kings 21. The context is certainly similar: the unhealthy accumulation of land (rather than smaller farms being tilled with love and respect by real farmers); and the violation of the relationship between the owner (the king) and the tenant, and between the owner and the land. Both of these tendencies lead to oppression and slavery. The same pattern is repeated when the poor, hungry, dispossessed farmers come from the east (the Okies among them):

> And the dispossessed, the migrants, flowed into California, two hundred and fifty thousand, and three hundred thousand. Behind them new tractors were going on the land and the tenants were being forced off. And new waves were on the way, new waves of dispossessed and the homeless, hardened, intent, and dangerous. And while the Californians wanted many things, accumulation, social success, amusement, luxury, and a curious banking security, the new barbarians wanted only two things – land and food; and to them the two were one.[243]

Here is a perfect description of the failure of the promised land, although Steinbeck reminds us that it is nothing new as such a failure had already happened in the Bible:

> 'An' it'd be nice under the trees, workin' in the shade. I'm scared of stuff so nice. I ain't got faith. I'm scared somepin ain't so nice about it.' Tom said, 'Don't roust your faith bird-high an' you won't do no crawlin' with the worms'. 'I know that's right. That's Scripture, ain't it?' 'I guess so', said Tom. 'I never could keep Scripture straight sense.'[244]

Like Fitzgerald and others, Steinbeck presents the idea that although we are yet to discover the promised land, it must exist somewhere, and we need only the time, patience, and resolution to find it. Such a belief is depicted in the novel by the deceitful handbills inviting migrant workers to California. Steinbeck has Ma Joad say: 'I seen the han'bills fellas pass out, an' how much work they is, an' high wages an' all? an' I seen in the paper how they want folks to come an' pick grapes an' oranges an'

243. Steinbeck, *The Grapes of Wrath*, 300.
244. Ibid., 117.

peaches. That'd be nice work.'[245] He is aware, nonetheless, that such an idea is naive and that the promised land, if it ever existed, can never be re-established:

> But you can't start. Only a baby can start. You and me – why, we're all that's been. The anger of a moment, the thousand pictures, that's us. This land, this red land, is us; and the flood years and the dust years and the drought years are us. We can't start again.[246]

Interestingly, and it cannot be dismissed as simply a naive idea, the American dream never fully dies but is carried into the next generation as if the people still believed, after so many disappointments, that the promised land can be reached:

> Behind the hunger for the land expressed in both the narrator's and the characters' words lies Jefferson agrarianism, a quintessential element in the American Dream, but a Jefferson agrarianism that is questioned and revised in the course of the novel. Behind the exodus from the Dust Bowl to the Eden of California lies the inevitable human need to believe in a new beginning, a second chance, the possibility of Eden rediscovered.[247]

Despite his suggestion that no one can start again, Steinbeck fails to come to terms with the death of the American dream. Donohue suggests that Rose of Sharon's stillborn baby symbolizes the fact that no Messiah will come again to redeem the world,[248] but the final scenes of humankind joined together in 'selfless' unions[249] and Rose of Sharon's breastfeeding of a starving old man do hold out at least some hope of rediscovering the promised land.

The idea of a new beginning when everything has failed and the known world has completely collapsed is deeply biblical. We saw it in the unconditional promise of land made to the exiles (Jer. 30.22; 32.38; Ezek. 37.27) and the promise of a new heart and the renewal of God's allegiance to the people of Israel: 'And they shall be my people and I will be their God'. The promise can be interpreted spiritually and eschatologically as the promise of the heavenly Jerusalem, or as the restoration of the earthly Jerusalem as presented in Ezra and Nehemiah.

---

245. Ibid.
246. Ibid., 113.
247. Owens, *The Grapes of Wrath*, 8.
248. Donohue, 'The Endless Journey to No End', 265.
249. The idea of 'selfless' unions is of course completely naive and must be attributed to Steinbeck's socialist background.

The Grapes of Wrath has enjoyed a rich history of interpretation in numerous scholarly disciplines. One interpretation that I believe has the potential to inspire the realm of biblical criticism is to speak of the 'sin' of the disembodied banks, who disrespected the land by buying it up, driving out the farmers, and joining the plots together into one huge latifundia. This is a violation of the land law just as we saw in 1 Kings 21 and the story of Naboth's vineyard. The remote relationship between the king and his servants is one of disembodiment, and when Solomon comes, the servants finally become slaves.

The key concept which emerged in the discussion of Fitzgerald, especially in the light of Brueggemann, is the never-ending cycle of land-lessness and landedness, from one to the other and back again. A pattern evolves: people settle the land and drive away the indigenous people; they then exploit the land, so the land vomits them out; they become landless and search for a new land to settle. Despite all the apparent despair, there is still a chance of a new beginning as people cannot kill the land in such a way as to prevent it from rising from the ashes. Although the western shore has been reached, a new promised land still awaits the new Israel, albeit not in America, or on Earth, but in heaven.

The soul's journey towards the promised land: East of Eden

East of Eden is one of Steinbeck's most mature novels, but despite his wish to make it his best, critics found it less passionate and inspiring than *The Grapes of Wrath*.[250] There is something to be said for this critique, as Fontenrose concludes:

> If Steinbeck had delved into a father's ambivalent feelings for his sons, his awareness of favoring one son over the other, his fairness or unfairness to either son, and the moral and spiritual problems arising from his relation to his sons, then East of Eden might have been a great novel. As it is, we do not understand Adam's actions; in this novel we cannot resort to saying that they just happened.[251]

---

250. 'I think perhaps it is the only book I have ever written. I think there is only one book to a man.' Steinbeck, *Journal of a Novel*, 5. The journal was a series of letters written to Steinbeck's editor Pascal Covici during the writing of *East of Eden*. The letters were never intended for publication. Interestingly, the passion that some find lacking in the novel seems to be present in the journal.

251. Fontenrose, *John Steinbeck*, 126. See also, Leo Gurko, 'Steinbeck's Later Fiction', *Nation*, no. 175 (1952): 235–6. Some scholars nonetheless appreciate Stein-beck's characters as true and lively enough. Prescott, for example, calls the characters

Numbering *East of Eden* among the 'moralities' written during the period of intellectual and psychological evaluation of the terrors of the Second World War,[252] Fontenrose asks whether the novel's message arises organically from the text or is imposed on the reader; he settles, reluctantly, on the latter.[253] However, if we look at the book as Steinbeck's attempt to write a story about good and evil for his two young sons,[254] we should hesitate before calling it merely schematic. Although the basic backdrops indicate that Steinbeck is seeking a clear direction and points of departure, the full picture is not so simple. Steinbeck's letters tell us he had always wanted to write a book about good and evil but had waited until he felt intellectually ready and in possession of the skills required to carry it off.[255]

Steinbeck saw the story of Cain and Abel in Genesis 4 as the most obvious biblical narrative for his story of good and evil, and the novel is framed by his never-ending search for the promised land. Genesis 4 also gave him his title:

> And now I had set down in my own hand the 16 verses of Cain and Abel and the story changes with flashing lights when you write it down. And I think I have a title at last, a beautiful title, East of Eden. And read the 16th verse to find it. And Salinas Valley is surely East of Eden.[256]

'strong and weak, wise and stupid'. Orville Prescott, 'Books of the Times', *New York Times*, 19 September, 1952. See also, W. Max Gordon, 'Steinbeck's New Book, *East of Eden*, Tells of "His People" in Our Valley', *Salinas Californian* 1952 (14 September): 4. Much of the criticism of the characters is valid, however. Although the background to Cathy's wretchedness is painted clearly enough, her evil conduct is not fully believable. Similarly, Adam is supposed to be a 'good man' but most of his actions do not lead to a good end.

252. Fontenrose, *John Steinbeck*, 118.

253. Ibid., 126.

254. Steinbeck, *Journal of a Novel*, 4. *East of Eden* includes the story of Steinbeck's mother's family, the Hamiltons.

255. Ibid., 3–6.

256. Steinbeck, *Journal of a Novel*, 104. Meyer argues that *East of Eden* is largely influenced by Milton's *Paradise Lost*: 'Yet a third Steinbeck book related to Milton's epic is *East of Eden*, in which Steinbeck portrays Adam Trask and his deceitful wife Cathy trying to reclaim Eden in southern California, offering a parallel not only to the original Adam and Eve but also to the fallen angels in hell trying to recreate a home to rival Heaven, even though they have been exiled'. Michael Meyer, 'Paradise Lost', in Railsback and Meyer, eds, *A John Steinbeck Encyclopedia*, 268–9.

East of Eden has three basic story lines, two fictional and one historical, which intertwine through the novel and eventually merge. The names of the characters in the two fictional story lines – the stories of the Trask family and of Cathy Ames – are schematic: the 'bad' Cain-like characters all have names beginning with 'C' (Cyrus, Charles, Cal, Cathy); the 'good' Abel-like characters have names beginning with 'A' (Adam, Aaron, Abra). In the novel, the biblical story of Cain and Abel is played out in two generations of brothers. Adam Trask, the main 'A' character, plays the Abel role in the first story (the story of Adam and his brother Charles) and the role of Abel's father Adam in the second story (the story of his sons Cal and Aaron). The basic element in the story of the Trasks is their move from the family farm in Connecticut to the Salinas Valley in California. The second narrative line is the story of Cathy Ames, which merges at one point with the Trask story and then leaves it again. The third story line, the 'historical' story, is that of 'Steinbeck's own people in the land'.[257] The main character in this narrative, which begins with an extensive description of the history of California, is Sam Hamilton, Steinbeck's maternal grandfather. This line also merges with the Trask narrative and stays with it until the end. There are many other parallels to the story of Cain and Abel, such as the birthday gifts from the sons to their fathers, one gift accepted and one rejected, and the mark of Cain borne by all the 'C' characters, which could indeed suggest that criticism of *East of Eden* as schematic and simplistic is justified.

Nevertheless, there are elements that testify to Steinbeck's profound understanding of the problem of good and evil and his ability to convey it in a novel. Cain and Abel are the first names Sam thinks of when it comes to naming Adam's twins,[258] but Adam refuses to name his children this way and risk setting their lives on the same unfortunate course as the biblical brothers, and the search begins anew. Here Steinbeck introduces the motif of the promised land when Sam suggests the names Joshua and Caleb, because 'of all the people who started out of Egypt only two came to the Promised Land'.[259] Adam has a military past and does not like the army, so Joshua, the soldier, is rejected. The name Caleb is accepted, and to keep the 'C's and 'A's in balance, the other boy is named Aaron (later spelled 'Aron'). Steinbeck suggests Aron's Abel-like fate in Samuel's reminder that: 'he did not make it to the Promised Land'.[260]

257. Steinbeck, *Journal of a Novel*, 4.
258. John Steinbeck, *East of Eden*, 2nd print (London: Penguin, 1992), 266.
259. Ibid., 271.
260. Ibid., 272.

The naming of the twins prompts a long discussion between Adam, Sam and the Chinese servant Lee about interpretations of the story of Cain and Abel, which Wright calls a midrash of Genesis 4.[261] Much has been written about the Hebrew verb 'timshol', which Steinbeck quotes here and tries to make sense of; Brueggemann refers to Steinbeck's use of the term in his commentary on Genesis 4.[262] Steinbeck suggests that the story of Cain and Abel is a model for God's preference of the Israelites over the Canaanites. Abel, a model of the Israelite, was chosen because he was a shepherd and not a farmer, while Cain, a model of the farming Canaanites, was condemned. Aware of such an interpretation,[263] Steinbeck begins to work with it but eventually rejects it.[264] More than anything else in this story, Steinbeck is interested in the possibility of overcoming evil. He is

261. Terrence Wright, 'Cain and Abel: John Steinbeck', in *The Genesis of Fiction: Modern Novelists as Biblical Interpreters*, ed. Terrence Wright (Aldershot: Ashgate, 2007), 51–2.

262. Although Brueggemann quotes extensively from the parts of *East of Eden* that deal with the Hebrew word 'timshol', he makes no attempt to interpret Steinbeck's contribution to the topic: 'Steinbeck has seen that much hangs on this strange word to Cain. It is invitation, challenge, promise. The different translations indicate the ambiguity of the verbal form. It is a statement which admits of more than one rendering. But any way it is taken, the interaction between Cain and the destructive power at work on him has been redefined.' Brueggemann, *Genesis*, 59.

263. See also: 'I remember that this story was written by and for a shepherd people. They were not farmers. Wouldn't the god of shepherds find a fat lamb more valuable than a sheaf of barley? A sacrifice must be the best and most valuable'. Steinbeck, *East of Eden*, 269.

264. See also: 'God did not condemn Cain at all. Even God can have a preference, can't he? Let's suppose God liked lamb better than vegetables... And God said, "I don't like this. Try again. Bring me something I like and I'll set you up alongside your brother." But Cain got mad. His feelings were hurt. And when a man's feeling are hurt he wants to strike at something, and Abel was in the way of his anger... I think everyone in the world to a large or small extent has felt rejection. And with rejection comes anger, and with anger some kind of crime in revenge for the rejection, and with the crime guilt – and there is the story of mankind. I think that if rejection could be amputated, the human would not be what he is... "He did a thing in anger, Adam, because he thought you had rejected him. The result of his anger is that his brother and your son is dead." Cal said, "Lee – you can't!" "I have to," said Lee... "I have the choice." He said sharply, "Your son is marked with guilt out of himself – out of himself – almost more than he can bear. Don't crush him with rejection. Don't crush him, Adam." ..."Let him be free. That's all a man has over beasts." ...Adam looked up with sick weariness... His whispered word seemed to hang in the air. "Timshel!"' Steinbeck, *East of Eden*, 269, 270, 602.

puzzled by the difference between the translations of Gen. 4.7 in the King James (KJV) and newly published American Standard (ASV) Bibles. Where the KJV has: 'Thou shalt rule over it', the ASV translates: 'Do thou rule over it'. Steinbeck in fact prefers the translation offered by his editor Pascal Covici: 'Thou mayest rule over it'. He even made Covici learn the original Hebrew word (timshol) and confirm the legitimacy of such an interpretation with a Jewish scholar, Dr Louis Ginzberg.[265] Steinbeck's preferred translation is, of course, an attempt to emancipate human beings from the determinism so deeply rooted in the American context as a result of its Puritan-Calvinist heritage. Steinbeck drew from the positive view of a freer and more independent human person in Emerson's transcendentalism, and unlike Brueggemann believes it is one's own choice, not socio-economic determinism, that has the greatest bearing on whether we head for the promised land or slip back into slavery.

Steinbeck points us towards an important and rarely discussed feature. In the story of Cain and Abel, good is only assumed and derived from what we learn about evil. We know nothing about Abel in the biblical story and we discover little about Adam and Aaron in the novel. Adam is supposed to be good, but aside from his tireless and loving care for Cathy, which seems more like a sign of his stupidity, nothing in his life indicates that he is a good man: he has no love for his father or his son Cal, and he takes no real care of his sons until forced to by Sam. We have only Steinbeck's ever-reassuring word on this. Furthermore, the 'good characters' Adam and Aaron (not Aaron's sweetheart Abra) seem weak and indifferent, unreal and enigmatic, if not ghostly. Abel's name (הבל) in Hebrew could be rendered as 'breath' or 'vanity', something 'fleeting', which could well describe all the 'A' characters, and which has nothing to do with goodness. Fontenrose shares a similar conviction:

---

265. See also: 'Your new translation of the story has one most important change. It is the third version. The King James says of sin crouching at the door, "Thou shalt rule over it." The American Standard says, "Do thou rule over it." Now this new translation says, "Thou mayest rule over it." This is the most vital difference. The first two are 1, a prophecy and 2, an order, but 3 is the offering of free will... I was very glad of your last letter. And the translation of the word. Don't worry about it. I will have to get the best answers... We may have to go outside of rabbinical thought to pure scholarship which may be non-Jewish. What American university has a good Hebrew department? Dr Ginzberg, dealing in theology, may have a slightly different attitude from that of a pure etymologist.' Steinbeck, *Journal of a Novel*, 107–8, 121–2. For further discussion on this matter, see ibid. See also, Wright, 'Cain and Abel: John Steinbeck'; Alec Gilmore, 'A Steinbeck Midrash on Gn 4:7', http://www.gilco.org.uk/eos/a-steinbeck-midrash-on.html; Ferrell, *John Steinbeck: The Voice of the Land*, 58.

The positive behavior of the 'good' characters is at best unpleasant. Aron is selfish, inconsiderate, unloving. Adam neglects his boys for twelve years, never loves anybody except Cathy, and loves her blindly. His rejection of Cal's gift was brutal, unfeeling, and this after he had begun a cordial relationship with his son.[266]

While he firmly believes in free will and the ability of human beings to choose the good, Steinbeck's Puritan background leads him to suggest that it is actually evil that makes us human. And since Abel was killed almost at the start of the biblical story, and it was Cain who had the descendants, everyone is ultimately an heir of Cain.[267]

The motif of the promised land in *East of Eden* tends to be overlooked despite the fact that Steinbeck speaks repeatedly about the 'E-motif' for Eden in his journal: 'Right now I am so deeply immersed in E that I have a difficulty thinking outside of it'.[268] We have dealt with the Abel-like character of Adam, but he also bears some of the attributes of his biblical namesake. America's flag as the new promised land is therefore flown high in this novel. Wright acknowledges Steinbeck's introduction to the novel, which is fully devoted to a description of the Salinas Valley in California – the assumed earthly paradise – but claims that this is for the sake of stressing the duality of good and evil.[269] This feels like an oversimplification as there is no doubt in my mind that the description is given to provide a parallel between the Salinas Valley and the promised land:

> On the wide level acres of the valley the topsoil lay deep and fertile. It required only a rich winter of rain to make it break forth in grass and flowers. The spring flowers in a wet year were unbelievable. The whole valley floor, and the foothills too, would be carpeted with lupins and poppies.[270]

The valley is rich, delightful, and promising, but we learn that there are dry years, 5–6 years at a time, when the valley becomes a waste land.

> I have spoken of the rich years when the rainfall was plentiful. But there are very dry years too, and they put a terror on the valley. The water came in a thirty-year cycle. There would be five or six wet and wonderful years when there might be nineteen to twenty-five inches of rain, and the land would

266. Fontenrose, *John Steinbeck*, 126.
267. Steinbeck, *Journal of a Novel*, 128.
268. Ibid. See also ibid., 127, 131, 133.
269. Wright, 'Cain and Abel: John Steinbeck', 61.
270. Steinbeck, *East of Eden*, 4.

shout with grass. Then would come six or seven pretty good years of twelve
to sixteen inches of rain. And then the dry years would come, and sometimes
there would be only seven or eight inches of rain. The land dried up and the
grasses headed out miserably a few inches high and great bare scabby places
appeared in the valley.[271]

Wright may be correct in one sense: the two faces of the Salinas Valley
could point to the assertion that good and evil are a duality; one cannot
be without the other as one is always described in contrast to the other.
Steinbeck could equally be describing a promised land which reverts to
being Egypt, just as it does in *To a God Unknown* and *The Grapes of
Wrath*. Philo's allegorical understanding of the journey to the promised
land, taken up by Origen and Dante, suggests that the exodus from Egypt
and settlement of the promised land reflects the everyday struggle of the
human soul on its way from earthly enslavement in the body (Egypt/hell)
to the presence of God (the promised land/heaven), a struggle between
the good that nudges the soul forward and closer to God and the evil that
pushes it back. It is clear, however, that the American dream of an earthly
paradise is understood in a spiritual and eschatological way. Steinbeck's
description of California suggests that the new promised land will never
exist on earth, not even in California. Like *To a God Unknown* and *The
Grapes of Wrath*, *East of Eden* suggests two respects in which California
is in fact a land of slavery: the enslavement of the people, and the trans-
formation of the rich and fruitful land into a waste land. Fontenrose
sees Adam and Sam as heirs of the legacy that says America is the new
promised land but argues that Sam was at least aware that the promised
land of California was like Canaan in also presenting a threat:

> Both Adam and Sam shared the dream of all settlers in the Salinas Valley,
> that there the American earthly paradise would be realized, but Sam felt
> a sinister influence too: 'There's blackness on this valley... It's as though
> some old ghost haunted it out of the dead ocean below and troubled the air
> with unhappiness.'[272]

Adam and Sam could be said to represent two sides of Steinbeck's
attempt to come to terms with the American dream. Each is aware of these
two sides, but whereas Adam stubbornly believes he will discover the lost
paradise for himself and his wife Cathy (who is not in fact interested),
Sam seems to be aware of the potential sting in the tail. Owens suggests
a similar allegorical interpretation of *East of Eden*:

271. Ibid., 5.
272. Fontenrose, *John Steinbeck*, 122–3.

And in the most allegorical of his novels, East of Eden (1952), Steinbeck creates an explicit American Adam in the character of Adam Trask, who, in a self-destructive search for his own unfallen Eden, flees from his Calvinistic Jehovah-like father on the eastern seaboard and settles in Salinas Valley in California.[273]

Despite Steinbeck's introduction to *East of Eden*, which bears a remarkable resemblance to the inter-chapter of *The Grapes of Wrath* mentioned above, Steinbeck scholars tend either to overlook the promised land motif in *East of Eden* or to acknowledge only the allegorical meaning, as we have seen in Wright. The introduction nonetheless provides a survey of the history of the expulsions that had taken place in California and reminds us that the motif of the promised land, with all its negative aspects, is an indisputable part of the novel. As in *The Grapes of Wrath*, Steinbeck offers a critical account of the greed and carelessness of the American settlers who disrespected both the people and the land. As we noted when discussing Brueggemann and ideology critique, promised land theology must always include a history of expulsion, not only in biblical times but also in New England and California. Steinbeck explains:

And that was the long Salinas Valley. Its history was like that of the rest of the state. First there were Indians, an inferior breed without energy, inventions or culture, a people that lived on grubs and grasshoppers and shellfish... Then the hard, dry Spaniards came exploring through, greedy and realistic, and their greed was gold or God. They collected souls as they collected jewels. They gathered mountains and valleys, rivers and whole horizons, the way a man might now gain title to building lots... Then the Americans came – more greedy because there were more of them. They took the lands, remade the laws to make their titles good.[274]

The narrative line of the novel also follows the westward movement from slavery to the promised land. Adam marries Cathy and moves with her from the family farm in Connecticut to the Salinas Valley. Their move west repeats the journeys of the Waynes in *To a God Unknown* and the Joads in *The Grapes of Wrath*. It is the same journey taken by the pioneers of centuries past. Steinbeck wanted Adam to move to California from the very beginning and has him mention this intention more than once.[275] When the time comes, the move is described as what we might now call a no-brainer:

273. Owens, *The Grapes of Wrath*, 50.
274. Steinbeck, *East of Eden*, 6–7.
275. Ibid., 71, 103, 106, 125.

The long Salinas Valley was part of the exploitation. Adam had seen and studied a fine color broadside which set forth the valley as that region which heaven unsuccessfully imitated. After reading the literature, anyone who did not want to settle in the Salinas Valley was crazy.[276]

The concepts of the garden of Eden and the promised land of Canaan merge in *East of Eden*. As we know from the Puritans, this is nothing new. The new promised land and new Eden of California contain their darker sides that transform them into their complete opposites. The new promised land dries up just like the land of slavery in Egypt and vomits out its inhabitants by means of the newcomers who do not respect the aboriginals. Adam moves with his wife to the new promised land of California, but on arrival they realize they must first create it.[277] At this point, the new promised land turns into a new Eden:

'Look, Samuel, I mean to make a garden of my land. Remember my name is Adam. So far I've had no Eden, let alone been driven out.' 'It's the best reason I ever heard for making a garden', Samuel exclaimed. He chuckled. 'Where will the orchard be?' Adam said, 'I won't plant apples. That would be looking for accidents.' 'What does Eve say to that? She has a say, you remember. And Eves delight in apples.'[278]

While Cathy is the only aspirant for the Eve role, she is far from Eve-like. She is a persistent reminder that the new promised land, the new Eden in the Salinas Valley, is an illusion, and that it has always been Adam's illusion. Fontenrose suggests that Adam loses his Eden, a happy life with Cathy, when she leaves the family, but this is not so.[279] Adam's life had never been a happy Eden, so he could not lose it. When Cathy deserts her husband and two new-born boys, the absence of an Eden only becomes clearer. What she in fact represents is the threat within the new Eden. Steinbeck describes her as a personification of evil, as the serpent of the new Eden with a serpentine look, as a bringer of treason:

276. Ibid., 134.
277. Ferrell argues that although Adam thought he was creating an earthly paradise, it was not so from the very beginning: 'The Eden that Adam hoped to create was no Eden at all, but a dead, stultifying life, the price for which was tragically borne by his sons Cal and Aron. Steinbeck was retelling the biblical story of Cain and Abel, using that story as a metaphor for the suffering that humans cause one another.' Ferrell, *John Steinbeck: The Voice of the Land*, 58.
278. Steinbeck, *East of Eden*, 169.
279. Fontenrose, *John Steinbeck*, 121.

And just as there are physical monsters, can there not be mental or psychic monsters born? The face and body may be perfect, but if a twisted gene or a malformed egg can produce physical monsters, may not the same process produce a malformed soul?[280]

There was a time when a girl like Cathy would have been called possessed by the devil.[281]

As though nature concealed a trap, Cathy had from the first a face of innocence. Her hair was gold and lovely; wide-set hazel eyes with upper lids that drooped made her look mysteriously sleepy. Her nose was delicate and thin, and her cheekbones high and wide, sweeping down to a small chin so that her face was heart shaped. Her mouth was well shaped and well lipped but abnormally small – what used to be called a rosebud. Her ears were very little, without lobes, and they pressed so close to her head that even with her hair combed they made no silhouette.[282]

The tension between landlessness and landedness sketched out in the novel can be described in terms of being 'listening and open' or 'closed off and stubborn': the main 'sin' in the novel, the sin which drives the people out of the promised land, is that they were closed off and unable to listen. It is a sin committed many times by the supposedly good Adam because he was landed: 'Adam sat as a contented cat on his land'.[283] Adam never listens to what people are telling him. He does not listen when his brother Charles warns him away from Cathy, saying she is not a good person. He does not listen to Cathy when she keeps telling him that she does not want to go to California. When Adam is 'landed' in his grief after Cathy's departure, he does not listen to Sam, who begs him not to neglect his sons. Adam is landed and wants to manage his future, the land, and the people. Managing land and people has always led to landlessness. Managing one's future obviously leads to 'futurelessness' (Mt. 16.25). When people are 'landed', they are closed off, and the promised land slips away from them. But when they are not sure of their conduct and start to 'wander', when they are landless, the promised land draws nearer. This happens when Cal admits his fault and pleads guilty of his brother's death and when Adam forgives Cal on his death bed. These are the moments when the doors of the promised land are wide open for them to enter, or at

280. Steinbeck, *East of Eden*, 72.
281. Ibid., 73.
282. Ibid.
283. Ibid., 156.

least to approach. Steinbeck does not give up on his idea of the promised land altogether: 'Although East of Eden is not Eden, it is not insuperably far away'.[284]

Many of the themes in *East of Eden* – the struggle between good and evil, the promised land motif – are worked out on the allegorical level. The everyday struggle of the human soul is to escape the earthly troubles of the body in Egypt and attain a trouble-free life with God in the heavenly promised land. The tension between landedness and landlessness takes place in the characters' minds and on their lips. The servant Lee declares: 'I think this is the best-known story in the world because it is everybody's story. I think it is the symbol story of the human soul.'[285] Lee is talking about the tension between good and evil, but we could translate it into patristic allegory and call it the story of the soul wandering towards the promised land. Steinbeck might have been correct to write 'the only story' in the world; perhaps he had always been writing it, but it was a different story. It was the story of the American dream, the search for paradise, and if not an earthly paradise then at least a heavenly one, as that has always been the motivation to conquer evil and promote the good.

284. Steinbeck, *Journal of a Novel*, 116.
285. Steinbeck, *East of Eden*, 270.

Conclusion

Not long into this exploration of the motif of the promised land I began to fear that it might appear more like a depiction of a land without promise or a promise without the land. Why was this, I wondered. Although the biblical roots of the motif are beyond question, the words 'promised land' appear not once in the whole Hebrew Bible. There must be a reason for that. Developing his own understanding of the motif, Walter Brueggemann introduces the metaphorical concept of landlessness and landedness and establishes a tension between the two which can never be overcome in one's earthly life. A similar tension had been described in Antiquity by Origen, who insisted that conquering the promised land is not a one-off event but a never-ending process which requires continual human effort if it is to remain conquered. Writing almost two millennia apart, Brueggemann and Origen each suggest that the promised land is something we will always strive for but never attain: the moment we try to take hold of it, it will slip through our fingers. The concept is therefore an illusion and appears always to have been so.

The history of the interpretation of the promised land motif is a story of two intermingling streams: the literal (physical and territorial) and the allegorical (metaphorical, spiritual and eschatological). Each of these streams can be found in both biblical and literary scholarship. The allegorical line in both disciplines is undoubtedly traced to Philo of Alexandria, who recognized something deeply existential and personal in the concept of the promised land: the soul's struggle and its longing for God is easily understood and applies to every individual regardless of their historical context. In *East of Eden*, the concept of the promised land encapsulates the eternal fight between light and darkness, love and hatred, openness and closedness, and, ultimately, good and evil. Here, unlike Brueggemann, for whom a person's socio-economic context appears to be the decisive factor in the battle for their soul, Steinbeck conquers his determinist Puritan heritage and champions free will:[1] despite our nature, despite our context, we are all free to decide; the battle for the promised land is won or lost according

---

1. This is not the case in *The Grapes of Wrath*, which is as fatalistic as Brueggemann.

to a free choice. In Milton, the promised land (Eden) is lost because of free will; in Steinbeck it is re-gained on the same basis.

The literal – physical, territorial – interpretations of the promised land are no less important. The idea of the elect, and the land to which they were elected, moved in both time and space, from ancient Israel, to medieval Britain, to the post-Reformation New World. Although the geography of the promised land is never clearly outlined, even in the Bible, the physical and territorial realm plays an important role, especially at times of political uncertainty.

In these closing comments, I will look back on the reception of the promised land motif in the Bible, Christian culture, and the novels of John Steinbeck through the lens of Hans-Georg Gadamer's approach to understanding, interpretation, and application.

Gadamer's unique approach emphasizes the equality of the scientific and artistic paths towards understanding and knowledge and their equal status in the hermeneutical process. The literary scholar Hans Jauss and the biblical scholar Anthony Thiselton both attempted to systematize Gadamer's approach and make it more practical and applicable, although Evans would argue, and I would agree, that their efforts took away from the brilliance of Gadamer's hermeneutic. Indeed, various interpretations over time have simply resembled extensions of previous interpretations, appropriated for new 'horizons of expectation' but leaving no space for originality or dissent so as to maintain continuity with tradition.

My approach emphasizes the originality and creativity of the artist's genius but seeks to avoid lapsing into unlimited subjectivism. Several mechanisms can help to keep artistic ingenuity on a leash while still making the most of it. In addition to profiting from the artist's contribution to the process of understanding, I take advantage of the diachronic aspects of Gadamer's hermeneutic, which explain why understanding is always historical and cannot be otherwise. These diachronic aspects, rightly exalted by scholars of reception history such as Jauss and Thiselton, can nevertheless overshadow the synchronic aspects, which are equally present in Gadamer's hermeneutic, and in my own approach are repre-sented by the original input of the artist. These inputs are legitimized not only by tradition or the horizon of expectation (Jauss and Thiselton) but also by the interpretive community (Fish and Clines).

Literal and/or allegorical face of the promised land

The mingling of the literal and allegorical interpretations of the promised land has been a feature of this whole exploration. Most New Testament scholars – but certainly not all of them – argue that after the incarnation, crucifixion, and resurrection of Jesus Christ, the promise of land ceases to be interpreted in the territorial and political sense that we encounter in the Hebrew Bible. But what if we were to approach the whole matter from a different angle and ask if it is indeed possible to separate the literal from the allegorical, the political from the eschatological, the territorial from the spiritual.

While we may claim that in certain periods the promise of land was understood more politically than it was in others, it is almost impossible to draw strict lines and reject the spiritual-eschatological dimension altogether. From the very beginning, when the promise was given to Abraham and the patriarchs and subsequently to the whole of Israel, the land clearly referred to a specific territory defined by both its geography ('from the river of Egypt to the great river, the river Euphrates', Gen. 15.18b) and its inhabitants ('the land of the Kenites, the Kenizzites, the Kadmonites, the Hittites, the Perizzites, the Rephaites, the Amorites, the Canaanites, the Girgashites, and the Jebusites', Gen. 15.19-21). However vague the actual location – there are differences between the various biblical descriptions of both the land and the people – it was nonetheless clearly a physical stretch of land in the Near East. However, because the promise given to the whole of Israel in Exod. 3.8 was of a land flowing with milk and honey, the land also acquires paradisiacal attributes that refer to a transcendental horizon. We could still argue nonetheless that until the exile, the promise of this somewhat idealized land was largely understood in political and territorial terms.

The first substantial shift in understanding took place when Israel was taken into exile in Babylon. Second and third Isaiah, second Jeremiah, and Ezekiel now begin to interpret the promise of land spiritually and eschatologically, most likely to comfort a broken people who have lost the essence of their identity: 'Israel without land is no people'.[2] Indeed, Israel without land is no people of God, whose attachment to the people was defined by the promise of land. With the gradual Hellenization of the Near East, these late postexilic books interpret the promise of land spiritually. The exceptions are Ezra and Nehemiah, who insist that the promised land is a discernible territorial entity – Jerusalem and its surroundings – with clear religious and political ambitions. The New Testament continues in the tone of the apocalyptic books and has little interest in political or territorial claims. Christianity extended the ethnic, local cult of the God YHWH into the global context and makes no plea for a definable territory, as Charles Talbert argues: 'In this context, the promise to inherit the world refers not to taking possession of the land of Israel but to gaining life in

2. Brueggemann, *The Land*, 111.

the New World beyond the resurrection'.[3] The well-known reference to 'inheriting' the land in the Beatitudes (Mt. 5.5) is understood as a spiritual and eschatological event that takes place in heaven. Ben Witherington suggests that, 'those who are totally dependent on God will in due course inherit the land. It would appear that Jesus did believe in an eschatological restoration of the land to those whom God had chosen, but not before the eschaton.'[4] The Jewish thinkers Philo of Alexandria and Flavius Josephus, despite their different contexts – one an exile from North Africa, the other an inhabitant, for most of his life, of Israel-Palestine – show an extraordinary lack of interest in the promise of land in the political and territorial sense. Josephus's feverish support for the Maccabean revolt which took place some hundred years before the revolt against the Romans of which he disapproved so vociferously is strange indeed. The fact that he remained a faithful Jew while siding with the Romans strongly suggests a lack of attachment to a political interpretation of the promised land. Philo's commentaries, which portray the promised land as a spiritual and eschatological concept, influenced the theological treatises of the Church Fathers and the fiction of the Middle Ages, such as Dante's brilliant apocalyptic vision of the soul's journey from the 'hell' of the earthly body to the 'heaven' of eternal dwelling with God.

The second paradigmatic shift came with the Reformation and the rise of national churches. Newly independent from Rome, the churches curried favour with local political leaders: Luther sought the support of the prince of Saxony; the Church of England was tightly bound to the crown from its very inception. It is no surprise, then, that the religious and the political began to merge, and with significant consequences. The execution of Charles I in England in 1649 and the successful overthrow of the monarchy led the revolutionaries to believe they were God's 'newly elect', the 'new Israel'. In the first and only such revolt in Europe, they had removed the fake king and installed the only true king, God the Almighty, as their ruler. The promised land was now securely located in the British Isles and very clearly a political and territorial entity. It was also now a national rather than merely personal concern, and no longer an allegory of the soul's longing for the presence of God but an existential battle between the new Israelites (the revolutionaries) and the Canaanites (the royalists). Milton's highly influential *Paradise Lost* is a political allegory of the revolution. The poet's tangible preference for the new monarch-less Commonwealth made *Paradise Lost* a seminal text for the revolutionary developments in eighteenth-century America and

3. Talbert, *Romans*, 119.
4. Witherington, *Matthew*, 121.

the struggle for independence from Britain. When the revolt was finally suppressed and the Commonwealth overthrown, those faithful to the revolution lost their illusion that England was their promised land. Many of the revolutionaries were Puritans. Unhappy with developments after the Reformation, they criticized the Church of England for what they saw as its perilous proximity to the 'old orders', including the Catholic Church. Persecuted for their outspoken beliefs, the nonconformists set sail for North America with a clear vision of being the 'new elect' and finally establishing the 'new promised land' that had failed to materialize in England. Puritan ministers took their zeal and their redemptive-historical faith to New England and became the 'voice crying out in the wilderness', preparing the way for the kingdom of heaven to come on earth. Their belief in the promised land was religious-political and it was territorial. Soon after their arrival, however, the promised land began to resemble a wilderness with all its struggles and hardships. The redemptive-historical self-understanding of these first immigrants as the 'new elect' in the new promised land would have a powerful influence on generations to come.

The synergy between belief in the freedom of the individual and life in the communal and political new promised land of America was a challenge from the start and soon proved untenable. Despite this, many of the authors we have discussed appeared unable to drop the ideal. The most obvious interest in the land as physical earth – but with clear political overtones – was presented by Thomas Jefferson in his *Notes on the State of Virginia*. Jefferson agrarianism insisted that the most natural occupation for Americans was husbandry and that manufacturing should be left for the Old Continent; a small plot of land for every farmer would secure democracy and freedom for all. This was a political statement par excellence which came straight out of biblical land theology: the idea that the land is YHWH's inheritance and God gives it to the people of Israel. The idea proved to be utopian, however, and Jefferson's dream of an 'Empire for Liberty' in which farmers husbanded small portions of land transformed into the nightmare of slaves toiling on vast plantations owned by faceless others. Steinbeck believed the practice of latifundi-alization destroyed both the people and the land and he described the process in *The Grapes of Wrath*. George and Lennie in *Of Mice and Men* dreamed of owning a piece of land that would secure their freedom and independence. The dream failed because of their inability to exercise any kind of self-control.

The idea of America as the new promised land is discussed at length in Walt Whitman's collection of poems *Leaves of Grass*. For Whitman, America fulfilled all the requirements of a land of promise: a unique and virgin land, fertile and full of natural riches. Whitman presents the idea of a people moving ever westward, bringing progress as they go. If failure comes, the promised land will appear over the next mountain range. Not so, says Steinbeck. In *Pastures of Heaven, To a God Unknown, The Grapes of Wrath*, and *East of Eden* the author shows that the promised land was not to be found even on the western shore. The search should not be abandoned, however, just re-directed, from the communal, territorial, and political realm to the individual, spiritual, and eschatological.

Steinbeck and Brueggemann

The American Hebrew Bible scholar Walter Brueggemann has proved a worthy interpretive partner for John Steinbeck. Brueggemann clearly sets out the dialectic of the promise and loss of land and its corollary in the dialectic of landlessness and landedness: neither state is definitive or permanent, and the two are always in tension. When people are landless, they are 'on the way' to the promised land; when they are securely landed, they begin to lose it. Brueggemann's intuition turned out to be universally applicable when we discovered a similar dividing line between the landlessness and landedness of many characters in Steinbeck's novels. The tension is clearly visible in *To a God Unknown*. While the landless Joseph Wayne is seeking his promised land in rich and fruitful California, the promise is before him. When he finally begins to feel settled, has a wife and a child, and everything is under control, everything changes and the promised land becomes a land of slavery, dry and barren, and full of death. A similar scenario appears in *The Grapes of Wrath*. The landed Okies oppress and exploit the Native Americans followed by the land they take from them; when they themselves are evicted, when they become landless, they help other migrants on the way to California and when they reach their final destination. Being landless in the land of promise, which turns out to be a land of slavery, motivates the Okies to stick together and help each other. In *East of Eden*, landlessness and landedness are evident on both the literal and the allegorical levels. Adam's landlessness and his search for the promised land lasts until he becomes landed in the Salinas Valley, but just as in *The Grapes of Wrath*, the promised land in California is an illusion. There never was a promised land for Adam and his family, not even from the beginning. Adam has been searching for it but is doomed never to reach it. His wife Cathy, who always intends to leave him (and keeps repeating this threat but Adam never listens), never allows him even a foretaste of the promised land. The literal earthly new promised land with his new Eve (Cathy) never materializes, although it does so on the allegorical level. *East of Eden* tells the story of the souls of Adam and Cal wandering from the slavery of their earthly bodies. 'Landedness' tied them to their respective 'good' and 'evil' natures, although they are both shown to be closed-minded. Finally, they are invited to approach the promised land by opening their hearts and forgiving each other and themselves.

Steinbeck and Brueggemann are equally critical of the idea of the 'elect' and the attitude of the elect towards both the land and the native inhabitants. The two concerns are connected and follow on from the landless-landed principle and the human response to it. The landed are inclined to *manage* – in Brueggemann's words *misuse* – both the people and the land, for example by violating the law of the Sabbath for the land. They treat the land not as an inheritance but as a possession, and one for which they have little respect. Steinbeck uses his intuition and creativity as a literary author to describe the same phenomenon and in so doing becomes a source of influence for biblical scholarship.

The dialectic of landlessness and landedness has its roots in the dialectic of land that is freely given and the conditions set out for 'tenants', a dialectic which in the Hebrew Bible is never clearly defined but is nevertheless always present. The free gift of land to the patriarchs and the whole of Israel (Gen. 15.7; Exod. 3.8) is set off against the threat of the land vomiting out the wicked who sin against God, the land, and the people (Lev. 18.25). These biblical illustrations are clear and comprehensible. The trouble comes when Brueggemann applies his principle of landedness and landlessness to the present-day conflict in Israel-Palestine, where inexplicably, the timeless and general applicability of the pattern disappears. Rather than keeping the dialectic in a productive tension, Brueggemann assigns the interested parties clear and unchanging roles and in so doing creates an ideology just like the one he criticizes the Israeli leadership for promulgating. Steinbeck coped with this problem more skilfully. When he criticizes the attitude of the incomers towards the native inhabitants (the Native Americans in Oklahoma, the Okies in Oklahoma, the Mexicans in California), he always stresses that the pattern of colonizing the natives is the 'story of the West', that it has always been like this, and that the pattern is timeless and universally applicable: the oppressor and the oppressed can switch roles at any time. In his introduction to *East of Eden* and in the inter-chapters in *The Grapes of Wrath*, Steinbeck was at great pains to stress that this pattern can involve anyone and everyone because 'land by violence' is the unavoidable fate of humanity.

Concern for both the physical soil and the land as a symbol of the relationship between God and God's people has been a permanent feature of the American religious-political and cultural identities of which Brueggemann and Steinbeck are both heirs. It is Steinbeck, however, who appears to have the keener eye for environmental and humanitarian concerns and who is sensitive to the land as well as to the native inhabitants. His agrarian concern, which develops into considerations comparable to the current environmental discourse, helps him to remember the need for careful cultivation of the promised land and to be critical when this requirement is not met. Steinbeck's upbringing and his marriage to Carol Henning and friendship with Tom Collins, both activists in the field of care for the socially disadvantaged during the Great Depression, lead Steinbeck to open a discussion on the moral responsibility of those in power. He not only discusses the poor and the dislocated during the time of the Great Depression but also considers the colonization of the Native Americans by the original settlers from Europe. Unlike Brueggemann, Steinbeck maintains the timeless character of the relationship between the oppressors and the oppressed by insisting that the oppressed Okies were once the oppressors of the Native Americans. There are some who criticize Steinbeck for not addressing the issue of the Native Americans of his own time.[5] The criticism may be valid, but we should remember that Steinbeck was writing novels, not academic articles about the complex sociological problems of the disadvantaged in America.

As a child of the first half of the twentieth century, Steinbeck begins criticizing land ideologies much earlier than his fellow interpreter, the younger Walter Brueggemann. That there is no sign of such criticism in the works of the biblical scholars Gerhard von Rad and Claus Westermann, who are closer contemporaries of Steinbeck than is Brueggemann, testifies to the fact that art and literature can play a prophetic role and sometimes set the agenda for other disciplines. Ideology critique was not taken up in biblical studies until the end of the twentieth century.

Steinbeck's contribution to the interpretation of the promised land motif

This much should now be clear: artistic interpretations such as the novels of John Steinbeck can contribute to a profound understanding of biblical motifs, both in Scripture and in its afterlife in culture. They are beneficial

---

5. Nellie McKay, '"Happy[?]-Wife-and Motherdom": The Portrayal of Ma Joad in John Steinbeck's *The Grapes of Wrath*', in Bloom, ed., *John Steinbeck*, 41.

on many levels. They provide an original perspective, a new hermeneutic that allows the interpreter extensive freedom. Such interpretations are informed by tradition but are by no means fettered by it. Artistic interpreters play a prophetic role in society and often serve as forerunners to paradigm shifts. Such prophecy is not always welcomed, of course. Although Steinbeck's *The Grapes of Wrath* with its great drive and social-revolutionary appeal won a Pulitzer Prize, it was criticized as a deeply perverted view of the world and by the Association Farmers of Kern County, California, as 'obscene sensationalism'.[6]

F. Scott Fitzgerald had already offered a critical evaluation of the American dream and the idea of the American 'elect', but his work says little about the need to re-evaluate our attitude to the environment. Steinbeck, however, especially in *To a God Unknown*, written as early as 1933, shows a level of concern for environmental matters unknown among his contemporaries. Joseph Wayne's deeply existential struggle between submitting to nature and mastering it is extraordinary. The Puritan fathers had tussled with hostile nature and sought to conquer it, but in Steinbeck, natural catastrophes have a human origin. Wayne never succeeds in his attempts to live in harmony with the natural world, not because of the hostility of nature but because of his failure to pay proper respect to his environment.

At the time Steinbeck was writing, the American Episcopal Church was not yet ready to admit the need to reconsider the idea of the American 'elect' and its consequences on the environment and the country's native inhabitants. Steinbeck's novels are therefore some distance ahead of his religious context, but could, arguably, have helped to trigger the paradigm shift in the Episcopalian Church which took place a few decades later. Steinbeck's love–hate relationship with his Christian heritage, especially the Episcopal Church as the heir of Puritanism in America, is clearly visible in all his works – his criticism of religious fundamentalism in the accounts of Grandma Liza Hamilton in *East of Eden*, and of the pastoral praxis of Jim Casy in *The Grapes of Wrath* – but his copious use of biblical imagery suggests an inability to bid a final farewell to Christian tradition. Nonetheless, his novels did not fit within the paradigm of the biblical scholars of his time. His interpretation of Scripture and its legacy are unique and have been influential in many ways. Our aim here has been to present that influence in the realm of the motif of the promised land and its socio-political and religious-cultural impact on Western culture.

6. Owens, *The Grapes of Wrath*, 11.

Brueggemann quotes from Steinbeck on occasion, usually to illustrate his argument, but makes no further evaluation of his interpretations, which are nonetheless worthy of further exploration. In addition to serving the arguments of others, Steinbeck himself has something relevant to say about biblical interpretation. Some of his ideas are original, promising, and inspiring, particularly those regarding the need to care for the land and the environment, but also for people, especially the indigenous people, who in his time were still of no interest to the mainstream.

Another great advantage of artistic interpretations is their form. A work of fiction is much closer to 'lay' readers than is a biblical commentary. *East of Eden* is a story about good and evil which Steinbeck writes for his two sons. It is a story which for maximum effect Steinbeck provides a biblical setting – the most obvious story about good and evil, the story of Cain and Abel in Genesis 4, a story known to almost everyone, including those who do not practise the Christian religion or participate in any institutionalized Christian worship. Such a familiar setting serves to provoke prejudice and facilitates the first encounter between the story and its reader. Steinbeck does not simply re-narrate the story but uses an American context that is well known to his sons. To draw them even closer, he throws in the story of his own family, thus fulfilling Gadamer's insistence on contextualization. To go further than Brueggemann, however, who simply quotes Steinbeck, I have brought an evaluation of Steinbeck's own imprint on the well-known story, that is, his own original interpretation and his life-long disapproval of the traditional interpretation. Steinbeck rejects black-and-white perspectives on this paradigmatic story about good and evil. The story does not begin and end in Genesis. For Steinbeck it is an eternal story which concerns every one of us. It is a story about landedness and landlessness, a story about longing for the promised land and about its subsequent loss. This is an interpretation on which Brueggemann and Steinbeck agree. However, where Steinbeck surpasses Brueggemann, and indeed surpasses his own earlier works, is the point where he gives up the Puritan legacy of determinism and the inevitable consequences of evil human inclinations and tells us that the promised land is there, somewhere, for anyone who chooses to look for it.

BIBLIOGRAPHY

Adorno, Theodore. *Aesthetic Theory*. Athlone Contemporary European Thinkers. London: Continuum, 2002.

Allen, Leslie C. *Ezekiel 20–48*. Word Biblical Commentary 29. Dallas, TX: Word, 1990.

Alter, Robert. *Canon and Creativity: Modern Writing and the Authority of Scripture*. New Haven, CT: Yale University Press, 2000.

Alter, Robert. *The World of Biblical Literature*. London: SPCK, 1992.

Alter, Robert, and Frank Kermode. *The Literary Guide to the Bible*. Boston, MA: Harvard University Press, 1983.

Attridge, Harold W. *The Epistle to the Hebrews: A Commentary on the Epistle to the Hebrews*. Hermeneia. Minneapolis, MN: Fortress, 1989.

Auerbach, Erich. *Mimesis: The Representation of Reality in Western Literature*. Princeton, NJ: Princeton University Press, 2003.

Ausloos, Hans. *The Deuteronomist's History: The Role of the Deuteronomist in Historical-Critical Research into Genesis–Numbers*. Oudtestamentische Studiën 67. Leiden: Brill, 2015.

Ausloos, Hans. '"A Land Flowing with Milk and Honey". Indicative of a Deuteronomistic Redaction?' *Ephemerides Theologicae Lovanienses. Louvain Journal of Theology and Canon Law* 75 (1999): 297–314.

Bailey, Lloyd R. *Leviticus–Numbers*. Smyth & Helwys Bible Commentary. Macon, GA: Smyth & Helwys, 2005.

Balentine, Samuel E. *Leviticus*. Westminster: John Knox, 2002.

Barrett, Charles K. *A Critical and Exegetical Commentary on the Acts of the Apostles: In Two Volumes*. Vol. 1. Preliminary Introduction and Commentary on Acts I–XIV. International Critical Commentary. Edinburgh: T. & T. Clark, 1994.

Barthes, Roland. *The Rustle of Language*. Berkeley, CA: University of California Press, 1989.

Benson, Jackson J. 'An Introduction to John Steinbeck'. In *A John Steinbeck Encyclopedia*, edited by Brian Railsback and Michael J. Meyer, xli–xlvii. Westport, CT: Greenwood, 2006.

Benson, Jackson J. *The True Adventures of John Steinbeck, Writer*. New York: Viking, 1984.

Bercovitch, Sacvan. *The American Jeremiad*. Madison, WI: University of Wisconsin Press, 1978.

Blenkinsopp, Joseph. *Ezekiel*. Interpretation: A Bible Interpretation for Teaching and Preaching. Louisville, KY: John Knox, 1990.

Bloom, Harold. *F. Scott Fitzgerald's the Great Gatsby*. New York: Infobase, 2010.

Bouwsma, William J. 'John Calvin'. *Britannica Academic*, www.academic.eb.com/EBchecked/topic/90247/John-Calvin.

Bray, Gerald. *Biblical Interpretation: Past and Present*. Leicester: Apollos, 1996.

Breneman, Mervin. *Ezra, Nehemiah, Esther*. Nashville, TN: B&H, 2009.

Brooker, Jewel Spears, and Joseph Bentley. *Reading 'The Waste Land': Modernism and the Limits of Interpretation*. Amherst, MA: University of Massachusetts Press, 1990.

Browne, Stephen. 'Samuel Danforth's Errand into the Wilderness and the Discourse of Arrival in Early American Culture'. *Communication Quarterly* 40, no. 2 (1992): 91–101.

Brueggemann, Walter. *1 & 2 Kings*. Smyth & Helwys Bible Commentary. Macon, GA: Smyth & Helwys, 2000.

Brueggemann, Walter. *A Commentary on Jeremiah: Exile and Homecoming*. Grand Rapids, MI: Eerdmans, 1998.

Brueggemann, Walter. *First and Second Samuel*. Interpretation: A Bible Commentary for Teaching and Preaching: O.T. Louisville, KY: John Knox, 1990.

Brueggemann, Walter. *Genesis*. Interpretation. Atlanta, GA: John Knox, 1983.

Brueggemann, Walter. 'The God of Joshua… Give or Take the Land'. *Interpretation: A Journal of Bible and Theology* 66, no. 2 (2012): 164–75.

Brueggemann, Walter. *The Land: Place as Gift, Promise, and Challenge in Biblical Faith*. 2nd ed. Minneapolis, MN: Fortress, 2003.

Brueggemann, Walter. 'Reading the Bible amid the Israeli–Palestinian Conflict'. *Theology Today* 73, no. 1 (2016): 36–45.

Brueggemann, Walter. *Reverberations of Faith: A Theological Handbook of Old Testament Themes*. Louisville, KY: Westminster John Knox, 2002.

Brueggemann, Walter. *The Theology of the Book of Jeremiah*. Old Testament Theology. New York: Cambridge University Press, 2007.

Brueggemann, Walter. *To Build, to Plant: A Commentary on Jeremiah 26–52*. International Theological Commentary. Grand Rapids, MI: Eerdmans, 1991.

Brueggemann, Walter. *To Pluck Up, to Tear Down: A Commentary on the Book of Jeremiah 1–25*. International Theological Commentary. Grand Rapids, MI: Eerdmans, 1988.

Brueggemann, Walter, and Rebecca J. Kruger Gaudino. *Theology of the Old Testament: Testimony, Dispute, Advocacy*. Minneapolis, MN: Fortress, 1997.

Brueggemann, Walter, and Patrick D. Miller. *Like Fire in the Bones: Listening for the Prophetic Word in Jeremiah*. Minneapolis, MN: Fortress, 2006.

Brueggemann, Walter, and Patrick D. Miller. *Old Testament Theology: Essays on Structure, Theme and Text*. Minneapolis, MN: Fortress, 1992.

Bryer, Jackson R., Alan Margolies, and Ruth Prigozy, eds. *F. Scott Fitzgerald: New Perspectives*. Athens, GA: University of Georgia Press, 2000.

Burge, Gary M. *Jesus and the Land: The New Testament Challenge to 'Holy Land' Theology*. Grand Rapids, MI: Baker Academic, 2010.

Burge, Gary M. 'The Land: Who Owns the Holy Land? (The Land: Place as Gift, Promise and Challenge in Biblical Faith) (Book Review)'. *Books & Culture* 9, no. 4 (2003): 40.

Calvin, John. *Commentaires de Jean Calvin sur l'ancien testament*. Edited by André Malet. Geneva: Labor et Fides, 1961.

Carlson, Eric W. 'Symbolism in *The Grapes of Wrath*'. In *A Case Book on The Grapes of Wrath*, edited by Agnes McNeill Donohue, 96–102. New York: Thomas Y. Crowell, 1970.

Carpenter, Frederic I. 'The Philosophical Joads'. In *A Case Book on The Grapes of Wrath*, edited by Agnes McNeill Donohue, 80–9. New York: Thomas Y. Crowell, 1970.

Chance, J. Bradley. *Acts*. Smyth & Helwys Bible Commentary 20. Macon, GA: Smyth & Helwys, 2007.

Childs, Brevard S. *Exodus: A Commentary*. London: SCM, 1974.

Clements, Ronald Ernest. *Jeremiah*. Interpretation: A Bible Interpretation for Teaching and Preaching. Atlanta, GA: John Knox, 1988.

Clines, David J. *Interested Parties: The Ideology of Writers and Readers of the Hebrew Bible*. Sheffield: Sheffield Academic, 1995.

Clines, David J. *On the Way to the Postmodern: Old Testament Essays, 1967–1998*. Sheffield: Sheffield Academic, 1998.

Colacurcio, Michael J. *The Province of Piety: Moral History in Hawthorne's Early Tales*. Durham, NC: Duke University Press, 1995.

Coote, Robert B. 'Land'. In *The Oxford Encyclopedia of the Bible and Theology. 2. Kin - Wor*, edited by Samuel E. Balentine, 27–32. Oxford: Oxford University Press, 2015.

Cotter, David W., Jerome Thomas Walsh, and Chris Franke. *Genesis*. Berit Olam: Studies in Hebrew Narrative & Poetry. Collegeville, MN: Liturgical, 2003.

Cotton, John. 'An Abstract of the Lawes of New England'. In *The New England Way*, edited by John Cotton. Library of American Puritan Writings 12. New York: AMS, 1984.

Craigie, Peter C., David Allen Hubbard, and Page H. Kelley. *Jeremiah 1–25*. Word Biblical Commentary 26. Waco, TX: Word, 1991.

Cranfield, Charles E. *A Critical and Exegetical Commentary on the Epistle to the Romans: In Two Volumes*. International Critical Commentary. Edinburgh: T. & T. Clark, 1985.

Crockett, H. Kelly. 'The Bible and *The Grapes of Wrath*'. In *A Case Book on The Grapes of Wrath*, edited by Agnes McNeill Donohue, 105–14. New York: Thomas Y. Crowell, 1970.

Danforth, Samuel. 'A Brief Recognition of New-England's Errand into the Wilderness: Made in the Audience of the General Assembly of the Massachusetts Colony at Boston in N.E. on the 11th of the Third Month, 1670, Being the Day of Election There by Samuel Danforth'. Printed by S.G. and M.J. in Cambridge, Massachusetts, 1671.

Dante Alighieri. *The Divine Comedy*. London: Bibliophile, 1988.

Davenport, John, and Samuel Whiting. 'The Life of Mr. John Cotton'. In *The New England Way*. Library of American Puritan Writings 12. New York: AMS, 1984.

Davies, William David. *The Gospel and the Land: Early Christianity and Jewish Territorial Doctrine*. Berkeley, CA: University of California Press, 1974.

Davies, William David, and Dale C. Allison. *A Critical and Exegetical Commentary on the Gospel according to Saint Matthew: In Three Volumes*. International Critical Commentary. Edinburgh: T. & T. Clark, 1997.

Davis, Ellen F. *Scripture, Culture, and Agriculture: An Agrarian Reading of the Bible*. New York: Cambridge University Press, 2009.

De Man, Paul. 'Introduction'. In *Toward an Aesthetic of Reception*, edited by Hans Robert Jauss, vii–xxv. Minneapolis, MN: University of Minnesota, 1982.

De Vries, Simon John, David Allen Hubbard, John D. Watts, and Ralph P. Martin. *1 Kings*. Word Biblical Commentary 12. Waco, TX: Word, 1985.

DeMott, Robert. 'Introduction'. In *The Grapes of Wrath*, edited by Robert DeMott, liv. Penguin Twentieth-Century Classics. London: Penguin, 1992.

DeMott, Robert. 'Introduction'. In *Working Days: The Journal of The Grapes of Wrath*, edited by Robert DeMott, xvii–lvii. New York: Viking, 1989.

Dohmen, Christoph. *Exodus 1–18*. Freiburg: Herder, 2015.

Donohue, Agnes McNeill. '"The Endless Journey to No End": Journey and Eden Symbolism in Howthorne and Steinbeck'. In *A Casebook on the Grapes of Wrath*, edited by Agnes McNeill Donohue, 257–66. New York: Thomas Y. Crowell, 1970.

Dougherty, Charles T. 'The Christ-Figure in *The Grapes of Wrath*'. In *A Case Book on The Grapes of Wrath*, edited by Agnes McNeill Donohue, 115–17. New York: Thomas Y. Crowell, 1970.

Doyle, Brian. *The Apocalypse of Isaiah Metaphorically Speaking: A Study of the Use, Function and Significance of Metaphors in Isaiah 24–27*. Bibliotheca Ephemeridum Theologicarum Lovaniensium 151. Leuven: Peeters, 2000.

Dozeman, Thomas B. *Commentary on Exodus*. Grand Rapids, MI: Eerdmans, 2009.

Dunn, James D., David Allen Hubbard, and John D. Watts. *Romans 1–8*. Word Biblical Commentary 38a. Waco, TX: Word, 1988.

Durham, John I. *Exodus*. Word Biblical Commentary 3. Waco, TX: Word, 1987.

Durham, M. *Methodist Hymn Book*, www.ccel.org/ccel/walker/harmony2.H51.html?

Edwards, Jonathan. *Sermons and Discourses, 1720-1723*, edited by Wilson Kimnach. The Works of Jonathan Edwards 10. New Haven, CT: Yale University Press, 1992.

Eisinger, Chester E. 'Jefferson Agrarianism in *The Grapes of Wrath*'. In *A Case Book on The Grapes of Wrath*, edited by Agnes McNeill Donohue, 143–50. New York: Thomas Y. Crowell, 1970.

Eliot, Thomas Stearns. *The Waste Land and Other Poems*. London: Faber & Faber, 1971.

Elliger, Karl, and Wilhelm Rudolph, eds. *Biblia Hebraica Stuttgartensia*. 4. Aufl. Stuttgart: Deutsche Bibelgesellschaft, 1990.

Emerson, Ralph Waldo. 'Nature'. In *Nature, the Conduct of Life and Other Essays*, edited by Sherman Paul, 1–38. London: Dent, 1970.

Evans, Robert. *Reception History, Tradition and Biblical Interpretation: Gadamer and Jauss in Current Practice*. London: Bloomsbury, 2014.

Farmer, William Reuben. *Maccabees, Zealots, and Josephus: An Inquiry into Jewish Nationalism in the Greco-Roman Period*. New York: Greenwood, 1973.

Ferrell, Keith. *John Steinbeck: The Voice of the Land*. Lanham, MD: Rowman & Littlefield, 2015.

Fish, Stanley E. *Is There a Text in This Class? The Authority of Interpretive Communities*. Cambridge, MA: Harvard University Press, 1980.

Fish, Stanley E. 'Literature in the Reader: Affective Stylistics'. In *Reader-Response Criticism: From Formalism to Post-Structuralism*, edited by Jane P. Tompkins, 70–100. Baltimore, MD: Johns Hopkins University Press, 1980.

Fitzgerald, Francis Scott. *The Great Gatsby*. Wordsworth Editions. Wordsworth Classics 18. Ware: Wordsworth, 1993.

Fitzmyer, Joseph A. *The Acts of the Apostles: A New Translation with Introduction and Commentary*. Anchor Bible 31. New York: Doubleday, 1998.

Fitzmyer, Joseph A. *Romans: A New Translation with Introduction and Commentary*. Anchor Bible 33. New York: Doubleday, 1993.

Flavius Josephus. 'Antiquities of the Jews', www.gutenberg.org/files/2848/2848-h/2848-h. htm#link42HCH0008

Fohlen, Claude. *Thomas Jefferson*. Nancy: Presses universitaires de Nancy, 1992.

Fontenrose, Joseph. *John Steinbeck: An Introduction and Interpretation*. New York: Holt, Rinehart & Winston, 1963.

Frankel, David. *The Land of Canaan and the Destiny of Israel: Theologies of Territory in the Hebrew Bible*. Winona Lake, IN: Eisenbrauns, 2011.

Freedman, Harry, ed. *Genesis*. 3. Midrash Rabbah 1. London: Soncino, 1983.

French, Warren, ed. *A Companion to The Grapes of Wrath*. New York: Viking, 1963.

French, Warren, ed. *John Steinbeck*. Boston: Twayne, 1975.

Fretheim, Terence E. *Jeremiah*. Smyth & Helwys Bible Commentary 15. Macon, GA: Smyth & Helwys, 2002.

Frye, Northrop. *The Great Code: The Bible and Literature*. London: Routledge & Kegan Paul, 1982.

Gadamer, Hans-Georg. *Truth and Method*. London: Continuum, 2004.

Gibson, Walker. 'Authors, Speakers, Readers, and Mock Readers'. In *Reader-Response Criticism: From Formalism to Post-Structuralism*, edited by Jane P. Tompkins, 1–11. Baltimore, MD: Johns Hopkins University Press, 1980.

Gilmore, Alec. 'A Steinbeck Midrash on Gn 4:7', www.gilco.org.uk/eos/a-steinbeck-midrash-on.html.

Gordon, Robert P. *Hebrews*. Sheffield: Sheffield Academic, 2000.

Gordon, W. Max. 'Steinbeck's New Book, *East of Eden*, Tells of "His People" in Our Valley'. *Salinas Californian* (14 September 1952): 4.

Gottwald, Norman K. *The Hebrew Bible: A Socio-Literary Introduction*. Philadelphia, PA: Fortress, 1985.

Gottwald, Norman K. *The Tribes of Yahweh: A Sociology of the Religion of Liberated Israel 1250–1050 B.C.E.* London: SCM, 1980.

Gray, John. *I & II Kings: A Commentary*. London: SCM, 1964.

Greenberg, Mosheh. *Ezekiel 1–20*. Anchor Bible 22. New York: Doubleday, 1983.

Greisch, Jean. 'Ou Passe Le Rubicon? Un Problème de Geographie Spirituelle'. In *Une Analytique de Passage: Rencontre et Confrontations Avec Emmanuel Falque*. Paris: Editions Franciscaines, 2016.

Gunkel, Hermann. *The Legends of Genesis*. Chicago, IL: Open Court, 1901.

Gurko, Leo. 'Steinbeck's Later Fiction'. *Nation*, no. 175 (1952): 235–6.

Habel, Norman Charles, and Walter Brueggemann. *The Land Is Mine: Six Biblical Land Ideologies*. Overtures to Biblical Theology. Minneapolis, MN: Fortress, 1995.

Habermas, Jürgen. 'The Entry to Postmodernity: Nietzsche as a Turning Point'. In *Postmodernism: A Reader*, edited by Thomas Docherty, 51–62. New York: Columbia University Press, 1993.

Hagner, Donald A., David Allen Hubbard, and John D. Watts. *Matthew 1–13*. Word Biblical Commentary 33a. Waco, TX: Word, 1993.

Hamilton, Victor P. *Exodus: An Exegetical Commentary*. Grand Rapids, MI: Baker Academic, 2011.

Hartley, John E., David Allen Hubbard, John D. Watts, and Ralph P. Martin. *Leviticus*. Word Biblical Commentary 4. Waco, TX: Word, 1992.

Hass, Andrew H. 'Artist Bound: The Enslavement of Art to the Hegelian Other'. *Literature and Theology* 25, no. 4 (2011): 379–92.

Henry, Matthew, and Thomas Scott. *A Commentary upon the Holy Bible: With Numerous Observations and Notes from Other Writers, Also Maps of the Countries Mentioned in Scripture and Various Useful Tables*. London: Religious Tract Society, 1834.

Hiebert, Theodore. 'Land'. In *Eerdmans Dictionary of the Bible*, edited by David Noel Freedman, 788–9. Grand Rapids, MI: Eerdmans, 2000.

Holloway, Emory. 'Introduction'. In *Leaves of Grass*, vii–xxxii. London: Everyman's Library, 1971.

Huey, F. B. *Jeremiah, Lamentations*. The New American Commentary 16. Nashville, TN: B&H, 1993.

Huttunen, Niko. 'The Bible, Finland, and the Civil War of 1918: Reception History and Effective History of the Bible as Contextualized Biblical Studies'. *Studia Theologica - Nordic Journal of Theology* 65 (2011): 146–71.

Hyatt, Philip. *Commentary on Exodus*. London: Oliphants, 1971.

Hymnal According to the Use of the Protestant Episcopal Church in the United States of America. New York: James Pott, 1874.

Iser, Wolfgang. 'The Reading Process: A Phenomenological Approach'. In *Reader-Response Criticism: From Formalism to Post-Structuralism*, edited by Jane P. Tompkins, 50–69. Baltimore, MD: Johns Hopkins University Press, 1980.

Jack, Alison M. *The Bible and Literature*. London: SCM, 2012.

Janzen, Waldemar. 'Land'. In *The Anchor Bible Dictionary, vol. 4. K–N*, edited by David Noel Freedman, 143–54. New York: Doubleday, 1992.

Jaubert, Annie. 'Introduction'. In *Homélies Sur Josué*, by Origen. Sources Chrétiennes 71. Paris: Cerf, 1960.

Jauss, Hans Robert, ed. *Toward an Aesthetic of Reception*. Minneapolis, MN: University of Minnesota Press, 1982.

Jefferson, Thomas. 'The Declaration of Independence'. In *The Declaration of Independence and the Constitution of the United States*: U.S. Citizenship and Immigration Services.

Jefferson, Thomas. *Jefferson's 'Original Rough Draft' of the Declaration of Independence*, https://jeffersonpapers.princeton.edu/selected-documents/jefferson%E2%80%99s-%E2%80%9Coriginal-rough-draught%E2%80%9D-declaration-independence-0

Jefferson, Thomas. *Notes on the State of Virginia*. Boston, MA: Lilly & Wait, 1832.

Jewett, Robert. *Romans: A Commentary*. Edited by Roy D. Kotansky and Eldon Jay Epp. Hermeneia 59. Minneapolis, MN: Fortress, 2007.

Johnston, William. *Exodus 1–19*. Smyth & Helwys Bible Commentary. Macon, GA: Smyth & Helwys, 2014.

Josephus Flavius. *Josephus: The Jewish War: Newly Translated with Extensive Commentary and Archaeological Commentary and Archaeological Background Illustrations*. Edited by Gaalyah Cornfeld, Benjamin Mazar, and Paul L. Maier. Grand Rapids, MI: Zondervan, 1982.

Keener, Craig S. *Acts: An Exegetical Commentary. 1. Introduction and 1:1–2:47*. Grand Rapids, MI: Baker Academic, 2012.

Killingsworth, Jimmie. *Walt Whitman and the Earth: A Study in Ecopoetics*. The Iowa Whitman Series. Iowa, IA: University of Iowa, 2004.

Klammer, Martin. *Whitman, Slavery, and the Emergence of Leaves of Grass*. University Park, PA: The Pennsylvania State University Press, 1996.

Koci, Katerina. 'On the Legacy of the Land: Ideology Criticism of Walter Brueggemann and John Steinbeck'. *Theology Today* 78, no. 1 (2021): 13–28.

Koci, Katerina 'Reception of the "Promised Land" in the Pauline Letters'. *Communio Viatorum* 56, no. 1 (2014): 35–55.

Koester, Craig R. *Hebrews: A New Translation with Introduction and Commentary*. Anchor Bible 36. New York: Doubleday, 2001.

Kolodny, Annette. *The Lay of the Land: Metaphor as Experience and History in American Life and Letters*. Chapel Hill, NC: University of North Carolina Press, 1975.

Kwakkel, Gert. 'The Land in the Book of Hosea'. In *The Land of Israel in Bible, History and Theology: Studies in Honour of Ed Noort*, edited by Cornelis De Vos and Jacques Van Ruiten, 167–81. Leiden: Brill, 2009.

Lakoff, George, and Mark Johnson. *Metaphors We Live By*. Chicago, IL: University of Chicago Press, 1980.

Lane, William L., David Allen Hubbard, John D. Watts, and Ralph P. Martin. *Hebrews 9–13*. Word Biblical Commentary 47b. Waco, TX: Word, 1991.

Langston, Scott M. 'Exodus in Early Twentieth-Century America: Charles Reynolds Brown and Lawrence Langner'. In *The Oxford Handbook of Reception History of the Bible*, edited by Michael Lieb and Emma Mason, 433–47. Oxford: Oxford University Press, 2011.

Lemmelijn, Bénédicte. 'Influence of a So-Called P-redaction in the "Major Expansion" of Exod ⱽ–11? Finding Oneself at the Crossroads of Textual and Literary Criticism'. In *Textual Criticism and Dead Sea Scrolls Studies in Honour of Julio Treble Barrera. Florilegium Complutense*. Edited by Andreés Piquer Otero and Pablo Torihano Morales, Supplements to the Journal for the Study of Judaism 158. Leiden: Brill, 2012.

Levenson, Jon. 'Is There a Counterpart in the Hebrew Bible to New Testament Antisemitism?' *Journal of Ecumenical Studies* 22, no. 2 (1985): 242–60.

Levering, Matthew. *Ezra & Nehemiah*. London: SCM, 2008.

Library of Congress. 'Great Depression and World War II (1929–1945)', www.loc.gov/teachers/classroommaterials/presentationsandactivities/presentations/timeline/depwwii/depress/hoovers.html

Lieb, Michael, and Emma Mason, eds. *The Oxford Handbook of the Reception History of the Bible*. Oxford: Oxford University Press, 2011.

Lisca, Peter. *John Steinbeck: Nature and Myth*. New York: Thomas Y. Crowell, 1987.

Loughlin, Gerard. *Telling God's Story: Bible, Church and Narrative Theology*. Cambridge: Cambridge University Press, 1996.

Louw, Johannes P., and Eugene Albert Nida, eds. *Greek-English Lexicon of the New Testament Based on Semantic Domains*. New York: United Bible Societies, 1989.

Luz, Ulrich. *Matthew 1–7: A Commentary*. Rev. edn. Hermeneia. Minneapolis, MN: Augsburg Fortress, 2007.

Luz, Ulrich. *Matthew in History: Interpretation, Influence, and Effects*. Minneapolis, MN: Fortress, 1994.

Mann, T. W. Review of *The Land: Place as Gift, Promise, and Challenge in Biblical Faith. Theology Today* 35, no. 2 (1978): 217–20.

Martino, Daniel. 'Postcolonial Biblical Hermeneutics: Interpreting with a Genuine Attunement to Otherness'. *Analecta Hermeneutica*, no. 4 (2012): 1–21.

Mather, Increase. 'An Earnest Exhortation to the Inhabitants of New England (1676)'. Edited by Reiner Smolinski. *Electronic Texts in American Studies*, no. 31 (1676): 1–34.

Mather, Increase. *Jeremiads*. Edited by Sacvan Bercovitch. Library of American Puritan Writings 20. New York: AMS, 1984.

Matterson, Stephen. *The Great Gatsby: An Introduction to the Variety of Criticism*. The Critics Debate. London: Macmillan Education, 1990.

Mazzeo, Joseph Anthony. *Medieval Cultural Tradition in Dante's 'Comedy'*. Westport, CT: Greenwood, 1968.

McEntyre, Marilyn Ch. 'Bible'. In *A John Steinbeck Encyclopedia*, edited by Brian Railsback and Michael J. Meyer, 28–9. Westport, CT: Greenwood, 2006.

McKay, Nellie Y. '"Happy[?]-Wife-and Motherdom": The Portrayal of Ma Joad in John Steinbeck's *The Grapes of Wrath*'. In *John Steinbeck*, edited by Harold Bloom, 33–51. Bloom's Modern Critical Views. New York: Infobase, 2008.

Meyer, Michael J. 'Paradise Lost'. In *A John Steinbeck Encyclopedia*, edited by Brian Railsback and Michael J. Meyer, 268–9. Westport, CT: Greenwood, 2006.

Milgrom, Jacob. *Leviticus 23–27: A New Translation with Introduction and Commentary*. Anchor Bible 3B. New York: Doubleday, 2001.

Millar, J. G. 'Land'. In *New Dictionary of Biblical Theology*, edited by T. Desmond Alexander, 623–7. Leicester: Inter-Varsity, 2003.

Milton, John. *Paradise Lost*. Edited by Alastair Fowler. Harlow: Pearson & Longman, 2007.

Minear, Paul S. 'Promise'. In *The Interpreter's Dictionary of the Bible*, edited by George Arthur Buttrick, 3:893–6. New York: Abingdon, 1962.

Moore, Stephen, and Yvonne Sherwood. *The Bible in Theory: Critical and Postcritical Essays*. Atlanta, GA: SBL, 2010.

Morgan, Jonathan. 'Transgressing, Puking, Covenanting: The Character of Land in Leviticus'. *Theology* 112 (2009): 172–80.

Myers, Jacob Martin. *Ezra, Nehemiah*. Anchor Bible 14. New York: Doubleday, 1965.

Nelson, Richard D. *First and Second Kings*. Interpretation: A Bible Interpretation for Teaching and Preaching. Louisville, KY: John Knox, 1987.

Niccacci, Alviero. *The Syntax of the Verb in Classical Hebrew Prose*. Journal for the Study of the Old Testament. Supplement Series 86. Sheffield: JSOT, 1990.

Nielsen, Kirsten. 'The Holy Spirit as Dove and as Tongues of Fire: Reworking Biblical Metaphors in a Modern Danish Hymn'. In *Gåder Og Billeder: Studier Til Ære for Tryggve N. D. Mettinger*, edited by Göran Eideval and Blazenka Scheuer, 239–56. Winona Lake, IN: Eisenbrauns, 2011.

Nietzsche, Fridrich. *Kritische Studienausabe*, vol. 8, 189, frgm 11/2.

Noble, Tim. *The Poor in Liberation Theology: Pathway to God or Ideological Construct?* Cross Cultural Theologies. Sheffield: Equinox, 2013.

Noth, Martin, and Bernhard W. Anderson. *A History of Pentateuchal Traditions*. Englewood Cliffs, NJ: Prentice Hall, 1972.

Odell, Margaret S. *Ezekiel*. Smyth & Helwys Bible Commentary. Macon, GA: Smyth & Helwys, 2005.

Origen. *Homélies sur l'Exode*. Sources Chrétiennes 16. Paris: Cerf, 1947.

Origen. *Homélies sur la Genèse*. Sources Chrétiennes 7. Paris: Cerf, 1944.

Origen. *Homélies sur Josué*. Sources Chrétiennes 71. Paris: Cerf, 1960.

Origen. *Homélies sur les Nombres*. Sources Chrétiennes 29. Paris Cerf, 1951.

Ottosson, Magnus. 'ארץ'. In *Theological Dictionary of the Old Testament*, edited by Helmer Ringgren, 1:388–405. Grand Rapids, MI: Eerdmans, 1977.

Owens, Louis. *The Grapes of Wrath: Trouble in the Promised Land*. New York: Twayne, 1989.

Owens, Louis. *John Steinbeck's Revision of America*. Athens, GA: University of Georgia Press, 1985.

Owens, Louis. '*Of Mice and Men*: The Dream of Commitment'. In *John Steinbeck*, edited by Harold Bloom, 17–22. Bloom's Modern Critical Views. New York: Infobase, 2008.

Parris, David Paul. *Reception Theory and Biblical Hermeneutics*. Eugene, OR: Pickwick, 2009.

Pelikan, Jaroslav Jan. *Acts*. Theological Commentary of the Bible. London: SCM, 2006.

Pelzer, Linda Claycomb. *Student Companion to F. Scott Fitzgerald*. Student Companions to Classic Writers. Westport, CT: Greenwood, 2000.

Philo of Alexandria. *De Abrahamo*. Edited by Jean Gorez. Les Oeuvres de Philon d'Alexandrie 20. Paris: Cerf, 1966.

Philo of Alexandria. *Quaestiones et solutiones in Exodum I et II e versione armeniaca et fragmenta graeca*. Edited by Abraham Terian. Les Oeuvres de Philon d'Alexandrie 34c. Paris: Cerf, 1992.

Philo of Alexandria. *Quaestiones et solutiones in Genesim III-IV-V-VI: e versione armeniaca*. Edited by Charles Mercier. Les Oeuvres de Philon d'Alexandrie 34b. Paris: Cerf, 1984.

Plaut, Wolf, and Annette Böckler. *Die Tora: in jüdischer Auslegung. 1. Bereschit.* Dt. Erstausg. Gütersloh: Kaiser, Gütersloher Verl-Haus, 1999.

Poole, Gary William. 'Josephus Flavius'. *Britannica Academic*, www.academic.eb.com/ EBchecked/topic/306479/Flavius-Josephus/3765/Josephus-as-historian?anchor =ref72691

Poulet, Georges. 'Criticism and the Experience of Interiority'. In *Reader-Response Criticism: From Formalism to Post-Structuralism*, edited by Jane P. Tompkins, 41–9. Baltimore, MD: Johns Hopkins University Press, 1980.

Pratt, John Clark. 'To a God Unknown'. In *A John Steinbeck Encyclopedia*, edited by Brian Railsback and Michael J. Meyer, 378–81. Westport, CT: Greenwood, 2006.

Prescott, Orville. 'Books of the Times'. *New York Times*, 19 September 1952.

Prior, Michael. 'The Bible and the Redeeming Idea of Colonialism'. *Studies in World Christianity* 5, no. 2 (1999): 129–55.

Prior, Michael. *A Land Flowing with Milk, Honey and People*. Lattey Lecture 1997. Cambridge: Von Hügel Institute, 1997.

Quinones, Ricardo J. 'Dante'. *Encyclopedia Britannica Online*, www.britannica.com/ biography/Dante-Alighieri#toc22149

Rad, Gerhard von. *Theologie des Alten Testaments, Band 1: Die Theologie der geschichtlichen Überlieferung Israels*. Munich: Chr. Kaiser, 1957.

Rad, Gerhard von. *Theologie des Alten Testaments, Band 2: Die Theologie der prophetischen Überlieferung Israels*. Munich: Chr. Kaiser, 1967.

Rendtorff, Rolf, and John J. Scullion. *The Problem of the Process of Transmission in the Pentateuch*. Journal for the Study of the Old Testament: Supplement Series 89. Sheffield: JSOT, 1990.

Ricoeur, Paul. *From Text to Action: Essays in Hermeneutics II*. London: Athlone, 1991.

Riffaterre, Michael. 'The Stylistic Approach to Literary History'. *New Literary History* 2, no. 1 (1970): 39–55.

Roberts, Jonathan. 'Introduction'. In *The Oxford Handbook of Reception History of the Bible*, edited by Michael Lieb and Emma Mason, 1–8. New York: Oxford University Press, 2011.

Rosenblatt, Louise M. *The Reader, the Text, the Poem: The Transactional Theory of the Literary Work*. Carbondale, IL: Southern Illinois University Press, 1978.

Ryken, Leland, ed. 'Land'. In *Dictionary of Biblical Imagery*, 487–8. Downers Grove, IL: InterVarsity, 1998.

Ryken, Leland. 'Land Flowing with Milk and Honey'. In *Dictionary of Biblical Imagery*, 488. Downers Grove, IL: InterVarsity, 1998.

Ryken, Leland. 'Promised Land'. In *Dictionary of Biblical Imagery*, 665–6. Downers Grove, IL: InterVarsity, 1998.

Sand, A. 'Ἐπαγγελία'. In *Exegetical Dictionary of the New Testament*, edited by Gerhard Schneider, 13–16. 2. Grand Rapids, MI: Eerdmans, 1990.

Sarna, Nahum M. *Exodus: The Traditional Hebrew Text with the JPS Translation.* תומש. Philadelphia, PA: Jewish PublSoc, 1991.

Sasse, Hermann. 'Κόσμος'. In *Theological Dictionary of the New Testament*, edited by Gerhard Kittel, 867–98. 3. Grand Rapids, MI: Eerdmans, 1981.

Schmid, H. H. 'קרא'. In *Theological Lexicon of the Old Testament*, edited by Claus Westermann and Ernst Jenni, 1:172–9. Peabody, MA: Hendrickson, 1997.

Schniewind, Friedrich. 'Ἐπαγγελία'. In *Theological Dictionary of the New Testament*, edited by Gerhard Kittel, 576–86. 2. Grand Rapids, MI: Eerdmans, 1964.

Schulman, Lydia Dittler. *Paradise Lost and the Rise of the American Republic*. Boston, MA: Northeastern University Press, 1992.

Schweinitz, George de. 'Steinbeck and Christianity'. In *A Case Book on The Grapes of Wrath*, edited by Agnes McNeill Donohue, 103–4. New York: Thomas Y. Crowell, 1970.

Sheehan, Bernard. 'Jefferson's "Empire for Liberty"'. *Indiana Magazine of History* 100, no. 4 (2004): 346–63.

Shockley, Martin. 'Christian Symbolism in *The Grapes of Wrath*'. In *A Case Book on The Grapes of Wrath*, edited by Agnes McNeill Donohue, 90–5. New York: Thomas Y. Crowell, 1970.

Skinner, John. *A Critical and Exegetical Commentary on Genesis*. 2nd edn. Edinburgh: T. & T. Clark, 1951.

Smith, John. 'A Description of New England'. New York: AMS, 1986.

Speiser, Ephraim A. *Genesis: Introduction, Translation and Notes*. Garden City, NY: Doubleday, 1964.

Steinbeck, John. *America and Americans*. New York: Bantam, 1968.

Steinbeck, John. *East of Eden*. 2nd print. London: Penguin, 1992.

Steinbeck, John. *The Grapes of Wrath*. 1st Penguin ed. New York: Penguin, 1976.

Steinbeck, John. *Journal of a Novel: East of Eden Letters*. New York: Viking, 1969.

Steinbeck, John. *Of Mice and Men*. London: Penguin, 2000.

Steinbeck, John. *The Pastures of Heaven*. London: Duality, 1946.

Steinbeck, John. *To a God Unknown*. New York: Bantam, 1955.

Steinbeck, John, and Robert J. DeMott. *Working Days: The Journals of the Grapes of Wrath 1938–1941*. New York: Viking, 1989.

Steinbeck, John, Elaine Steinbeck, and Robert Wallsten. *Steinbeck: A Life in Letters*. New York: Viking, 1975.

Talbert, Charles H. *Romans*. Smyth & Helwys Bible Commentary 24. Macon, GA: Smyth & Helwys, 2002.

Talstra, Eep. 'A Hierarchy of Clauses in Hebrew Bible Narrative'. In *Narrative Syntax and the Hebrew Bible: Papers of the Tilburg Conference 1996*, edited by Ellen van Wolde, 85–118. Leiden: Brill, 1997.

Terian, Abraham. 'Introduction'. In *Quaestiones et Solutiones in Exodum I et II E Versione Armeniaca et Fragmenta Graeca*. Les Oeuvres de Philon d'Alexandrie 34c. Paris: Cerf, 1992.

The Book of Common Prayer and Administration of the Sacraments and Other Rites and Ceremonies of the Church according to the Use of the Protestant Episcopal Church in the United States of America. New York: Oxford University Press, 1929.

The Book of Common Prayer and Administration of the Sacraments and Other Rites and Ceremonies of the Church according to the Use of the Protestant Episcopal Church in the United States of America Together with the Psalter or Psalms of David. New York: James Pott, 1892.

Theodoret of Cyrus, 'Genesis, Exodus'. In *The Questions on the Octateuch*, edited by John Petruccione and Robert Hill. Library of Early Christianity 1. Washington, DC: Catholic University of America, 2007.

Thiselton, Anthony C. *1 & 2 Thessalonians: Through the Centuries*. Blackwell Bible Commentaries. Chichester: John Willey & Sons, 2011.

Thiselton, Anthony C. 'Communicative Action and Promise in Interdisciplinary, Biblical and Theological Hermeneutics'. In *The Promise of Hermeneutics*, edited by Roger Lundin, Anthony Thiselton, and Clarence Walhout 133–239. Grand Rapids, MI: Eerdmans, 1999.

Thiselton, Anthony C. 'Reception Theory, H. R. Jauss and the Formative Power of Scripture'. *Scottish Journal of Theology* 65, no. 3 (2012): 289–308.

Throntveit, Mark A. *Ezra–Nehemiah*. Interpretation: A Bible Interpretation for Teaching and Preaching. Louisville, KY: John Knox, 1992.

Tompkins, Jane P. 'An Introduction to Reader-Response Criticism'. In *Reader-Response Criticism: From Formalism to Post-Structuralism*, edited by Jane P. Tompkins, ix–xxvi. Baltimore, MD: Johns Hopkins University Press, 1980.

Towner, Wayne Sibley. *Genesis*. Louisville, KY: John Knox, 2001.

Turner, Laurence A. *Genesis*. Sheffield: Sheffield Academic, 2000.

Van Seters, John. *Abraham in History and Tradition*. London: Yale University Press, 1975.

Van Seters, John. *The Life of Moses: The Yahwist as Historian in Exodus–Numbers*. Louisville, KY: Westminster John Knox, 1994.

Van Wijk-Bos, Johanna W. H. *Ezra, Nehemiah, and Esther*. Louisville, KY: Westminster John Knox, 1998.

Vervenne, Marc. 'The "P" Tradition in the Pentateuch: Document and/or Redaction? The Sea Narrative' (Ex 13,17–14,31) as a Test Case'. In *Pentateuchal and Deuteronomistic Studies: Papers Read at the XIIIth IOSOT Congress Leuven 1989*, edited by C. Brekelmans and J. Lust. Bibliotheca Ephemeridum Theologicarum Lovaniensium 94. Leuven: Peeters, 1990.

Von Rad, Gerhard. *Old Testament Theology*. New York: Harper & Row, 1962.

Von Rad, Gerhard. 'The Promised Land and Yahweh's Land in the Hexateuch'. In *The Problem of the Hexateuch*, 79–93. Edinburgh: Oliver & Boyd, 1966.

Von Rad, Gerhard. 'Typological Interpretation of the Old Testament'. In *Essays on Old Testament Interpretation*, edited by Claus Westermann, 17–39. London: SCM, 1963.

Warrior, Robert A. 'Canaanites, Cowboys, and Indians'. *Union Seminary Quarterly Review* 59, no. 1–2 (2005): 1–8.

Wenham, Gordon J. *Genesis 1–15*. Edited by David Allen. Word Biblical Commentary 1. Waco, TX: Word, 1987.

Westermann, Claus. *Genesis 1–11: A Continental Commentary*. Minneapolis, MN: Fortress, 1994.

Westermann, Claus. *The Promises to the Fathers*. Philadelphia, PA: Fortress, 1980.

Westphal, Merold. 'The Philosophical/Theological Response'. In *Biblical Hermeneutics: Five Views*, edited by Stanley E. Porter and Beth M. Stovell, 162–4. Downers Grove, IL: IVP Academic, 2012.

Westphal, Merold. *Whose Community? Which Interpretation? Philosophical Hermeneutics for the Church*. Grand Rapids, MI: Baker Academic, 2009.

Wheeler, Rachel M. 'Edwards as Missionary'. In *The Cambridge Companion to Jonathan Edwards*, 196–214. Cambridge: Cambridge University Press, 2007.

Whitman, Walt. *Leaves of Grass*. London: Everyman's Library, 1971.

Wilken, Robert Louis. *The Land Called Holy: Palestine in Christian History and Thought*. New Haven, CT: Yale University Press, 1992.

Williamson, Hugh Godfrey Maturin, David Allen Hubbard, and John D. Watts. *Ezra, Nehemiah*. Word Biblical Commentary 16. Waco, TX: Word, 1985.

Winthrop, John. 'A Model of Christian Charity. A Reader's Edition', edited by John B. Uebersax (2014), http://www.john-uebersax.com/pdf/John%20Winthrop%20-%20 Model%20of%20Christian%20Charity%20v1.01.pdf.

Witherington, Ben. *Matthew*. Smyth & Helwys Bible Commentary 19. Macon, GA: Smyth & Helwys, 2006.

Wright, Christopher J. H. 'ארץ'. In *New International Dictionary of Old Testament Theology and Exegesis*, edited by Willem A. VanGemeren, 1:518–24. Carlisle: Paternoster, 1997.

Wright, Terrence R. 'Cain and Abel: John Steinbeck'. In *The Genesis of Fiction: Modern Novelists as Biblical Interpreters*, edited by Terrence R. Wright. Aldershot: Ashgate, 2007.

Wykes, David L. 'Henry, Matthew (1662–1714)'. *Oxford Dictionary of National Biography*, www.oxforddnb.com/view/article/12975

Zane, Nancy. 'America and Americans'. In *A John Steinbeck Encyclopedia*, edited by Brian Railsback and Michael J. Meyer, 9–11. Westport, CT: Greenwood, 2006.

Ziff, Larzer. *Puritanism in America: New Culture in a New World*. New York: Viking, 1973.

INDEX OF REFERENCES

Index of Authors

Printed in Great Britain
by Amazon

57430817R00156